CAMBRIDGE

Economics

for Cambridge IGCSE™ and O Level

COURSEBOOK

Susan Grant

Third edition with Digital access

CAMBRIDGE
UNIVERSITY PRESS & ASSESSMENT

Shaftesbury Road, Cambridge CB2 8EA, United Kingdom

One Liberty Plaza, 20th Floor, New York, NY 10006, USA

477 Williamstown Road, Port Melbourne, VIC 3207, Australia

314–321, 3rd Floor, Plot 3, Splendor Forum, Jasola District Centre, New Delhi – 110025, India

103 Penang Road, 05–06/07, Visioncrest Commercial, Singapore 238467

Cambridge University Press & Assessment is a department of the University of Cambridge.

We share the University's mission to contribute to society through the pursuit of education, learning and research at the highest international levels of excellence.

www.cambridge.org
Information on this title: www.cambridge.org/9781009814577

First published 2014
Second edition 2018
Third edition 2025
20 19 18 17 16 15 14 13 12 11 10 9 8 7 6 5 4 3 2 1

Printed in Italy by L.E.G.O S.p.A

A catalogue record for this publication is available from the British Library

ISBN   978-1-009-81457-7   Coursebook with Digital Access
ISBN   978-1-009-81456-0   Digital Coursebook
ISBN   978-1-009-81458-4   Coursebook eBook

Additional resources for this publication at www.cambridge.org/9781009814577

For EU product safety concerns, contact us at Calle de José Abascal, 56, 1°, 28003 Madrid, Spain, or email eugpsr@cambridge.org.

2024 Cambridge Dedicated Teacher Awards

Our **Cambridge Dedicated Teacher Awards** are an opportunity to show appreciation for the incredible work teachers do every day.

Thank you to everyone who nominated this year; we have been inspired and moved by all of your stories. Well done to all of our nominees for your dedication to learning and for inspiring the next generation of thinkers, leaders and innovators.

Congratulations to our winners!

Global Winner
Southeast Asia & Pacific
Sydney Engelbert
Keningau Vocational College, Malaysia

East Asia
Pengfei Jiang
Zhuji Ronghuai Foreign Language School, China

Pakistan
Saeeda Salim
SISA – School of International Studies in Sciences & Arts, Pakistan

South Asia
Meena Mishra
Dr Sarvepalli Radhakrishnan International School, India

Middle East and North Africa
Gina Justus
Our Own English High school Sharjah-Girls, United Arab Emirates

Sub-Saharan Africa
Tajudeen Odufeso
Isara Secondary School, Nigeria

Europe
Aynur Bayazit
Menekşe Ahmet Yalçınkaya Kindergarten, Türkiye

Latin America & the Caribbean
Ramon Majé Floriano
Montessori sede San Francisco, Colombia

North America
Maria Medvetz Santos
Seminole Ridge Community High School, United States

For more information about our dedicated teachers and their stories, go to
dedicatedteacher.cambridge.org

CAMBRIDGE

> Contents

> How to use this series

This suite of resources supports students and teachers following the Cambridge IGCSE™, IGCSE (9–1) and O Level Economics syllabuses (0455/0987/2281) for examination from 2027. All of the components in the series are designed to work together and help students develop the necessary knowledge and skills for this subject.

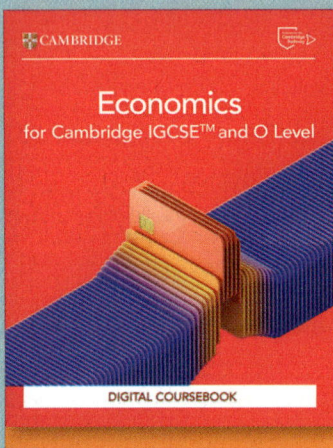

The Coursebook is designed for students to use in class with guidance from the teacher. It offers complete coverage of the Cambridge IGCSE™ , IGCSE (9–1) and O Level Economics syllabuses (0455/0987/2281). The Coursebook contains in-depth explanations of economics concepts, a variety of independent and group activities, engaging new features and images to help students make real-world connections.

A digital version of the Coursebook is included with the print version, and available separately. It includes access to video content to further support students' learning, as well as simple tools for students to use in class or for self-study.

The Workbook provides further practice of all the skills presented in the Coursebook and is ideal for use in class or as homework. It provides engaging activities, worked examples and opportunities for students to evaluate sample answers so they can put into practice what they have learnt.

A digital version of the Workbook is included with the print version. It includes simple tools for students to use in class or for self-study, as well as downloadable templates to complete some of the activities.

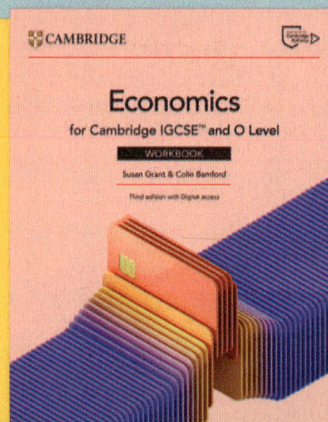

The Digital Teacher's Resource provides everything teachers need to deliver the course. It is packed full of useful teaching notes and lesson ideas, with suggestions for differentiation to support and challenge students, ideas for formative assessment, overcoming common misconceptions and language support.

The Digital Teacher's Resource contains downloadable resource sheets and worksheets.

All answers are available on Cambridge GO.

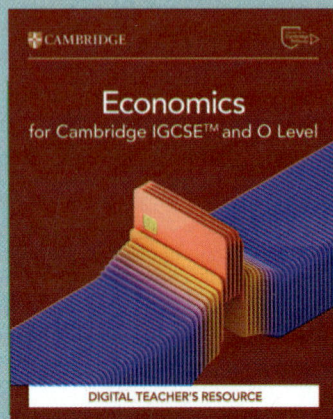

> How to use this book

Throughout this Coursebook, you will notice some features that are designed to help your learning. Here is a brief overview of what you will find.

LEARNING INTENTIONS

Learning intentions open each chapter. These help you with navigation through the Coursebook and indicate the important topics in each chapter.

ECONOMICS IN CONTEXT

Economics in context introduces you to the content in a chapter. These place some of the key ideas contained in the chapter into a real-world business setting. Each one contains questions that allow you to discuss the topic.

KEY TERMS

Key vocabulary is highlighted in the text when it is first introduced. An accompanying definition tells you the meanings of these words and phrases. You will also find definitions of these words in the Glossary at the back of this book.

TIPS

Tips are provided throughout this Coursebook to help with your learning. The tips might cover how to avoid common errors or misconceptions, advice on answering questions or key skills for your course.

LINKS

These explain the links between topics in different sections of the Coursebook.

DISCUSSION

Discussion questions are used throughout this Coursebook to prompt thinking at key points within each chapter.

ACTIVITY

There are various activities throughout this Coursebook. These give you opportunities to discuss topics or produce your own work either individually, in pairs or in groups.

ECONOMICS IN ACTION

Economics in action provides you with an opportunity to apply economics principles to current events in various international settings. You will look at your life through an economics lens, and also apply your analysis skills and use evidence to look at the world of work. Designed to encourage group discussion, the short case studies and accompanying questions will help you to make connections between employment and studying economics.

REFLECTION

Reflection questions direct you to look back on an activity and encourage you to think about your learning. You will reflect on and assess the process that you used to arrive at your answers.

SUMMARY

At the end of each chapter, you will find a list that brings together the key information you have learnt. This list can also be used as a useful revision aid.

CHECK YOUR PROGRESS

Each chapter ends with a grid showing the Learning intentions from the start of the chapter. When you are revising, you might find it helpful to rate how confident you are for each of these statements. You should also provide an example to support your score.

End-of-chapter practice questions

Each chapter contains a set of multiple-choice questions, as well as a set of four-part questions. You can use these to assess the knowledge you have gained on this section of the syllabus.

End-of-section practice questions

Each section ends with a set of more demanding questions that includes an extended case study. These can be used to assess what you have learnt across several chapters of the Coursebook.

> Introduction

Cambridge IGCSE™ and O Level Economics introduces you to a subject that will provide you with the skills and information to explore some of the key issues and challenges facing the world today.

The Coursebook will help you develop your skills in interpreting economic information, explaining economic ideas, applying those ideas to current issues and drawing clear, accurate and well-labelled economic diagrams.

The Coursebook is divided into six sections and has 36 chapters. Each chapter has features to help you increase your understanding and enjoyment of the subject. The features include 'Economics in context', activities, key terms, tips, key links and 'Economics in action'.

The activities give you the opportunity to use and strengthen your understanding of economic topics. Key terms define what economic words mean. You will find that some words in economics, such as 'demand', have a rather different meaning in economics than in everyday language. You will also come across new words, such as 'fiscal policy'.

Tips may remind you of a key point, warn you about a common confusion or recommend something you could do to increase your understanding. Links are given to parts of other chapters where concepts can help you understand topics. 'Economics in context' aims to get you started thinking and discussing a topic. 'Economics in action' puts you in the role of an economist.

At the end of each chapter is a summary of the main points of the chapter. There are also multiple-choice questions and four-part questions where you can assess your understanding. At the end of each section, you will find further practice questions based on source material and stimulus material.

Economics is an exciting subject. Economists play a key role in the world. They give advice to firms and governments to improve their performance and also comment on their success or failure. The work of economists can make a significant difference to people's lives. For instance, the policies they recommend to governments may increase employment, reduce poverty and improve the quality of the environment.

> Section 1

The basic economic problem

> Chapter 1

The nature of the basic economic problem

LEARNING INTENTIONS

By the end of this chapter, you will be able to:

- define and give examples of the basic economic problem
- explain the concept of scarcity
- give examples of the basic economic problem in the context of consumers, workers, producers/firms, governments
- explain the key resource allocation decisions answering the three basic economic questions of what to produce, how to produce and for who to produce
- explain the difference between economic goods and free goods.

Introduction

Do you have everything you need to live? What about everything you would like to have? Some people do not have basic goods and services needed to live as they do not have enough food, clothing or adequate housing. Once our needs for sufficient food, clothing and housing are met, we will still want other products. Indeed, our **wants** are unlimited. The richer we get, the more, and the better, quality products we would like. Many of us would like, for instance, more holidays and the latest smartphone. This chapter will look at why we cannot have everything we would like.

KEY TERM

wants: desires for goods and services.

ECONOMICS IN CONTEXT

Stuck in traffic

In October 2023, people sat in their cars for three hours, stuck in a traffic jam in Panathur, India. As a result, workers were late for work, students missed lessons and friends did not meet up. In many towns and cities throughout the world, drivers and their passengers waste time and often become stressed when stuck in long queues of slow-moving or stationary traffic (see Figure 1.1).

Traffic jams occur because the number of cars and other vehicles grows faster than road space. Every year more people own a car and some people own more than one car. The average number of cars per household in India is rising every year.

Discuss in a pair or group:

1   Does everyone who wants a car own a car?

2   Is there enough spare land available where you live to build more roads?

Figure 1.1: Increasing car ownership can cause problems

1.1 Finite resources and infinite wants

There is no limit to people's wants. Wants are infinite (unlimited) while the **resources** that are required to make the things people want are finite (limited). For instance, people want more and better clothing, more and better healthcare and improved transport infrastructure. In contrast, resources, that is the number of workers, machines, offices, factories, raw materials and land used to produce goods and services, are scarce. For example, at any given time there are only a limited number of workers, and they can produce only a specified amount (see Figure 1.2).

The mismatch between what people want and the maximum that can be produced gives rise to **the basic economic problem**. The basic economic problem of not being able to satisfy everyone's wants arises because of the **scarcity** of resources. Choices have to be made about how resources are to be used.

KEY TERMS

resources: inputs used to produce goods and services.

the basic economic problem: where unlimited wants are greater than finite resources.

scarcity: a situation where there are not enough resources to satisfy everyone's wants.

Figure 1.2: There is a limit to how much workers can produce

TIP

It is very important to learn definitions of economic terms. The more you apply a term, such as 'scarcity', in your work, the sooner you will get used to using it. You may also want to compile your own economics dictionary by writing down terms in alphabetical order as you come across them.

The continuing nature of the basic economic problem

Scarcity continues to exist. More goods and services are being produced today than ever before, but the growth in wants is exceeding the growth of economic resources. People still want more products than the available resources can produce. Over time, wants continue to grow and change.

The basic economic problem in different contexts

The fact that people have to choose which products to buy, which subjects to study, what jobs to do and which products to produce shows that there are insufficient (not enough) resources. As consumers, we cannot have everything we want. We have limited incomes. Students have to select which courses to study. It is not always possible to study economics and chemistry at the same time. Workers have to make choices about what jobs they do. Some teachers may carry out other work in the evening, but when they are teaching they are not working as writers! Time is in limited supply. Producers have to decide what to make. Farmers cannot grow rice and wheat on the same land. They have to select one crop as land is scarce. The government has to decide how to spend tax revenue. Deciding to build a new hospital may mean that it is not possible to build a new school.

DISCUSSION

In your group, discuss and decide which of the following are scarce:

a vacancies for university degree courses

b food

c healthcare.

Note down the group's decision in each case and why you reached your decision.

ECONOMICS IN ACTION

Challenges facing the tourism industry in the Maldives

The Maldives is a country with more than a thousand islands. It is now one of the world's most popular places to go for a holiday. The country opened its first holiday resort in 1972 and attracted a thousand tourists (see Figure 1.3). By 2023, 1.8 million tourists visited the country. Many Maldivian workers are employed directly in tourism or indirectly in jobs involved in supplying goods and services used in tourism. Some of the most popular islands now have no space left for hotels, restaurants or souvenir shops. Tourists also increase the amount of waste in the country, including plastic waste. Most of this waste is burnt which causes air pollution and some leaks into the sea which pollutes the water around the Maldives.

Figure 1.3: Tourism is an important industry for the Maldives

1 What may limit the number of holidays abroad a person can take?

2 What may limit the number of foreign tourists the Maldives can host?

1.2 Resource allocation decisions

All economies have to answer three fundamental economic questions:

1 What to produce?

2 How to produce it?

3 Who is to receive the products produced?

The economic questions arise because of the basic economic problem of infinite wants exceeding finite resources. A decision has to be made as to how the economy's resources are to be allocated. For example, how many resources should be allocated to healthcare, how many to leisure goods and services and how many to education.

Once the decision is made, an economy has to decide on how the products are to be produced, for example, whether a large number of workers should be used in agriculture or more machines used. Finally, because it is not possible to produce enough goods and services to satisfy the wants of everyone, it is necessary to decide how the products should be distributed. Should products be distributed to people according to their needs or their ability to earn a high income?

ACTIVITY 1.1

Decide whether each of the questions in Table 1.1 relates to **what to produce**, **how to produce** or **who to produce for**. Copy and complete the table.

Table 1.1

Question		Key resource allocation decision
1	Should a car manufacturer focus on producing electric cars?	
2	Should a government provide free healthcare to all of its citizens?	
3	Should everyone have the same income?	
4	Should farmers make use of drones?	
5	Should farmers use more of their land to grow maize and less to grow millet?	
6	Should workers be used to produce luxury goods or necessities (essential goods)?	

REFLECTION

Compare your answers with another student. If you disagreed on any of the questions, were you able to explain your answer? If some of your answers were not correct, what strategy did you use to increase your understanding?

1.3 Economic goods and free goods

Most goods and services are **economic goods**. Resources are used to produce economic goods, and so they are limited in supply. For example, a carpet is an economic good (see Figure 1.4). The material and labour used to produce it could have been used to make another good (or goods). It is easy to find examples of economic goods. Almost every good and service you can think of is an economic good. Your education is an economic good, since your teachers and the other resources used to provide it could have been employed to make other products.

KEY TERM

economic good: a product which requires resources to produce it.

Figure 1.4: Carpets are an economic good

Free goods are much rarer. When most people talk about free goods, they mean products they do not have to pay for. These are not usually free goods in the economic sense since resources have been used to produce them. Economists define a free good as one that takes no resources to make it. It is hard to think of examples of free goods. Sunshine is one such example, and so is water in a river (see Figure 1.5). However, as soon as this water is processed for drinking or used for irrigation of fields, it becomes an economic good.

Figure 1.5: Water in a river is a free good

KEY TERM

free good: a product which does not require any resources to make it.

LINK

There is another difference between an economic good and a free good. This is covered in Chapter 3.2 (Influence of opportunity cost on decision-making – Economic goods and free goods).

TIP

In economics, what determines whether a product is a free good is not whether people have to pay for it, but whether it takes resources to produce it.

ACTIVITY 1.2

In a group of five, each person chooses one of the options below. Each person has 60 seconds to explain to the rest of the group whether their option is an economic good or a free good and why.

1 air

2 bicycle tyres

3 newspapers

4 public libraries

5 state education.

SUMMARY

You should now know:

- People's wants continue to grow.

- Resources such as workers, machines and land are limited in supply.

- The economic problem is that infinite wants exceed finite resources.

- The three key resource allocation decisions are what to produce, how to produce it and who to produce for.

- Economic goods take resources to produce them.

- Free goods exist without the use of resources.

Chapter 1 practice questions

1   What is the reason for the existence of scarcity?

    A   each year workers tend to produce less than previously

    B   machines wear out with time

    C   there are not sufficient resources to produce all the products people want

    D   there is a limit to people's wants   [1]

2   What will cause scarcity to continue to be a problem in the future?

    A   prices will rise

    B   the quantity of resources will decline

    C   wants will continue to increase

    D   world population will fall   [1]

3   Which combination would increase the basic economic problem?

	Resources	Wants
A	Decrease by 5%	Decrease by 20%
B	Increase by 10%	Increase by 14%
C	Increase by 20%	Remain unchanged
D	Remain unchanged	Decrease by 5%

[1]

4   Which is a free good?

A   products given away by a supermarket to attract customers

B   recycled paper

C   vaccination provided without charge by the state

D   wind coming in from the sea   [1]

Total: [4]

5   a   What is meant by 'the basic economic problem'?   [2]

b   Explain why a car is an economic good.   [4]

Total: [6]

CHECK YOUR PROGRESS

How well do you think you have achieved the learning intentions for this chapter?
Give yourself a score from 1 (still need a lot of practice) to 5 (feeling very confident)
for each learning intention. Provide an example to support your score.

Now I can...	Score	Example
define the basic economic problem		
explain the concept of scarcity		
give examples of the basic economic problem		
explain the key resource allocation decisions		
explain the difference between economic goods and free goods.		

> Chapter 2

Factors of production

LEARNING INTENTIONS

By the end of this chapter, you will be able to:

- define the factors of production: land, labour, capital and enterprise
- identify the rewards to the factors of production: rent, wages, interest and profit
- analyse the causes of changes in the quantity and quality of the factors of production.

Introduction

People are living longer. In 1963, the average life expectancy in Bangladesh was 47 years of age. By 2023, it had risen to 74 years. The Japanese could expect to live until 85 years in 2023. Figure 2.1 shows how the global average life expectancy has increased over the same period.

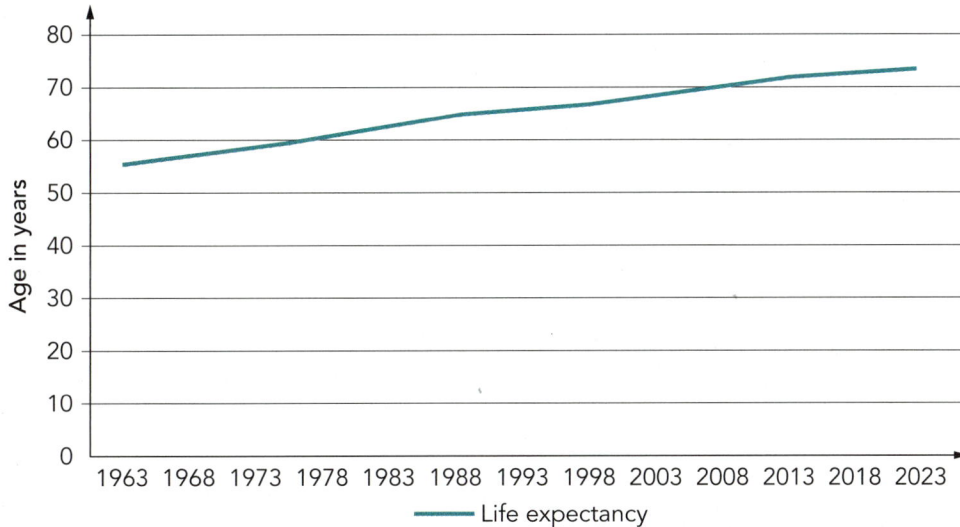

Figure 2.1: Global average life expectancy, 1963–2023

People are living longer because healthcare, education, housing, sanitation (systems for taking dirty water and waste products away from buildings) and nutrition have improved. This, in turn, is because of increases in the quantity and quality of **factors of production**. Factors of production is another term for economic resources. Factors of production can also be called inputs. Chapter 1 explained that economic resources are used to produce goods and services, and that they are in limited supply.

> **KEY TERM**
>
> **factors of production:** the economic resources of land, labour, capital and enterprise.

ECONOMICS IN CONTEXT

Taking a risk

Nguyen Thi Phuong Thao is a very successful businessperson. She made her first million dollars by selling office machinery when she was at university studying economics. Later she made a $2.7 billion fortune through co-founding Vietjet, an international airline (see Figure 2.2). Nguyen makes important decisions about which planes to buy, which routes to fly and how many workers to employ.

If Vietjet continues to be successful, Nguyen will add to her fortune. However, there is a chance that she could lose money if the airline runs into difficulties.

Figure 2.2: Flying towards success?

Discuss in a pair or group:

1 What difficulties might an airline experience?

2 What other decisions may Nguyen make in running Vietjet?

2.1 The factors of production

Most economists identify four factors of production:

1 land

2 labour

3 capital

4 enterprise.

Land

Land generally includes the earth in which crops are grown, and on which offices and factories are built. In economics, land has a wider meaning. Land covers any natural resource which can be used in production. So, besides the land itself, it also includes:

- what is beneath the land, such as coal

- what occurs naturally on the land, for example, rainforests, the sea, oceans and rivers and what is found in them, such as fish (see Figure 2.3).

Land can be described as the gifts of nature available for production, as the term covers things that occur in nature without any human intervention. So, for example, crops grown by farmers are not land, since they have not occurred naturally. They may be output sold directly to consumers, such as onions, or may be used as raw materials, such as cotton.

> **KEY TERM**
>
> **land:** natural resources used in production.

Figure 2.3: Rainforest: a natural resource

To attract tourists, for example, a travel company will show water in swimming pools, as well as the good climate and beaches in the holiday advertising it provides. Similarly, the land used by a safari park includes not only the grass on which some of the animals graze, but also the animals themselves.

Labour

Labour covers all human effort used in production. Human effort includes both the mental and the physical effort involved in producing goods and services. A road sweeper, a steel worker and a bank manager all contribute their labour.

The education, training and experience that workers have gained can be called human capital. The more human capital workers have, the more goods and services they should be able to produce.

Capital

Capital is any artificial (manufactured) good used to produce other goods and services. It includes offices, factories, machinery, railways and tools, for example.

Capital is also referred to as **capital goods** and producer goods. Economists distinguish between capital goods and consumer goods. Capital goods are not wanted for their own sake, but for what they can produce, for example, equipment to build a road. In contrast, **consumer goods**, such as food, clothing and entertainment, are wanted for the satisfaction they provide to their buyers.

To decide whether a good is a capital or a consumer good, it is necessary to consider who the user is and the purpose of its use. A computer, for example, will be a capital good if it is used by an insurance company to process insurance claims – it is producing a service. However, if the computer is used by an individual to play games, it is a consumer good.

KEY TERMS
labour: human effort used in production.
capital / capital goods: artificial goods used in production.
consumer goods: goods and services purchased by households for their own satisfaction.

DISCUSSION

In your group, discuss which of the following are capital goods and which are consumer goods:

a   a chocolate bar

b   a car

c   a child's toy

d   a farm tractor

e   a dentist's drill

f   a courtroom.

TIP

Capital in everyday language usually means money that is used to start a business or expand an existing one. However, this money is not capital in an economic sense. This is because capital does not, itself, produce anything. It is the machines purchased with the money that are capital, for example. You can refer to money as financial capital but only use the term 'capital' for artificial goods used in production.

Enterprise

Enterprise is the willingness and ability to take risks and to make decisions in a business. **Entrepreneurs** are the people who organise the other factors of production and who crucially bear the risk of losing their money if their business fails. Entrepreneurs decide what to produce by taking into account consumer demand and how to produce it. Some of the risks faced by a business can be insured against, for example, fire, flood and theft. Other risks have to be accepted by entrepreneurs. This is because some risks cannot be insured against. These include the uninsurable risks of other firms bringing out rival products and the rising costs of production.

The two key tasks of an entrepreneur can be carried out by different people. In large companies, it is the shareholders who run the risk of losing their money if the companies go out of business, while the managing director takes production decisions and organises the factors of production.

> **KEY TERMS**
>
> **enterprise:** risk-taking and key decision-making in business.
>
> **entrepreneur:** a person who takes the risks and makes the key decisions in a business.

ACTIVITY 2.1

Table 2.1 shows a list of economic resources. In each case, decide whether the resource is an example of land, labour, capital or enterprise. Copy and complete the table.

Table 2.1

Economic resources	Factor of production
1 Chemical fertiliser	
2 A school	
3 A lake	
4 The work of a nurse	
5 The initiative needed to set up and run a bicycle repair shop	

Share your answers with another student. Discuss any that you have decided differently.

> **LINK**
>
> Wages are explored in detail in Chapter 17.1 (Factors affecting an individual's choice of occupation – Wages).

2.2 Rewards for the factors of production

Rewards for the factors of production are the payments made for the use of the factors. The rewards or factor payments can also be called factor incomes and factor earnings. Firms pay wages for the services of the workers. For taking uncertain risks and organising the other factors of production, entrepreneurs earn profit. Landowners receive rent, and interest is a payment for capital.

It may seem strange that interest is the reward to capital. However, entrepreneurs may have to borrow money to buy capital goods and will have to pay interest on the money they borrow. So, they are only likely to buy the capital goods if they think they will earn an amount at least equal to the rate of interest. If anyone else wants to make use of the capital goods, the payment received will again have to be at least equal to the rate of interest.

ACTIVITY 2.2

In a pair, produce a poster, based on the table below. Include a picture for each of the factors of production. Display the poster on your classroom wall if you are permitted to do so.

Factor of production	Definition	Example	Reward	Picture

REFLECTION

Did making the poster help you to understand the key features of the four factors of production?

2.3 Causes of changes in the quantity and quality of the factors of production

The quantity of land

The amount of physical land can be increased by land reclamation and decreased by soil erosion. A number of countries, including China, Dubai, the Maldives, the Netherlands and Singapore, have reclaimed land to use for farming and to build towns and cities on (see Figure 2.4). One cause of soil erosion is changes in how land is used. For example, the destruction of rainforests due to timber firms and farmers cutting down trees results in the release of carbon dioxide and other greenhouse gases and reduces the future capture of greenhouse gases. Pollution contributes to a rise in the world's average temperature. This climate change is causing more hurricanes, floods and droughts which result in widespread damage including soil being eroded.

Figure 2.4: Housing built on reclaimed land

Some natural resources are renewable while others are non-renewable. For example, renewable resources, such as wind power, are replaced by nature and can be used again and again. In contrast, non-renewable resources, such as gold and oil, are reduced by use. There is a risk that renewable resources can be turned into non-renewable resources if they are overexploited (used at a faster rate than they are replenished). Overfishing and the hunting of wildlife can reduce numbers to a point where they cannot be restored.

The quality of land

There are a number of reasons why the quality of natural resources may increase. Fertilisers can be used to increase the fertility of the land. The purity of rivers, and so the health of fish in the rivers, can be improved by stopping the pollution of rivers. Providing good drainage can increase the yield from fruit trees.

The quantity of labour

The quantity of labour is influenced by two key factors. One is the number of workers available and the second is the number of hours they work.

The number of available workers is determined by:

- **The size of the population.** The larger the population, the more workers there are likely to be.

- **The age structure of the population.** A country with a high proportion of people of working age will have more workers than a country with the same population size, but a higher proportion of people who would be too young or too elderly to work.

- **The retirement age.** The higher the retirement age, the more potential workers there will be.

- **The school-leaving age.** Raising the school-leaving age would reduce the number of workers.

- **Attitude to women in the labour force.** Countries where it is acceptable for women to work have more workers to draw on.

KEY TERM

labour force: people in work and those actively seeking work.

People who are working and those seeking work form the labour force. The labour force is also known as the workforce or working population. People of working age are everyone between the school-leaving age and the retirement age. In Singapore in 2023, the labour force included people aged between 16 and 63 years. Singapore plans to raise the retirement age to 65 years in 2030.

Not everyone of working age is in the labour force. Some may be in full-time education, some may have retired and some may be unable to work due to sickness or disability.

The number of hours which people work may be influenced by:

- the length of the average working day (for example, full-time workers in the USA tend to work for longer hours than those in European Union countries)

- whether they work full time or part time (for example, more people in the UK work part time than those in France)

- the amount of overtime a person may work

- the length of holidays taken by workers

- the amount of time lost through illness.

The quality of labour

As with all the factors of production, it is not only the quantity of labour that is important but also the quality. More can be produced with the same number of workers if the workers become more skilled. An increase in **productivity**, including **labour productivity**, is a major cause of an increase in a country's **output**.

The quality of labour can be improved as a result of better education, better training, more experience and better healthcare. A better educated, better trained and more experienced labour force will be able to carry out more difficult tasks, work with more complex machinery and equipment and produce more and better quality products (see Figure 2.5). A healthier labour force will be able to concentrate more, be stronger for any manual tasks and will have fewer days off sick.

Figure 2.5: An apprentice aircraft engineer learns skills that will contribute to the quality of labour

TIP

Increase your understanding of economics in the real world by finding out what has happened to the size of your country's labour force in the last ten years and why it has changed.

KEY TERMS

productivity: the output per factor of production in an hour.

labour productivity: output per worker hour.

output: goods and services produced by the factors of production.

ACTIVITY 2.3

Decide which of the following would raise labour productivity:

1   improved education and training

2   better equipment

3   worse working conditions.

Write your answers in your notebook. Include reasons for your decision.

The quantity of capital

The quantity of capital is influenced by **investment** and tends to increase with time. Every year some capital goods physically wear out and some become outdated, for example, a farmer's barn may fall down, and some machinery may be replaced by newer, more efficient machinery.

New capital goods usually take the place of worn-out or outdated goods that firms are unable (or choose not) to use anymore. Capital goods produced to replace those capital goods that cannot be repaired or are obsolete are referred to as replacement capital. The total value of the output of capital goods produced is known as **gross investment**. The value of replacement capital is called **depreciation** or capital consumption.

Net investment is the value of the extra capital goods made. It is equal to gross investment minus depreciation. For example, if a country produces $200 million of capital goods one year and there is depreciation of $70 million, net investment is $130 million. The country will have more capital goods. These additional capital goods will allow it to produce more goods and services.

Occasionally, gross investment may be lower than depreciation. This means that some of the capital goods taken out of use are not replaced. This is known as **negative net investment**.

The quality of capital

Advances in technology enable capital goods to produce a higher output and a better quality output. For example, the development of robotics in car production has greatly increased the number of cars that a car factory can produce (see Figure 2.6).

Figure 2.6: Robotics improves car production

KEY TERMS

investment: spending on capital goods.

gross investment: total spending on capital goods.

depreciation (capital consumption): the value of capital goods that have worn out or become obsolete.

net investment: gross investment minus depreciation.

negative net investment: a reduction in the number of capital goods caused by some obsolete and worn-out capital goods not being replaced.

ACTIVITY 2.4

A firm produces air conditioning units. It is currently using 12 machines. Each machine can produce 100 units, giving it a capacity to make 1 200 units. Three of the machines will wear out during the year. The firm expects to sell 1 600 units next year.

1   Individually:

    a   decide how many replacement machines the firm should buy

    b   calculate how many machines it should buy to expand its capacity

    c   calculate how many machines in total it should buy.

Share your answers with others in the group.

2   Discuss why, in the future, fewer machines are likely to be needed to produce the same output.

DISCUSSION

Discuss how advances in technology have changed:

a   students' learning experience

b   people's medical care

c   food production.

ECONOMICS IN ACTION

The development of AI

More of the machines and devices we use employ artificial intelligence (AI). This is the technology that enables machines to learn from the data they gather, to solve problems and to learn from past mistakes. For instance, AI can enable your smartphone to recommend products to you based on your previous spending patterns, and a video game you play may be adapted based on the skills you show.

In a few years' time, many people may have a home heating or cooling system controlled by AI, work with machines that use AI and travel on driverless buses (see Figure 2.7).

AI will enable machines to think and make decisions more like humans. Scientists disagree about whether or not machines will ever become more intelligent than humans. Both scientists and economists debate whether AI will be good for people. Some economists suggest that it will cause jobs to be lost. Others argue that it will increase output and create new jobs.

Figure 2.7: Driverless buses will make use of AI to take decisions based on road and traffic conditions

1   How is AI likely to affect the quantity and quality of capital goods?

2   Why might the development of AI result in the loss of jobs?

The quantity of enterprise

The quantity of enterprise will increase if there are more entrepreneurs. A good education system, including university degree courses in economics and business studies, may help to develop entrepreneurs in an economy. Lower taxes on firms' profits (corporate taxes) and a reduction in government regulations may encourage more people to set up their own businesses. A disproportionate number of migrants become entrepreneurs. These are people who have had the drive to leave where they have been living in search of a better or different life. This drive often leads them to become entrepreneurs in another country or a different region of their own country.

The quality of enterprise

The quality of enterprise can be improved if entrepreneurs receive better education, better training, better healthcare and gain more experience. More experience can be very important in the case of entrepreneurs. Very successful entrepreneurs have often set up businesses in the past, some of which may have failed. The knowledge and understanding they have gained of the products people like to buy and the best sources of raw materials can help them make a success of a new business.

ACTIVITY 2.5

In a group:

1   Research which entrepreneur founded each of the following firms and whether they have a university degree:

- Biocon, a biotechnology firm

- Lenovo, a computer firm

- Silverbird Group, a group of property, media and entertainment companies

- Sofizar, an internet marketing firm.

2   Find an example of a successful entrepreneur who does not have a degree.

3   Produce a poster from the information you have found.

SUMMARY

You should now know:

- The four factors of production are land, labour, capital and enterprise.

- Land is a term covering all natural resources.

- Labour involves the mental and physical effort workers put into producing goods and services.

- Capital goods are used to make other goods and services.

- Enterprise involves taking risks and making production decisions.

CONTINUED

- Land receives rent, labour receives wages, capital receives interest and enterprise receives profit.

- Some natural resources are renewable whereas others are non-renewable.

- Labour involves the mental and physical effort workers put into producing goods and services.

- The quantity of labour is influenced by the number of workers and the number of hours they work.

- The size of the labour force is influenced by the size and age structure of the population, the school-leaving age, the retirement age and attitudes to women in the workforce.

- Net investment increases a country's stock of capital goods.

- Improved education, lower taxes and less regulation can encourage enterprise.

Chapter 2 practice questions

1 Which factor of production's function is to make the key business decisions and take risks?

   A capital

   B enterprise

   C labour

   D land   [1]

2 Which type of factor of production is a road?

   A capital

   B enterprise

   C labour

   D land   [1]

3 A country produces 3 000 new capital goods in a week. Of these, 500 replace worn-out capital goods. What is the net investment made?

   A 500

   B 2 500

   C 3 000

   D 3 500   [1]

4   What is the difference between rent and wages?

   A   rent is a payment to capital, while wages are a payment to entrepreneurs

   B   rent is a payment to a factor of production that is scarce, whereas wages are a payment to a factor of production that is infinite

   C   wages are paid to a human resource, whereas rent is a payment to a natural resource

   D   wages are paid every day, whereas rent is paid annually   [1]

5   It is decided to cut down a forest and build a new factory on the cleared site. What effect will this have on the quantity of capital and the quantity of land?

	Quantity of capital	Quantity of land
A	Decrease	Increase
B	Increase	Decrease
C	Increase	Remain unchanged
D	Remain unchanged	Increase

[1]

Total: [5]

6   a   Identify **two** non-human factors of production.   [2]

   b   Explain **two** causes of an increase in the quantity of labour.   [4]

   c   Analyse why the quality of labour may increase over time.   [6]

Total: [12]

CHECK YOUR PROGRESS

How well do you think you have achieved the learning intentions for this chapter? Give yourself a score from 1 (still need a lot of practice) to 5 (feeling very confident) for each learning intention. Provide an example to support your score.

Now I can...	Score	Example
define the factors of production: land, labour, capital and enterprise		
give examples of the factors of production		
identify the rewards to the factors of production: rent, wages, interest and profit		
analyse the causes of changes in the quantity and quality of the factors of production.		

> Chapter 3

Opportunity cost

LEARNING INTENTIONS

By the end of this chapter, you will be able to:

- define opportunity cost
- give examples of opportunity cost in different contexts
- explain the influence of opportunity cost on decisions made by consumers, workers, producers/firms and governments when allocating their resources.

Introduction

There are many subjects that schools could teach. Several examination boards offer numerous subjects. Each school offers only a proportion of the subjects on offer. Why is this? It is because schools do not have enough classrooms, teachers and equipment to teach all subjects. For example, a classroom can be used to teach English or economics in the same room, but not at the same time.

There are not enough economic resources to produce all the goods and services we may like to have, as we saw in Chapter 1 (The nature of the basic economic problem). Land, labour, capital and enterprise are scarce, so decisions have to be made about the method and purpose of their use. In deciding what to use the classroom for, and in making other decisions, the concept of opportunity cost is important.

ECONOMICS IN CONTEXT

Making the best choice

Choices are not always easy. In 2023, work started on the construction of a large onshore wind farm in Golden Plains in the state of Victoria, Australia. The wind farm is expected to bring major benefits over the course of the next 30 years. It will produce enough clean, renewable energy to supply electricity to least 450 000 homes a year. This will reduce the need to use fossil fuels, such as coal, which causes pollution. It is also predicted that the wind farm will create approximately 700 jobs.

The site of the wind farm is near a small town. It is being built on agricultural land previously used to grow crops and raise livestock.

The wind farm is funded jointly by a French firm and the Australian government. Some Australians argue that government money could be better spent on a new hospital, for example.

Figure 3.1: A wind farm or a hospital? How do governments decide which project to fund?

Discuss in a pair or group:

1   What may have happened to agricultural output in Victoria as a result of the building of the wind farm?

2   Should the Australian government have spent the money building the wind farm or a new hospital?

3.1 The meaning of opportunity cost

When we decide to do one thing, we are also deciding not to do something else. To ensure that we make the right decisions, it is important that we consider the alternatives, particularly the best alternative. **Opportunity cost** is the cost of a decision in terms of the best alternative given up to achieve it. For example, there are a variety of things you could do tomorrow between 5 p.m. and 6 p.m.

KEY TERM

opportunity cost: the best alternative forgone.

These may be to go shopping, to read a chapter of an economics book, to do some paid work or to visit a friend (see Figure 3.2). You may narrow those choices down to reading the chapter or visiting a friend. You will have to consider very carefully which one will give you the best return. If you choose to read the chapter, you will not be able to visit your friend and vice versa.

Figure 3.2: Reading has an opportunity cost

LINK

We have unlimited wants but only limited resources. So, we have to make choices, and these choices involve an opportunity cost – see Chapter 1.1 (Finite resources and infinite wants).

TIP

When explaining opportunity cost, it is always useful to give an example.

ECONOMICS IN ACTION

The importance of opportunity cost

Opportunity cost is one of the key concepts used in economics. The concept can be used to analyse almost every issue in economics and in your everyday life. For example, you may find it helpful to spend time at the end of the week to review the work you have done in the different subjects you are studying. You have limited time, so you need to consider carefully how you use it. If you decide to spend 15 minutes producing a mind map on factors of production, you may have to sacrifice three mathematics practice questions you could have answered.

1   If you decide to go on to study A levels, how may the concept of opportunity cost be useful in making your choice?

2   How may opportunity cost be applied to a football manager's decision on who should take a penalty kick? (See Figure 3.3.)

Figure 3.3: Choosing one player to take a penalty kick involves an opportunity cost

3.2 Influence of opportunity cost on decision-making

Opportunity cost and consumers

Consumers are buyers and users of goods and services. We are all consumers. Most of us cannot buy everything we like. You may have to choose which economics dictionary to buy, for example. You will probably consider several different ones, taking into account their prices. The choice will then tend to settle on two of them. You are likely to select the one with the widest and the most accurate informative coverage. The closer the two dictionaries are in quality and price, the harder the choice will be.

Opportunity cost and workers

An individual working in one job involves an opportunity cost. People employed as teachers might also be able to work as civil servants. They need to carefully consider their preference for the jobs available. This would be influenced by a number of factors, including the wage paid, chances of promotion and the job satisfaction to be gained from each job. If the pay of civil servants or their working conditions improve, the opportunity cost of being a teacher will increase. It may even increase to the point where some teachers resign and become civil servants instead.

DISCUSSION

Discuss why the opportunity cost of working as an accountant is likely to be higher than that of working as a window cleaner.

Opportunity cost and producers

Producers have to decide what to make. If a farmer uses a field to grow oilseed, they cannot keep cattle on that field. If a car producer uses some of their factory space and workers to produce one model of a car, they cannot use the same space and workers to make another model of the car at the same time.

In deciding what to produce, private sector firms will tend to choose the option which will give them the maximum profit. This will involve the firm considering the demand for different products and the cost of producing those products.

ACTIVITY 3.1

In 2023, a firm spent a month producing four types of naan (see Figure 3.4). It calculated the profit earned per hour from the sale of the different types of naan as:

- garlic naan: $45
- paneer naan: $39
- keema naan: $48
- peshwari naan: $50.

CONTINUED

Figure 3.4: Naan, a type of flatbread

As a result, the firm decided to concentrate on making peshwari naan.

By 2025, costs and prices had changed. The firm decided to try producing the four types again, to see which would be the most profitable. This time it finds that the profit that can be earned is:

- garlic naan: $52
- keema naan: $26
- paneer naan: $43
- peshwari naan: $55.

In a pair, discuss these questions. Then write out your answers individually. Remember to explain your answers.

1   What was the opportunity cost of producing peshwari naan in 2023?

2   What happened to the opportunity cost of producing peshwari naan in 2025?

TIP

Opportunity cost is one of the most important concepts in economics. You will find that you can use it in answers to a wide range of structured questions.

Opportunity cost and the government

Government has to carefully consider its expenditure of tax revenue on various things. If it decides to spend more on education, the opportunity cost involved may be a reduced expenditure on healthcare. Government could, of course, raise tax revenue in order to spend more on education. In this case, the opportunity cost would be put on the taxpayers. To pay higher taxes, people may have to give up the opportunity to buy certain products or to save.

ACTIVITY 3.2

In a pair, copy and complete Table 3.1 by giving a possible opportunity cost of each decision.

Table 3.1

	Decision	Possible opportunity cost
Consumers	Travel by car	
	Buy basmati rice	
	Buy clothing online	
Workers	Work overtime	
	Work in a foreign country	
	Work full-time	
Producers	Rent an office building	
	Employ more workers	
	Produce skincare cream	
Government	Build new schools	
	Instruct state schools to start at 9 a.m.	
	Employ foreign economic advisers	

REFLECTION

How did your understanding of opportunity cost help you to choose appropriate examples in Activity 3.2? Has the activity helped to reinforce your understanding of the concept of opportunity cost?

ACTIVITY 3.3

In a group, discuss what might be the opportunity cost in each of the following examples:

1   A person wanting to buy fruit, decides to buy apples.

2   A person decides to study economics at a university.

3   A factory is built on farmland.

Now each share an example of an opportunity cost in your daily lives. How do your opportunity costs vary?

Economic goods and free goods

Resources are used to produce economic goods, so their production involves an opportunity cost. In contrast, no resources are used to produce free goods, so they do not involve an opportunity cost.

LINK

The difference between economic goods and free goods explains why economic goods involve an opportunity cost while free goods do not – see Chapter 1.3 (Economic goods and free goods).

SUMMARY

You should now know:

- Opportunity cost is an important concept as it emphasises that people should consider what they are sacrificing when they make a decision.

- Consumers, workers and producers should consider opportunity cost when deciding what to buy, what job to do and what to produce.

- Governments should take opportunity cost into account when deciding what to spend their tax revenue on.

- Economic goods have an opportunity cost whereas free goods do not.

Chapter 3 practice questions

1   A person decides to go to university for three years to study economics. If they had not gone to university, they could have taken up a job which would have paid them $15 000 a year. After the person graduates, they expect to find a job paying them $40 000 a year. What is the opportunity cost of going to the university for them?

   A $15 000

   B $40 000

   C $45 000

   D $120 000   [1]

2   What are the characteristics of a free good?

A	Has an opportunity cost	Takes resources to produce it
B	Has an opportunity cost	Takes no resources to produce it
C	Has no opportunity cost	Takes no resources to produce it
D	Has no opportunity cost	Takes resources to produce it

[1]

3 When Kamran reaches 16 years of age, he receives $200 from his aunt, $50 of which he decides to save. He is taken out by his father to watch a movie at a local cinema. His father pays for the cinema tickets. Kamran spends the afternoon playing football. Which of these activities involves an opportunity cost?

	Watching the movie	Playing football	Saving
A	No	No	No
B	No	No	Yes
C	No	Yes	Yes
D	Yes	Yes	Yes

[1]

4 A person receives an invitation to a free lunch. What is a possible opportunity cost to them of accepting the invitation?

A the food that could have been eaten by another person

B the food that they do not select from the menu

C the time taken to produce the food they eat

D the time they could have spent playing tennis [1]

5 A firm can produce gloves and scarves. The table shows the combination of the two products it could make.

Pairs of gloves	Scarves
0	85
18	70
34	50
48	26
60	0

Based on the data, if the firm is currently producing 18 pairs of gloves and 70 scarves, what would be the opportunity cost of producing 16 more pairs of gloves?

A 15 scarves

B 20 scarves

C 50 scarves

D 85 scarves [1]

Total: [5]

6 a Define 'opportunity cost'. [2]

b Explain why opportunity cost is an important concept for producers. [4]

c Analyse what effect the building of an airport may have on the decision of how to use an area of land nearby. [6]

Total: [12]

CHECK YOUR PROGRESS

How well do you think you have achieved the learning intentions for this chapter?
Give yourself a score from 1 (still need a lot of practice) to 5 (feeling very confident)
for each learning intention. Provide an example to support your score.

Now I can...	Score	Example
define opportunity cost		
give examples of opportunity cost in different contexts		
explain the influence of opportunity cost on the decisions made by consumers, workers, producers and governments.		

> Chapter 4

Production possibility curve diagrams

LEARNING INTENTIONS

By the end of this chapter you will be able to:

- define a production possibility curve (PPC)
- draw a PPC
- interpret points under, on and beyond a PPC
- analyse movements along a PPC
- analyse the causes and consequences of shifts in a PPC in terms of an economy's growth.

Introduction

The USA produces many more goods and services than Mauritius. In 2023, the output of the USA was valued at $26 265 billion, whereas it was only $14 billion in Mauritius. This is because the USA has a much larger economy with a much larger labour force, more capital equipment, more entrepreneurs and more natural resources.

The productive potential of an individual, producer/firm or a country can be shown on a production possibility curve (PPC) diagram. A PPC diagram can also illustrate opportunity cost and efficiency.

ECONOMICS IN CONTEXT

Changes in the quantity and quality of factors of production

The number and quality of resources are regularly changing. For example, between 2000 and 2023, the labour force of India increased from 400 million workers to 525 million (see Figure 4.1). More workers increase the total output a country can produce. The availability of more workers usually results in the country producing more goods and services.

Over the same period, the labour force of Latvia, a small European country, fell from 1.1 million to 0.9 million workers. Some Latvian workers left the country to live and work in other European countries. They were attracted by higher wages in countries such as Germany. However, despite the fall in the number of workers that Latvia had, its total output increased. This was because it had an increase in another factor of production, capital, and because the quality of its remaining labour force rose with improved education and training.

More and better factors of production increase the potential output of a country, but countries do not always make use of the factors of production they have. Not using factors of production means that a country is not producing as much as it could be.

Discuss in a pair or group:

1 Do you think your country has more factors of production than it did five years ago?

2 What would you advise your school/college to do with extra factors of production?

Figure 4.1: Office workers in India

4.1 Production possibility curves

A **production possibility curve (PPC)** shows the maximum output of two types of products and combinations of those products that can be produced with the existing quantity and quality of resources and technology. A production possibility curve is also known as a production possibility frontier or a production possibility boundary.

Figure 4.2 shows that a country can produce either 200 capital goods or 300 consumer goods or a range of combinations of these two types of goods.

KEY TERM

production possibility curve (PPC): a curve that shows the maximum output of two types of products and combination of those products that can be produced with existing resources and technology.

Capital goods

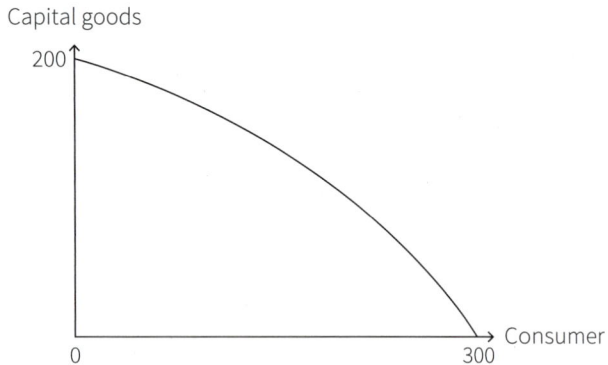

Figure 4.2: A production possibility curve (PPC)

4.2 Points under, on and beyond a PPC

While a PPC shows the maximum amount that can currently be produced, a production point shows what is being produced or what may be produced in the future. A point anywhere on the curve, such as Point Y in Figure 4.3, means that resources are used optimally. This is an efficient output. Any point inside the curve, that is to the left of the curve, means there is not full use of resources. Point X in the diagram shows output is being produced where there are unemployed resources.

There are not enough resources to produce outside the limit set by the PPC. So, a point such as Z is not currently achievable.

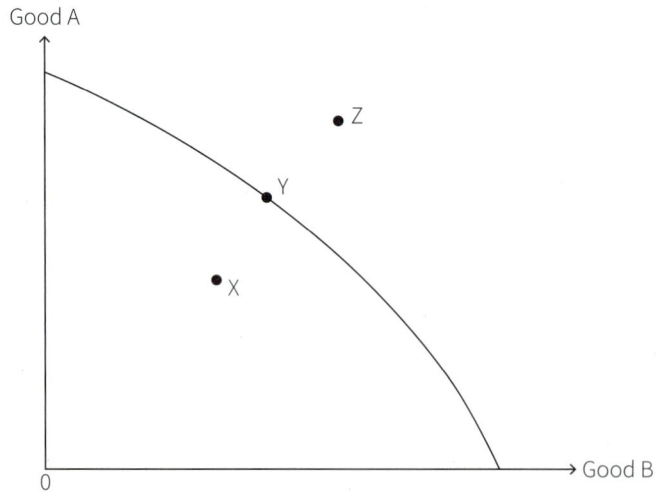

Figure 4.3: A PPC and production points

ACTIVITY 4.1

Figure 4.4 shows a country's PPC. Before looking at the questions below, discuss the diagram with another student. Then, individually, write your answers in your notebook.

1   If a country is producing at Point X, what is its output of capital goods and consumer goods?

2   If a country's output moves from Point X to Point Y, how many more capital goods and how many more consumer goods will it produce?

3   What is the maximum number of capital goods that can be produced if all resources are devoted to capital goods?

Share your answers with your partner.

Capital goods

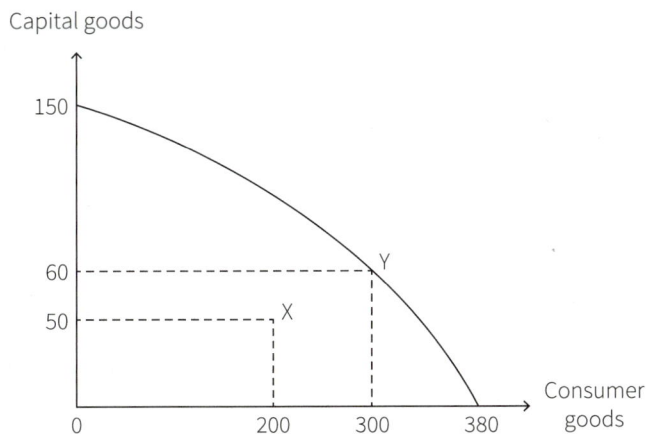

Figure 4.4: A country's PPC

REFLECTION

Were you confident in your answers to Activity 4.1? Did you find it helpful to discuss the PPC diagram with a partner before you looked at the questions? Did you reread Sections 4.1 and 4.2 to ensure you fully understood the information on PPC diagrams before jotting down your answers?

4.3 Movements along a PPC

A movement along a PPC shows that resources are being reallocated. It also shows the opportunity cost of that decision. Figure 4.5 shows a country initially deciding to produce 80 units of manufactured goods and 75 units of agricultural goods. If the country then decides to produce 100 units of agricultural goods, it will have to switch resources away from producing manufactured goods. The diagram shows the reduction of output of manufactured goods to 60 units. In this case, the opportunity cost of producing 25 extra units of agricultural goods is 20 units of manufactured goods.

Manufactured goods

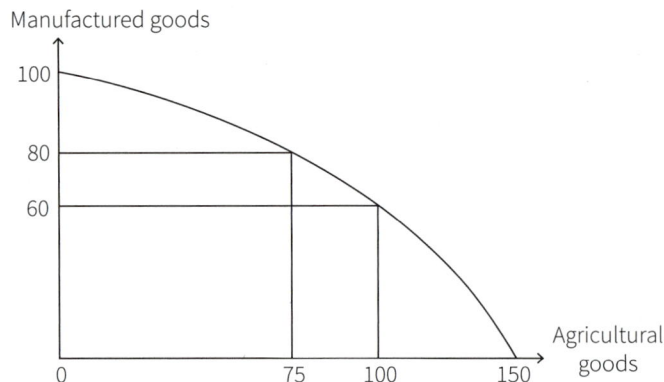

Figure 4.5: A movement along the PPC

LINK

PPC diagrams are a good way to analyse the opportunity cost involved in deciding what to produce – see Chapter 3.2 (Influence of opportunity cost on decision-making).

REFLECTION

Check your answers with another student. If you disagree, can you explain how you arrived at your answers? If you think you have made a mistake, think why this has occurred. Are there aspects of PPCs that you need to check over?

ACTIVITY 4.2

Figure 4.6 shows a country's PPC. Write down your answers to the questions.

1   What is the maximum number of capital goods the country can produce if it devotes all its resources to making capital goods?

2   Calculate the opportunity cost of increasing the output of consumer goods from 80 to 90 units.

Capital goods

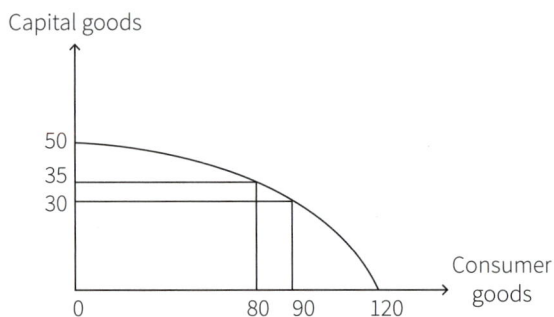

Figure 4.6: A country's PPC

The shape of the PPC

PPCs are usually bowed outwards as shown in Figures 4.2–4.6. This is because the best resources are used first to produce a particular type of product. In Figure 4.5, we noted the opportunity cost of increasing the output of manufactured goods from 60 to 80 was 25 agricultural goods.

To increase the output of manufactured goods by a further 20 to 100 would involve a higher opportunity cost of 75. The last resources switched from producing agricultural goods would have been the least suited to producing manufactured goods.

In the less common situation where resources are equally suited to producing both types of products, the opportunity cost remains constant. In this case, the PPC is shown as a straight line, as shown in Figure 4.7.

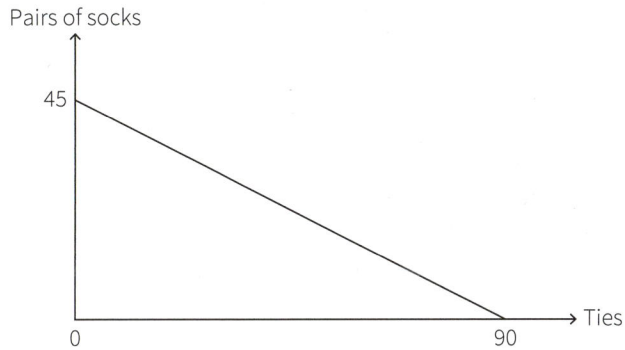

Figure 4.7: A straight-line PPC

The opportunity cost of producing 1 more pair of socks remains at 2 ties as the output of socks changes.

4.4 Shifts of a PPC

Causes of shifts of a PPC

The PPC will shift to the right if there is an increase in the quantity or quality of resources (see Figure 4.8). For example, if there is an increase in the size of the labour force, the maximum output that a country can produce will increase.

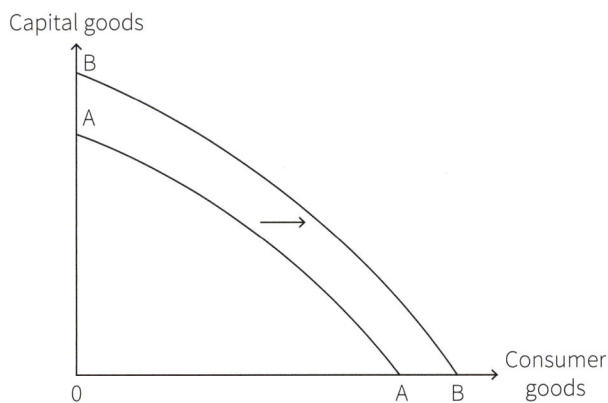

Figure 4.8: A shift in a PPC

A shift to the left of the PPC will be caused by a reduction in the quantity or quality of resources.

ACTIVITY 4.3

In a group, discuss and decide whether scenarios in Table 4.1 will cause a shift of a country's PPC to the left or the right. Individually, copy and complete the table. Explain each of your decisions. One has been done for you.

Table 4.1

		Does the PPC shift right or left?	Explanation
1	Advances in technology		
2	A rise in the retirement age	Right	An increase in the quantity of labour
3	Improved education		
4	Widespread floods		
5	Worn-out capital goods not being replaced		

DISCUSSION

Discuss how a production point to the right of an economy's current PPC could be achieved in the future.

Consequences of a shift of the PPC

A shift to the right of the PPC increases a country's productive potential. The country will be able to produce more. This is referred to as potential economic growth. To take advantage of this increased capacity, extra or better quality resources have to be used. Figure 4.9 shows both the PPC and the production point moving to the right, so output increases. A rise in a country's output is actual economic growth.

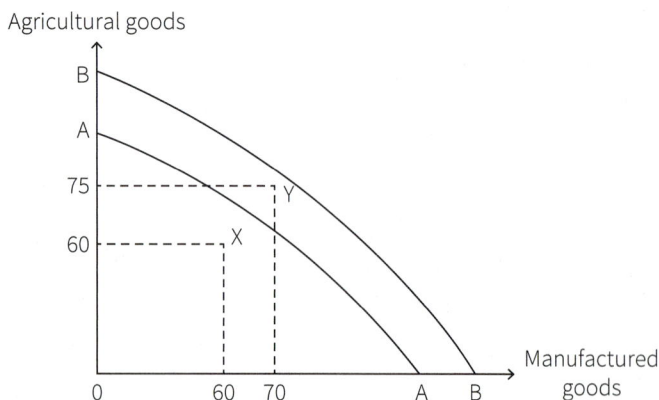

Figure 4.9: Economic growth

LINK

The reasons why economic growth, and so a movement of the production point and/or a shift of the PPC to the right may occur, are discussed in Chapter 26.2 Economic growth (causes).

ECONOMICS IN ACTION

The use of PPCs

Economists use PPCs to illustrate the choices facing individuals, producers/firms and economies, how resources are currently being used and the effects of changes in the quality and quantity of resources.

One change which is altering the PPCs of many countries is the increase in the average age of populations. Having a higher proportion of older people and a smaller proportion of children may change the pattern of demand. For example, more holidays or leisure activities for retired people may be demanded while fewer children's video games may be demanded (see Figure 4.10). A change in the pattern of demand can alter how firms allocate their resources. An older population may also alter the number of workers available to an economy and the skills of the workers. For example, older workers may be more experienced but may not be as up to date with advances in technology.

PPCs can be used to model the effects of a range of issues facing individuals, producers/firms and the economy, including the effects of an ageing population.

1   What is the difference between how a change in resource allocation is shown in a PPC diagram and how a change in the quantity of resources is shown?

2   How would a failure to make full use of advances in technology be shown in a PPC diagram?

Figure 4.10: An art class for older people

SUMMARY

You should now know:

- A PPC can be used to illustrate opportunity cost. It shows what can be produced with existing resources and current technology.

- A point inside a curve indicates unemployed resources, a point on the curve shows full use of resources and a point to the right of the curve is currently unachievable.

- A movement along a PPC shows a reallocation of resources and the opportunity cost involved.

- A bowed outwards PPC shows an increasing opportunity cost, whereas a straight-line PPC shows a constant opportunity cost.

- An increase in the quantity or quality of resources will cause a shift of the PPC to the right and an increase in productive potential.

Chapter 4 practice questions

1   A country experiences a fall in unemployment. How would this be shown on a PPC diagram?

    A   a movement of the production point away from the curve

    B   a movement of the production point towards the curve

    C   a shift of the PPC to the left

    D   a shift of the PPC to the right   [1]

2   Which points in the diagram are attainable?

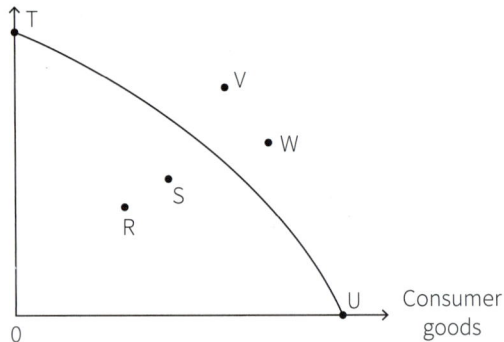

    A   R and S

    B   V and W

    C   R, S, T and U

    D   T, U, V and W   [1]

3   The diagram shows a country's production possibility curve (PPC) showing the potential output of movies and TV programmes. The PPC is a downward sloping straight line. What can be concluded from the shape of the PPC?

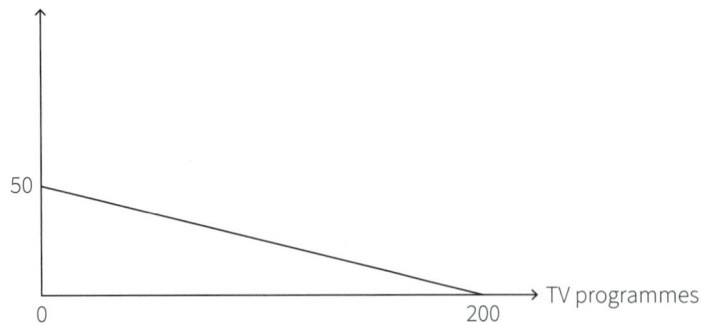

    A   all resources are equally good at producing movies and TV programmes

    B   resources cannot be switched between producing movies and TV programmes

    C   the country is able to produce 50 movies and 200 TV programmes

    D   TV programmes take more resources to produce than movies   [1]

4   The diagram shows a production possibility curve (PPC) with two different types of goods: basic goods and luxury goods. What would be the opportunity cost of increasing the output of luxury goods from 25 to 35?

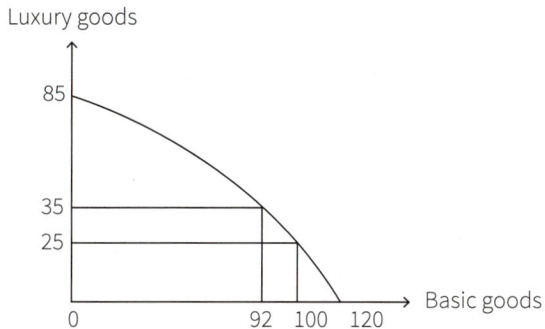

- **A**   8 basic goods
- **B**   10 luxury goods
- **C**   25 luxury goods
- **D**   92 basic goods   **[1]**

5   The diagram shows a production possibility curve (PPC) with two goods: food and clothing. What could have caused the change in the shape of the PPC shown below?

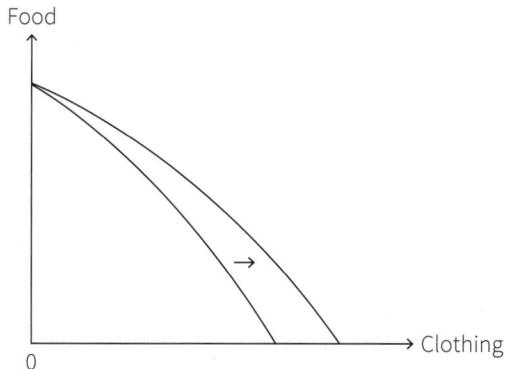

- **A**   a change in consumer preferences towards clothing
- **B**   advances in technology in the clothing industry
- **C**   an increase in the size of a country's labour force
- **D**   more resources being devoted to producing clothing   **[1]**

                                                                          Total: [5]

6   **a**   What is the difference between a point inside and a point on a PPC?   **[2]**

   b   Explain **two** causes of a shift in a PPC.   **[4]**

   c   Analyse how a PPC illustrates scarcity, opportunity cost and efficiency.   **[6]**

                                                                          Total: [12]

CHECK YOUR PROGRESS

How well do you think you have achieved the learning intentions for this chapter?
Give yourself a score from 1 (still need a lot of practice) to 5 (feeling very confident)
for each learning intention. Provide an example to support your score.

Now I can...	Score	Example
define a production possibility curve (PPC)		
draw a PPC		
interpret points under, on and beyond a PPC		
analyse movements along a PPC		
analyse the causes and consequences of shifts of a PPC.		

Section 1 practice questions

1 Read the source material carefully before answering all parts of the question.

CASE STUDY: AGRICULTURAL OUTPUT IN AFRICA

The output of more fertilisers and better irrigation have contributed to higher agricultural output for each unit of land in Africa in recent years. More significant, however, has been the increase in the quantity of land used for agriculture, particularly to grow crops.

Despite the rise in agricultural output, the quantity of high-quality food that people would like to consume is not keeping pace with the rise in population in all African countries. Africa's population is set to double by 2050, which will increase the demand for food even further. As incomes increase in Africa, the desire for a range of products is increasing. People in Africa are, for example, wanting more and better housing. Indeed, the desire for housing usually outstrips the growth in resources devoted to housing. People constantly strive for better living standards.

The expansion of the housebuilding industry is encouraging some farm workers to switch to working in the building industry. Changes in the pattern of demand are causing not only agricultural workers but also other workers to change their occupation and where they work.

Agricultural output can fluctuate quite significantly as it can be influenced by, for example, floods, droughts and heatwaves. The contribution of agricultural output varies between countries. For example, in 2023, agriculture accounted for a much lower percentage of South Africa's total output than of Nigeria's total output (see Table 1).

The total output a country produces is influenced by the size of the labour force. Table 1 shows the size of the labour force and total output for a group of selected African countries.

Africa fact file	
Land used for agriculture in 1975	12%
Land used for agriculture in 2023	36%
Agriculture's contribution to South Africa's total output in 2023	3%
Agriculture's contribution to Nigeria's total output in 2023	21%

Table 1: The labour force and total output of five African countries

Country	Labour force (millions)	Total output ($ billions)
Ethiopia	60	126
Ghana	15	73
Mali	8	19
Nigeria	73	476
South Africa	25	406

Refer to the information in the source material in your answers.

  a   Calculate the value of agricultural output in South Africa in 2023. **[2]**

  b   Identify **two** reasons why the productivity of land has increased in Africa. **[2]**

  c   Explain the opportunity cost of working on a farm. **[2]**

  d   Explain **two** examples of the economic problem. **[4]**

  e   Analyse the relationship between the size of a country's labour force and its output, as shown in the table. **[4]**

  f   Discuss whether or not an increase in the output of food will reduce the output of other products. **[6]**

Total: [20]

2   In 2023, a floating turbine, moored in the sea off the coast of the north of the UK, started to produce electricity from wave power. More entrepreneurs are becoming interested in making use of wave power, which is a free good. All four factors of production are employed in making use of wave power, including labour. The quality of labour usually increases over time. However, it can be more difficult to predict what may happened to the quantity of labour in a country in the future.

  a   Define 'entrepreneur'. **[2]**

  b   Explain the difference between a free good and an economic good. **[4]**

  c   Analyse, using a production possibility curve (PPC), the effect on an economy of an increase in the supply of labour. **[6]**

  d   Discuss whether or not the quantity of labour in your country is likely to increase in the future. **[8]**

Total: [20]

> Section 2

The allocation of resources

> Chapter 5

The role of markets in allocating resources

LEARNING INTENTIONS

By the end of this chapter, you will be able to:

- define a market
- gives examples of markets
- explain the roles of buyers and sellers.

Introduction

We all buy goods and services. Sometimes we may also sell a good or service. For example, you may buy a laptop on an online selling platform. When you want to replace the laptop, you may try to sell your old laptop on the same platform. The aims you may have as a buyer and a seller may differ.

ECONOMICS IN CONTEXT

A market for spices

The Dubai Spice Souk is one of the oldest spice markets in the world (see Figure 5.1). At the market, a variety of spices including cardamom, chilli, frankincense, ginger, saffron and turmeric are offered for sale.

People from Dubai and tourists from across the world come to the market to buy spices. Most buyers and sellers haggle over the price of the spices. People from Dubai have more experience in knowing what prices the sellers will accept. The amount of each spice purchased varies between buyers depending on what they require. A chef working in a Dubai hotel is likely to buy more than a tourist, for example.

Figure 5.1: At the Dubai Spice Souk, sellers want to sell their goods for the highest price while buyers bargain for the lowest price

Discuss in a pair or group:

1. What price would you initially offer for a small bag of ginger if you are willing to pay $6?

2. What advantages might buyers receive from having a large number of sellers to choose from?

5.1 How markets work

Many people think that a **market** is always a particular place, such as the Dubai Spice Souk or a shop. In economics, the term 'market' means any arrangement that allows goods and services to be traded. For example, it may include a furniture manufacturer making contact with potential buyers of its chairs by placing advertisements in magazines. Many markets are now online. Online banking allows bank customers and their banks to exchange payments and services over the internet.

Markets can be studied on different levels in terms of product and geography. For example, the market for carrots in Phuket in Thailand has far fewer buyers and sellers than the global market for vegetables.

Besides what products are traded and where they are traded, markets can also be examined in terms of how many firms compete to sell the product.

KEY TERM

market: an arrangement which brings buyers into contact with sellers and which includes all the buyers and sellers.

LINK

Chapter 21.1 (Competitive markets) outlines some of the advantages consumers may gain from having a number of sellers in a market.

ACTIVITY 5.1

In a pair, research what products are bought and sold in the following markets:

1   City God Temple Market, Shanghai, China

2   Forex Market, London, UK

3   Kawran Bazaar, Dhaka, Bangladesh

4   Rahba Kedima Souk Smarine, Marrakesh, Morocco

5   Royal Flora Holland, the Netherlands.

Produce a poster about a market. The market could be one of the above or another market of your choice. The poster could include the products traded, the age of the market, its busy times and images of the market.

ECONOMICS IN ACTION

The growing video games market

The video games market is one of the fastest growing markets in the world (see Figure 5.2). It is expected to be worth over $550 billion by 2030. Advances in technology are increasing the quality of both the platforms games can be played on, including smartphones, laptops, tablets and TVs, and the games themselves. In 2023, nearly 3 billion people worldwide played video games. The market for video games contains people of all ages including some with high incomes.

1   What may be the opportunity cost of a senior accountant playing a video game?

2   On what basis do you think economists make predictions about the future value of a product's sales?

Figure 5.2: More people are playing video games

5.2 The role of buyers and sellers

Buyers buy products from sellers. Buyers are sometimes called **consumers**. They may be individuals, **firms** or governments. Individuals may buy food for themselves and for their families to eat. Firms buy **raw materials** such as flour purchased by bakers and machines such as cameras bought by movie makers. Governments may buy MRI scanners for its state hospitals.

Sellers sell products to buyers. An individual may sell a bicycle they no longer use. Firms may sell cars, insurance or jewellery. Governments may sell goods and services through the firms they own such as a state-owned railway firm. Workers also sell their labour.

KEY TERMS

consumers: people who buy goods and services for their own or their family's use.

firm: a business organisation that produces goods and services.

raw materials: basic materials used to produce goods.

DISCUSSION

Discuss why you think the price of some earbuds is higher than other earbuds.

ACTIVITY 5.2

This activity will help you to understand the roles of buyers and sellers in a market. Your class is going to role-play the buyers and sellers. Your teacher will give you a set of blank cards, five envelopes and some blank paper. Prepare the cards the cards by writing on the following roles:

- Seller of an economics workbook (on two cards)
- Seller of a set of pens (on two cards)
- Seller of A4 paper (on two cards)
- Seller of a ruler (on two cards)
- Seller of a college bag (on two cards)
- Buyer (on 20 cards)

Write the name of the item to be sold on each envelope (economics workbooks, pens, paper, rulers, college bags).

Shuffle the cards. Place them face down. Each member of the class picks up the top card in the pack to decide their role.

Each buyer has $60. They have to spend all of their money on up to **four** of the items. Each buyer should consider how they want to spread the $60 between four items. For example, they may be prepared to spend $25 on a college bag, $15 on an economics workbook, $10 on a set of pens and $10 on A4 paper. They should then put a folded bid with their name on it in each of the five envelopes with a 'no bid' in one envelope. When all the bids are made, each of the sellers should consider which two bids they will accept and let the successful bidders know.

REFLECTION

Did Activity 5.2 help you to understand the roles of buyers and sellers? If not, what will you do to improve your understanding of the aims of buyers and sellers?

SUMMARY

You should now know:

- A market is an arrangement that brings buyers and sellers into contact with each other and includes all those involved in the exchange of the product.
- Buyers and sellers may meet face-to-face in a shop or by using technology such as the internet, for example.
- Buyers purchase what is produced, and sellers provide the products for buyers to purchase.

TIP

Try to follow changes in a major global market such as the oil market. This will help you see how a real-world market works, and you may be able to use some of the knowledge you gain in your economics studies.

LINK

Chapter 18.1 (Different types of firms) looks at the different sectors firms operate in and the different sizes of firms.

Chapter 5 practice questions

1 What is a market?

    A   all the buyers of a product

    B   all the sellers of a product

    C   an arrangement which allows buyers to gain more than sellers

    D   an arrangement which allows products to be exchanged   [1]

2 If sellers find that no one will buy what they are trying to sell, what are they likely to do?

    A   increase their output

    B   increase the time buyers have to wait to get the product

    C   lower the price they charge

    D   reduce the quality of the product   [1]

3 There are 3 000 boxes of chocolates sold in a town in one month. What can be concluded from this information?

    A   there are 3 000 buyers

    B   there are three 3 000 sellers

    C   there is an equal amount bought and sold

    D   there is an equal number of buyers and sellers   [1]

Total: [3]

4 a   Define 'market'.   [2]

    b   Explain why a successful football club may build a larger stadium.   [4]

    c   Analyse how the key resource allocation decisions influence the products a consumer can buy.   [6]

Total: [12]

CHECK YOUR PROGRESS

How well do you think you have achieved the learning intentions for this chapter? Give yourself a score from 1 (still need a lot of practice) to 5 (feeling very confident) for each learning intention. Provide an example to support your score.

Now I can...	Score	Example
define a market		
give examples of markets		
explain the roles of buyers and sellers.		

› Chapter 6
Demand

LEARNING INTENTIONS

By the end of this chapter, you will be able to:

- define demand
- recognise the link between individual and market demand
- draw and interpret the demand diagram
- explain the causes of extensions and contractions in demand
- draw diagrams that illustrate movements along a demand curve
- analyse the causes of increases and decreases in demand
- draw diagrams that illustrate shifts of the demand curve.

Introduction

Imagine you find that the price of your favourite snack has been reduced. Would you buy more? If so, why? What happens to the quantity of ice cream people buy in hot weather? Why might people in low-income countries own fewer cars than people in high-income countries? Economists answer these and other questions by examining the influences on demand.

ECONOMICS IN CONTEXT

Demand for e-bikes

Each year more people buy electric bikes (e-bikes) (see Figure 6.1). In 2023, the value of e-bikes bought was $27 billion. It is predicted that by 2030, this will increase to $63 billion. There are a number of reasons why more people are buying e-bikes. These include increases in income, greater awareness of the health benefits of cycling and concern about the environment. Some people buy e-bikes to travel relatively short distances in city centres, while others buy e-bikes to travel longer distances, such as exploring different parts of the country.

People of a wide range of ages are buying e-bikes. They are easier for older people to ride than other types of bikes, but the largest age group currently buying them is between 25 and 34 years.

Figure 6.1: More people are buying and riding e-bikes

Discuss in a pair or group:

1   Are more people buying e-bikes in your country?

2   What would influence your decision of whether to buy an e-bike?

6.1 Individual and market demand

When economists discuss **demand**, they mean the *willingness* and *ability* to buy a product. We may want a product, but if we cannot afford the product, we will not be able to buy it. Alternatively, we may have the money to purchase the product, but if we do not want it, we will not buy it. So, if economists state that demand for a product is 2 000 at a price of $30, they mean that people are willing and able to buy that number (2 000) at that price ($30).

Demand and price are inversely related. Inversely related means that demand will rise as price falls and fall as price rises. A higher price will mean that fewer people will be able to afford the product. They will also be less willing to buy it and will be more likely to switch to rival products. So, as price rises, the willingness and ability to buy a product falls.

KEY TERM

demand: the willingness and ability to buy a product.

The link between individual and market demand

Economists study individual demand and, more commonly, **market demand**. Individual demand is the amount of a product an individual would be willing and able to buy, at different prices. Market demand is the total demand for a product at different prices. Market demand is found by adding up each individual's demand at different prices. The totalling of the demand of all of the potential buyers is sometimes referred to as **aggregation**.

KEY TERMS

market demand: total demand for a product.

aggregation: the addition of individual units to arrive at a total amount.

A demand schedule

A demand schedule lists the different quantities demanded of a product, at different prices over a particular time period. Table 6.1 shows a demand schedule for tickets on trains from Station X to Station Y.

Table 6.1: Daily demand for train tickets from Station X to Station Y

Price ($)	Quantity demanded
50	2 200
45	2 500
40	3 000
35	3 800
30	5 000
25	7 000

Drawing and interpreting the demand diagram

The information from a demand curve can be plotted on a diagram. Price is measured on the vertical y-axis (the line going up) and quantity demanded on the horizontal x-axis (the line going across). Figure 6.2 shows the information in Table 6.1 as a diagram.

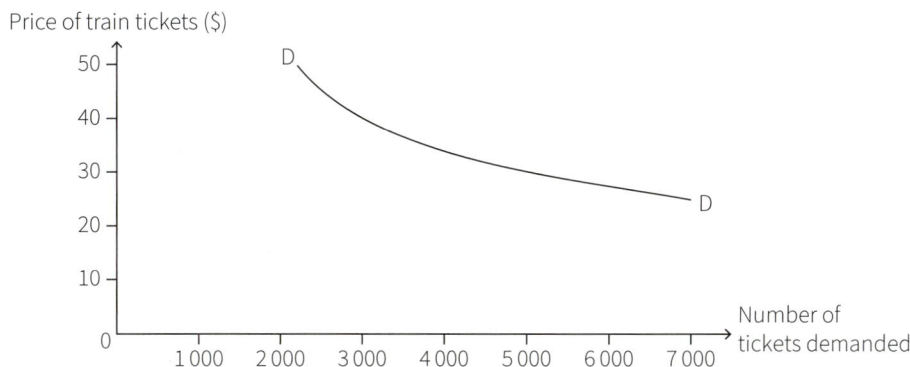

Figure 6.2: Daily demand (D) for train tickets from Station X to Station Y

The demand curve in Figure 6.2 and the demand schedule on which it is based (Table 6.1) do not show the demand over the full range of prices. It is possible to do this. Figure 6.3 illustrates this type of curve.

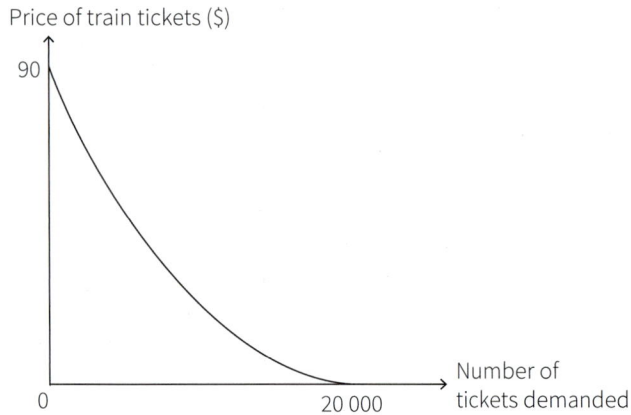

Figure 6.3: A demand curve over the full range of prices

TIP

When answering questions on demand and supply, you will find it helpful to draw diagrams. A diagram must be accurately and fully labelled. It should also be large enough and clear. It is advisable to use at least one-third of an A4-size page for drawing a diagram. Remember to explain the diagram in your text.

The curve shows the price, $90, at which people would stop buying tickets. At $90, the service is priced out of the market. It also shows how many tickets people would want if they were provided free of charge. As it is unusual for firms to charge either such a high price that demand is zero or a zero price, demand curves are often not taken to the axes.

To save time and for clarity, economists often draw demand curves as straight lines, as shown in Figure 6.4. Straight-line demand curves are still referred to as curves. Demand curves do not always show exact quantities and prices but can be used to illustrate the relationship between demand and price, and the effect of price changes on demand.

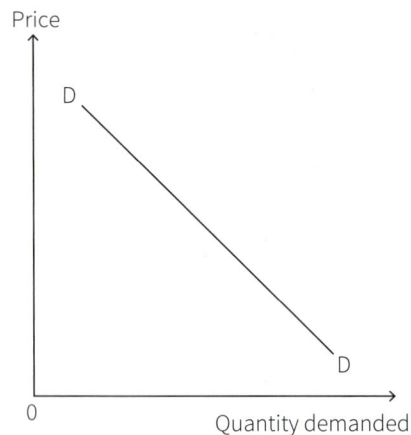

Figure 6.4: A straight-line demand curve

Using the demand schedule in Table 6.2, plot the demand curve for rooms in a hotel in Delhi.

Table 6.2: Demand for rooms in a hotel in Delhi

Price ($)	Number of rooms
800	10
700	20
600	35
500	55
400	80
300	110

6.2 Movements along a demand curve

Causes of extensions and contractions in demand

As mentioned earlier, a fall in the price of a product is likely to lead to a rise in demand for the product. Economists refer to this as **extension in demand** or a rise in the quantity demanded. When an economist sees the term 'extension in demand', or 'rise in the quantity demanded', they will understand that the cause of the alteration in demand is a change in the price of the product itself. A change like this can be illustrated on a demand curve, as shown in Figure 6.5.

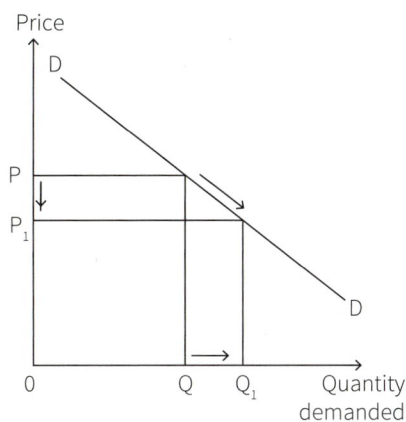

Figure 6.5: An extension in demand

The diagram shows that a fall in price from P to P_1 has caused the demand to extend from Q to Q_1. In contrast, a rise in price will cause a **contraction in demand** which can also be referred to as a fall in quantity demanded.

Figure 6.6 shows the impact of a rise in price. Demand contracts from Q to Q_1 as a result of a rise in price from P to P_1.

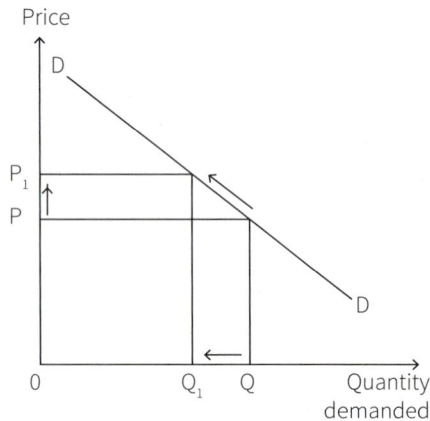

Figure 6.6: A contraction in demand

ACTIVITY 6.2

A shop changes the price of a can of soft drink from $3 to $2. As a result, demand changes from 40 cans a day to 50 cans. Illustrate this change on a demand curve.

Share your diagram with another student. Decide whether demand has extended or contracted.

6.3 Shifts of a demand curve

If people demand more or less of a product for a reason other than a change in its price, this is referred to as a **change in demand**. There are a range of causes of changes in demand. These reasons are sometimes known as the conditions of demand. For example, in a period of hot weather there is likely to be an **increase in demand** for ice cream (see Figure 6.7). The quantities demanded will rise at each and every price. A new demand schedule can be drawn up to show the higher level of demand (see Table 6.3).

Figure 6.7: There may be an increased demand for ice cream on a hot day

Table 6.3: Demand for ice cream

Price per ice cream	Quantities demanded per day	
$	Original demand	New demand
5	2 000	4 000
4	3 000	5 000
3	4 000	6 000
2	5 000	7 000
1	6 000	8 000

On a diagram, an increase in demand is shown by a shift to the right of the demand curve. Figure 6.8 shows that at any given price, a larger quantity is demanded. For example, at a price of $2, initially 5 000 ice creams would be demanded a day. The hot weather would encourage people to buy more ice creams. Demand would increase to 7 000.

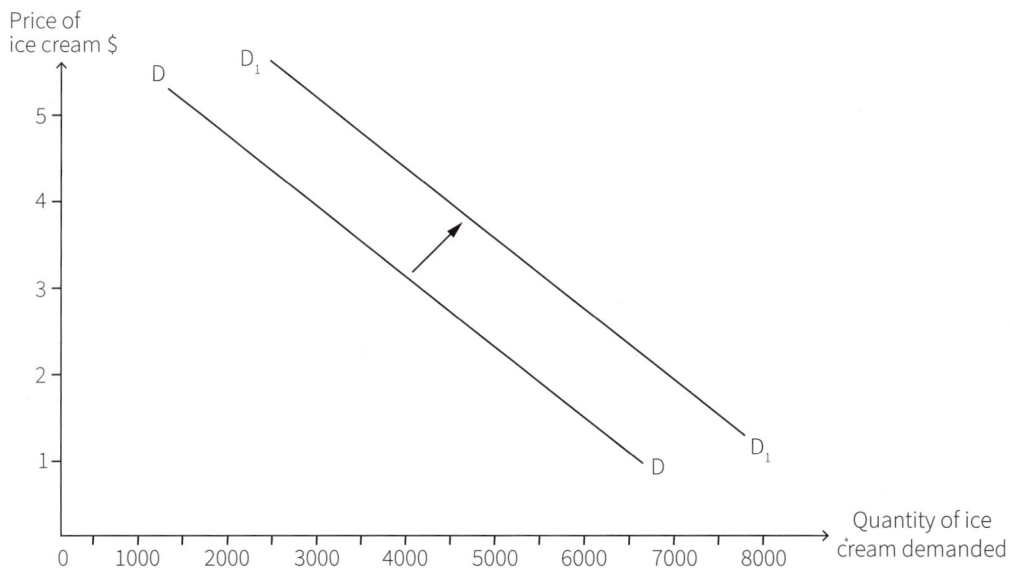

Figure 6.8: An increase in demand. The curve shifts to the right from D to D$_1$

TIP

Be careful to distinguish between a *movement* along a demand curve and a *shift* in demand. The only thing that can cause a movement *along* a demand curve is a change in the price of the product itself. Anything else that causes demand to change would be shown by a *shift* in the demand curve.

LINK

The effects that increases and decreases in demand have on a market are explored in Chapter 9.2 (The consequences of changes in demand).

Demand for ice cream may decrease too. During periods of cold weather, consumers tend to demand less ice cream. A **decrease in demand** is illustrated by a shift to the left of the demand curve, as shown on Figure 6.9.

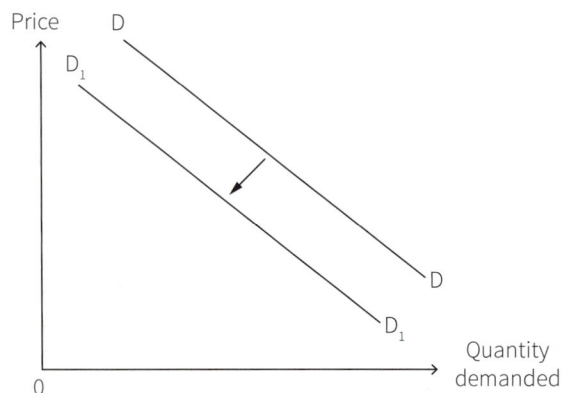

Figure 6.9: A decrease in demand. The curve shifts to the left from D to D_1.

KEY TERM

decrease in demand: a fall in demand at any given price, causing the demand curve to shift to the left.

ECONOMICS IN ACTION

Space tourism

Figure 6.10: Only a few space tourists have had the opportunity to see the Earth from space

Space tourism involves people travelling into space for pleasure (see Figure 6.10). Between 2001 and 2009, seven space tourists went into space on a Russian spaceship. It is thought that the price they were charged was $20 million each. In 2023, Virgin Galactic, a firm run by the UK entrepreneur Richard Branson, took six people, three crew members and three passengers, into space in its VSS Unity rocket. The firm is predicting that it will charge $450 000 for a ticket for the next trip. The US firm Orbital Assembly Corporation is planning to open a space hotel with room for up to 400 guests. These guests will be able to watch planet Earth while enjoying the comforts of a hotel, including a cinema and a gym.

1 Why is demand for space tourism currently low?

2 In examining why demand for space tourism is likely to be higher in the future, economists distinguish between an extension in demand and an increase in demand. Why is it important to make this distinction?

Causes of decreases and increases in demand

Among the factors that can cause consumers to demand different quantities of a product, even if the price has not changed, are changes in income, changes in the price of related products, advertising campaigns, changes in population and changes in taste and fashion.

Changes in income

An increase in income increases consumers' purchasing power. For most products, this results in an increase in demand. The positive relationship between income and demand is so common that such products are referred to as **normal goods**. A few products have a negative relationship with income. These products are called **inferior goods**. When income rises, demand falls as consumers switch to better quality products.

ACTIVITY 6.3

In China, the average income increased by 68% between 2015 and 2022. This contributed to a rise in demand for smartphones, making China the world's largest smartphone market. In your notebook:

1   Illustrate the change in demand for smartphones in China on a diagram.

2   What relationship have you assumed between an increase in income and demand? Explain your answer.

Changes in the price of related products

An increase in demand can be caused by a rise in the price of a **substitute** product. A substitute is a product that can be used instead of another product. For example, if the price of holidays to Morocco rises, demand for holidays to Mauritius may increase. Demand will also increase if the price of a **complement** falls. A complement is a product that can be used with another product. For example, if travel insurance becomes cheaper, demand for holidays to most of the destinations will increase.

DISCUSSION

Discuss whether each of the following is a substitute for or a complement to a Volkswagen car:

*   public transport

*   petrol

*   a Ford car.

Advertising campaigns

A successful advertising campaign will increase demand for a product. It may bring the product to the notice of some new consumers and may encourage some existing consumers to purchase larger quantities of the product (see Figure 6.11).

Figure 6.11: Advertising is all around us

Changes in population

The population of a country can change in terms of both size and age composition. If there is an increase in the number of people in the country, demand for most products will increase. If there is an **ageing population**, with people living longer, and a fall in the **birth rate**, demand for mobility aids is likely to increase while demand for toys is likely to decrease.

Changes in taste and fashion

Certain products may be influenced by changes in taste and fashion. These include food, clothing and entertainment. A rise in vegetarianism in a number of countries has caused the demand for meat to decrease. Health reports can have a significant influence on demand for particular foods. Designer trainers have become more popular in many countries. The rise in the popularity of football in Asia and the USA has increased demand for football shirts and football merchandise.

> **KEY TERMS**
>
> **ageing population:** an increase in the average age of the population.
>
> **birth rate:** the number of live births per 1000 of a country's population in a year.

ACTIVITY 6.4

Decide in each case whether the following would cause an extension in demand, a contraction in demand, an increase in demand or a decrease in demand for fish in a country.

1   a rise in the price of fish

2   a report that eating fish reduces heart disease

3   net emigration (with more people leaving the country than entering it)

4   a fall in the price of chicken.

Write your answers in your notebook, with reasons for your decisions.

Other factors

A range of other factors can influence demand for a product. It was mentioned earlier that a change in weather conditions will affect the demand for ice cream. Such a change would also shift the demand curve for umbrellas, soft drinks and clothing.

Expectations about future price rises can influence current demand. Demand for oil increased during the revolution in Libya in 2011. This was because it was widely expected that such an event would disrupt supplies of oil and raise prices. Special events can have an impact on demand for a particular product. For instance, the 2024 Paris Olympic Games may have increased the demand for holidays in France.

> **TIP**
>
> When exploring the causes of changes in demand for a product, you do not need to consider why the opposite is true. For example, focus on why the demand for smartphones may increase if incomes rise, and not also on why demand would decrease if income falls.

ACTIVITY 6.5

Young people throughout the world are increasingly getting information and entertainment from social media platforms. Newspaper sales are falling. For example, in the UK in 1973, 80% of 16–24-year-olds read a (paid for) national newspaper. By 2023, this percentage had fallen to 16%. Studies have found a number of reasons for this trend. These include young people having less time, less need, less interest and less opportunity to buy newspapers, and the declining importance of newspapers for them. There are now many rivals to newspapers on the internet. Those young people who do buy newspapers tell the researchers that they read them more for entertainment than news.

In a pair, produce a podcast on what you expect to happen to the demand for newspapers. You could make use of your answers to the following questions in your podcast:

1   What percentage of 16–24-year-olds did not read a 'paid for' national newspaper in 2023?

2   Explain two reasons why young people throughout the world are demanding fewer newspapers.

3   Does the extract suggest that social media and the internet is a substitute for or a complement to newspapers? Explain your answer.

4   Discuss two ways through which newspaper publishers could increase demand for their newspapers.

REFLECTION

In what ways did producing and giving a podcast help you understand the causes of an increase in demand? If you were not able to answer any of the questions, what would you do to ensure that you are able to answer similar questions in the future?

SUMMARY

You should now know:

- A fall in the price of a product will make people more willing and able to buy it.

- A demand schedule lists, and a demand curve shows, the different quantities of a product that would be demanded at different prices.

- An extension in demand is caused by a fall in the price of the product, whereas a contraction is caused by a rise in price.

- Causes of a change in demand include changes in income, changes in the price of substitutes and complements, advertising campaigns, changes in the size and age composition of the population and changes in taste and fashion.

- An increase in demand shifts the demand curve to the right.

- A decrease in demand shifts the demand curve to the left.

Chapter 6 practice questions

1   What is measured on the vertical axis of a demand diagram?

   A   cost

   B   price

   C   quantity demanded

   D   wants   [1]

2   What happens to people's willingness and ability to buy a product when its price falls?

	Willingness	Ability
A	increases	increases
B	increases	decreases
C	decreases	decreases
D	decreases	increases

[1]

3   What is an increase in demand represented by?

   A   a movement down the demand curve

   B   a movement up the demand curve

   C   a shift to the left of the demand curve

   D   a shift to the right of the demand curve   [1]

4   The price of a product rises. What will happen to the demand for its complement?

   A   it will contract

   B   it will decrease

   C   it will extend

   D   it will increase   [1]

5   What is most likely to cause an increase in demand for university places?

   A   a fall in graduate salaries

   B   a fall in the ratio of university lecturers to students

   C   a rise in the percentage of 1st class degrees

   D   a rise in university fees   [1]

                                                                  Total: [5]

6   a   Define 'market demand'.   [2]

    b   Explain the relationship between demand and a change in price.   [4]

    c   Analyse the effect of a rise in the price of tea on the demand for milk and the demand for coffee.   [6]

    d   Discuss whether or not the demand for bicycles will rise in the future.   [8]

                                                                     Total: [20]

CHECK YOUR PROGRESS

How well do you think you have achieved the learning intentions for this chapter? Give yourself a score from 1 (still need a lot of practice) to 5 (feeling very confident) for each learning intention. Provide an example to support your score.

Now I can...	Score	Example
define demand		
recognise the link between individual and market demand		
draw and interpret the demand curve		
explain the causes of extensions and contractions in demand		
draw diagrams that illustrate movements along a demand curve		
analyse the causes of increases and decreases in demand		
draw diagrams that illustrate shifts of a demand curve.		

> Chapter 7

Supply

LEARNING INTENTIONS

By the end of this chapter, you will be able to:

- define supply
- recognise the link between individual and market supply
- explain the causes of extensions and contractions in supply
- draw a diagram to illustrate a movement along a supply curve
- analyse the causes of shifts in the supply curve
- draw diagrams that illustrate shifts of a supply curve.

Introduction

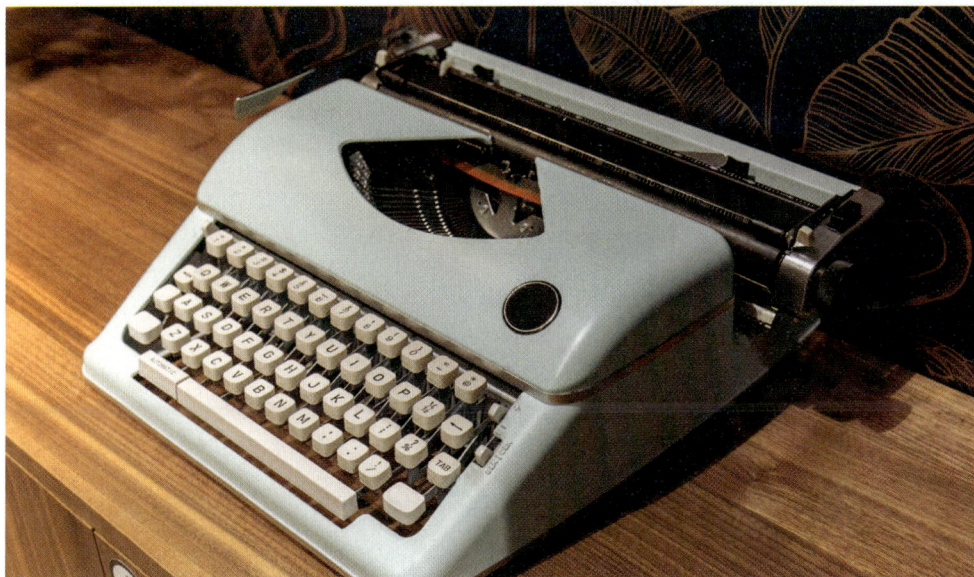

Figure 7.1: A typewriter was a common sight in offices in the 1970s

Have you seen a typewriter (Figure 7.1)? In the past, there were many firms producing typewriters. Now there are very few typewriters produced. In contrast, the number of coffee shops is increasing, and more and more trainers (sneakers) are being sold. Why does the supply of products change? Economists answers these questions by considering the influences on supply.

ECONOMICS IN CONTEXT

A growing market for pineapples

The number of Malaysian pineapples sold has increased in recent years. Malaysian farmers are offering more pineapples for sale both at home and in a range of foreign markets (Figure 7.2). These include China, Egypt, Germany, Saudi Arabia and the United Arab Emirates (UAE). More land is being used to grow pineapples and more workers are being employed in growing, and selling pineapples. The Malaysian government is providing pineapple farmers with advice and subsidised equipment.

Discuss in a pair or group:

1   Identify three factors of production which are used to supply pineapples.

2   Why do you think Malaysian farmers are growing more pineapples?

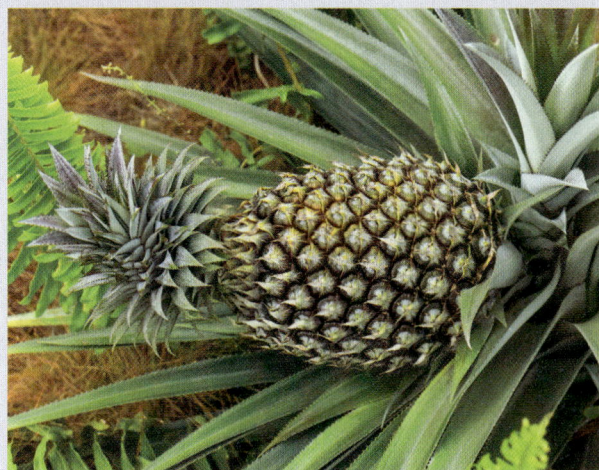

Figure 7.2: A pineapple nearly ready to sell

7.1 Individual and market supply

Supply is the willingness and ability to sell a product. It is important not to confuse supply with production. Supply is influenced by the amount produced but is not the same as production. This is because some of the amount produced today may be stored to be sold at a later date. It may also be that some of the output offered for sale today may have come from stocks.

Unlike demand, supply is directly related to price. A rise in price will lead to a rise in supply. Firms will be more willing to supply the product, as they are likely to earn higher profits. They will also be able to supply more, as the higher price will make it easier for them to cover the costs of production.

KEY TERMS

supply: the willingness and ability to sell a product.

market supply: total supply of a product.

The link between individual and market supply

Individual supply is the supply of one firm. **Market supply** is the total supply of a product supplied by all the firms in the industry. Market supply is calculated in a similar way to market demand. The quantities that would be supplied by each firm at each price are added up. Aggregation of the supply of each individual firm gives the market supply.

A supply schedule

A supply schedule records the different quantities supplied at different prices. Table 7.1 shows a supply schedule for train tickets from Station X to Station Y.

Table 7.1: Daily supply of train tickets from Station X to Station Y

Price ($)	Quantity supplied
50	6 000
45	5 000
40	4 300
35	3 800
30	3 600
25	3 500

From this information, a supply curve can be plotted, as shown in Figure 7.3.

As with demand curves, supply curves can be drawn as straight lines.

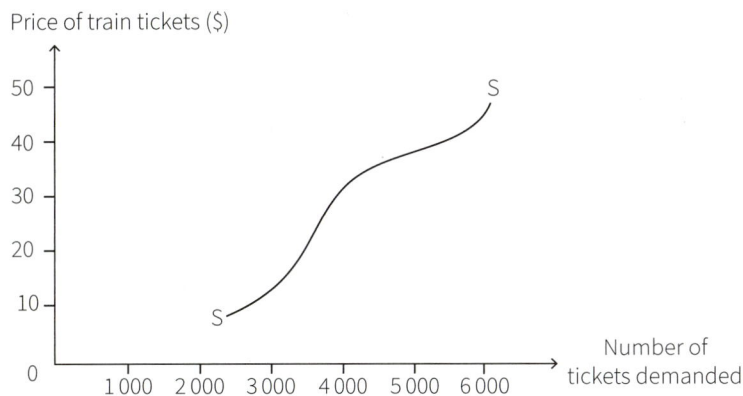

Figure 7.3: Daily supply (S) of train tickets from Station X to Station Y

7.2 Movements along a supply curve

Causes of extensions and contractions in supply

Like demand, a change in price of the product will cause an **extension in supply** (expansion or an increase in the quantity supplied) or a **contraction in supply** (a decrease in the quantity supplied). This time, however, it is a rise in price which will cause an extension in supply and a fall in price which will cause a contraction in supply. Figure 7.4 shows both these changes.

extension in supply: a rise in the quantity supplied caused by a rise in the price of the product itself.

contraction in supply: a fall in the quantity supplied caused by a fall in the price of the product.

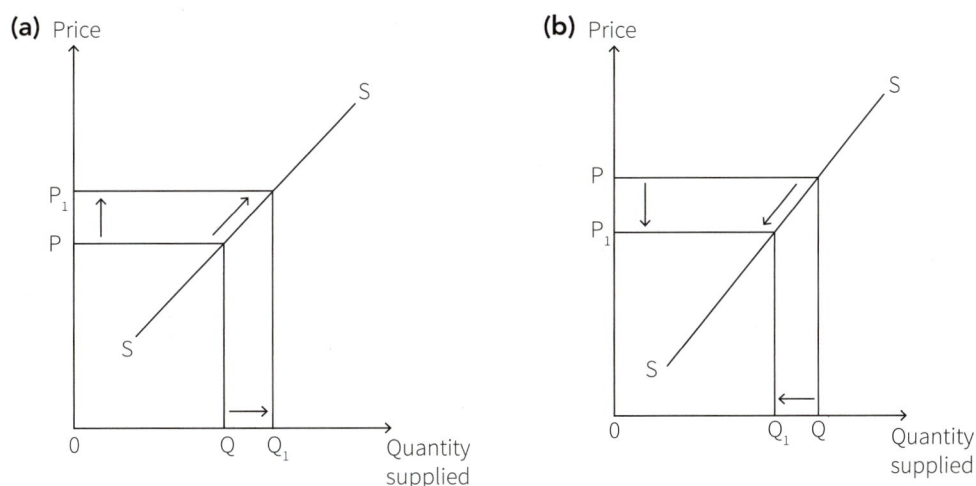

Figure 7.4: (a) An extension in supply   **(b)** A contraction in supply

ACTIVITY 7.1

Pakistan's paper industry is growing. In 2023, there were approximately 100 manufacturing firms producing writing paper, printing paper, wrapping paper and chip board.

Imagine you are an accountant in the finance department and your manager has asked you to prepare a three-minute presentation to give to the directors of a large paper products firm in Pakistan. Your presentation should explain:

1   what effect a rise in supply of the firm's products will have on the market supply of paper

2   what would cause an extension in the supply of paper. Remember to explain what 'an extension in supply' is.

7.3 Shifts of a supply curve

A **change in supply** occurs when the conditions faced by suppliers change. Where a condition changes, such as an improvement in technology, a different quantity will be offered for sale at each price. For instance, favourable weather conditions may lead to an increase in the rice crop in a country. Rice farmers will be able to supply more rice. Table 7.2 shows the original supply schedule in the previous season and the supply schedule in the current season.

Table 7.2: Rice production

Price per tonne ($)	Supply in previous season (millions of tonnes)	Supply in current season (millions of tonnes)
600	110	130
500	100	120
400	90	100
300	80	90
200	70	80
100	60	70

While a change in the price of the product itself causes a movement along the supply curve, a change in supply conditions causes the supply curve to shift. An **increase in supply** is shown by a shift to the right, as in Figure 7.5. At each and every price, more is supplied.

In contrast, a **decrease in supply** results in a movement of the supply curve to the left, as shown in Figure 7.6. Now whatever the price, less will be supplied.

KEY TERMS

change in supply: changes in supply conditions causing shifts in the supply curve.

increase in supply: a rise in supply at any given price, causing the supply curve to shift to the right.

decrease in supply: a fall in supply at any given price, causing the supply curve to shift to the left.

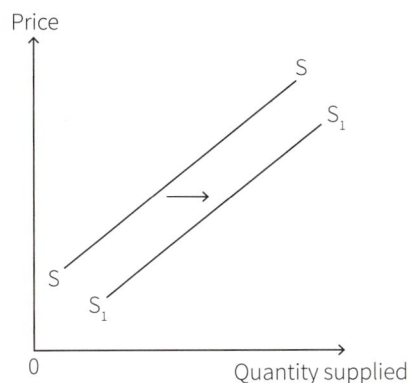

Figure 7.5: An increase in supply is shown by a shift to the right from S to S_1

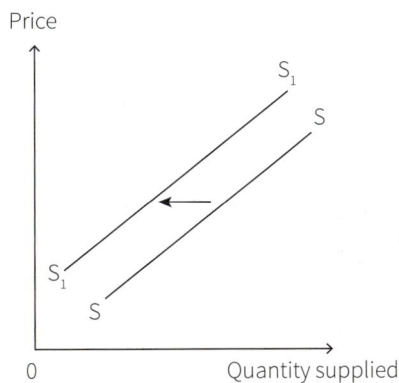

Figure 7.6: A decrease in supply is shown by a shift to the left from S to S_1

Causes of decreases and increases in supply

Changes in the costs of production

If there is an increase in the costs of producing a product, suppliers will want to sell the product at a higher price. For example, if it costs $200 to produce four units, firms would supply four units at a price of $50 per unit. If costs rise to $280, firms would want to sell each unit at a price of $70 or more.

The two basic reasons for a change in costs of production are:

- a change in the price of any of the factors of production
- a change in the productivity of any of the factors of production.

If, for example, the price of raw materials used increases, it will be more expensive to produce a product. One cost which changes frequently is the cost of transporting goods. This is because the price of oil used in petrol and diesel, is very volatile (may change suddenly and by a large amount) (see Figure 7.7).

Figure 7.7: A rise in the cost of fuel will increase the cost of production and is likely to result in a rise in price

A rise in the productivity of a factor of production will reduce unit cost. For example, if a worker who is paid $200 a week produces 100 units, the labour cost per unit is $2. If the worker's productivity rises to 200 units, the labour cost per unit would fall to $1.

An increase in the wages paid to workers would raise the costs of production and, therefore, cause a decrease in supply. However, if the increase in wages is accompanied by an equal rise in productivity, then **unit costs** and supply will remain unchanged.

> ### ACTIVITY 7.2
>
> A firm employs ten workers and pays $50 a day to each of them. The total output of ten workers is 100 units initially. The firm then raises the wage rate to $60 a day and the output per worker rises to 20.
>
> 1   Individually, work out the initial unit cost and the new unit cost. Share your answers with another student. Did you arrive at the same answers? If not, check your workings and correct answers where necessary.
>
> 2   In your pair, discuss if supply will decrease, stay the same or increase. Why do you think this?

Improvements in technology

Improvements in technology raise the productivity of capital, reduce costs of production and result in an increase in supply. It has become much cheaper to produce a range of products due to the availability of more efficient capital goods and methods of production. For example, while world demand for personal computers has increased in recent years, the supply has increased even more as it has become easier and cheaper to produce computers.

> ### ACTIVITY 7.3
>
> Since 2000, the world supply of rice has increased from 575 million tonnes to 786 million tonnes in 2022. This has largely been the result of breakthroughs in seed germination and cultivation techniques.
>
> 1   Draw a diagram showing the change in supply of rice since 2000.
>
> 2   Share your diagram with a partner. Discuss what factors could cause the supply curve for rice to move in the opposite direction.

Taxes

Direct taxes on firms, including corporate income tax (corporation tax), and **indirect taxes**, such as value-added tax and excise duty, are a cost that firms have to pay. Firms are likely to try to recover at least some of this extra cost by raising the price paid by consumers. Despite this, the firms themselves are largely responsible for passing on the revenue from the **tax** to the government. A rise in the rate of an existing tax or a new tax will make it more expensive to supply a product and so will reduce supply. In contrast, a cut in a tax or its removal will increase supply.

KEY TERM

unit cost: the average cost of production. It is found by dividing total cost by output.

LINK

Chapter 20.1 (Calculating the costs of production) explores the nature of costs of production.

KEY TERMS

improvements in technology: advances in the quality of capital goods and methods of production.

direct taxes: taxes on the income and wealth of individuals and firms.

indirect taxes: taxes on goods and services.

tax: a payment to the government.

Subsidies

A **subsidy** given to the producers provides a financial incentive for them to supply more of a product, for example, a subsidy given to farmers to encourage them to grow more fruit. Besides being paid by the consumer, the producer is now being paid by the government. As a result, the granting of a subsidy will cause an increase in supply while the removal of a subsidy will cause a decrease in supply.

Most countries throughout the world subsidise some agricultural products. A number of them also give subsidies to new and important industries.

Less frequently, a government may give a subsidy to consumers to encourage them to buy a particular product. For example, grants may be given to households to enable them to buy electric cars. In this case, it is demand and not supply conditions that change.

> **DISCUSSION**
>
> Discuss whether you think the supply of 3D printers will increase in the future.

Weather conditions and health of livestock and crops

Changes in weather conditions may affect some agricultural products. Good weather conditions around harvest time are likely to increase the supply of a number of crops. Very dry, very wet or very windy weather, however, is likely to damage a range of crops and reduce their supply. The amount of agricultural products produced and available for supply is also influenced by the health of livestock and crops. The outbreak of a disease, such as foot-and-mouth in cattle or blight in crops, will reduce supply (see Figure 7.8).

Figure 7.8: Bad weather can destroy a crop

Prices of other products

Firms often produce a range of products. If one product becomes more popular, its price will rise and supply will extend. In order to produce more of this product, the firm may switch resources from the production of other products. The prices of these other products have not changed, but the firm will now supply less at each and every price. For example, if a farmer grows both maize and soya beans, a rise in the price and profitability of soya beans is likely to result in the farmer growing more soya beans and growing less maize, causing the supply of maize to decrease,

Besides the products being supplied in a competitive environment, they can also be jointly supplied. This means that one product is automatically made when another product is produced, that is one product is a by-product of the other one. For example, when more soya bean oil is produced, more soya bean meal will be available to feed livestock.

In the case of products which are jointly supplied, a rise in the price of one product will cause an extension in supply of the other product. Firms make more of one product because its price has risen. The supply of the other product will increase automatically. More is produced, not because it has risen in price but because the price of a related product has risen.

Disasters and wars

Natural disasters, such as cyclones and floods, and wars can result in a significant decrease in supply. The earthquake and resulting tsunami that hit Japan in March 2011 caused extensive damage to infrastructure and killed workers. These effects reduced the supply of a range of products.

Discoveries and depletions of commodities

The supply of some primary products, such as coal, gold and oil, is affected by discoveries of new sources. For example, the discovery of deposits of gold will increase the supply of gold. In contrast, if copper is extracted rapidly from copper mines, the supply of copper will be reduced in the future.

ACTIVITY 7.4

In your group, discuss and decide whether the following would cause a decrease in the demand, an increase in the demand, a decrease in the supply or an increase in the supply of gold bracelets:

1   a decrease in income

2   a decrease in the cost of the equipment used to mine gold

3   an increase in the price of silver bracelets

4   an increase in the tax on gold

5   the discovery of new deposits of gold

6   a strike by gold mining workers.

Note down the group's decision in each case and the reasons for your decision.

ECONOMICS IN ACTION

The market for diamonds

Advances in technology are making it easier and cheaper to produce synthetic diamonds. These laboratory-grown diamonds are often sold at a third of the price of natural diamonds (see Figure 7.9).

Both synthetic and natural diamonds are easily stored. Demand for diamonds to use in industrial production and in jewellery tends to be high in most months. If, however, demand falls one month, the diamond firms can store any unsold diamonds. If the next month, demand increases, the diamond firms can sell not only the diamonds produced artificially or mined that month but also some they have in storage.

Figure 7.9: An unsold diamond may be stored without the quality being affected

1   Why do you think economists are predicting that synthetic diamonds will account for a larger percentage share of the diamond market in the future?

2   Explain the causes of an increase in the supply of diamonds.

ACTIVITY 7.5

In a pair, produce a worksheet of questions on the differences between demand and supply. Aim to include between four and six questions in your worksheet. Look through this chapter and Chapter 6 (Demand) to give you ideas for questions. Here's an example question you could ask:

How do the definitions of demand and supply differ?

As you write each question, write your answer on a separate sheet.

Swap your worksheet with another pair. When you have finished, check and discuss answers.

REFLECTION

Did writing the questions and answers for your worksheet help you to better understand the differences between and supply? Do you think producing a worksheet on other economics topics would help to reinforce your understanding?

SUMMARY

You should now know:

- Individual supply is the supply of one firm, whereas market supply is the supply of all the firms in the industry.

- A fall in the price of a product will make suppliers less willing and able to sell it.

- Supply schedules and supply curves show the relationship between the price and the quantity supplied.

- A fall in price causes a contraction in supply, whereas a rise in price causes an extension in supply.

- Causes of a change in supply include changes in the costs of production, improvements in technology, taxes, subsidies, weather conditions, health of livestock and crops, changes in the price of related products, natural disasters, wars and discoveries of new sources and depletion of commodities.

- An increase in supply shifts the supply curve to the right.

- A decrease in supply moves the supply curve to the left.

Chapter 7 practice questions

1 What is the relationship between a change in price and demand and the relationship between a change in price and supply?

	Relationship between a change in price and demand	Relationship between a change in price and supply
A	move in opposite directions	move in opposite directions
B	move in opposite directions	move in the same direction
C	move in the same direction	move in the same direction
D	move in the same direction	move in opposite directions

[1]

2 What does a market supply curve show?

A proportion of total output sold

B the proportion of total output produced by different firms in the industry

C the relationship between the total quantity supplied and demand for the product

D the relationship between the total quantity supplied and the price of the product [1]

3 How would an increase in supply be illustrated on a diagram?

A a movement down the supply curve

B a movement up the supply curve

C a shift to the left of the supply curve

D a shift to the right of the supply curve [1]

7 Supply

4   What would cause an increase in the supply of milk?

   A   an increase in the price of cattle feed

   B   an increase in wages paid to farmworkers

   C   the introduction of a subsidy to cattle farmers

   D   the outbreak of a disease affecting cows   [1]

5   What is supply?

   A   the quantity of a product that consumers are willing to buy

   B   the quantity of a product that consumers can afford to buy

   C   the quantity of a product that is offered for sale

   D   the quantity of a product that is produced   [1]

                                                     Total: [5]

6   **a**   Define 'supply'.   [2]

   b   Explain why supply and price are positively related.   [4]

   c   Analyse, using a supply diagram, the effect of an improvement in the quality of the training car manufacture workers receive on the supply of cars.   [6]

   d   Discuss whether or not changes in demand or changes in supply have a larger influence on the market for tomatoes.   [8]

                                                     Total: [20]

CHECK YOUR PROGRESS

How well do you think you have achieved the learning intentions for this chapter? Give yourself a score from 1 (still need a lot of practice) to 5 (feeling very confident) for each learning intention. Provide an example to support your score.

Now I can...	Score	Example
define supply		
recognise the link between individual and market supply		
distinguish between extensions and contractions in supply		
draw diagrams that illustrate movements along a supply curve		
analyse the causes of increases and decreases in supply		
draw diagrams that illustrate shifts of the supply curve.		

75

> # Chapter 8
> # Price determination

Introduction

Market traders of fresh fish are sometimes left with unsold fish, which they throw away at the end of the day. The next day they are likely to lower the price they charge for fish. On other occasions, they may find that they are selling out of fish very quickly. In this situation, they may decide to raise their price. In practice, it can be difficult for suppliers to know what the appropriate price to charge is. Suppliers may need to make adjustments to prevent shortages and surpluses.

ECONOMICS IN CONTEXT

The price of oranges

The supply of oranges decreased in 2022 due to bad weather and a disease that infected orange trees. Most oranges in the USA are grown in Florida (see Figure 8.1). In 2022, hurricanes and a citrus disease destroyed much of the year's crop. A number of Florida's orange farmers gave up farming and sold their land for other purposes. Some consumers and firms that produce orange juice found that they could not buy oranges at the market price. As a result, some firms offered to pay a higher price, and orange farmers adjusted their prices until the demand for oranges equalled the quantity of oranges that the farmers were willing and able to supply.

Figure 8.1: Orange farmers may need to alter the price of their crop when market conditions change

Discuss in a pair or group:

1   Why does the price of agricultural products often change?

2   What are the likely differences in the objectives of buyers and sellers?

8.1 The price mechanism

Resources move automatically as a result of changes in price. In turn, price changes are determined by the interaction of the market forces of **demand** and **supply**. Resources switch from products that are becoming less popular to those that are becoming more popular. Consumers signal to producers their changes in demand through the prices they are prepared to pay for different products. Figure 8.2 shows the effect of demand for bananas increasing while demand for apples decreases.

KEY TERMS

demand: the willingness and ability to buy a product.

supply: the willingness and ability to sell a product.

Bananas	Apples
Increase in demand	Decrease in demand
↓	↓
Rise in price	Fall in price
↓	↓
Rise in profit	Fall in profit
↓	↓
Firms produce more	Firms produce less
↓	↓
Hire more workers, use more capital and land	Reduce number of workers, capital and land employed

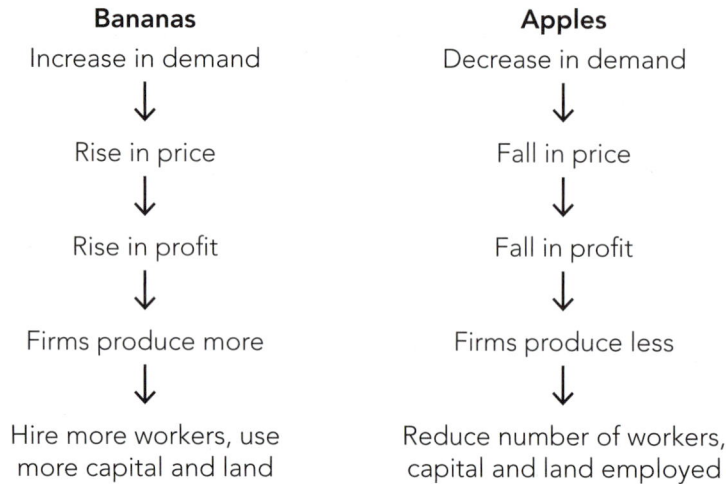

Figure 8.2: How the price mechanism can change the allocation of resources

The **price mechanism** provides an incentive for producers to respond to changes in market conditions. If consumers want more of a product, they will be willing to pay more for it. The higher price offered will encourage firms to produce the product in larger quantities as then the firms make more profit. In fact, the use of resources is changing all the time in response to changes in consumer demand and costs of production.

The price mechanism also rations out products when their supply falls short of demand. If, for example, a disease infects a potato crop, supply will decrease. Initially, the decrease in supply may result in a shortage of potatoes and potato-based products, with demand exceeding supply (see Figure 8.3). The shortage, however, will drive up prices until the market clears again, with demand equalling supply. The price mechanism decides who will receive the products by raising the price. The people who will be able to consume the product will be those who are able to pay the higher price.

Figure 8.3: The production of crisps may be affected by the supply of potatoes

KEY TERM

price mechanism: the way the decisions made by households (buyers or consumers) and firms (sellers) interact to decide the allocation of resources.

LINK

The price mechanism plays a key role in a market economic system – see Chapter 12.2 (Market economic system).

Copy and complete Table 8.1. Give one reason why the price will be higher in each case.

Table 8.1

Products	Which product has the higher price?	Reason why the product has the higher price
1 The price of a ticket at a World Cup football match and a ticket at a local non-league football game		
2 Gold and rice		
3 The services of a dentist and the services of a cleaner		

8.2 Market equilibrium

A **market is in equilibrium** when demand and supply are equal. In this situation, the **market price** charged will mean that the quantity consumers want and are able to buy is equal to the quantity producers are willing and able to sell. There will be no pressure for the price or the quantity in the market to change.

How prices are determined

Consumers want low prices while sellers want high prices. So, how is the price of a product determined (decided upon)? In some cases, there is direct bargaining between buyers and sellers. Buyers often haggle with market traders, seeking to drive the price down. Traders aim to keep the price relatively high. In other cases, the bargaining is more indirect. Firms estimate and then charge what they think the **equilibrium price** is. The equilibrium price is the price where demand and supply are equal (see Figure 8.4). If firms find that they cannot sell all of their output at this price, they will lower it. If firms find that consumers want to buy more than what they are offering for sale at this price, firms will raise the price.

KEY TERMS

market equilibrium: a situation where demand and supply are equal.

market price: the price at which a product is bought and sold.

equilibrium price: the price at which demand and supply are equal and there is no surplus and no shortage.

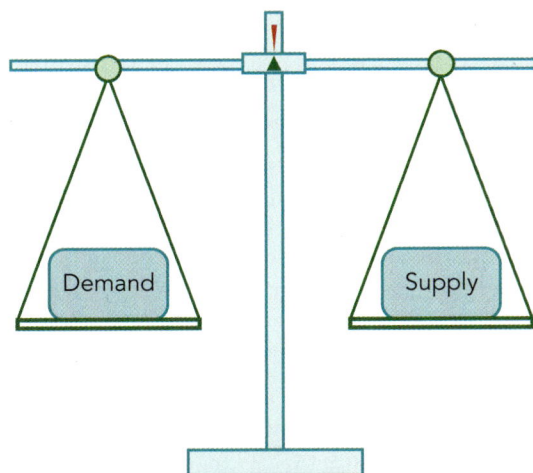

Figure 8.4: Equilibrium price is where demand and supply are equal

Equilibrium price and equilibrium quantity in a market

Equilibrium price is also sometimes referred to as the market clearing price. This is the point at which the price where demand and supply are equal, and so there are no shortages or surpluses of the product (the market clears). The equilibrium price of a product can be found by comparing the demand and supply schedules of the product and seeing where demand and supply are equal. Table 8.2 uses the information previously given on train tickets in Chapters 6 and 7.

Table 8.2: The daily demand for and supply of train tickets from Station X to Station Y

Price ($)	Quantity demanded	Quantity supplied
50	2 200	6 000
45	2 500	5 000
40	3 000	4 300
35	3 800	3 800
30	5 000	3 600
25	7 000	3 500

In this case, the equilibrium price is $35 as at this point, demand and supply are equal (at 3 800 units). The equilibrium price can also be found by looking at a demand and supply diagram. The equilibrium price occurs where the demand and supply curves intersect. Figure 8.5 shows that the equilibrium price is P and the **equilibrium quantity** is Q. Prices will stay at P and sales at Q until demand and supply conditions change.

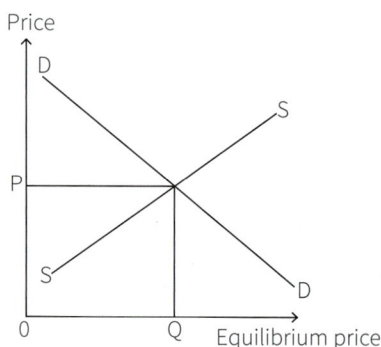

KEY TERM

equilibrium quantity: when the quantity demanded by buyers equals the quantity supplied by sellers, and so there is no surplus and no shortage.

Figure 8.5: Equilibrium price is where lines S and D intersect

8.3 Market disequilibrium

A **market is in disequilibrium** when there is an imbalance between demand and supply. In this case, the market price will not be the market equilibrium price. There will be a difference between the quantity demanded and the quantity supplied. There will be pressure for the price to change (see Figure 8.6).

KEY TERM

market disequilibrium: a situation where demand and supply are not equal.

Figure 8.6: Prices may be changed to move from market disequilibrium to market equilibrium

Surpluses and shortages

Market forces move price towards the equilibrium. If a firm sets the price above the equilibrium level, it will not sell all the products it offers for sale. There will be a **surplus** of products. To ensure the firm sells all the products it wants to, it will lower price until the market clears, with the quantity demanded equalling the quantity supplied. Figure 8.7 shows a market initially in a state of disequilibrium, with supply exceeding demand.

At $6, the firm is willing and able to sell 10 000 products, but consumers buy only 4 000. This leaves 6 000 unsold products. As a result, price will fall, causing demand to extend and supply to contract until price reaches the equilibrium level. Figure 8.8 shows this adjustment.

> **KEY TERM**
>
> **surplus:** the amount by which supply is greater than demand (excess supply).

> **TIP**
>
> When explaining how prices move from disequilibrium towards equilibrium, a demand and supply diagram will help you to illustrate this.

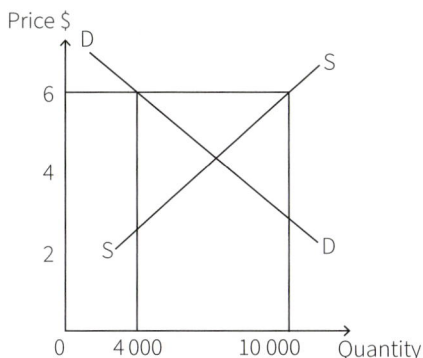

Figure 8.7: Supply exceeding demand

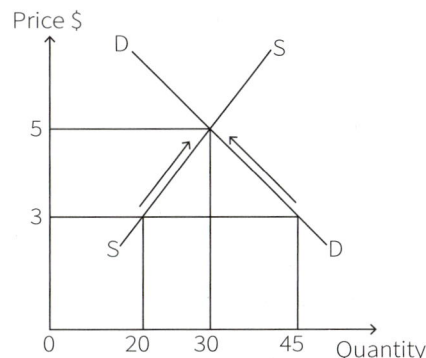

Figure 8.8: Return to equilibrium

Market forces will also move the price if it is initially set below the equilibrium level. In this case, there will initially be a **shortage** of the product with demand exceeding supply (excess demand), as shown in Figure 8.9.

Some consumers who are anxious to buy the product will be willing to pay a higher price. Suppliers that recognise this excess demand will raise the price. Figure 8.10 shows the price being pushed up to the equilibrium level of $5.

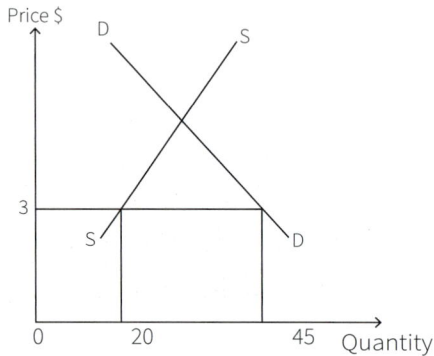

Figure 8.9: Demand exceeding supply

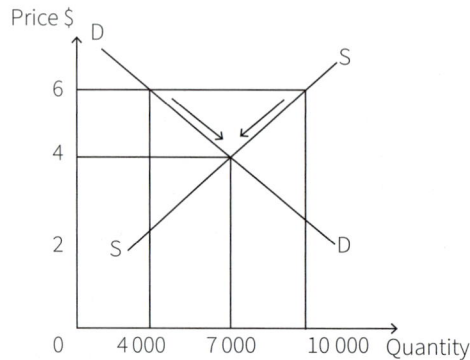

Figure 8.10: Return to equilibrium

KEY TERM

shortage: the amount by which demand is greater than supply (excess demand).

TIP

When drawing diagrams to show a market moving from disequilibrium to equilibrium, include arrows to show the movements along the demand and supply curves, as shown in Figure 8.10.

ACTIVITY 8.2

As the 2022 FIFA World Cup Final in Qatar approached, the sportswear firm that made Argentina's replica kit reported 'extraordinary high demand'. There was a global shortage particularly of the replica shirts, with demand outstripping supply.

In a group of three:

1   Individually, draw a demand and supply diagram to illustrate the global market for Argentina replica shirts before the World Cup. Remember to label your diagram clearly. Share your diagrams. Discuss any differences, and correct diagrams where necessary.

2   What do you think might have happened to the price of Argentina replica shirts in this situation? Why might you have expected this?

ECONOMICS IN ACTION

Setting prices

There are many restaurants in the city of Karachi in Pakistan. In 2023, a new restaurant opened in the city selling Lebanese food (see Figure 8.11). The quality of the food was good, the decoration of the restaurant was attractive, the service was excellent, and the restaurant was in a good location. However, in its first few days, the restaurant attracted only a few customers. After a week, the restaurant owner adjusted their prices. The restaurant soon became a success.

Figure 8.11: Preparing restaurant food

1   Why would an economist decide that the prices the restaurant owner originally charged for the different meals were not the equilibrium prices?

2   Is it likely that the restaurant owner raised or lowered their prices?

ACTIVITY 8.3

In a pair, use Table 8.3, which shows the demand and supply schedules, to answer the following questions.

Table 8.3

Price ($)	Quantity demanded	Quantity supplied
1	100	40
2	96	65
3	88	88
4	74	100
5	61	110
6	41	115

1   What is the equilibrium price?

2   At which price is the surplus greatest?

3   At which price is the shortage greatest?

Discuss your answers with the rest of the group. Think about whether there is anything you need to do to increase your understanding of market equilibrium and market disequilibrium.

DISCUSSION

Discuss how buyers may be affected by a market moving from disequilibrium to equilibrium.

SUMMARY

You should now know:

- The price mechanism provides an incentive for producers to respond to changes in market conditions.

- Price is determined by the interaction of demand and supply.

- Market equilibrium occurs where demand is equal to supply.

- A diagram shows equilibrium price and quantity where the demand curve and supply curve intersect.

- If a market is in disequilibrium initially, market forces will move it towards equilibrium.

- A diagram will show there is market disequilibrium when demand and supply are not equal at the market price.

- If price is above the equilibrium price, there will be a surplus (excess supply).

- If price is below the equilibrium price, there will be a shortage (excess demand).

Chapter 8 practice questions

1   Which price is the equilibrium price?

   A   everything that is produced is sold

   B   supply exceeds demand

   C   the amount consumers demand is equal to the amount sellers supply

   D   the number of buyers equals the number of sellers   [1]

2   A market is experiencing a shortage. What will happen to price and sales as the market moves back to equilibrium?

	Price	Sales
A	decrease	fall
B	decrease	rise
C	increase	fall
D	increase	rise

[1]

3   If there is excess demand in a market, what is the relationship between price and equilibrium price, and sales and equilibrium sales?

	Price	Sales
A	above equilibrium	above equilibrium
B	above equilibrium	below equilibrium
C	below equilibrium	below equilibrium
D	below equilibrium	above equilibrium

[1]

4   The demand and supply schedules of a product are:

Price	Quantity demanded	Quantity supplied
10	78	22
20	66	38
30	54	54
40	32	70
50	20	86
60	8	102

Using the data, what is the equilibrium price?

A $20

B $30

C $40

D $50

[1]

5   The diagram shows the market for biscuits with a price of P.

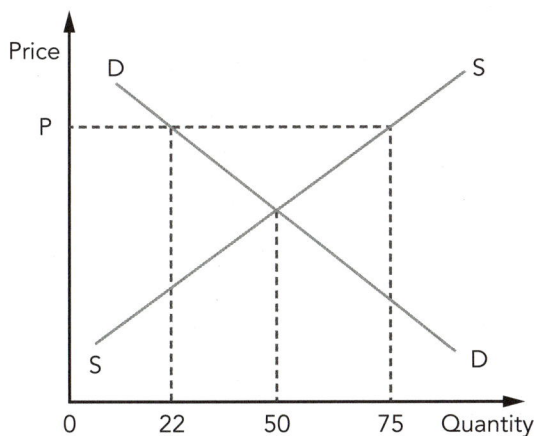

What evidence is there that the market is in disequilibrium?

A   an excess demand of 25

B   an excess demand of 28

C   an excess supply of 22

D   an excess supply of 53

[1]

Total: [5]

6   a   What may be the opportunity cost of buying apples?   [2]

    b   Explain why the market for apples may be in disequilibrium.   [4]

    c   Analyse, using a demand and supply diagram, why a surplus of
        apples will be eliminated.   [6]

    d   Discuss whether or not consumers will benefit from a market being
        in disequilibrium.   [8]

                                                            Total: [20]

CHECK YOUR PROGRESS

How well do you think you have achieved the learning intentions for this chapter?
Give yourself a score from 1 (still need a lot of practice) to 5 (feeling very confident)
for each learning intention. Provide an example to support your score.

Now I can...	Score	Example
explain how the price mechanism provides answers to the basic resource allocation questions		
define market equilibrium		
interpret equilibrium price and quantity in a market using demand and supply schedules		
draw and interpret equilibrium price and quantity using demand and supply curves		
define market disequilibrium		
interpret disequilibrium prices and quantities in a market using demand and supply schedules		
draw and interpret disequilibrium prices and quantities using demand and supply curves		
explain shortages and surpluses.		

> Chapter 9
Price changes

LEARNING INTENTIONS

By the end of this chapter, you will be able to:

- analyse how changes in demand supply can cause price changes
- use demand and supply diagrams to illustrate how changes in demand and supply affect price
- analyse the consequences of price changes.

Introduction

The price of food and vegetables can change greatly from month to month. The price of calculators has been falling for a number of years, while the price of housing in many countries has been rising. There are a number of reasons why prices change.

ECONOMICS IN CONTEXT

Solar power in Thailand

Demand for solar power is increasing throughout the world. In Thailand, for example, more homes and more firms are using solar power. One major Thai food producer has installed solar panels to generate energy at all of its nearly 200 farms, feed mills and processing factories.

In 2021, Thailand opened the world's largest floating solar farm (see Figure 9.1). The farm has 145 000 solar panels and is the first of 16 projects planned in the country's reservoirs.

Advances in technology are reducing the cost of producing solar power. It is predicted that the price of solar power in Thailand will be 42% lower in 2030 than in 2023.

Figure 9.1: A floating solar farm in Thailand

Discuss in a pair or group:

1   Why is the increase in demand for solar power not increasing its price?

2   What may happen to the supply curve for solar power between 2023 and 2030?

9.1 Causes of price changes

Price changes when market conditions change. A change in demand, a change in supply or a combination of the two would cause a change from one equilibrium price to a new equilibrium price. For example, an increase in supply would cause the supply curve to shift to the right and the equilibrium price to fall. These changes and how they affect the market depend on the initial cause of the change in price, as discussed in the rest of the chapter.

9.2 The consequences of changes in demand

Changes in demand will cause a change in price and a movement along the supply curve. Figure 9.2 shows the effect of an increase in demand. Initially, there is a shortage of xy. This shortage forces the price to move up.

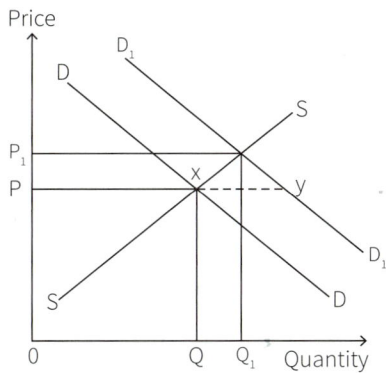

Figure 9.2: The effect of an increase in demand

The higher price encourages an extension in supply until a new equilibrium price of P_1 is reached. At this price, demand and supply are again equal with higher sales of Q_1. In contrast, a decrease in demand will cause a fall in equilibrium price and a contraction in supply. Figure 9.3 shows demand decreasing from D to D_1. With lower demand, there will be a surplus of unsold products at the initial price of P.

This surplus pushes down the price. As a result, supply contracts until the new equilibrium price of P_1 and a new quantity of sales, Q_1, are reached.

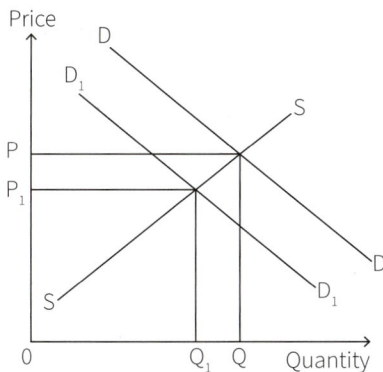

Figure 9.3: The effect of a decrease in demand

ACTIVITY 9.1

What is likely to happen to the market for economics books in India in the following situations:

1   a successful advertising campaign by the publishers of economics books.

2   a decrease in the number of students studying economics.

Use a demand and supply diagram in each case to illustrate the impact of changes in market conditions.

ECONOMICS IN ACTION

The growing golf market

Figure 9.4: Golf is a popular leisure activity

Golf is a very popular sport worldwide (see Figure 9.4). The number of people playing golf increased from 67 million in 2016 to 70 million in 2023. The largest increase was in Asia, where the number rose from 25 million to 27 million over the same period. In Bangladesh, membership of golf clubs has increased. One Bangladeshi golf club with 5 000 members and a waiting list of 2 000 doubled its fees in 2023. Other golf clubs in Bangladesh also saw increased membership, and many clubs increased their membership fees. Those playing golf in Bangladesh and most other countries also had to pay higher prices in 2023 than in 2016 for golf equipment including golf clubs and golf balls.

1 Explain what evidence there is that demand for membership of golf clubs has increased.

2 Explain the relationship between the demand for golf clubs and the demand for golf balls.

9.3 The consequences of changes in supply

Changes in supply cause a change in price and a movement along the demand curve. Initially, an increase in supply will cause a surplus. The surplus will drive down the price and result in an extension in demand, as shown in Figure 9.5. Equilibrium price falls to P_1 and sales rise to Q_1.

A decrease in supply will have the opposite effect. It will cause a rise in equilibrium price, which in turn will cause a contraction in demand, as shown in Figure 9.6. In this case, sales fall to Q_1.

LINK

Chapter 11 (Price elasticity of demand (PES)) explores the extent to which supply extends or contracts when there is a change in price.

TIP

Whenever you are looking at the effect on the market of a product, make sure you take into account demand, supply and price. Also, be careful to get the order of events right. For example, an increase in demand will first cause a rise in price and then an extension in supply.

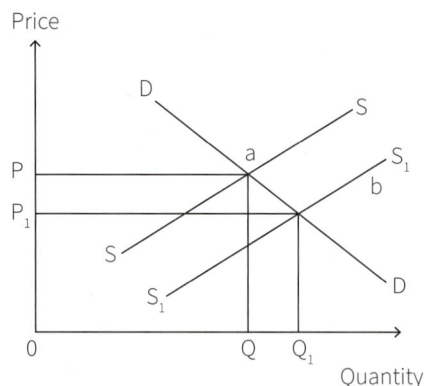

Figure 9.5: The effect of an increase in supply

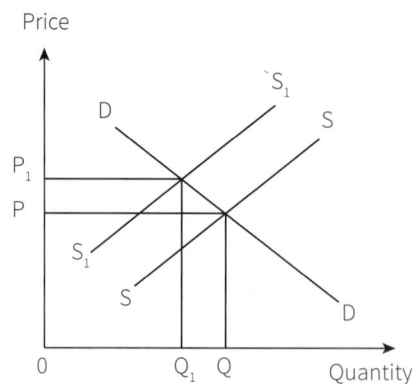

Figure 9.6: The effect of a decrease in supply

ACTIVITY 9.2

Ghana's men's football team is known as the Black Stars. Fans of the national team buy replica football shirts. Like any goods, the market for Ghana replica football shirts will be affected by demand and supply. For each of the situations below, draw a demand and supply diagram and explain the effect on the market. Copy and complete Table 9.1. The first one has been done for you.

Table 9.1

	Demand and supply diagram	Effect on the market
1 A fall in incomes in Ghana and neighbouring countries	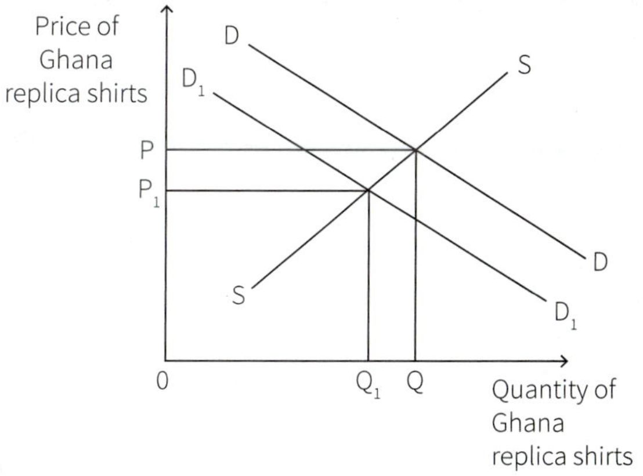	A replica football shirt is a normal good. Demand would decrease, causing a fall in price and a contraction in supply.
2 A rise in the productivity of workers making Ghana replica shirts		
3 Ghana winning the Africa Cup of Nations		
4 A tax being placed on Ghana replica shirts		
5 New, cheaper, but more efficient machinery being introduced to make Ghana replica shirts		

9.4 The consequences of changes in demand and supply

It is possible for both the conditions of demand and the conditions of supply to change at the same time. In this case, the impact on the market will depend not only on the direction of the changes but also on the size of the changes. For example, a report that eating apples is good for you may be trending on social media. At the same time, good weather contributes to a bumper harvest (see Figure 9.7).

Figure 9.7: A bumper apple harvest will cause the price of apples to change

As a result, both demand and supply will increase. The quantity being bought and sold will rise. The effect on price, however, will depend on relative strengths of shifts in demand and supply. Figure 9.8 shows the increase in demand being greater than the increase in supply. As a result, the equilibrium price rises.

In contrast, Figure 9.9 shows the increase in supply exceeding the increase in demand, causing price to fall.

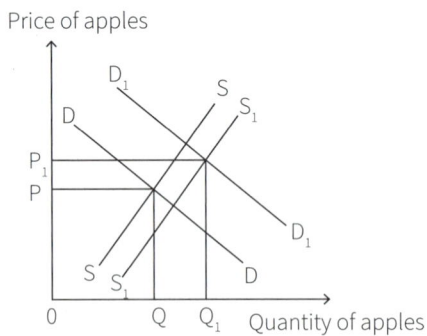

Figure 9.8: The effect of demand increasing more than supply

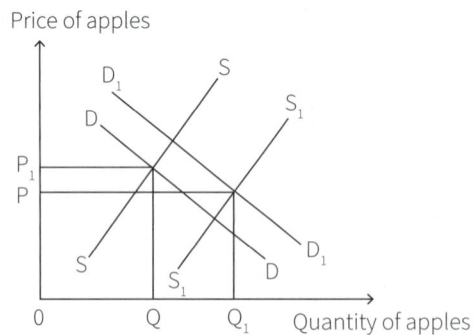

Figure 9.9: The effect of supply increasing more than demand

ACTIVITY 9.3

In a group of four, choose a product such as dates. Now make the following four sets of cards:

Set 1 – 4 cards. For your chosen product, write one cause of an increase in demand on one card, one cause of a decrease in demand on a second card, one cause in increase in supply on a third card and one cause in decrease in supply on a fourth card.

Set 2 – 12 cards. Write 'a rise in price' on 6 cards. Repeat with 'a fall in price' on the other 6 cards.

Set 3 – 16 cards. On 4 cards, write 'a contraction in demand'. Repeat this with 'extension in demand', 'contraction in supply' and 'extension in supply' on the other sets of 4 cards.

Set 4 – 16 cards. On 4 cards, draw a diagram showing the effect of a shift to the right of the supply curve. Repeat with the remaining cards to show a shift to the right of the demand curve, a shift to the left of the demand curve and a shift to the left of the supply curve.

Shuffle the cards in set 1 and place them in a pile face downwards. One person takes the top card from set 1, then chooses a card from each of sets 2–4 that best links to the card from set 1. The person should explain what links the cards. Repeat for everyone in the group.

DISCUSSION

In a group, discuss why the demand for and supply of rice may vary between your country and another country. Make a podcast of your discussion.

REFLECTION

Economics uses diagrams to help you understand concepts. You also need to draw diagrams to explain different situations. Do you find understanding diagrams challenging? Do you find drawing diagrams a challenge? If so, what could you do to help you use diagrams more easily?

SUMMARY

You should now know:

- An increase in demand will shift the demand curve to the right, raise equilibrium price, cause an extension in supply and a rise in sales.

- A decrease in demand will shift the demand curve to the left, lower equilibrium price, cause a contraction in supply and a fall in sales.

- An increase in supply will shift the supply curve to the right, lower the equilibrium price, cause an extension in demand and a rise in sales.

- A decrease in supply will shift the supply curve to the left, raise the equilibrium price and cause a contraction in demand and sales.

Chapter 9 practice questions

1   The diagram shows a change in the market for coffee. What could explain this change?

   A   a health report indicating that drinking coffee can cause headaches

   B   a rise in the price of coffee

   C   a rise in the price of tea

   D   a successful advertising campaign for tea   [1]

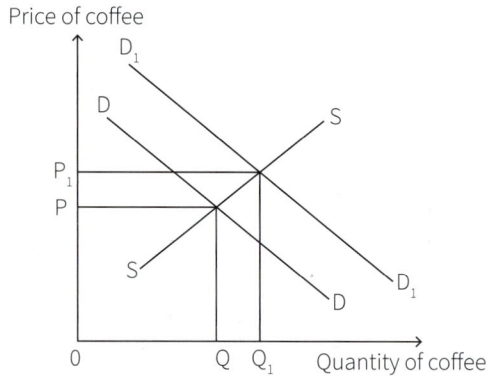

2   The diagram shows the demand for and supply of a product. The initial equilibrium is at Point x. The cost of raw materials used to produce the product falls. Which point represents the new equilibrium?

   A   A

   B   B

   C   C

   D   D   [1]

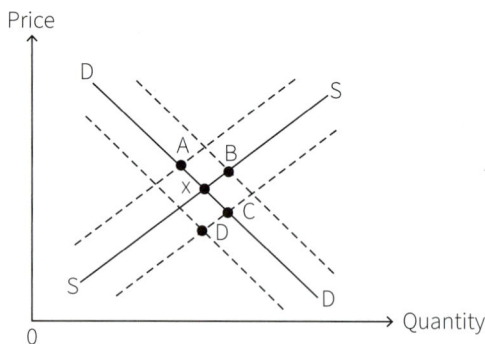

3   Which diagram best illustrates the effect of an increase in income on the market for an inferior good?

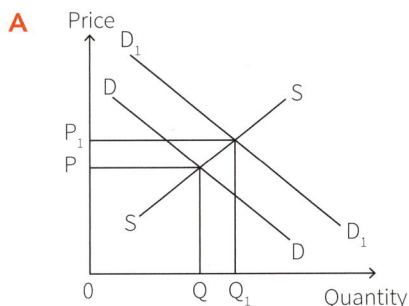

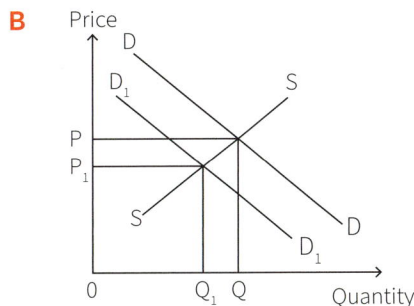

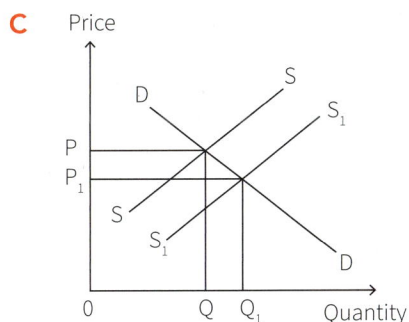

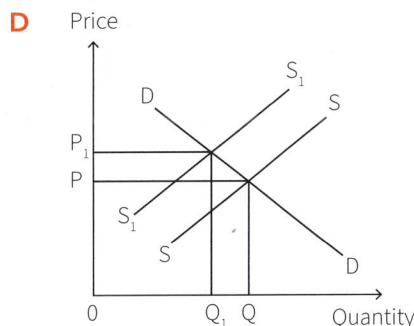

[1]

4   What effect would a decrease in supply of a product have on its price and demand?

	Price	Demand
A	decreases	contracts
B	decreases	extends
C	increases	contracts
D	increases	extends

[1]

5   What would cause a fall in the price of bicycles and an extension in demand for bicycles?

A   a shift to the left of the demand curve

B   a shift to the left of the supply curve

C   a shift to the right of the demand curve

D   a shift to the right of the supply curve

[1]

Total: [5]

6   a   Identify **two** causes, apart from an increase in income, of an increase in demand for a product.   [2]

     b   Explain why an increase in wages is likely to increase demand but may reduce supply.   [4]

     c   Analyse, using a demand and supply diagram, the granting of a subsidy to the producers of a product.   [6]

     d   Discuss whether or not the price of air travel is likely to rise in the future.   [8]

                                 Total: [20]

CHECK YOUR PROGRESS

How well do you think you have achieved the learning intentions for this chapter? Give yourself a score from 1 (still need a lot of practice) to 5 (feeling very confident) for each learning intention. Provide an example to support your score.

Now I can...	Score	Example
analyse how changes in demand and supply can cause price changes		
use demand and supply diagrams to illustrate how changes in demand and supply affect price		
analyse the consequences of price changes.		

> Chapter 10

Price elasticity of demand (PED)

LEARNING INTENTIONS

By the end of this chapter, you will be able to:

- define price elasticity of demand (PED)
- calculate price elasticity of demand
- interpret the significance of the PED value: perfectly inelastic, inelastic, unitary elastic, elastic, perfectly elastic
- draw and interpret demand curve diagrams to show PED
- analyse the main influences on whether demand is elastic or inelastic
- explain the relationship between PED and the amount spent by consumers and revenue raised by firms
- discuss the implications of PED for decision-making by consumers, workers, producers/firms and government.

Introduction

Would you expect a rise in the price of bread to have much impact on the demand for bread? Probably not. You are more likely to think that the demand for a luxury watch will be sensitive to price changes. Bread may be regarded as a need, while a luxury watch is a want. Whether a product is a necessity or a luxury is one influence on how responsive demand is to a change in price.

ECONOMICS IN CONTEXT

Popularity of coffee shops in China

Demand for coffee is growing faster in China than in most other countries. More people in China are also visiting coffee shops (see Figure 10.1). Every year, more coffee shops are opened in China. In 2023, there were more than 120 000 coffee shops in the country with one Chinese firm operating more than 10 000 coffee shops. In most Chinese cities, the coffee shops are located close together.

Figure 10.1: Serving the growing Chinese market for coffee

Discuss in a pair or group:

1   How are coffee shop owners' pricing decisions likely to be influenced by rival coffee shops nearby?

2   Why do you think the demand for coffee has increased?

10.1 What is price elasticity of demand (PED)?

Price elasticity of demand (PED) measures the extent to which the quantity demanded changes when the price of the product changes. The formula used to calculate price elasticity of demand is:

$$PED = \frac{\text{Percentage change in quantity demanded}}{\text{Percentage change in price}}$$

The formula is often abbreviated to:

$$PED = \frac{\%\Delta QD}{\%\Delta P}$$

KEY TERM

price elasticity of demand (PED): a measure of the responsiveness of the quantity demanded to a change in price.

10.2 Calculating PED

To work out price elasticity of demand, first you need to calculate the percentage change in quantity demanded and the percentage change in price. To do this, the change in quantity demanded is divided by the original demand and multiplied by 100. The same process is used to work out the percentage change in price.

For example, the quantity demanded may rise from 200 to 240 as a result of price falling from $10 to $9. In this case, the percentage change in quantity demanded is:

$$\frac{\text{Change in demand}}{\text{Original quantity demanded}} \times 100 = \frac{40}{200} \times 100 = 20\%$$

The percentage change in price is:

$$\frac{\text{Change in price}}{\text{Original price}} \times 100 = \frac{-\$1}{\$10} \times 100 = -10\%$$

When these changes have been calculated, the percentage change in quantity demanded is divided by the percentage in price to give the PED. In this case, this is:

$$\frac{-20\%}{10\%}$$

Remember that a division involving different signs gives a minus figure. So the PED is –2.

ACTIVITY 10.1

1   Calculate the PED for each of the following:

   a   A fall in price from $4 to $3 causes the demand to extend from 60 to 105.

   b   Demand falls from 200 to 180 when price rises from $10 to $12.

   c   A reduction in price from $12 to $6 results in an extension in demand from 100 to 140.

   Share your answers with another student.

2   Demand for a product extends from 80 to 100 a day when price falls from $40 to $35.

   a   In a pair, discuss each of the options below and select the correct one.

      A   –0.5

      B   –0.7

      C   –2.0

      D   –4.0

   Write some notes about each option: why you selected your answer and why each of the other options is incorrect. Share answers in your group.

   b   Now, individually or in a pair, write your own PED calculation question like the one above:
   Demand for a product extends from … to … when price falls from … to … .

   Make sure that each of the incorrect options is based on figures that those answering the question might select.

   Ask other members of the group to answer your question and provide feedback.

Interpreting the significance of the PED value

The PED figure provides two pieces of information. One is given by the *sign*. In most cases, the sign will be a minus. The minus sign tells us that there is an inverse relationship between the quantity demanded and price: a rise in price will cause a contraction in demand, and a fall in price will cause an extension in demand.

The second piece of information is provided by the *size* of the figure. The size of the figure shows the extent by which demand will extend or contract when price changes. A figure of −2, for example, shows that a 1% change in price will cause a 2% change in quantity demanded.

ACTIVITY 10.2

Demand for a luxury product falls from 500 to 200 when price rises from $2 000 to $2 200.

1 Calculate the PED.

2 The price rises by 1%. What percentage would demand contract by?

Share your answers with another student.

Elastic and inelastic demand

Most products have either elastic or inelastic demand. **Elastic demand** occurs when a percentage change in price results in a greater percentage change in quantity demanded, giving a PED figure (ignoring the sign) of more than 1 but less than infinity.

When demand is elastic, price and total revenue (the amount of money earned from selling the product) and price and total spending move in opposite directions. For example, ten products may initially be demanded at a price of $5 each, giving a total revenue of $50. If the price falls to $4 each and demand rises to 20 (giving a PED of −5, that is $\frac{100\%}{-20\%}$), then the total revenue would increase to $80. In the case of elastic demand, a firm can raise total revenue by lowering the price, but it must be aware that if it raises the price, its total revenue will fall. Elastic demand is usually illustrated by a shallow demand curve, as shown in Figure 10.2. The diagram shows that the percentage change in quantity demanded is greater than the percentage change in price.

KEY TERM

elastic demand: when the quantity demanded changes by a greater percentage than the percentage change in price.

Figure 10.2: Elastic demand

Inelastic demand is when the quantity demanded changes by a smaller change than the price and the PED is less than 1 but greater than zero. In this case, price and total revenue and price and total expenditure move in the same direction. If the price is raised, the quantity demanded will fall but by a smaller percentage than the change in price, and so more revenue will be earned. If the price is lowered, more products will be demanded, but not enough to prevent the total revenue from falling. In this case, if a firm wants to raise revenue, it should raise its price.

> ### KEY TERM
>
> **inelastic demand:** when the quantity demanded changes by a smaller percentage than the percentage change in price.

> ### TIP
>
> When defining elastic demand, it is not accurate to state that it is when a change in price causes a large change in quantity demanded. This is because the change in price may have been larger than the change in quantity demanded. Elastic demand is when a percentage change in price causes a greater *percentage* change in the quantity demanded. The same care must be taken with inelastic demand. In this case, it is a smaller *percentage* change in quantity demanded.

> ### LINK
>
> Chapter 35.4 (Effects of changes in foreign exchange rates) explains how the effect of a change in the foreign exchange rate on export revenue is influenced by price elasticity of demand.

Inelastic demand is usually represented by a steep demand curve, as shown in Figure 10.3.

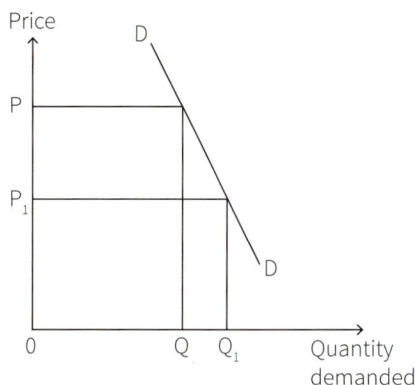

Figure 10.3: Inelastic demand

TIP

As shown in this chapter, elastic demand is often shown by a shallow demand curve and inelastic demand by a steep demand curve. To be certain that this is the case, however, it would be necessary to know how the axes are measured.

The most common degrees of elasticity are elastic and inelastic. Other degrees of elasticity sometimes occur.

Perfectly elastic demand

Perfectly elastic demand occurs when a change in price causes a complete change in the quantity demanded. A firm can sell any quantity at the going market price, for example Q or Q_1, but nothing above this price. For example, if one of the many wheat farmers raises their price, they may lose all of their sales with buyers switching to rival farmers. In this case, PED is infinity and is represented by a horizontal straight line, as shown in Figure 10.4.

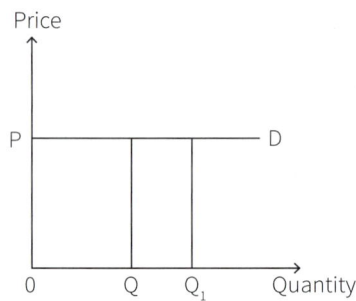

KEY TERMS

perfectly elastic demand: when a change in price causes a complete change in the quantity demanded.

perfectly inelastic demand: when a change in price has no effect on the quantity demanded.

Figure 10.4: Perfectly elastic demand

Perfectly inelastic demand

Perfectly inelastic demand is when the quantity demanded does not change when price changes. For example, demand for some medicines may be perfectly inelastic over a given price range. Consumers may buy the same quantity despite an alteration in price and PED is zero. Figure 10.5 shows demand remaining unchanged at Q as price rises from P to P_1.

Figure 10.5: Perfectly inelastic demand

Unitary elastic demand

Unitary elastic demand exists when a percentage change in price results in an equal percentage change in quantity demanded, giving a PED of one (unitary). When PED is unitary, the area under the demand curve stays the same as price changes, showing that total revenue and total spending remain unchanged as price changes. Figure 10.6 illustrates unitary elasticity of demand.

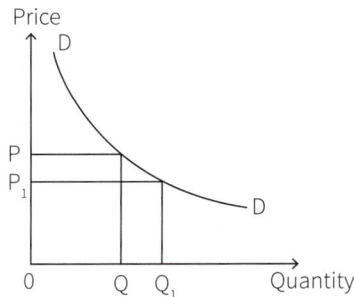

Figure 10.6: Unitary elastic demand

KEY TERM

unitary elastic demand: when a percentage change in price causes an equal percentage change in the quantity demanded, leaving total revenue unchanged.

10.3 Influences on PED

The main influences on whether demand is elastic or inelastic are described below.

Availability of substitutes

The availability of substitutes is the main factor that influences whether demand is elastic or inelastic. If a product does have a close substitute of a similar quality and price, it is likely to have elastic demand. In this case, a rise in price will be likely to cause a significant fall in the quantity demanded as consumers will switch to the substitute. However, if there is no close substitute available, demand will probably be inelastic. The quantity demanded will not fall much in response to a rise in price because there is no suitable alternative to switch to. Some of the other influences on whether demand is elastic or inelastic are linked to the availability of substitutes.

The proportion of income spent on the product

If people only need a small proportion of their income to purchase a product, demand is likely to be inelastic. For example, if the price of salt rose by 20%, the quantity demanded is likely to alter by a much smaller percentage. This is because a 20% rise in price is likely to mean consumers pay only a little more. In fact, some consumers may not even notice the rise in price.

Demand is like to be elastic where a large proportion of people's income is required to buy a product. For example, a 20% rise in the price of a new car would mean consumers would have to pay much more. So, a 20% rise in the price of a new car would be likely to cause a greater percentage contraction in demand.

Figure 10.7: A consumer may choose a budget-priced tyre instead of a more expensive brand

Whether the product is a necessity or a luxury

Luxury products usually have elastic demand. They do not have to be purchased, so a rise in price may result in a greater percentage fall in quantity demanded. If their prices fall, however, the quantity demanded is likely to rise by a greater percentage, as more of the population can now afford to buy them. In contrast to luxuries, necessities such as soaps tend to have inelastic demand. People cannot cut back significantly on their use, even if the prices of soaps rise.

Whether the product is addictive

People may find it difficult to cut back on purchases of products which are addictive, such as cigarettes and coffee. Addictive products therefore have inelastic demand. If the purchase of a product can be delayed, demand tends to be elastic. A rise in price will result in a greater percentage fall in the quantity demanded, as people will postpone the purchase of the product, hoping that its price will drop back in the future. If it does, the quantity demanded will rise by a greater percentage, with the build-up of sales.

Complements

A product may be purchased to be used with a more expensive product (Figure 10.8). In this case, a rise in the price of the cheaper product may not have a significant impact on the overall price of the two products combined. For example, if the price of a portable phone charger rises by 20%, it may increase the combined price of a charger and smartphone by only 1%. In this case, the demand for the charger is likely to be inelastic. So, demand for a complement is likely to be inelastic if it accounts for a small proportion of the combined amount spent on the two connected products.

Figure 10.8: People are buying more virtual reality headsets as complements to gaming consoles

How the market is defined

The more narrowly defined a product is, the more elastic its demand is. Demand for one brand of tea is more elastic than demand for tea in general and even more elastic than demand for hot drinks in general. This is because the narrower the definition, the more substitutes a product is likely to have.

The time period under consideration

Demand also becomes more elastic if the time period under consideration is long. This is because it gives consumers more time to switch their purchases. In the short term, if the price of a product rises, customers may not have enough time to find alternatives, and if it falls, new customers will not have sufficient time to notice the change in price and switch away from rival products.

ACTIVITY 10.3

In a group, decide whether demand for each of the following products is likely to be elastic or inelastic and why. Copy and complete Table 10.1.

Table 10.1

Example	Elastic or inelastic?	Reason
1 cut flowers		
2 gold jewellery		
3 coffee		
4 train travel by commuters		
5 food		

Differences in PED

PED for the same products can differ with time. What were once seen as luxuries can turn into necessities as people become richer. This changes their demand from elastic to inelastic. Many people have a smartphone, and a rise in price would not discourage them from buying the latest model. A wide range of other products, including washing machines and cars, are now seen as being essential.

Due to different tastes, different income levels and different cultures, PED may vary between countries. Demand for rice is more inelastic in Bangladesh than it is in the USA, where it is included in a smaller number of meals. In India, where professional cricket has a huge following, demand for tickets to international cricket matches is more inelastic than it is in the Netherlands, where cricket attracts a smaller following.

DISCUSSION

Discuss how climate change is likely to affect the PED for air conditioners.

PED and the total spending on a product and revenue gained

As mentioned above, when demand is inelastic, a change in price will cause total spending (and total revenue) to move in the same direction. So, a rise in price will cause total spending and total revenue to rise. When demand is perfectly inelastic, a change in price will not only cause spending and revenue to move in the same direction but also by the same percentage. For instance, the price may originally have been $10 and 50 units may have been sold. Total spending and total revenue would have been $500. If the price rose by 20% to $12, the quantity demanded would stay the same at 50, and so total spending and revenue would also rise by 20% to $600.

When demand is elastic, a change in price results in total spending and total revenue moving in the opposite direction. In this case, a rise in the price will cause total spending and total revenue to fall. In the case of perfectly elastic demand, a rise in price will cause demand to fall to zero.

In the case of unitary elastic demand, price and the quantity demanded change by the same percentage, and so total spending and total revenue remain unchanged. It is important to understand that it is the quantity demanded which remains unchanged when price changes in the case of perfectly inelastic demand, whereas it is total spending and total revenue which do not change in the case of unit price elasticity of demand.

10.4 Changes in PED

PED becomes more elastic as the price of a product rises. Consumers become more sensitive to price changes, the higher the price of the product. So, a 10% rise in price when the price was initially $10 000 would mean consumers have to spend considerably more ($1 000) to buy the product. If a supplier kept on raising the price, the product would eventually be priced out of the market. At this point, demand would be perfectly elastic.

As the price falls, demand becomes more inelastic. For example, a 10% fall in price when the price was initially $1 is not very significant and is unlikely to result in much extra demand. If the price falls to zero, there will be a limit to the amount people want to consume. At this point, demand is perfectly inelastic. Figure 10.9 shows how PED varies over a straight-line demand curve. At the midpoint there is unit PED, with the percentage change in quantity demanded matching the percentage change in price.

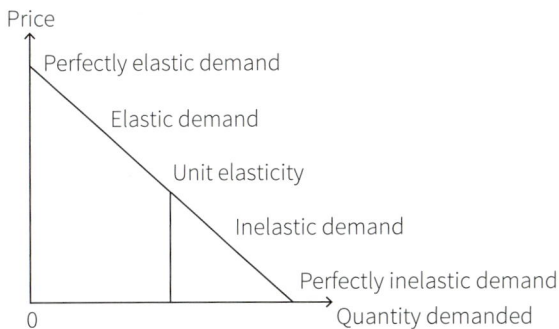

Figure 10.9: Variation of PED over a demand curve

PED also changes when there is a shift in the demand curve. The more consumers want and are able to buy a product, the less sensitive they are to price changes. So, a shift in the demand curve to the right reduces PED at any given price. In Figure 10.10, PED is initially $-5\left(\frac{50\%}{-10\%}\right)$ when price falls from $10 to $9. Then, when demand increases to D_1, PED falls to $-2.5\left(\frac{25\%}{-10\%}\right)$.

> **TIP**
>
> Remember that inelastic demand does alter when price changes but by a smaller percentage than the percentage change in price. It is only when demand is perfectly inelastic that demand does not change with price.

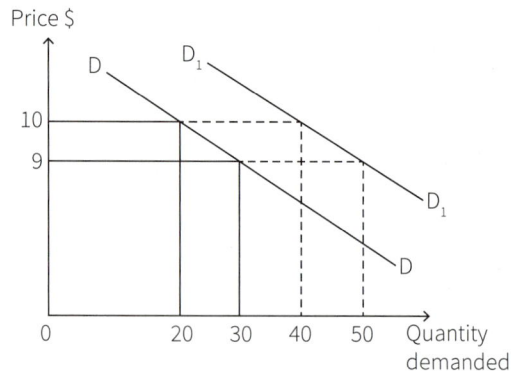

Figure 10.10: The effect of an increase in demand on PED

When demand decreases, consumers become more sensitive to price changes and demand becomes more elastic. Figure 10.11 shows PED rising from $-5\left(\dfrac{50\%}{-10\%}\right)$ to $-10\left(\dfrac{100\%}{-10\%}\right)$.

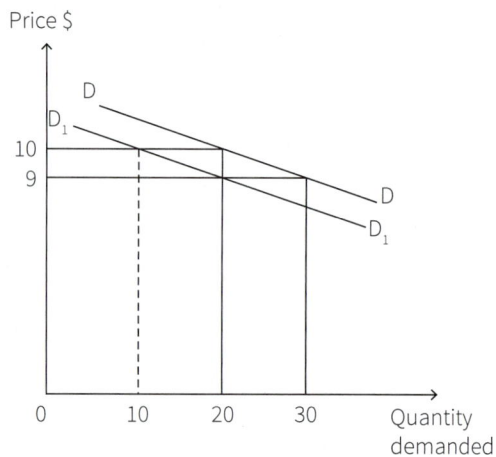

Figure 10.11: The effect of a decrease in demand on PED

ACTIVITY 10.4

In a pair, calculate the PED for each of the following examples. Then discuss and decide if the PED is elastic, inelastic, perfectly elastic, perfectly inelastic or unitary elastic.

1 The price of a product falls from $8 to $6, causing demand to extend from 10 000 to 12 500.

2 Demand contracts from 500 to 400 when price rises from $40 to $42.

3 Demand extends from 2 000 to 2 800 when price falls from $20 to $18.

4 Price rises from $15 to $30, but demand stays unchanged at 5 000.

5 An increase in price from $80 to $90, and as a consequence, a decrease in quantity demanded from 400 to 300.

CONTINUED

You could present your answers in a table like this:

Example	PED	Degree of elasticity

10.5 Significance of PED for decision-making

A change in a product's price is often the main influence on its demand. This is one of the reasons why economists study the effect of a price change in some depth. The implications of PED for the decision-making of different groups are explained below.

Consumers

Consumers are more likely to benefit from lower prices and higher quality when demand is elastic. This is because producers would be reluctant to raise price as demand would contract by a greater percentage and revenue would fall. The quality may also be high if the elastic demand results from the existence of close substitutes. In this case, a producer may have to provide a good quality product to remain competitive (Figure 10.12).

Figure 10.12: A consumer compares the price of rival brands of cooking oil

Workers

Workers' wages and employment can be influenced by the price elasticity of demand for labour. If demand for labour is inelastic, it will be easier for workers to push up wages without losing any jobs. For example, if the wage of hospital doctors rises, it is likely that demand for doctors will fall by a smaller percentage. This is because it is difficult to replace most doctors by machines. However, in the future, developments in artificial intelligence (AI) may reduce the use of doctors in initial medical diagnosis and may make demand for doctors more elastic.

Producers/firms

It is widely recognised that a fall in price will result in an extension in demand. A firm, however, in considering whether to cut the price of a product will need to know the extent of any rise in demand. If demand is going to rise by only a small amount, there may be no benefit to the firm in reducing the price. For instance, the firm may be currently selling 100 units a day at $4 each and earning a total revenue of $400. If it is expected that by lowering its price to $3, demand will only rise to 120, the firm would experience a fall in revenue of $40.

A firm may try to make their product more recognisable through the use of a special design or slogan to encourage brand loyalty. This would discourage consumers switching to other firms' products, as they would not be seen as such close substitutes. It would make demand for the firm's product more price inelastic and would give the firm more power to raise price.

Government

When taking a decision on subsidy and taxation policies, a government needs to know the responsiveness of the quantity demanded to a change in price. For instance, the government may have a policy to discourage consumption of a certain product. In this case, the policy is more likely to be successful if demand is elastic. If, however, demand for a product does not alter much with a change in price, placing a tax on the product will not be a very effective way of achieving their aim.

On the other hand, if a government wants to raise tax revenue, it will be more successful if demand is inelastic. This is because the contraction in demand will be less. If, for example, a government places a tax of $2 on a product and demand falls from 100 to 80, $160 tax revenue would be raised. In contrast, if the PED was higher, and demand falls from 100 to 50, only $100 tax revenue would be raised.

LINK

Chapter 17.3 (Effects of changes in demand and supply in the labour market – The extent to which wages change) looks at the influence of the elasticity of demand for labour on how changes in labour markets affect the wage paid.

ECONOMICS IN ACTION

The importance of the internet

Figure 10.13: Ordering online is now an important part of everyday life

Life without access to the internet is difficult. We use the internet in our work and in our leisure activities. We order goods online, many people bank online, we may play games online and we may do research online. In most countries, there are several firms providing internet services. These firms generally charge a similar price. When internet service providers increase their prices, there tends to be little change in demand.

1   Why is demand for internet services not very responsive to rises in price?

2   Why is important for firms to know not only that demand is likely to extend if they lower prices but also to know by how much demand might extend?

SUMMARY

You should now know:

- Economists, producers/firms and the government need to know the extent to which the quantity demanded changes as a result of a change in price.

- Price elasticity of demand (PED) is a measure of the extent to which the quantity demanded changes as a result of a change in price.

- The most common types of PED are elastic and inelastic.

- The main factor that influences whether demand is elastic or inelastic is the availability of close substitutes of the product.

- Demand for a product is likely to be inelastic if it has no close substitutes, takes up a small proportion of income to be bought, is a necessity, addictive or its purchase cannot be postponed.

- PED can vary with time and between countries.

- The categories of PED are elastic, inelastic, perfectly elastic, perfectly inelastic and unitary elastic.

- As price rises, demand becomes more elastic.

- An increase in demand will make demand more inelastic.

- Consumers tend to benefit from demand being elastic whereas workers and firms tend to benefit from inelastic demand.

- To reduce consumption, governments need demand to be elastic.

- To raise tax revenue, governments need demand to be inelastic.

Chapter 10 practice questions

1   What is price elasticity of demand?

   A   a measure of the extent to which price changes when the quantity demanded changes

   B   a measure of the extent to which price changes when total revenue changes

   C   a measure of the extent to which the quantity demanded changes when price changes

   D   a measure of the extent to which total revenue changes when price changes   [1]

2   Demand for a product is inelastic. What effect will a fall in price have?

   A   demand will change by a greater percentage

   B   demand will not change

   C   total revenue will fall

   D   total revenue will rise   [1]

3   What characteristic is likely to make the demand for a product elastic?

   A   it is a necessity

   B   it is habit-forming

   C   it is relatively cheap

   D   it has close substitutes   [1]

4   The price of a product rises from $60 to $90. This causes demand to contract from 800 to 600. What type of price elasticity of demand does this product have over this price range?

   A   elastic

   B   inelastic

   C   perfectly inelastic

   D   unitary elastic   [1]

5   Price is initially $20 and demand is 600. Price falls to $18 and the PED is −3. What will the new demand be?

   A   420

   B   582

   C   618

   D   780   [1]

                                                                            Total: [5]

6   a   Define 'price elasticity of demand'.   [2]

   b   Explain the difference between inelastic demand and perfectly
       inelastic demand.   [4]

   c   Analyse how the price elasticity of demand of a product influences
       the relationship between changes in price and total revenue.   [6]

   d   Discuss whether or not demand for laser eye surgery will become
       more inelastic over time.   [8]

                                                                        Total: [20]

CHECK YOUR PROGRESS

How well do you think you have achieved the learning intentions for this chapter?
Give yourself a score from 1 (still need a lot of practice) to 5 (feeling very confident)
for each learning intention. Provide an example to support your score.

Now I can...	Score	Example
define price elasticity of demand (PED)		
calculate price elasticity of demand (PED)		
interpret the significance of the PED value: elastic, inelastic, perfectly elastic, perfectly inelastic and unitary elastic		
draw and interpret demand curve diagrams to show PED		
analyse the main influences on whether demand is elastic or inelastic		
explain the relationship between PED and the amount spent by consumers and revenue raised by firms		
show in a diagram how price changes affect the amount spent by consumers and revenue raised by firms		
discuss the implications of PED for decision-making by consumers, workers, producers/firms and government.		

> Chapter 11

Price elasticity of supply (PES)

LEARNING INTENTIONS

By the end of this chapter, you will be able to:

- define price elasticity of supply (PES)
- calculate price elasticity of supply (PES)
- draw and interpret supply curve diagrams to show different PES
- interpret the significance of the PES value: perfectly inelastic, inelastic, unitary elastic, elastic, perfectly elastic
- analyse the main influences on whether supply is elastic or inelastic.

Introduction

Why does the supply of container ships change less quickly than the supply of pens when their price changes? Why would an increase in demand and a rise in price have no impact on the number of seats offered for sale at a football match between Barcelona and Real Madrid? How are advances in technology, such as the development of 3D printing and AI, affecting the supply of car parts? All of these questions relate to the extent to which supply adjusts to changes in price.

ECONOMICS IN CONTEXT

Changes in window cleaning

Traditional window cleaning, where window cleaners climb ladders to clean upper-floor windows, has existed for centuries. Recently, there has been a growth in other methods of window cleaning. These include mobile electronic platforms and abseiling to clean the windows of tall buildings. The largest growth has been in the use of telescopic, water-fed poles. This method of window cleaning involves the window cleaner, at ground level, operating a long pole to clean windows on upper floors. The use of water-fed poles is safer and quicker than traditional methods. Improved safety increases the number of people willing and able to clean windows. Being quicker allows more windows to be cleaned in a given time period. As a result of the greater use of water-fed poles, the supply of window cleaning services can be adapted more easily to any changes in demand and the resulting change in prices.

Figure 11.1: The use of water-fed poles is speeding up window cleaning

Discuss in a pair or group:

1   Why is it reasonably easy for the supply of window cleaning to extend when demand increases and price rises?

2   How will consumers benefit if supply is responsive to changes in price?

11.1 What is price elasticity of supply (PES)?

Economists use **price elasticity of supply (PES)** to study how responsive supply is to a change in price. PES measures the extent to which the quantity supplied changes when the price of a product changes.

The formula is:

$$PES = \frac{\text{Percentage change in quantity supplied}}{\text{Percentage change in price}}$$

The formula is often abbreviated to:

$$PES = \frac{\%\Delta QS}{\%\Delta P}$$

KEY TERM

price elasticity of supply (PES): a measure of the responsiveness of the quantity supplied to a change in price.

11.2 Calculating PES

PES is calculated in the same way as price elasticity of demand (PED). This time, however, it is the percentage change in quantity supplied which is calculated. PES is found by dividing the change in quantity supplied by the original quantity supplied and multiplying by 100. Similarly, the percentage change in price is calculated by dividing the change in price by the original price and multiplying by 100. For example, the quantity supplied may rise from 100 to 130 as a result of price increasing from \$10 to \$12. In this instance, the percentage change in quantity supplied is:

$$\frac{\text{Change in quantity supplied}}{\text{Original quantity supplied}} \times 100 = \frac{30}{100} \times 100 = 30\%$$

and the percentage change in price is:

$$\frac{\text{Change in price}}{\text{Original price}} \times 100 = \frac{\$2}{\$10} \times 100 = 20\%$$

This means that the PES is:

$$\frac{30\%}{20\%} = 1.5$$

ACTIVITY 11.1

Calculate the PES for each of the following:

1   A fall in price from \$5 to \$4 causes supply to contract from 10 000 to 4 000.

2   Supply extends from 200 to 210 when price rises from \$10 to \$14.

3   An increase in price from \$4 000 to \$4 400 results in an extension of supply from 80 to 90.

Share your answers with another student.

> **TIP**
>
> When calculating PES (and PED), remember to divide the change by the original figure and multiply by 100 to give the percentage.

Interpreting the significance of the PES value

As the quantity supplied and price are directly related, PES is a positive figure. The figure indicates the degree of responsiveness of the quantity supplied to a change in price. The higher the figure, the more responsive supply is. A PES of 2.6, for example, means that a 1% rise in price will cause a 2.6% extension in supply.

ACTIVITY 11.2

Supply of a product rises from 5 000 to 7 000 due to a rise in price from \$4 to \$5.

1   Calculate the PES.

2   The price rises by 1%. What percentage would supply extend by?

Share your answers with another student.

Elastic and inelastic supply

Supply is usually elastic or inelastic. **Elastic supply** is when the percentage change in quantity supplied is greater than the percentage change in price. In this case, PES is greater than 1, but less than infinity. The higher the figure, the more elastic supply is. Elastic supply is usually illustrated by a shallow curve, as shown in Figure 11.2. A straight-line supply curve illustrating elastic supply would touch the vertical axis.

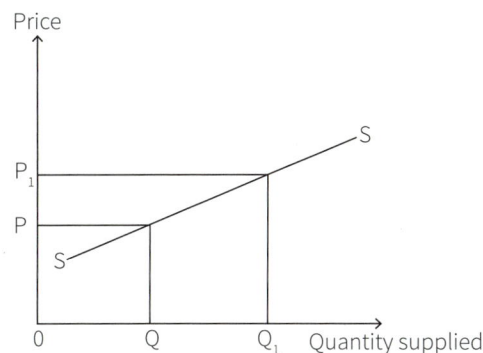

Figure 11.2: Elastic supply

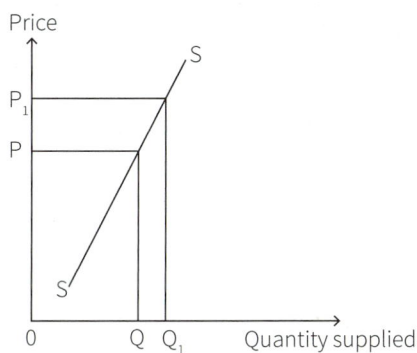

Figure 11.3: Inelastic supply

In contrast, **inelastic supply** is when the percentage change in quantity supplied is less than the percentage change in price, and so PES is less than 1, but greater than zero. A PES of 0.2 would mean that supply is more inelastic than that for a PES of 0.7. Figure 11.3 illustrates inelastic supply. The supply curve is steep, showing that the quantity supplied changes by less than the price in percentage terms. A straight-line supply curve illustrating inelastic supply would touch the horizontal axis.

As well as elastic and inelastic supply, three other degrees of elasticity sometimes occur.

Perfectly inelastic supply

Perfectly inelastic supply is when the quantity supplied does not alter with price changes and PES is zero. If, for example, more people are demanding to see a movie at a particular cinema, ticket prices may rise (see Figure 11.4). However, it is unlikely to increase the seating capacity in the short run. In the longer run, if demand remains high, the owners of the cinema are likely to increase its size.

KEY TERMS

elastic supply: when the quantity supplied changes by a greater percentage than the percentage change in price.

inelastic supply: when the quantity supplied changes by a smaller percentage than the percentage change in price.

KEY TERM

perfectly inelastic supply: when a change in price has no effect on the quantity supplied.

Figure 11.4: With a fixed number of seats available, not everyone may get into the cinema to see the movie

Figure 11.5 shows perfectly inelastic supply. A rise in price from P to P_1 leaves the quantity supplied unchanged at Q.

Perfectly elastic supply

Perfectly elastic supply is when a change in price will cause an infinite change in supply, giving a PES of infinity. PES may come close to infinity in very competitive markets. The market for paper clips, for example, may include very many firms selling almost identical paper clips. In this case, if one firm tried to charge a higher price than the rest, it is likely to lose all of its sales. The very high level of competition is likely to drive price down to its lowest level that still covers the cost of producing the paper clips. If price were to fall below this level, all the firms may stop producing paper clips.

Figure 11.6 illustrates perfectly elastic supply.

KEY TERM

perfectly elastic supply: when a change in price causes a complete change in quantity supplied.

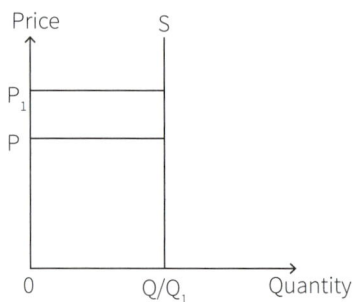

Figure 11.5: Perfectly inelastic supply

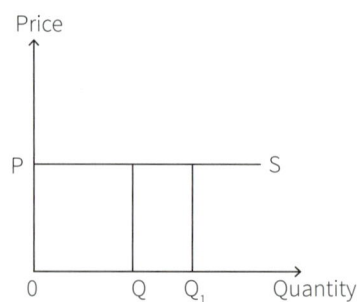

Figure 11.6: Perfectly elastic supply

Unitary elastic

Unitary elastic occurs when a given percentage change in price causes an equal percentage change in supply. Unitary elastic is illustrated by any straight line that goes through the origin (the point where the vertical and horizontal axes intersect), as shown in Figure 11.7.

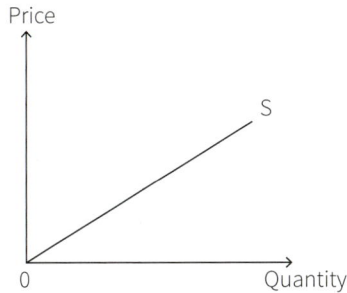

Figure 11.7: Unitary elastic

11.3 Influences on PES

The main influences which determine the PES of a product are:

- **The time taken to produce it.** If the product can be made quickly, supply is likely to be elastic. If it takes a long time to make a product, it may not be easy to change the quantity supplied quickly and supply is likely to be inelastic (see Figure 11.8).

- **The cost of altering supply.** If production involves the use of expensive capital equipment or highly paid labour, firms are likely to consider carefully whether to alter supply, and this may make supply inelastic.

LINK

Chapter 17.3 (the extent to which wage changes) looks at the influence of the elasticity of supply of labour on how changes in labour markets affect the wage paid.

Figure 11.8: Production of chairs may take time

- **Mobility of factors of production.** The more mobile factors of production are, the more elastic supply is likely to be. This is because it will be reasonably easy for firms to increase their supply by employing more factors of production. If, however, it is difficult for workers, capital, land and enterprise to move from one industry to another, supply will be inelastic.

- **Level of capacity.** If most factors of production are in use, it will be difficult to increase production and so will restrict any rise in supply. However, if there is spare capacity in the economy, firms would be able to expand their output and increase their supply by recruiting unemployed resources. Firms may also have resources that they are not using fully. For example, firms may have machines that are being used for only a few hours a day.

- **Whether or not the product can be stored.** If the product can be stored, the quantity supplied can be adjusted relatively easily in the event of a price change, and supply will be elastic. If the price falls, firms will remove some products from the market and place them in storage. Whereas, if price rises, firms may sell some of their stock of the product.

- **The time period involved.** The longer the time period, the more opportunity firms will have to alter the quantity of factors of production they employ and, if appropriate, change their methods of production.

- **Depletion of natural resources.** If natural resources are being depleted, it will become increasingly difficult to extend the supply of those products that use these natural resources.

Supply of many agricultural products is inelastic. It takes time for crops to grow and livestock to mature, and many agricultural products cannot be stored. If the price of apples falls, for example, the quantity offered for sale is unlikely to fall significantly. This is because once picked, apples have a fairly short shelf life. If the price of apples rises, farmers will not be able to substantially alter the quantity supplied. It can take years before new apple trees are mature enough to crop. However, the supply of apples in one area or one country may be relatively elastic if apples can be moved from one place to another in response to a difference in demand and so in price.

ACTIVITY 11.3

In a group, decide whether supply for each of the following products is likely to be elastic or inelastic, giving a reason for your decision. Copy and complete Table 11.1.

Table 11.1

Example	Elastic or inelastic?	Reason
1 rubber bands		
2 t-shirts		
3 aircraft		
4 pencils		
5 lamb		

As already suggested, PES can vary with time. The supply for most products becomes more elastic as the time period increases. This is because producers have more time to adjust their supply. This may involve switching production from or to other products and building new factories and offices or selling off existing plants.

Advances in technology, by reducing the production period and lowering costs of production, make supply more elastic. In recent years, it has become much easier and cheaper to produce magazines. As a result, not only has the number of magazines on offer increased, but also the speed with which new titles appear and titles which are declining in popularity disappear.

ECONOMICS IN ACTION

The development of flat pack housing

Economists analyse how changes in price elasticity of supply of different products affect the performance of markets. One market where a change in price elasticity of supply is having an impact is the housing market. The supply of housing has been inelastic for some time. It can take at least seven months to build a house. With inelastic supply, any change in demand results in a relatively large change in price and a relatively small extension in supply.

The development of flat pack housing is changing the price elasticity of supply in a number of countries. Flat pack housing, sometimes called modular housing, involves constructing the parts of a house or flat in a factory. It is then delivered to the site and fitted together there (see Figure 11.9). This method has the advantage that it is not affected by bad weather. It has been estimated to be at least 25% cheaper than the traditional method of building houses. It is also much quicker, with houses and flats being constructed in weeks rather than months.

Figure 11.9: Flat pack houses make the supply of housing more elastic

1   Why is the supply of flat pack houses more responsive to a fall in price than traditional housing?

2   Why, in practice, may it be difficult to measure price elasticity of supply?

ACTIVITY 11.4

In a pair, produce a poster on elastic and inelastic supply. This could compare:

- a definition

- value of PES

- example of a product

- reason for the product's PES

- shape of the supply curve.

You could include several features on the poster, for example, symbols showing the difference in the value of PES, with elastic supply having a PES >1. You could also include diagrams with inelastic supply being shown by steep, upward supply curve that would touch the horizontal axis.

REFLECTION

What kind of activities in this chapter helped you further your understanding of PES?

Was there any aspect of PES that you found difficult to understand? If so, what will you do to gain a better understanding?

SUMMARY

You should now know:

- PES is a measure of the responsiveness of the quantity supplied to a change in price.

- The most common types of PES are elastic and inelastic supply.

- The main factors that influence whether supply is elastic or inelastic are whether production can be changed cheaply and quickly and whether the product can be stored.

- Supply of a product is likely to be inelastic if it takes a long time to produce it, if it is expensive to alter production, if there is little or no spare capacity and if the product cannot be stored.

- Supply tends to become more elastic with time.

- The categories of PES are elastic, inelastic, perfectly elastic, perfectly inelastic and unitary elastic.

Chapter 11 practice questions

1 What is the formula for PES?

A $\dfrac{\text{change in quantity supplied}}{\text{change in price}}$

B $\dfrac{\text{change in quantity supplied}}{\text{change in quantity demanded}}$

C $\dfrac{\text{percentage change in quantity supplied}}{\text{percentage change in price}}$

D $\dfrac{\text{percentage change in quantity supplied}}{\text{percentage change in quantity demanded}}$ [1]

2 What does a PES of 0.8 indicate?

A supply is elastic

B supply is inelastic

C supply is perfectly elastic

D supply is perfectly inelastic [1]

3 In which circumstance would supply of a product be elastic?

A it is costly to produce

B it takes time to produce

C it can be stored

D it uses resources which are in short supply [1]

4 Which diagram illustrates elastic supply?

[1]

5   Supply of a product falls from 820 to 656 when price falls from $8 to $4.
    What is the PES?

    A   0.4

    B   1.0

    C   1.9

    D   2.5   [1]

                                                               Total: [5]

6   a   Define 'perfectly inelastic supply'.   [2]

    b   Explain how an economist can determine whether the supply of
        a product is elastic or inelastic.   [4]

    c   Analyse why the supply of agricultural products tends to be
        more inelastic than the supply of manufactured products.   [6]

    d   Discuss whether or not producers would want the demand
        and supply of their product to be more price elastic.   [8]

                                                              Total: [20]

CHECK YOUR PROGRESS

How well do you think you have achieved the learning intentions for this chapter?
Give yourself a score from 1 (still need a lot of practice) to 5 (feeling very confident)
for each learning intention. Provide an example to support your score.

Now I can...	Score	Example
define price elasticity of supply (PES)		
calculate PES		
interpret the significance of the PES value: perfectly inelastic, inelastic, unitary elastic, elastic, perfectly elastic		
analyse the main influences on whether supply is elastic or inelastic.		

Market economic system

Introduction

A number of countries are increasing the role of market forces of demand and supply and reducing the role of the government in their economies. For example, Cuba is increasing the role of market forces in its economy. The country's government has legalised the private sale of cars and homes and removed some price controls and regulations. Why is it making these changes?

ECONOMICS IN CONTEXT

Trying to catch a bargain

Market forces can be seen in operation in the Noryangjin Fish Market in Seoul, Republic of Korea (see Figure 12.1). Every day, except Sunday, people come to the market to buy seafood from the nearly 700 retail seafood stores and to eat in the seafood restaurants in the market. There are crabs, octopus and shrimps and a wide variety of fish such as mackerel, marlin, salmon and stingrays on sale.

Some consumers bargain for the produce with the store staff. Consumers start by offering a lower price than they are willing and able to pay. Some store staff initially ask for a higher price than they are willing and able to accept. The price finally agreed upon is usually somewhere in the middle.

On the second floor of the market, fish and seafood are auctioned. The fishers sell their catches to the owners of the seafood stores in the market, to seafood stores throughout the city and to food processing firms throughout the country. The auction starts at 1 a.m. The buyers bid against each other to buy the fish and seafood. Those with the greatest willingness and ability to buy leave the market with their purchases. Fishers who find that

they have difficulty selling their catch at a price they find acceptable may decide to switch to catching seafood that is sold at a higher price.

Discuss in a pair or group:

1   Why are some consumers prepared to pay a higher price for salmon than other consumers?

2   Why might the price a seafood store charges for mackerel change throughout the day?

Figure 12.1: Noryangjin Fish Market

12.1 Different economic systems

There are three main **economic systems**. One is a **planned economic system**. An economy which operates a planned economic system may be called a planned, centrally planned, command or collectivist economy. A planned economic system is an economy in which the state (government) makes the decisions about what to produce, how to produce it and who receives the products. The state owns most or all of the land and capital and employs workers. The state gives **directives** (instructions) to **state-owned enterprises (SOEs)** on what to produce and how to produce it. The state determines who receives the products that are produced. It does this in two main ways. One is by deciding on the wages paid to workers. Those who are paid more will be able to buy more products. The state will also usually provide basic necessities and

KEY TERM

economic system: the institutions, organisations and mechanisms that influence how an economy works and determine how resources are allocated.

important products, such as housing, transport and education, free of cost or at a low price. This is so that everyone can have access to these products.

The other two types of economic systems are a market economic system and a mixed economic system. This chapter looks at the market economic system. (Chapter 14 looks at the mixed economic system.)

Examples of the different economic systems

To a certain extent, all economies are mixed economies. This is because there is some government intervention in all economies and some private sector production. The term 'mixed economy', or 'mixed economic system', however, is largely used to describe an economy which has private and public sectors of reasonably similar sizes. An example of such an economy is Sweden.

While there is no economy without a public sector, the USA is often described as a market economy. The US government does carry out some functions, for example, providing defence. The economy is, nevertheless, considered to be a market economy, as most capital and land is owned by individuals and groups of individuals, and market forces play the key role in deciding the fundamental economic questions.

In Democratic People's Republic of Korea, there is a very limited degree of small-scale private sector agricultural production, but the economy is largely a planned economy. The government owns most land and capital and it makes most of the decisions as to what to produce, how to produce it and who receives the output.

Changes in economic systems

In the 1980s and 1990s, a number of economies, including the UK and New Zealand, moved from being largely mixed economies to being mainly market economies. The role of the government was reduced by removing a number of government regulations, selling off SOEs and parts of SOEs (privatisation) and lowering taxation.

There was an even more dramatic change in the economies of Eastern Europe, including Poland and Russia, in the 1990s. They moved from being planned economies towards market economies. These economies have experienced a significant increase in consumer choice and a rise in the quality of products produced. However, they have also seen a rise in income inequality and poverty.

Likewise, there has been an increasing role of market forces in a number of economies in Asia, including China and India, and in Africa, including South Africa. In contrast, there has been a rise in government intervention in a number of Latin American economies, including Bolivia and Venezuela.

12.2 Market economic system

An economy which operates a market economic system is known as a market economy or a free enterprise economy. In a market economic system buyers (also known as consumers) determine what is produced. Buyers signal their preferences to sellers through the price mechanism.

KEY TERMS

planned economic system: an economic system where the government makes the main decisions, land and capital are state-owned and resources are allocated by directives.

directives: instructions given by the state (government) to state-owned enterprises.

state-owned enterprises (SOEs): organisations owned by the government which sell products and provide services.

market economic system: an economic system where consumers determine what is produced, resources are allocated by the price mechanism and land and capital are privately owned.

mixed economic system: an economy in which both the private and public sectors play an important role.

In a market economic system, governments rarely intervene in decisions about what to produce, how to produce it and who receives it. Land and capital are privately owned. Private sector firms decide how to produce the products consumers want to buy. Some firms, for instance steel firms, may employ large amounts of capital relative to labour. Others, for example, rely mainly on labour (see Figure 12.2). In making their decision on which factors of production to employ, firms will seek to achieve the lowest cost method of production, while producing the highest quality of products. This may also involve the use of new, more productive capital equipment to replace older equipment.

Figure 12.2: Labour employed in a restaurant kitchen

LINK

For an explanation of the role of the price mechanism in allocating resources – see Chapter 8.1 (The price mechanism).

TIP

Remember the key role the price mechanism and demand and supply play in determining what products are produced in a market economy.

LINK

Capital-intensive production and labour-intensive production both have advantages and disadvantages – see Chapter 19.2 (Labour-intensive and capital-intensive production).

ACTIVITY 12.1

Individually, think about the answers to this question:

How are the following questions likely to be answered in a market economic system?

1   What is produced?

2   How is output produced?

3   Who gets the products produced?

Discuss your answers with another student. Then share your answers with the rest of your group or class. Make sure you are able to explain your answers.

How a market economic system works

Resources move towards those products for which demand is rising and away from those which are becoming less popular. Figure 12.3 shows an increase in demand for air travel and a decrease in demand for sea travel.

(a)

Air fares

(b)

Sea fares

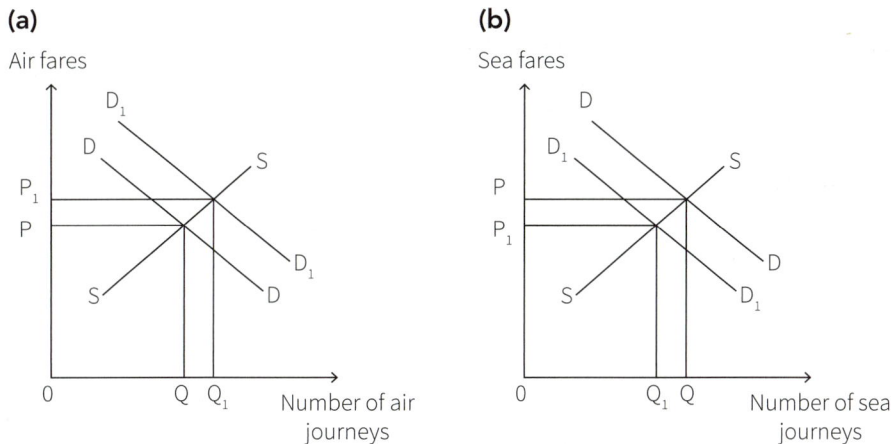

Figure 12.3: (a) Change in the market for air travel **(b)** Change in the market for sea travel

The changes in demand cause prices to change. These alterations in price encourage firms to switch their resources from sea travel to air travel.

ACTIVITY 12.2

The price of onions rose significantly in India in 2021. Traders blamed the rise in price on a poor crop after unusually light monsoon rains. In the same year in India, the price of tomatoes rose, largely due to higher demand caused by an increase in incomes.

1   Draw a diagram, for each case, to show why the price of onions and the price of tomatoes rose in India in 2021.

2   Give an explanation how, in each case, the markets responded to changing circumstances.

Share your answers with another student. Did you make the same points as other students in your explanation?

The importance of competition and incentives

The advantages of a market economic system largely rely on competitive pressures. One of the benefits of a market system is *choice*. If several firms produce a product, consumers will have a choice of producers. Producers should then compete with each other to meet consumer demand. In such a case, consumers are said to be *sovereign* (consumers have power to determine what should be produced).

Competition, whether actual or potential, should also result in low prices. Actual competition arises when there are rival firms in the industry. Potential competition occurs when it is easy for firms to enter or leave the industry. If it is possible for consumers to switch from high-price firms to low-price firms, there will be pressure on firms to keep their prices low in order to stay in business. To remain in business, firms will try to keep their costs low. The more successful a firm is in keeping its costs low and the more it provides what consumers want, the more efficient the firm is likely to be.

The market economic system encourages efficiency by rewarding entrepreneurs and workers who respond to market signals and punishes those who do not. This is sometimes referred to as the market system providing both a *carrot* (a reward) and a *stick* (punishment) to encourage efficiency.

Entrepreneurs who are quick to pick up on changes in consumer demand are likely to earn high profits. High profits then provide businesses with the incentive and ability to innovate and expand. In contrast, entrepreneurs who are unresponsive to changing consumer demand are likely to suffer losses.

In labour markets, workers increase their chance of earning high wages by developing the skills which are in high demand, working hard, accepting more responsibility and by being willing to change what they do and their place of work. Workers who are not prepared (or able) to work, who lack the appropriate skills and who are not able to change where they work (geographically immobile) may receive no or low incomes.

Private and public sectors

The private sector includes business organisations owned by shareholders or individuals. Business organisations in the private sector respond to changes in market forces and aim to make a profit.

The **public sector** is controlled by the government. It includes services run by the government and state-owned enterprises (SOEs). SOEs are called nationalised industries (see Figure 12.4). The government's priority may be to promote the welfare of the country's population.

Figure 12.4: Qatar Airways is a public sector business. The airline is wholly owned by the Qatari government

LINK

The advantages and disadvantages of state-owned enterprises (public sector firms) and private sector firms are explored in Chapter 14.3 (Government measures intervention to address market failure – Nationalisation and Privatisation).

KEY TERM

public sector: the part of the economy controlled by the government.

TIP

Be careful with the word 'public'. Sometimes, it refers to the government as in 'public expenditure' and 'public sector'. It can also refer to people as a whole, as in the 'general public', or open to all people, as in a 'public limited company'.

ACTIVITY 12.3

India has a long tradition of government planning. In 1991, the government began to reduce its intervention in the economy by selling parts of its state-owned enterprises (SOEs). It divided up the ownership of some of its SOEs into shares and sold the shares to the private sector. The sale of SOEs is known as **privatisation**. The process of privatisation sped up in the first decade of the 2000s. It slowed down in the second decade and first half of the third decade, but there is still some debate about whether a number of state-run enterprises, including the national rail industry, Indian Railways, should be transferred from the public to the private sector.

Explain one reason for better performance of a firm when:

1   it is in the private sector

2   it is in the public sector.

Write your answers in your notebook. Then share your answers with your group. You may want to add additional points in your notebook.

KEY TERM

privatisation: the sale of public sector assets to the private sector.

12.3 Arguments for and against the market economic system

A market economic system has the potential to provide some significant advantages.

- **Resources should change automatically and quickly to reflect changes in consumer demand.** There are three reasons why this happens.

    1   The price mechanism in a market economic system provides information on which products are increasing in demand and which ones are falling in demand.

    2   The market economic system provides an incentive for resources to move in response to changes in demand. For example, if demand for books is increasing while the demand for cinema tickets is falling, profits and wages will be rising in the publishing industry, while they will be falling in the film industry. These changes will encourage some firms to switch production and some workers to change their jobs.

    3   The market economic system punishes those firms, workers and owners of capital and land who do not respond to changing demand. For example, if a firm continues to produce a product which is falling in demand, it will make a loss.

- **The market system provides consumers, firms and workers with choice.** Consumers can choose which products to buy and which firms to buy from. Firms can also decide what they want to produce, and workers can choose who to work for.

- **Costs and prices may be low.** The profit motive and competition promote efficiency. The firms which produce at the lowest costs and are able to charge the lowest prices, are likely to sell more and earn more profit. In contrast, those firms which produce products of the same quality at a higher price are likely to go out of business. By rewarding efficiency, and punishing inefficiency, the market economic system should encourage the production of the goods and services that consumers want and are prepared to pay for, in the right quantities and at the lowest possible cost per unit.

- **Quality may be high.** Market forces may encourage better methods of production and a rise in the quality of products made. It does this by putting competitive pressure on firms, and by providing them with the profit incentive to try to gain more sales by making their products more attractive to consumers.

There is a risk that the market forces of demand and supply may not work well. In fact, **market failure** may occur, with market forces failing to ensure the maximum benefit for society. There are a number of reasons for this.

- **Consumers and private sector firms may only take into account the costs and benefits to themselves.** They may not consider the costs and benefits of their decisions to others. For example, some people may smoke cigarettes, even if it endangers the health of those around them. Another example is that to keep their costs and prices down, firms may dump waste material in rivers rather than process it to protect the environment.

- **Competition between firms should ensure efficiency but, in practice, there may be little competition.** A market may become dominated by one or a few firms. These firms have considerable market power leading to limited or no choice for consumers. They can raise the prices of their products and produce poor quality products, as people have no choice but to buy from them.

- **Even when there is competition and firms want to respond to desires of consumers, they may not be able to do this.** This may be because firms cannot attract more workers, as workers lack the right skills or are geographically immobile.

- **Firms will not make products unless they think they can charge for them.** There are some products, such as street lighting, which most people want and expect, but firms know that they cannot restrict the light provided by street lighting to those who are prepared to pay for it. There will be others who do not pay who will be able to benefit from the light (see Figure 12.5). In such cases, people can act as **free riders**. They benefit from the product even if they do not pay for it. When it is not possible to exclude non-payers, private sector firms do not have the financial incentive to produce the product.

- **Advertising can influence consumer choice by persuading people to buy products they would not otherwise have wanted or encourage them to buy larger quantities.** Consumers and producers may also lack information and so may make inefficient choices.

- **Differences in income will increase over time.** Those earning high incomes can afford to save and buy shares. Their savings and shares will earn them interest and dividends (a share of a company's profits). In contrast, people living in poverty cannot afford to save. The children of the rich will be more likely than the children of those living in poverty to earn high incomes. This is because their parents are able to spend more on their education, provide better equipment, such as digital devices, and so they are likely to have high hopes of what they can achieve.

As well as market forces sometimes failing to achieve efficiency, they may result in inequitable (unfair) outcomes. In a market economic system, some consumers will

TIP

Efficiency is a key economic concept. When assessing the performance of an economy or firm, consider whether it is efficient or not. Are costs and prices low and quality high?

KEY TERMS

market failure: market forces resulting in an inefficient allocation of resources.

free rider: someone who consumes a good or service without paying for it.

have a lack of income. There can be a very uneven distribution of income, with some people being very rich and others living in poverty. The sick and people with disabilities may find it difficult to earn incomes. Older people may not have sufficient savings for their retirement. Some workers may become unemployed and may find it difficult to find new jobs.

Figure 12.5: Street lighting is an example of where there are free riders

LINK

Differences in income and wealth can have a number of consequences. These consequences are why governments take measures to reduce income and wealth inequality – see Chapter 22.1 (Reasons why governments aim to redistribute income) on unfairness.

ACTIVITY 12.4

In the USA, there is a big gap between the rich and people living in poverty.

In a group, discuss how in a market economy, some people can be rich, and some people experience poverty. Note down the main points on sticky notes. At the end of the discussion, use the sticky notes to write the reasons why there may be a gap between poverty and wealth in a market economy.

REFLECTION

Do you find taking part in a discussion or listening to a discussion helpful for your understanding?

ECONOMICS IN ACTION

Changes in the ownership of the water supply in Ghana

Until 2008, a state-owned enterprise (SOE) provided water to households and firms in Ghana. The SOE was then privatised. The government hoped that a private sector firm would be more efficient and would provide a better service to consumers. It was thought that a private sector firm would respond more quickly to changes in demand and supply. However, in 2013, the government returned water supply to government control. It was concerned that there were still water shortages, because the private sector had not spent much on buying capital goods and employing more workers to expand water provision. The private sector firm was criticised for putting profits before improving water provision.

Figure 12.6: Water is an essential good

1   Is demand for water elastic or inelastic?

2   Do you think water should be supplied by a state-owned enterprise or a private sector firm?

ACTIVITY 12.5

Bata Pakistan Limited is a shoe producer and retailer. In recent years, it has expanded the range of products it produces. It now, for example, also produces and sells handbags. The firm has faced increased competition which has reduced the growth of its profits.

1   What evidence is there in the passage that Bata may have been responding to consumer demand?

2   How may consumers benefit from the high profits earned by a firm?

Write your answers in your notebook.

DISCUSSION

Discuss whether you would like to live in a country that relies on a market economic system. You could produce a podcast of your discussion.

SUMMARY

You should now know:

- The main factor that determines the type of economic system is how resources are allocated.

- The market system relies on the price mechanism to allocate resources.

- Competition and incentives, including higher profits and higher wages, play key roles in a market system.

- The main advantages of a market economy are that output reflects consumer tastes, consumers have greater choice, competition promotes efficiency which lowers prices and increases quality, and financial incentives encourage hard work and enterprise.

- The main disadvantages of a market economy are that output may not reflect the full costs and benefits, private sector firms may abuse their market power, workers may lack skills and resources may be geographically immobile, products that consumers want but cannot be charged for directly cannot be produced, and there may be poverty.

- In a mixed economy, resources are allocated by means both of the price mechanism and government decision.

Chapter 12 practice questions

1   What is an advantage of a market economy?

    A   an absence of poverty

    B   consumer sovereignty

    C   firms having considerable market power

    D   full employment   [1]

2   What encourages firms to produce what consumers demand?

    A   the chance to earn a high profit

    B   the chance to experience high unit costs of production

    C   the desire to attract new firms into the industry

    D   the desire to keep revenue as low as possible   [1]

3   What is found in a market economy?

    A   entrepreneurs making profits and losses

    B   government controls on the price of most products

    C   most firms being in the public sector

    D   most people working for SOEs   [1]

4   In a market system, what encourages firms to keep their costs low?

    A   competition

    B   government regulations

    C   subsidies

    D   taxation   [1]

5   How is the key resource allocation decision of what to produce made
    in a market economy?

    A   by the aims of the government

    B   by the cost of production

    C   by the preferences of consumers

    D   by the size of the population   [1]

                                                         Total: [5]

6   a   Identify **two** differences between the private sector and the public sector.   [2]

    b   Explain why consumers are said to be sovereign in a market
        economic system.   [4]

    c   Analyse the role of profit in a market economic system.   [6]

    d   Discuss whether or not prices will be low in a market economic system.   [8]

                                                        Total: [20]

CHECK YOUR PROGRESS

How well do you think you have achieved the learning intentions for this chapter?
Give yourself a score from 1 (still need a lot of practice) to 5 (feeling very confident)
for each learning intention. Provide an example to support your score.

Now I can...	Score	Example
define market economic system		
discuss the arguments for and against the market economic system.		

Chapter 13

Market failure

LEARNING INTENTIONS

By the end of this chapter, you will be able to:

* define market failure
* explain key terms associated with market failure: public goods, merit goods, demerit goods, private benefits, external benefits, social benefits, private costs, external costs, social costs, monopoly
* explain the causes of market failure relating to public goods, merit goods, demerit goods, external costs, external benefits and abuse of monopoly power
* analyse the consequences of market failure.

Introduction

Do you think education and healthcare receive sufficient resources in your country? Do you think too many resources in the global economy are used to produce things that may damage people's health and well-being, such as sugary drinks and cigarettes? Are you worried about the level of pollution in your country and the world? Why do market forces sometimes result in a misallocation of resources?

Chapter 12 described the benefits when markets work well. In practice, however, there are a number of reasons why markets may fail to be efficient. These reasons were introduced in the previous chapter and are explained in more depth here. Some of the measures that governments can take to correct market failure are also outlined.

ECONOMICS IN CONTEXT

Are soft drinks too sweet?

It has long been known that high-sugar drinks are bad for dental health. Some soft drinks contain as much as eight teaspoons of sugar per can or small bottle. Sugary drinks can cause tooth decay, the need for fillings and sometimes tooth loss. Drinking sugary drinks as part of a high-sugar diet can contribute to obesity, which puts people at risk of diseases such as diabetes and heart disease.

Treating patients with diabetes or heart disease uses healthcare resources. If people cut back on sugar in their daily nutrition, including sugary drinks, waiting lists for medical treatment would be reduced, fewer working days would be lost to illness and people would be likely to live longer.

Some people are still unaware of the health risks of drinking sugary drinks. Others are aware but enjoy the taste and are prepared to take the risks (see Figure 13.1).

Figure 13.1: Drinking lots of sugary drinks can damage health

Discuss in a pair or group:

1   Who may suffer as a result of people drinking sugary drinks?

2   How may producers of sugary drinks respond to the knowledge of the health risks?

13.1 What is market failure?

Market failure occurs when market forces fail to produce the products in the right quantities and at the lowest possible cost. Market failure arises when markets are inefficient. There are a number of indicators of market failure, including lack of information, high prices, poor quality and lack of innovation.

If left to market forces, some products may be underproduced, some overproduced and some may not be produced at all. Prices may be high due to lack of competitive pressure and difficulties in lowering the costs. A lack of investment and less expenditure on research and development can also slow down the improvement of products.

13.2 Causes and consequences of market failure

The market forces of demand and supply do not always result in the best use of resources. There are a number of reasons why there may be a misallocation of resources. Some of these causes and their consequences are explored below.

Failure to take into account all costs and benefits

The consumption and production of some products may affect people who are not directly involved in their consumption or production (people indirectly affected are often referred to as **third parties**). For example, a firm producing chemicals may allow waste products to leak into a river, harming wildlife and making the water unsafe for humans. In such cases, the total benefits and total costs to society are greater than the benefits and costs to the consumers and producers.

The total benefits and total costs to society are called **social benefits** and **social costs**. The benefits and costs to the consumers and producers are known as **private benefits** and **private costs**. So, the social costs of the firm producing chemicals will include costs not only to the firm but also to people living nearby and the environment.

Costs to third parties are called **external costs**. Among the private costs to the firm will be the cost of buying raw materials, fuel and wages. The external costs imposed on those living nearby may include noise pollution, air pollution and water pollution. If the decision to produce chemicals is based only on the private costs to the firm, there will be overproduction. Figure 13.2 shows that if only the private costs to the firm are taken into account then the supply would be curve S, whereas the full cost to society is higher at curve S$_x$. The difference between the two is accounted for by the external costs. The allocatively efficient output is Q$_x$, but the market output is Q.

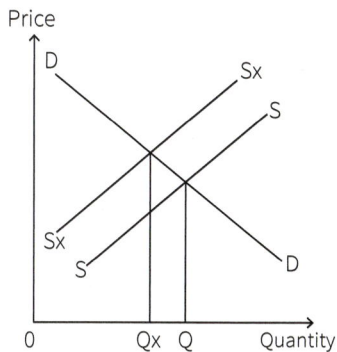

Figure 13.2: Overproduction

> ### KEY TERMS
>
> **third parties:** those not directly involved in producing or consuming a product.
>
> **social benefits:** the total benefits to a society of an economic activity.
>
> **social costs:** the total costs to a society of an economic activity.
>
> **private benefits:** benefits received by those directly consuming or producing a product.
>
> **private costs:** costs incurred by those directly consuming or producing a product.
>
> **external costs:** costs imposed on those who are not involved in the consumption and production activities of others directly.

Demand, based just on the private benefits to those consuming the product, will lead to underconsumption and so to underproduction if the total benefit to society is greater. For example, among the benefits students may receive by undertaking university degree courses are greater numbers of career choices, higher future earnings, life-long interests and life-long friends. The social benefits include not only these private benefits, but also the benefits to other people (**external benefits**) who will be able to enjoy a higher quantity and quality of output as graduates are usually highly productive workers. In Figure 13.3, the demand for degree courses, based on private benefits, is curve D, while the total benefit to the economy is shown by curve D_x. The number of degree courses that would be undertaken, if left to market forces, is Q, whereas the number which would cause the maximum benefit to the society is Q_x.

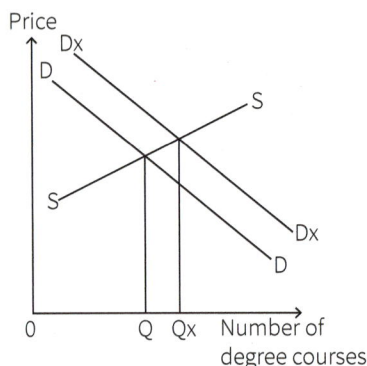

Figure 13.3: Underproduction

KEY TERMS

external benefits: benefits enjoyed by those who are not directly involved in the consumption and production activities of others.

socially optimum output: the level of output where social cost equals social benefit and society's welfare is maximised.

Whenever there is a gap between the total effects on society, and the effects on those directly consuming and producing the products, markets will fail to allocate resources efficiently. The level of output which will result in maximum benefit to the society (**socially optimum output**) will occur when the social benefit of the last unit produced is equal to the social cost of that unit. If the social cost exceeds the social benefit, it means that too many resources are being allocated to the production of the product. Society would benefit from reducing its output. In contrast, if the benefit society would gain from producing more of the product is greater than the cost to society of producing more output, then more resources should be allocated to its production.

A case where the social cost (in most countries) exceeds the social benefit is the use of road space by private cars. When people decide to make a trip in their car, they take into account the private costs and benefits, that is the cost and benefits to themselves. If the benefits received by them by going on the journey exceed the costs (for example, the cost of petrol and wear and tear on the vehicle), they will make the journey. What they do not consider is the external costs caused by them, such as air pollution, noise pollution, congestion and accidents (see Figure 13.4). A number of governments, including Singapore and the UK, have introduced road pricing schemes. These seek to charge the full costs of their journeys. Different amounts are charged according to when and where people drive. Someone driving along an empty country road is likely to cause lower external costs than someone driving into a city centre at peak time.

Figure 13.4: Pollution is an external cost

> ### TIP
>
> Students often confuse social and external costs and benefits. Try to remember: social costs and benefits are the total costs and benefits of an economic activity. Social costs and benefits include both the external and private costs and benefits.

ACTIVITY 13.1

In November 2023, thousands of people in Panama demonstrated against the government giving a 20-year licence to a Canadian firm to reopen a copper mine. They were worried about the environmental impact mining would have, including water pollution. The government said reopening the mine would create thousands of jobs.

In a pair, produce a poster identifying examples of the possible private costs, external costs, private benefits and external benefits of reopening the copper mine.

Information failure

For consumers to buy the products that will give them the highest possible satisfaction at the lowest possible prices, they have to be fully informed about the nature of the products on offer, the benefits they can receive from them and their prices. Workers need to know what jobs are on offer, the location of the workplace, the qualifications required and the remuneration (wages) they would receive. They should also be aware about the nature of jobs for which their skills are best suited.

Similarly, producers need to know what products are in demand, where good quality raw materials can be purchased at lowest possible prices and what are the most cost-effective methods of production. If they lack this information, they will make decisions that are not in their best interests. As well as consumers paying more than required and buying products of lower quality than other available, workers may end up in the wrong jobs, and producers' costs may be higher and revenues lower than possible due to **information failure**.

> ### KEY TERM
>
> **information failure:** a lack of information, inaccurate information or asymmetric information which may result in inefficient choices.

Information failure can occur in a number of ways. There may be a lack of information or inaccurate information. There may also be asymmetric information which occurs when consumers and suppliers do not have equal access to information. For instance, if a car mechanic tells a motorist that their car needs an expensive repair, the motorist may lack the technical knowledge to question the advice.

Merit goods

In the case of some products, there is both the problem of information failure and the problem of social benefits or costs being greater than the private benefits or costs.

Merit goods are products that are more beneficial to the consumers than they themselves realise. Merit goods have benefits for those who are not involved in their consumption directly, that is external benefits. This failure of the consumers to acknowledge the true value to themselves, and to others, means that these products would be underconsumed and so underproduced, if left to market forces.

Healthcare is an example of a merit good. For instance, some people may not recognise the importance of regular medical check-ups and/or visiting a doctor. They are unlikely to take into account the benefits of their fitness to others. The external benefits may include higher output as a result of workers having less time off work (being more productive) and the prevention of spread of diseases.

There are various measures that a government may adopt to overcome the problem of underconsumption of merit goods. One is by providing information on the benefits of consuming the products. If successful, there should be an increase in demand. In the absence of an increase in demand, the government may need to try another approach. Figure 13.5a shows the demand that will exist if left to market forces, D, and demand based on the full benefits to society, D_x. To persuade consumers to purchase the allocatively efficient quantity of Q_x, the price of the product needs to fall to P_1. Figure 13.5b shows this being achieved, as a result of a subsidy shifting the supply curve to the right.

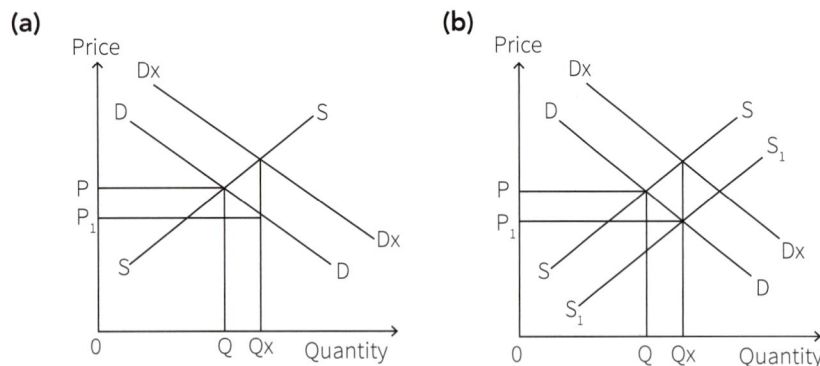

> **KEY TERM**
>
> **merit goods:** products which the government considers consumers do not fully appreciate the benefits of and so will be under-consumed if left to market forces.

(a)

(b)

Figure 13.5: (a) Underconsumption of a merit good if left to market forces, **(b)** The effect of subsidy on the market of a merit good

> **LINK**
>
> Governments directly provide a range of goods and services – see Chapter 14.3 (Direct provision of goods and services).

If a government thinks that consumers undervalue the importance of the product or there are considerable external benefits, it may provide the product free to consumers and/or make its consumption compulsory. For example, inoculation against a range of diseases is provided free, and the wearing of seat belts in cars is compulsory in the UK.

ACTIVITY 13.2

Some African countries, such as Kenya, Togo and Mozambique, provide free primary education. In a number of other African countries, state schools charge fees. Discuss the following with another student.

1   Give two arguments for providing free primary education.

2   Education is likely to be underconsumed if left to market forces. Do you agree? Give your reasons.

Make notes of the main points.

ECONOMICS IN ACTION

The tomato market

Many people believe tomatoes are a vegetable, but tomatoes are actually fruit. Economists measure which countries produce the most tomatoes, which consume the most tomatoes and which consume the most tomatoes per head of the population. In 2023, the largest growers of tomatoes were China, India, Pakistan, Türkiye and Egypt; the largest consumers, in total, were China, India, the USA, Egypt and Türkiye; and the largest consumers per head of population were Türkiye, Egypt, the USA, China and India.

Tomatoes contain potassium and vitamins, and they have several health benefits. Consuming tomatoes can reduce diabetes, improve digestion, protect against UV skin damage, maintain eye health and even protect against cancer.

Tomato consumption is increasing throughout the world. Schools in a number of countries, such as Belarus, Belgium and Japan, are including more tomatoes in the meals they provide to students.

More families are increasing their daily intake of tomatoes. Some governments are also keen to encourage people to eat more fruit and vegetables.

1   Why may tomatoes be regarded as a merit good?

2   Apart from greater awareness of health benefits, what else might encourage people to eat more fruit and vegetables?

Figure 13.6: Eating tomatoes can be good for you

Demerit goods

Demerit goods are the opposite of merit goods. Demerit goods are more harmful to consumers than they realise and generate external costs. For example, cigarettes are a demerit good. Some people do not fully realise the damage that smoking can do to their health. Their smoking also imposes external costs on people around them by polluting the air, causing some people to develop cancer through passive smoking, and generating litter.

Demerit goods are overconsumed and so overproduced. To tackle this problem, a government could raise the price of demerit goods by imposing a tax on them. It could also try to discourage consumption by providing information about their

KEY TERM

demerit goods: products which the government considers consumers do not fully appreciate how harmful they are and so will be overconsumed if left to market forces.

harmful effects. If a government believes that the consumption of certain products causes serious problems it may ban them.

Many countries now have a ban on smoking in public places. This measure is designed not only to discourage smoking, but also to protect the health of non-smokers. Other measures that governments use to reduce smoking include government-sponsored health campaigns, placing health warnings on packets of cigarettes, taxation and banning the advertising of cigarettes. The UK government is seeking to phase out smoking by raising, each year, the age at which people can smoke. Bhutan has banned the purchase of cigarettes in the country.

> ### DISCUSSION
> Discuss whether video games are a demerit good.

Public and private goods

Public goods

The degree of market failure is greater in the case of **public goods** than merit goods and demerit goods. While too few merit goods and too many demerit goods will be produced if left to market forces, no public goods would be made.

Public goods have two main characteristics:

- **They are non-excludable.** In Chapter 12 (Market economic system), we learned that private sector firms will not make products they cannot charge for. It is not possible to exclude non-payers from taking advantage of the benefits of products such as defence. If these public goods are provided for some people, others can consume them without paying for them. Those who do take advantage in this way are called free riders. For example, if a flood defence system is built to protect a coastal town, all homes in the area would be protected whether their owners are prepared to pay for it or not (see Figure 13.7).

- **They are non-rival.** Consumption of the product by one more person does not reduce someone else's ability to consume it. For example, one more person walking down a lit street does not reduce the benefit that other people receive from the streetlights.

Public goods usually have two other characteristics:

1 **They are non-rejectable.** It is not possible for people to reject the services of the police, for example.

2 **The cost of supplying a public good to one more consumer is often zero.** Defending one more person in the country will be unlikely to cost its defence forces anything.

Markets will not supply public goods. Non-provision of public goods is a consequence of market failure. Public goods have to be financed through taxation. The government can then produce them itself or pay a private sector company to produce them.

> ### KEY TERM
> **public good:** a product which is non-rival and non-excludable and so needs to be financed by taxation.

Figure 13.7: Flood defences are a public good

Private goods

Most products, including merit and demerit goods, are **private goods**. Private goods are both rival and excludable. In these cases, it is possible to stop non-payers from enjoying the products, and if one person consumes a unit of the product, someone else cannot. For example, an individual cannot take a computer out of a shop without paying for it, and if they do buy it, no one else can have that particular computer.

Even though healthcare and primary and secondary education are not directly charged for in some countries (such as Greece, Sri Lanka and Brazil), they are nevertheless private goods. This is because they can be charged for, and also because they are rival goods (in some cases). If one student is occupying a place in a class or one patient is occupying a hospital bed, no one else can occupy these places. Of course, education and healthcare are examples of a special type of private goods – that is, merit goods.

Markets will supply private goods, although not necessarily in the right quantities. They will not, however, supply public goods.

ACTIVITY 13.3

Are the following private goods or public goods? Copy Table 13.1.
Put a tick (✓) in the correct column.

Table 13.1

		Private good	Public good
1	biscuits		
2	lighthouse protection for shipping		
3	flood control systems		
4	public car parking spaces		
5	public library services		

KEY TERM

private good: a product which is both rival and excludable.

TIP

In deciding whether a good is a private or a public good, the key thing to consider is not whether a price is charged for it, but whether a price could be charged for it.

TIP

You may find it useful to create a set of cards with examples of different types of products, for example, products with elastic demand, those with inelastic demand, those with elastic supply, those with inelastic supply, merit goods, demerit goods as well as private and public goods.

Abuse of monopoly power

Market failure can arise due to producers having more market power than consumers. If one firm dominates a market, the firm may not be efficient. It will lack competitive pressure to respond to consumer demands, to keep its costs low and to improve its product. It may restrict the supply so as to push up price. If the firm is the only one selling the product, the firm is a **monopoly**. Consumers will have no choice but to buy from it, even if the price of the product is high, the product does not meet the needs of the consumers or the quality is poor.

Abuse of market failure can also occur when there is more than one firm producing the product. If there are, for example, five major producers in a market there is a risk that they may join together to reduce competition and, in effect, act as one seller. For example, they may all agree to charge the same high price. This is referred to as **price fixing**.

There are various ways in which governments try to promote competition and prevent firms from abusing their market power. These include removing restrictions on the entry of new firms into a market and making uncompetitive practices such as price fixing illegal. They may also stop some firms from merging (joining together to form one new firm), if it is thought that the merged firm will act against the interests of consumers by charging high prices and producing poor quality products.

KEY TERMS

monopoly: a market with a single supplier.

price fixing: when two or more firms agree to sell a product at the same price.

LINK

A firm with considerable market power, such as a monopoly, may act in ways that disadvantage consumers – see Chapter 21.2 (Monopoly markets).

ACTIVITY 13.4

In recent years, a number of agreements have been signed between different countries to allow more airlines to fly between particular locations, including between Heathrow Airport, London, and the USA. Until 2008, only four airlines – British Airways (BA), Virgin Atlantic, American Airlines and United Airlines – were permitted to fly between London and New York. Now a range of airlines, including Air France, Air India, British Airways, Delta, Lufthansa, KLM and Virgin Atlantic, fly between Heathrow Airport and the USA.

In a pair, research the number of airlines that fly between an airport in your capital city and an airport in the capital city of another country. Produce and give a presentation that covers:

*   the findings of your research

*   what may encourage more airlines to fly on the route

*   the benefits consumers may gain from increased competition on the route.

REFLECTION

Do you find explaining points using a real-world example helps you to further your understanding of economic concepts?

13.3 Other consequences of market failure

Immobility of resources

To achieve a socially optimum output, it is necessary for resources to move from producing products that are decreasing in demand towards those which are experiencing an increase in demand. This requires resources to be both occupationally and geographically mobile. In practice, some resources may be immobile (unable to move). If, for example, demand for a country's financial services is increasing while demand for its steel is decreasing, there may be a shortage of financial services, unemployment of workers and underutilisation of capital equipment if resources cannot easily move between the two.

The main measures a government can take to promote occupational mobility of labour are to improve education and to provide training in the new skills needed. Also, governments can provide investment grants to make it easier for firms to change the use of land and buildings. Geographical mobility of workers can be encouraged by making it easier for workers to buy or rent housing in areas where demand for labour is high. This might be achieved by construction of more houses in such areas or by the government providing financial help for those workers who move to these locations.

> **LINK**
>
> There are a number of influences on the geographical and occupational mobility of labour – see Chapter 17.4 (Mobility of labour).

Short-termism

There is a risk that market forces may not result in sufficient resources being allocated to capital goods. If a country produces a high quantity of consumer products, people can enjoy a high living standard. For people to enjoy more consumer products in the future, some resources have to be reallocated to making capital goods. Private sector firms may be interested in making quick profits and may not plan for the future. Such a short-sighted approach can result in a lack of investment. As a result, a government may have to stimulate private sector investment by, for example, cutting taxes on firms and undertake some investment itself.

ACTIVITY 13.5

1   Decide what type of product the word cloud below relates to. Share your answer with another student.

non-excludable
non-rival
financed by government
free riders   lighthouses
provided to everyone

2   In your group, individually write down three words or terms associated with a demerit good. Discuss your responses. Then construct a word cloud based on demerit goods and ask another group if they can recognise a demerit good from your word cloud.

SUMMARY

You should now know:

- Market failure occurs when markets do not operate efficiently.

- If left to market forces, products whose social benefits are greater than their private benefits will be underconsumed and so underproduced.

- There will be overconsumption and overproduction of products, if their social costs exceed their private costs.

- Merit goods would be underconsumed if left to market forces.

- Demerit goods would be overconsumed in a market system.

- Public goods are both non-excludable and non-rival.

- Where there is a lack of competition, a firm may not keep its costs down, may charge a high price and may produce a poor quality product.

TIP

In discussing whether a market system works well, consider arguments for and against and, where appropriate, come to a conclusion.

Chapter 13 practice questions

1   In which case is market failure occurring?

   A   consumers determining what is produced

   B   firms producing above the lowest possible cost

   C   price falling as a result of a decrease in demand

   D   price rising as a result of an increase in costs of production   [1]

2   A merit good is one which:

   A   has an absence of external benefits

   B   has higher private benefits than consumers realise

   C   imposes costs on those who are not involved in its production directly

   D   is both non-excludable and non-rival   [1]

3   Which type of goods would be overproduced if left to market forces?

   A   basic necessities

   B   capital goods

   C   demerit goods

   D   public goods   [1]

4   What is a cause of market failure?

   A   competition between firms

   B   consumers lacking information about where the lowest prices can be found

   C   differences in pay between skilled and unskilled workers

   D   resources being both geographically and occupationally mobile   [1]

5   What would ensure that the socially optimum output is achieved?

   A   private benefit equals private cost

   B   private benefit exceeds private cost

   C   social benefit equals social cost

   D   social benefit exceeds social cost   [1]

                                                          Total: [5]

6   a   Define an 'external cost'.   [2]

     b   Explain the difference between a merit good and a demerit good.   [4]

     c   Analyse why the social benefit of education exceeds the private benefits.   [6]

     d   Discuss whether or not trees in the rainforests of Brazil should
          continue to be cut down.   [8]

                                                          Total: [20]

CHECK YOUR PROGRESS

How well do you think you have achieved the learning intentions for this chapter?
Give yourself a score from 1 (still need a lot of practice) to 5 (feeling very confident)
for each learning intention. Provide an example to support your score.

Now I can...	Score	Example
explain key terms associated with market failure: public goods, merit goods, demerit goods, private benefits, external benefits, social benefits, private costs, external costs, social costs		
explain the causes of market failure relating to public goods, merit goods, demerit goods, external costs, external benefits and abuse of market power		
analyse the consequences of market failure relating to the overconsumption of demerit goods and goods with external costs, the underconsumption of merit goods and goods with external benefits, the non-provision of public goods and restricted supply causing higher prices under a monopoly.		

> Chapter 14
Mixed economic system

LEARNING INTENTIONS

By the end of this chapter, you will be able to:

- define a mixed economic system and discuss its advantages and disadvantages
- define a maximum price, draw and interpret a diagram showing a maximum price and analyse its advantages and disadvantages
- define a minimum price, draw and interpret a diagram showing a minimum price and analyse its advantages and disadvantages
- define indirect taxation, draw and interpret a diagram showing the effect of an indirect tax and analyse its advantages and disadvantages
- define a subsidy and draw and interpret a diagram showing the effect of a subsidy
- define regulation and analyse its advantages and disadvantages
- define privatisation and analyse its advantages and disadvantages
- define nationalisation and analyse its advantages and disadvantages
- define direct provision of goods and services and analyse its advantages and disadvantages
- define quotas and analyse their advantages and disadvantages.

Introduction

Why do governments in every country intervene in the economy and why do they do this to a different extent? Can a government improve the performance of an economy? This chapter looks at how and why governments in mixed economic systems may intervene in the economy.

> **TIP**
>
> A market economic system and a mixed economic system are different. Be careful not to confuse them. In a market economic system, it is the price mechanism which allocates resources. In a mixed economic system, it is both the price mechanism and the government that decide the use of resources.

ECONOMICS IN CONTEXT

Is the cost of chocolate too high?

Many of us like chocolate. However, many of us are unaware that some farmers who grow the cocoa beans that are used to produce chocolate are paid very low prices by the firms that manufacture and sell chocolate. As well as not paying farmers enough to live on, some of these chocolate firms have been accused of being unconcerned about the child labour used in growing cocoa beans. It is thought that as many as 1.5 million children in Ghana and Côte d'Ivoire, the two main cocoa bean growing countries, are involved in the farming of cocoa beans.

Children kept out of school to work on farms miss out on education. Working long hours can also affect the health of children and some are injured in accidents. There are laws against child labour in both Ghana and Côte d'Ivoire. However, these laws are difficult to enforce as there are large areas to check.

Some chocolate firms do try to behave ethically. They pay a price that enables farmers to enjoy a reasonable quality of life and to keep their children in school. These firms ensure that child labour is not used. Some also provide training programmes aimed at increasing farmer productivity, and they support schools in the area.

Discuss in a pair or group:

1. What are the advantages and disadvantages of a law against child labour?

2. How might chocolate firms benefit from behaving ethically?

Figure 14.1: The ingredients of chocolate

14.1 What is a mixed economic system?

Governments intervene in a mixed economic system. A **mixed economic system** includes features of a planned and a market economic system. Some firms are privately owned (in the private sector) and some are government owned (in the public sector). Some prices are determined by the market forces of demand and supply, and some are set by the government. In this type of economic system, both consumers and the government influence what is produced.

14.2 Arguments for and against the mixed economic system

A mixed economy aims to combine the advantages of both a market and a planned economy, while avoiding their disadvantages. Some products produced by the private sector may provide choice, increase efficiency and create incentives. There may also be benefits to be gained from state intervention. They may include:

- The government should take into account all the costs and benefits that will arise from their decisions. This should mean, for example, that even if a railway line and station would not make a profit in the private sector, they would be maintained by the state if the benefit to society is greater than the cost.

- Government can also encourage the consumption of products that are more beneficial for consumers and others than they realise by granting subsidies, providing information or passing legislation (see Figure 14.2).

- Government can discourage the consumption of products that are more harmful for consumers and others than they realise by imposing taxes on such products, providing information or passing legislation.

- Government can finance the production of products that cannot be charged for directly, for example, defence.

- Government can seek to prevent private sector firms from taking advantage of consumers by charging high prices.

- Government is likely to seek to make maximum use of resources, including labour, and so try to ensure that those people willing and able to work can find jobs.

- There is a possibility that the government will plan ahead to a greater extent than private sector firms and may devote more of its resources to capital goods.

- Government can help vulnerable groups, ensuring that they have access to basic necessities. It can also create a more even distribution of income, by taxing the rich at a high rate.

There are, nevertheless, also disadvantages to a mixed economic system. There is no guarantee that it will perform better than the other two types of systems. Market failure can occur and government intervention may make the situation worse.

Figure 14.2: The government in a mixed economy may promote a healthy lifestyle policy

14.3 Government intervention to address market failure

Maximum and minimum prices in product markets

A government may limit firms' ability to set their own prices by imposing price controls.

A government may set a maximum ceiling on the price in order to enable those living in poverty to afford basic necessities. To have any impact, a maximum price has to be set below the equilibrium price. Figure 14.3 shows a maximum price being set at P_x below the equilibrium price of P. Some people will now be able to purchase the product at a lower price. The problem is, however, that a shortage will be created, as at this lower price the quantity demanded exceeds the quantity supplied. To prevent the development of an illegal market in the product, some method of its allocation will have to be introduced. This might be through queuing, **rationing** or even a **lottery**.

KEY TERMS

rationing: a limit on the amount that can be consumed.

lottery: the drawing of tickets to decide who will get the products.

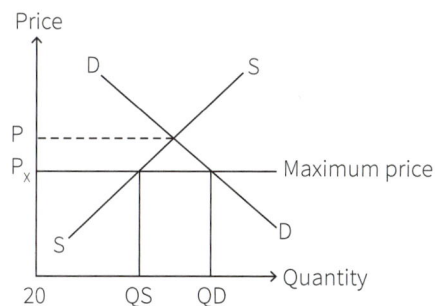

Figure 14.3: The effect of setting a maximum price

To encourage production of a product, a government may set a minimum price (P_x). This is a price floor, as it represents the lowest price producers are allowed to charge. To have an impact on a market, the price floor will have to be set above the equilibrium price, as shown in Figure 14.4. This time the problem created is a surplus, with the quantity supplied being greater than the quantity demanded. To prevent the price being driven down, the surplus will have to be bought up by the government or some other official body.

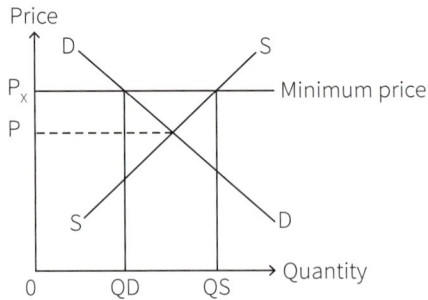

Figure 14.4: The effect of setting a minimum price

A minimum price may also be set on the price of labour in the form of a minimum wage. The motives for such a move and its impact are discussed in Chapter 17 (Workers). In addition, a minimum price may be set on a demerit good to discourage people from buying it. In this case, there is a risk that an illegal market may develop with sellers offering the product and at less than the legal minimum price.

ACTIVITY 14.1

In March 2023, the Government of Laos imposed price controls on 23 basic necessities, including rice and natural gas. Its aim was to protect consumers from rapidly rising prices. Government officials were sent into markets and shops to check that sellers were not charging prices above the limit set by the government. Some sellers found charging more were fined, and a few were sent to prison. There was some evidence that the price controls distorted the market, and some sellers went out of business. Discuss the following questions with another student:

1   How are prices determined by the market?

2   How do price controls distort the market?

3   Do you think that the Laos government sets maximum or minimum prices on rice and natural gas? Give reasons.

Write down notes of the main points.

Indirect taxation and subsidies

All firms are likely to be affected by taxation in some way. Governments tax firms' profits, which has an impact on the ability and willingness of firms to invest. Indirect taxation raises firms' costs of production, while income tax lowers consumers' disposable income and, as a result, demand for firms' products. In contrast, subsidies may only be targeted at some of the country's firms.

Indirect taxation

The impact of a tax is influenced by the size of the tax and the price elasticity of demand. The higher the tax, the greater its impact. A tax on a product with inelastic demand would have a greater effect on price than the quantity sold. In the case of a product with elastic demand, it is the other way round.

If a government wants to raise revenue, it should tax products with inelastic demand. This is because the quantity sold will not fall by much. For example, a tax of $2 per product may be placed on a product that initially has sales of 2 000 a day. If the tax causes sales to fall to 1 800, the government will receive $3 600 in revenue. However, if the demand had been elastic and sales had fallen to 900, the government tax revenue would have been only $1 800.

In contrast, if the government's aim is to discourage the consumption of a product (in particular a demerit good) it will be more successful if demand is elastic. This is one of the problems in using taxation to discourage smoking, as demand for tobacco products is inelastic.

Subsidies

The effect of a subsidy given to producers is influenced by the size of the subsidy and the price elasticity of demand. As explained in Chapter 7 (Supply), as an extra payment to producers, a subsidy shifts the supply curve to the right. The larger the subsidy, the more increase there is in supply.

On a diagram, the size of the subsidy is represented by the distance between the two supply curves. In Figure 14.5, the subsidy per unit is SY. If all the subsidy is passed on to consumers, prices would fall to P_2. As demand is inelastic, producers have to pass on most of the subsidy to encourage an extension in demand. Price actually falls to P_1 with consumers receiving most of the benefit ($PSXP_1$) and the producers keeping the rest (P_1XYP_2).

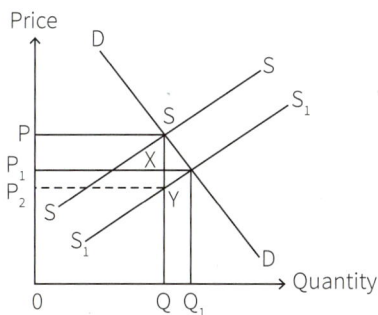

Figure 14.5: The effect of a subsidy in the case of inelastic demand

LINK

There are a number of influences on whether demand for a product is elastic or inelastic – see Chapter 10.3 (Influences on PED). Whether a product has elastic or inelastic supply is also influenced by various factors – see Chapter 11.3 (Influences on PES).

LINK

A subsidy is one of the reasons why the supply of a product may increase – see Chapter 7.3 (Shifts of a supply curve – Causes of decreases and increases in supply).

If demand is elastic, a subsidy will have more impact on the quantity sold and less on the price. In this case, the producers can keep more of the subsidy, as shown in Figure 14.6. In deciding whether to grant a subsidy, a government needs to consider the opportunity cost, as the money could have been used for another purpose.

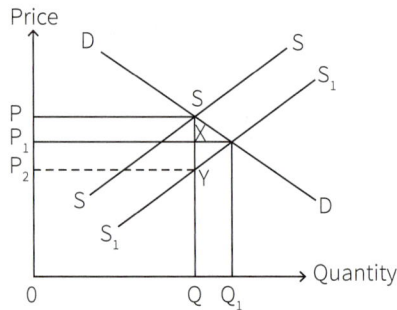

Figure 14.6: The effect of a subsidy in the case of elastic demand

---

TIP

When looking at information related to subsidies, identify whether the focus is on subsidies to producers (which would shift the supply curve) or subsidies to consumers (which would shift the demand curve). If the information simply refers to a subsidy, assume it likely to be a subsidy to a producer, as this is the most common form of subsidy.

DISCUSSION

Discuss whether you think train travel in your country should be subsidised.

ACTIVITY 14.2

Emissions of carbon dioxide from the aviation industry more than doubled between 1990 and 2022, and are forecast to double again by 2030. Under international law, aviation fuel for international flights is exempt from taxation. Environmentalists argue that airlines should be taxed for the pollution they cause.

Produce a report on the arguments for and against taxing aviation fuel. There is a range of arguments you may wish to consider, including the impact on the amount of air travel and tourism, employment in the industries and the external costs and external benefits that may be affected.

ECONOMICS IN ACTION

Should a government set maximum and minimum prices?

Figure 14.7: Can everyone afford to celebrate Diwali?

The Malaysian Family Maximum Price Scheme (SHMMP) aims to stabilise the price of essential goods. In November 2023, the SHMMP imposed maximum prices on essential foods, including red onions and lentils during Diwali (the festival of lights). The aim was to prevent prices being pushed up when people demand more food during the festival.

Maximum prices are also applied during other festivals, including Chinese New Year, and during periods of shortages. For example, in 2023, there was a shortage of chicken, and a maximum price was set at 15% below the market price.

Farmers and sellers, however, oppose maximum prices and argue that they should be able to charge higher prices if demand increases. Some farmers have asked the government to impose minimum prices on food. Such prices might provide farmers with more security and might encourage them to invest more.

Economists consider whether government intervention, in the form of maximum prices, minimum prices and other measures, may be necessary to correct market failure or reduce income inequality and poverty. They also assess whether any government intervention will be likely to improve market performance.

1   Will all consumers benefit from a maximum price being set on red onions during Diwali?

2   Do you think a subsidy given to chicken farmers would be more effective than a maximum price on chicken?

3   Why might it be possible to remove a minimum price on food after a period of time while keeping supply high?

Regulation

Regulation includes rules and laws which place restrictions on the activities of firms. Besides setting price controls, outlawing uncompetitive behaviour and limiting the amount of pollution emitted by a firm, a government may regulate the target audience for the product, the quality of products and the working conditions provided by firms. For example, a government may pass a law banning the sale of cigarettes to children. It may also require firms to ensure that the products produced by them meet certain standards and that they allow their workers a specified number of regular holidays. In addition, it may place restrictions on timing for opening/closing of shops and control the routes that buses must follow.

Governments may use regulation to promote competitive pressures and prevent firms from abusing their market power. There are several ways a government might be able to do this. These include prevention of mergers that it thinks will not be in the interest of consumers, removal of barriers to entry and exit into markets, and regulation of monopolies. A government may also ban uncompetitive practices such as a firm charging a price below the cost to drive a rival firm (or firms) out of the market.

Governments may also use regulation to protect the environment. For example, a government may place restrictions on the amount of pollutants emitted by firms into the air, sea and rivers. It may then fine any firms which exceed these limits.

As a measure to correct market failure, regulations have the advantages of being backed up by law and easily understood. The government does, however, have to check that the rules and laws are being followed, and this may be difficult and expensive. Also, a regulation works only if most people agree with it. For example, it would be difficult to enforce a law that everyone wears a safety helmet when riding a motorcycle if such a move is opposed by most of the riders. This is because too much time and money would need to be spent on prosecuting the offenders, and the government could become very unpopular.

There are a number of other problems with imposing regulations, for example, they do not directly compensate those who suffer as a result of market failure, and regulations may be too restrictive, reducing market flexibility.

Nationalisation

To benefit the public and to improve economic performance, a government may set up an industry or **nationalise** a private sector industry. Industries owned by the government are known as state-owned enterprises, **public corporations** and nationalised industries. The chairperson and board of managers are appointed by the government. They are responsible for the day-to-day management but are accountable to the government. There are no shareholders in state-owned enterprises (SOEs). The funds come from the government, from government-approved loans and from the private sector. SOEs do not always seek to make a profit. Their main aim is to work in the public interest.

Some of the advantages and disadvantages associated with state-owned enterprises are shown in Table 14.1.

Table 14.1: Main advantages and disadvantages of state-owned enterprises

Advantages	Disadvantages
SOEs base their decisions on the full costs and benefits involved.	SOEs can be difficult to manage and control. The large size of the organisations may mean that time has to be spent on meetings and communicating with staff, slowing down decision-making.
SOEs can be used to influence economic activity. To boost the country's output, public corporations can be directly encouraged to increase their output.	SOEs may become inefficient, produce low-quality products and charge relatively high prices due to a lack of competition and the knowledge that they cannot go bankrupt.
In cases where it is practical to have only one firm in the industry, such as rail infrastructure, a SOE may not abuse its market power.	SOEs will need to be subsidised if they are making a loss. The use of tax revenue to support them has an opportunity cost – it could be used to spend on training more teachers and nurses, for example.

nationalisation (nationalise): moving the ownership and control of an industry from the private sector to the government.

public corporation: a business organisation owned by the government which is designed to act in the public interest.

LINK

The case for and against state-owned enterprises is linked to the effects of leaving production to free market forces – see Chapter 12.3 (Arguments for and against the market economic system).

Advantages	Disadvantages
Ownership of a whole industry by the government makes planning and coordination easier, for example, if the state runs the train system, it can ensure that train timetables are coordinated.	SOEs cannot raise finance for expansion from shareholders. They may have limits imposed on reinvestment of any profits they earn.
It is important to ensure that essential industries, such as electricity and transport, continue to exist, charge low prices and produce good quality goods or services, as other domestic industries depend on them.	

Privatisation

Concern about the performance of state-owned enterprises and increased confidence in market forces has led a number of countries to sell their state-owned enterprises, or part of their state-owned enterprises, to the private sector. Those supporting this move argue that private sector firms are likely to produce the products desired by consumers, at a low cost and offer them at low prices. This is because market forces provide an incentive for firms to be efficient in the form of profit and a threat of bankruptcy if they are inefficient.

Besides low prices and high quality, privatisation may result in greater choice. Freedom from government regulation may reduce administration costs and enable managers to respond more quickly to changing conditions. There may also be less risk of underinvestment in the private sector. The funds available to a private sector firm for investment will depend on the profits it earns and its ability to convince shareholders and lenders of its success. Public corporations may be kept short of funds for investment, however successful they are, if the government wants to spend the money elsewhere.

There are also arguments against privatisation. There is no guarantee that private sector firms will face the full pressure of market forces. Some private sector firms may not face competition – they may be monopolies (the only firm selling the product). In this case, they can be inefficient, charge high prices and produce low-quality products without reducing profits. They may not take into account the total costs and benefits to the society of their actions. For example, they may cause pollution. Privatisation also reduces a government's control of the economy.

LINK

The private sector and the public sector differ in terms of who owns the firms that produce goods and services and the objectives these firms have – see Chapter 12.2 (Market economic system – How a market economic system works).

ACTIVITY 14.3

Copy and complete Table 14.2, which compares a state-owned enterprise and a private sector firm.

Table 14.2

	State-owned enterprise	Private sector firm
Ownership	The government	
Sector		Private
Aim	Acts in the public interest	

Direct provision of goods and services

A government may produce products which it believes are of key importance, the products that are produced by a **natural monopoly**, those which it thinks are essential and should be available to all and those which the private sector may under-produce or not produce (see Figure 14.8).

Figure 14.8: Having just one firm transmitting electricity may be the most efficient way to provide an essential product to all

KEY TERMS

natural monopoly: an industry where a single firm can produce at a lower average cost than two or more firms.

strategic industries: industries that are important for the economic development and safety of the country.

national champions: industries that are, or have the potential to be, world leaders.

Most countries seek to ensure that their key industries survive and do well. Key industries may be **strategic industries** or **national champions**. In China and France, for instance, such industries are often run by state-owned enterprises. In Italy, they receive favoured loans from banks. In a number of countries, the government also stops foreign companies from taking them over or merging with them, such as rail infrastructure which may be run or regulated by the government. This is, in part, to prevent consumers being exploited by a private sector firm charging a high price.

Most governments produce some goods and services that they think are essential. In some countries, such as Australia, China and Iran, governments provide affordable housing to rent. Housing, education and healthcare are seen as essential services. Some governments, such as the UK, Indonesia and Germany, produce them and provide them to people free of charge or at subsidised prices. Besides being essential products, education and healthcare are also merit goods. Governments also provide public goods such as prisons.

- To reduce market failure is one reason for government spending – see Chapter 23.2 (Reasons for government spending).

- If left to market forces, there would not be enough merit goods provided to achieve the best outcome for society – see Chapter 13.2 (Causes and consequences of market failure – Merit goods).

- There is no reason why public goods would be produced if left to market forces – see Chapter 13.2 (Causes and consequences of market failure – Public and private goods).

- Governments intervene in markets as markets do not all work efficiently and because the outcomes may not always be considered fair – see Chapter 12.3 (Arguments for and against the market economic system).

ACTIVITY 14.4

Guess the term! In a group of up to nine, write one of the following terms on a sticky note:

maximum price   minimum price   indirect taxation   subsidy   regulation
privatisation   nationalisation   direct provision of goods and services   quota

Each person takes a sticky note without looking at what is written on it, and places it on their forehead. (Smaller groups take more than one note each.) The person asks the group questions to help them guess the term. The questions have to be answered with either 'yes' or 'no'. Each person has a maximum of three questions to work out what the term is.

TIP

Find out what goods and services the government provides in the area where you live.

REFLECTION

Did this activity help to reinforce your understanding of the topics in this chapter? Would it help your learning to use this technique in other topics?

Quotas

Governments may place **quotas** (limits) on the extraction of natural resources. Their motives are likely to be to protect the environment and to ensure that future generations can benefit from the resources. For example, a government may place a quota on the number of trees that may be felled in a rainforest so that the same amount of carbon dioxide can be absorbed and the risks of climate change reduced. A government may also put a quota on the amount of fish that can be caught to maintain fish stocks (see Figure 14.9).

KEY TERM

quota: a limit placed on quantity or value.

Figure 14.9: There may be a restriction on the amount of fish that can be caught

Effectiveness of government intervention

While government intervention can reduce market failure, there is a risk, however, that government failure may occur. The government may overestimate the extent of the private benefits offered to the people by consuming merit goods. It may also find it difficult to calculate the most efficient quantity of public goods to supply.

Governments can take time to make decisions and those decisions may be influenced by political factors and, in some cases, corruption. For example, a government may decide not to raise the tax on petrol, despite concerns about the environment, because it may be politically unpopular and may lose it votes.

Government intervention may also reduce economic efficiency by reducing incentives. If taxes on earned income and unemployment benefits are high, some people may be discouraged from working. High taxes on firms' profits can reduce entrepreneurs' willingness and ability to invest.

There is also some debate as to whether public or private sector expenditure leads to a more efficient allocation of resources. Do households and firms make better decisions than the government? In practice, there are advantages and disadvantages of both private and public sector expenditure. A new airport, for example, could be built by the private or public sector. There may be a number of advantages in it being built by a private sector firm. The profit incentive and force of competition may imply that it will build a high-quality airport at low cost and in less time.

There is a risk, however, that a private sector firm may be a monopoly and hence may not be forced to keep its costs down. Thus, it may charge a high price for building the airport. A private sector firm will also take only private costs and benefits into account.

Using public expenditure to build an airport may also have its drawbacks. Knowing that the state is paying, a state-owned enterprise, or private sector firm hired by the government, may not keep its costs down. A state-owned enterprise may lack the commercial expertise to complete the project on time. There may also be delays in decision-making by the government to go ahead with the project. A major benefit, however, of a major investment project being undertaken by government is that it will base its decision (as to whether to proceed with it) on the consideration of all factors involved, that is social impact, costs and benefits.

Discuss whether dental treatment should be provided free by the government.

ACTIVITY 14.5

The private sector in China is responsible for a growing amount of output and employment. Some economists argue that private sector firms are more profitable and efficient than the state sector.

In a pair, write a script for a podcast to answer these questions:

1   How may the government benefit from private sector firms being more profitable?

2   Why may private sector firms be more efficient than state-owned enterprises?

SUMMARY

You should now know:

- In a mixed economic system, resources are allocated by means both of the price mechanism and government intervention to address market failure.

- Maximum prices are set below the equilibrium price. They lower prices but lead to shortages.

- Minimum prices are set above the equilibrium price. They can help producers but lead to surpluses.

- Indirect taxation and subsidies influence firms' output and the price they charge for their products.

- The impact of a subsidy or indirect taxation depends on its size and price elasticity of demand.

- Other types of government intervention to address market failure include regulation, privatisation, nationalisation, direct provision of goods and services, and quotas.

Chapter 14 practice questions

1   Which type of goods production has to be financed by the government?

    A   capital

    B   consumer

    C   merit

    D   public   [1]

2   A government decides to subsidise rail travel. What will be an external benefit of this move?

    A   a rise in government expenditure

    B   increased crowding on trains

    C   lower fares for train passengers

    D   reduced congestion on roads   [1]

3   A firm, concerned about its reputation, decides to install new equipment in order to reduce the pollution it creates. What impact will this have on private and external costs?

	Private costs	External costs
A	fall	fall
B	fall	rise
C	rise	fall
D	rise	rise

[1]

4   What is an argument for state intervention in an economy?

    A   to encourage the consumption of harmful products

    B   to increase the role of the price mechanism in allocating resources

    C   to make the distribution of income more uneven

    D   to prevent private sector firms from overcharging consumers   [1]

5   What is a possible disadvantage of a minimum price?

    A   excess demand

    B   lack of incentive to produce

    C   lack of resources

    D   unsold products   [1]

                                                                          Total: [5]

6   a   Define 'minimum price'.   [2]

    b   Explain how a maximum price will affect a market.   [4]

    c   Analyse **three** ways a government could encourage consumption of a merit good.   [6]

    d   Discuss whether or not consumers benefit more from a market economic system or a mixed economic system.   [8]

                                                                          Total: [20]

CHECK YOUR PROGRESS

How well do you think you have achieved the learning intentions for this chapter?
Give yourself a score from 1 (still need a lot of practice) to 5 (feeling very confident)
for each learning intention. Provide an example to support your score.

Now I can...	Score	Example
define a mixed economic system		
define a maximum price		
draw and interpret a diagram showing a maximum price		
analyse the advantages and disadvantages of a maximum price in product markets		
define a minimum price		
draw and interpret a diagram showing a minimum price		
analyse the advantages and disadvantages of a minimum price in product markets		
define indirect taxation		
draw and interpret a diagram showing the effect of indirect taxation		
analyse the advantages and disadvantages of indirect taxation		
define a subsidy		
draw and interpret a diagram showing the effect of a subsidy		
define regulation		
analyse the advantages and disadvantages of regulation		
define privatisation		
analyse the advantages and disadvantages of privatisation		
define nationalisation		
analyse the advantages and disadvantages of nationalisation		
define direct provision of goods and services		
analyse the advantages and disadvantages of direct provision of goods and services		
analyse the advantages and disadvantages of quotas.		

Section 2 practice questions

1   Read the source material carefully before answering all parts of the question.

CASE STUDY: TRANSPORT AND COTTON PRODUCTION

There is not much traffic on the motorway between Islamabad and Lahore. This first motorway built in Pakistan was opened in 1997. It cost $1.2 billion to construct. One reason for the lack of traffic on the motorway is the existence of a rival road, the Grand Trunk Road, which is shorter and toll-free.

Improvements in road infrastructure can bring a number of benefits to an economy. These include reducing costs of production faced by a number of industries, including construction materials, cotton and paper products.

Some economists, however, argue that less tax revenue should be spent by the government on roads and more on education. Higher spending on education can increase labour productivity which, in turn, can reduce unemployment and increase productive potential. Labour productivity, for example, is higher in the USA in the cotton industry than in the other major cotton producers. Figure 1 shows the share of the global output of cotton (25 million metric tonnes) in the five largest producers in 2023.

One of the reasons for the greater productivity in the USA is that workers work with more advanced farm machinery.

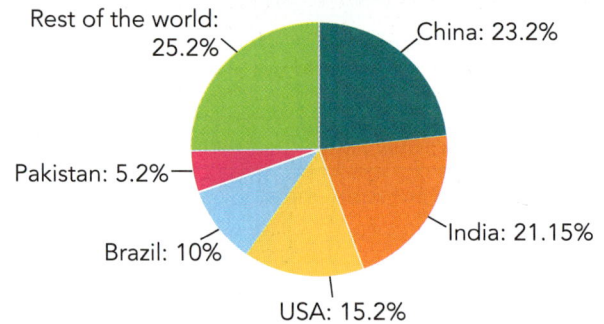

Figure 1: Percentage share of global cotton production

India is seeking to raise its labour productivity in a range of ways. These include reducing congestion on its roads. Between 2000 and 2023, the number of cars on India's roads quadrupled. The higher volume of traffic is causing considerable pollution. In 2022, India's capital city, Delhi, was named by the World Air Quality Report, produced by Swiss air technology firm IQAir, as the world's fourth most polluted city. The government has introduced new regulations, including stricter emissions standards for new vehicles, and has stopped subsidising diesel fuel in an attempt to reduce pollution. It is also increasing its investment to modernise and expand the country's train service.

Refer to the information in the source material in your answers.

a	Calculate Pakistan's output of cotton in 2023.	[2]
b	Explain **one** external cost.	[2]
c	Explain a possible opportunity cost of the Pakistan government building more roads.	[2]
d	Draw a demand and supply diagram to show the effect of improvements in road infrastructure on the market for cotton.	[4]
e	Analyse the pattern of cotton production.	[4]
f	Discuss whether or not regulation, in the form of stricter emission standards for new cars, is likely to reduce pollution.	[6]

Total: [20]

2 Read the source material carefully before answering all parts of the question.

CASE STUDY: JORDAN'S SEARCH FOR NEW SOURCES OF ENERGY

Jordan is currently trying to find new sources of energy for the country's firms, farms and households to use. It is exploring the possibility of nuclear power generation and has started to produce solar energy. The country benefits from long hours of sunshine, and the solar energy industry converts sunshine into power.

Jordan is not the only country to be developing a solar energy industry. Other countries include China, India, Italy, the UAE and the UK. Indeed, 2016 was the first year in which the world invested more in the industry than in coal- and gas-fired power generation. Solar power is seen as a cleaner and more environmentally friendly source of energy. With advances in technology, the price of solar panels is falling. This is reducing the cost of producing solar energy and its price to customers, increasing its price competitiveness. In a number of countries, the price of coal is rising which is reducing the sales of coal.

Jordan's agricultural industry needs a boost. The country lacks water and some of its land is not very fertile. It produces a range of agricultural products, including citrus fruits, tomatoes, cucumbers and olives. The country has benefited from an increased preference for fruit, but it has been estimated that the price elasticity of supply of fruit is only 0.25 in Jordan. In 2023, shortages of lemons, due to heat and lack of rain, pushed up their price. Table 2 shows how the price of lemons rose throughout October in 2023 and how this affected demand.

Agriculture is a small industry in the country. It only accounted for 4% of the country's output and employed only 2% of its 3 million workers in 2023. Most of the country's workers are employed in the public sector where wages are higher. For example, in 2023, 47 000 people were employed in the police force. This position is, however, changing. A number of the country's industries have been privatised and market forces are playing an increasing role in the economy.

Table 1: The price and demand for lemons in October in Jordan in 2023

Price of 1 kilogram of lemons (Jordanian dinars)	Daily demand for lemons (tonnes)
0.50	200
0.60	180
0.75	135
1.00	60

Refer to information in the source material in your answers.

   a   Calculate the number of agricultural workers in Jordan in 2023.   **[2]**

   b   Explain why demand for coal is likely to become more elastic in the future. **[2]**

   c   Calculate the effect that an 8% rise in the price of fruit would have on the supply of fruit in Jordan. **[2]**

   d   Draw a demand and supply diagram to show the effect of an increased preference for fruit on the market for fruit. **[4]**

   e   Analyse how changes in the price of lemons affected the price elasticity of demand for lemons in Jordan in October 2023. **[4]**

   f   Discuss whether or not governments have to produce public goods such as the police service. **[6]**

                                     Total: [20]

3   Qatar Airways is a state-owned airline. Most airlines are, however, in the private sector and the prices they charge move between equilibrium and disequilibrium as a result of changes in market forces. The price elasticity of demand for air travel differs from other forms of transport.

   a   Define 'market forces'. **[2]**

   b   Explain the difference between an equilibrium price and a disequilibrium price. **[4]**

   c   Analyse why different products have different price elasticities. **[6]**

   d   Discuss how useful knowledge of price elasticity is to an airline company. **[8]**

                                     Total: [20]

4   Gym membership is a normal good. More people throughout the world are joining gyms in a bid to get fitter. This change in demand is also affecting the demand for substitutes and complements to gym membership. In some countries, gym membership is taxed. Some economists argue that rather than taxing gym membership, governments should subsidise it.

   a   Define a 'normal good'. **[2]**

   b   Explain the difference between a complement and a substitute. **[4]**

   c   Analyse, using a demand and supply diagram, the effect of introducing a tax on gym membership. **[6]**

   d   Discuss whether or not governments should subsidise gym membership. **[8]**

                                     Total: [20]

Microeconomic decision-makers

> # Chapter 15
> # Money and banking

Introduction

Would you like more money? Most people would. What would you do with it? You might, perhaps, spend it. On the other hand, you might save it. You might even lend it to someone else. **Commercial banks** lend money to individuals and businesses, and they may look after our savings. Our lives are affected by banks more than we realise. The policy measures of the central banks of some countries can change the prices of products not only in their own countries but also in other countries.

ECONOMICS IN CONTEXT

What is the future of the sand dollar?

We are living in a time of significant developments in money and banking. More people are banking online, receiving and transferring money electronically. Technology is used to create different forms of digital currency. Digital currency is money which now exists only in an electronic form.

In October 2020, the Central Bank of the Bahamas introduced a digital currency known as the 'sand dollar'. The digital money exists alongside cash and bank accounts in the country. The Central Bank is keen to allow people who do not have easy access to a bank account to be able to make and receive payments. Perhaps more significantly, the Central Bank wants to make the transfer of money cheaper and quicker.

So far, not many people have converted their money into sand dollars, which have the same value as the traditional Bahamian dollar. However, as more people become confident about using digital money and as more central banks introduce digital currencies, the use of sand dollars is likely to increase. Throughout the world, people are making less use of coins and banknotes and many

are looking for more efficient ways of carrying out financial transactions.

Discuss in a pair or group:

1   How do you or your family make and receive payments?

2   Do you think we will still be using cash (coins and banknotes) in 20 years' time?

Figure 15.1: A quick way of making a payment

15.1 Money

Forms of money

The main forms of **money** used in most countries are coins, banknotes and bank accounts. Coins are often used to make small purchases and are given in change. Banknotes are used to buy more expensive items. In most countries, the main form of money is bank accounts. These are responsible for the largest proportion (in terms of value) of payments made. There are a number of ways of transferring money from one bank account to another. These include direct debits, credit cards and transactions using a smartphone.

KEY TERMS

commercial bank: a government-owned bank which provides banking services to the government and commercial banks and operates monetary policy.

money: an item which is generally acceptable as a means of payment.

Although bank accounts are the most important form of money, they are not legal tender. Legal tender is any form of payment which, by law, has to be accepted in settlement of a debt. Coins (up to a certain value) and banknotes are legal tender. Together, coins and banknotes are referred to as cash. So a person has to accept banknotes in payment, but they have the right to refuse, for example, a credit card. In practice, however, most people and firms find payment from bank accounts convenient and so are willing to accept it.

Digital currency is becoming increasingly important. There are three types of digital currency:

- Cryptocurrency is based online. Cryptocurrency does not have notes and coins. There are more than 10 000 cryptocurrencies. The best-known cryptocurrency is bitcoin. Cryptocurrencies are created by using algorithms and codes. They are used mainly for investment (people buy, store and sell cryptocurrencies to make a profit) and can be used as a method of payment. Cryptocurrencies can fluctuate (change) significantly in value.

- Stablecoins were developed to avoid fluctuations in value. They do this by linking their value to a currency, such as the US dollar, or a basket of goods. Stablecoins can be used to make payments.

- Central bank digital currencies (CBDCs). Some **central banks** have joined the Central Bank of the Bahamas by issuing their own digital currencies, and others are planning to. For example, the Central Reserve Bank of India and the People's Bank of China are developing their own CBDCs. CBDCs may be used as an additional method of payment alongside cash.

Digital currency has several advantages. It is the fastest way to carry out transfers of money. It is also cheap. People who use financial institutions to send money to relatives in other countries have to pay a larger transaction fee. Digital money also allows people who do not have bank accounts to make and receive payments. There is a risk, however, that digital currency can be hacked.

> **KEY TERM**
>
> **central bank:** a government-owned bank which provides banking services to the government and commercial banks and operates monetary policy.

The functions of money

Money has four functions. It acts as a:

1 **Medium of exchange.** Money allows people to buy and sell products. In carrying out this function, money is said to act as a medium of exchange. Products are exchanged for money, and that money is used to buy other products.

$$\text{Products} \rightarrow \text{Money} \rightarrow \text{Products}$$

Enabling people to exchange products is money's most important function (see Figure 15.2).

2 **Store of value.** Acting as a store of value means that money can be saved. It would be pointless to save eggs, for example, as eggs go bad over time and no one will be prepared to accept them a few weeks after they have been laid. Money, however, does not deteriorate with time and so will be acceptable in the future.

3 **Unit of account.** Money can also be used to place a value on an item. Prices are expressed in monetary terms. A newspaper may be priced at $2 and a book at $30. This function of acting as a unit of account, or measure of value (as it is sometimes called), enables buyers and sellers to agree on what items are worth,

relative to each other. In the example, one book is worth 15 newspapers. With $60 to spend, a person can either buy two books or 30 newspapers.

4   **Standard of deferred payments.** Money allows people to borrow and lend. Someone who wants to buy something now can get it by borrowing money from someone who does not want to use it now. They can make an agreement about the amount to be repaid in the future.

Figure 15.2: Cash is used as a medium of exchange to buy food in a market

The characteristics of money

To act as money, an item does not need to have intrinsic value (that is, an item does not have to be worth something in its own right). For example, both silver and banknotes can act as money, but whereas silver is wanted for a variety of purposes, banknotes have no intrinsic value. An item has to possess a number of characteristics for it to serve as money:

- The most important characteristic is that it should be generally acceptable (see Figure 15.2). If people are not prepared to accept the item as payment, it will not be able to carry out the functions of money.

- The item has to be in limited supply. Why, for instance, should people accept twigs as payment in a country with many trees?

- An item needs to be durable (will last some time),

- It needs to be portable (can be carried around easily), divisible (can be divided into units of different values),

- It should be homogeneous (every note or coin of the same value should be exactly the same).

- The item also has to be recognisable (people can easily see that the item is money).

TIP

Do not confuse the functions and characteristics of money. Remember: the functions concern the transactions/operations that money helps to make possible, whereas the characteristics are the features which an item needs to possess to act as money.

ACTIVITY 15.1

In a pair, discuss how many characteristics of money each of the following items possesses:

1 leaves

2 seashells

3 gold.

In your notebook, write up the characteristics alongside each item.

15.2 Banking

Commercial banks

Banking is a major industry in a number of countries. Banks enable people to borrow and lend and carry out a range of other financial activities. Banking services encourage more efficient use of resources and the growth of output of economies.

Commercial banks are also called retail banks. Both names tell us something about them. Commercial indicates that they are business organisations which usually seek to make a profit. Retail suggests that they are selling the public something – in this case, banking services. Commercial banks are the banks we are most familiar with.

The role and importance of commercial banks

Commercial banks have three main functions: to accept deposits, to lend and to enable customers to make payments (see Figure 15.3).

By accepting deposits, a bank's customers are able to keep their money in a safe place. Deposits can be made into two types of bank account: a current account and a savings account. A current account is sometimes called a demand account, demand deposit or sight account. There is easy and immediate access to money in a current account, but banks do not usually pay **interest** on money held in a current account. Customers use current accounts mainly to receive and make payments.

A savings account is also called a time account or time deposit. A period of notice may have to be given before money can be withdrawn from a savings account. Banks pay interest to customers on any money held in a savings account and, as its name suggests, customers use savings accounts as a way of saving.

There are two main ways of borrowing from a bank. An overdraft enables a customer to spend more than the amount of money in their account, up to an agreed limit. Interest is charged on the amount borrowed. This can be a relatively expensive way of borrowing and is mainly used to cover short-term gaps between expenses and income.

The other way of borrowing is by taking a loan. This is usually for a particular purpose and for a certain period of time. Interest is charged on the full amount of the loan, but the rate of interest is likely to be lower than that on an overdraft. A customer may be asked to provide some form of security, known as collateral, when taking a loan. This is to ensure that if the loan is not repaid, the asset given as collateral can be sold and the money recovered. In practice, though, banks try to avoid doing this

> ### KEY TERM
>
> **interest:** a payment for borrowing and a reward for saving.

by checking very carefully whether the person seeking a loan will be able to repay it. In the case of a firm, this is likely to involve careful inspection of the firm's accounts and business plan.

The first two functions of banks, that is borrowing from their customers and lending to them, means that banks act as financial intermediaries. They accept deposits from those with more money than they currently want to spend and lend it to those with an immediate requirement to spend more money than they have at hand. In other words, banks channel money from lenders to borrowers.

Lenders → Banks → Borrowers

Commercial banks make most of their profit by charging a higher interest rate to borrowers than they pay to people who save their money with them.

The third main function that banks carry out is to enable their customers to receive and make payments. This is referred to as acting as agents for payments and providing money transmission services. There is now a range of ways in which people can receive money and make payments out of their accounts. These include standing orders, direct debits, debit cards and online banking.

Commercial banks enable their customers to repay money borrowed on credit cards. Credit card companies allow people to borrow up to a maximum amount. Each month people get a statement on how much they owe. If this amount is repaid in full each month, they do not have to pay any interest. However, if not repaid each month, the amount owed can build up, and the interest charged is often high.

Figure 15.3: Commercial banks offer customers a range of financial services, such as personal loans and savings accounts

ACTIVITY 15.2

In 2022, the profits of Brazil's commercial banks increased by 20% from 2021. Their profits totalled $20bn. This was despite the high interest rates the banks were charging, particularly on overdrafts. Discuss these questions with another student. Make notes of the main points.

1   What is an overdraft?

2   Are Brazil's banks likely to continue to earn high profits?

Other functions of commercial banks

Commercial banks may offer customers a range of other services such as the purchase of foreign currency. Customers can safely store important documents, such as house deeds and small valuables, with their banks. Banks may also help with the administration of customers' wills.

They can provide advice and help with a number of financial matters, such as completion of tax forms, and the purchase and sale of shares. Many banks also now sell insurance and offer a wide variety of savings accounts, with a range of conditions and interest rates. Some now offer mortgage loans, which are loans to buy property.

DISCUSSION

Discuss which commercial bank you use or might use in the future to save any money you may have left over when you start working and possible reasons why.

ACTIVITY 15.3

A bank has $50 000 that it can lend. Six people apply for a loan. Their details are in Table 15.1.

Table 15.1

Person	Occupation	Income last year	Amount of loan requested	Credit history	Reason why loan requested
A	teacher	$45 000	$15 000	borrowed before and repaid on time	to have an extension to home built
B	actor	$12 500	$15 000	not borrowed from a financial institution before	to repay a loan from a friend borrowed during a period of unemployment
C	a student about to study medicine	$0	$10 000	not borrowed before	to pay first-year course fees
D	hospital porter	$16 000	$13 000	has borrowed from a money lender before and has repaid on time	to buy a car
E	lawyer	$100 000	$14 000	has borrowed from the bank four times before and has repaid on time	to have a swimming pool built
F	unemployed	state benefit of $7 000	$7 500	has not borrowed before	to buy IT equipment to set up as a web designer

CONTINUED

In a group of four, decide who should receive a loan.

Appoint someone in the group to write up the reasons for your decision. Choose a spokesperson to explain your decision to the rest of the class. Some things to think about before you complete the activity:

- People have to be able to pay back any loan with interest. Some uses of a loan can generate money, some of which can be used to repay the loan

- Commercial banks consider people's credit history

- The more that can be safely lent, the more interest can be earned.

Some things to think about individually after you compete the activity:

How easy did you find it to come to an agreement? What did you consider when making your decision?

The aims of commercial banks

The key aim of a commercial bank is to make a profit for its owners. Banks make their profits largely through loans on which banks charge customers interest. Banks earn most of the interest on long-term loans. Many long-term loans are for more than one year. Some can be for as long as 25 years.

However, banks' requirement to make a profit can conflict with their other aim – **liquidity**. Banks must ensure that they are able to meet their customers' requests to withdraw money from their accounts. To do this, banks must keep a certain amount of liquid assets (items which can be turned into cash quickly and without incurring loss). However, if banks tie up all their money in long-term loans, they would not be able to pay out cash to customers requesting it. Banks have to balance profitability and liquidity. They need to hold some assets that earn high interest but are illiquid (not liquid), and other assets earning low or no interest but being liquid.

> **KEY TERM**
>
> **liquidity:** being able to turn an asset into cash quickly without a loss.

Islamic finance

In a number of Islamic countries, commercial banks are not allowed to charge interest on bank loans. This is because many Muslims regard charging of interest, sometimes called usury, as a sin. Traditionally, Islamic banks have provided finance for firms by lending to them in return for a share in their profits. In recent years, more US and European commercial banks have expanded existing branches and opened up new branches in Islamic countries in the Middle East and Asia. Most employ Islamic sharia scholars and experts who can issue religious edicts (fatwas) that approve financial products including loans. The French bank BNP Paribas, for example, has created an independent sharia advisory board of Islamic scholars to offer it advice.

ACTIVITY 15.4

ICICI Bank is India's largest private sector bank. It has more than 6 000 branches in India and operates in more than 18 countries, including China, South Africa, the UAE, the UK and the USA. The bank's overseas branches aim their services mainly at Indian communities. They are, however, attracting a high number of non-Indian customers. The main reason why ICICI has been so successful is largely because the bank often pays a higher interest rate on deposits than rival banks.

1   What function of a commercial bank is mentioned in the extract?

2   Explain one other function of a commercial bank.

Write your answers in your notebook.

Central banks

A central bank is the single most important and influential bank in the country or, in the case of the European Union, the region. The five most well-known central banks in the world are probably the Federal Reserve Bank of the USA (often called the Fed), the European Central Bank (ECB), the Bank of England, the Reserve Bank of India and the People's Bank of China. Central banks are owned by governments and are responsible to the government (see Figure 15.4).

Figure 15.4: The Monetary Authority of Singapore is the country's central bank

Role and importance of a central bank

The role a central bank plays in an economy means that it can have a significant impact on households, producers/firms and the performance of the economy. Its functions include:

- **Acts as a banker to the government.** Tax revenue is paid into the government's account at the central bank, and payments by the government for goods and services are paid out of this account.

- **Operates as a banker to the commercial banks.** The commercial banks may use their accounts at the central bank to settle debts between each other and to draw out cash if their own customers are taking more cash from their branches than usual.

- **Acts as a lender of last resort.** The central bank may lend to banks which are temporarily short of cash. It may also lend to a commercial bank if it thinks that the closure of the commercial bank would reduce confidence in the banking system.

- **Manages the national debt.** The national debt is the total amount the government owes. Over time, government debt tends to build up. The central bank borrows on behalf of the government by issuing government securities, for example government bonds, pays interest on the bonds and repays them when they fall due.

- **Holds the country's reserves of foreign currency and gold.** The central bank keeps foreign currency and gold to influence the exchange rate.

- **Issues banknotes.** The central bank is responsible for printing notes and destroying notes which are no longer suitable for circulation. It also authorises the minting of coins.

- **Implements the government's monetary policy.** The prime aim of monetary policy is to keep inflation low and steady. This involves controlling the money supply and influencing interest rates throughout the economy by changing the interest rate it charges on its loans. The government may instruct the central bank to increase or decrease the money supply. In some cases, central banks implement interest rate changes decided by their own government. In other cases, central banks have been given the responsibility to set interest rates.

- **Controls the banking system.** Many central banks play a key role in regulating and supervising the banking system.

- **Represents the government.** At meetings with other central banks and international organisations such as the World Bank and the International Monetary Fund it represents the government.

LINK

Central banks keep foreign currencies and gold to influence the price of the country's currency against other currencies – see Chapter 35.3 (Determination of a foreign exchange rate in foreign exchange markets – Causes of foreign exchange rate fluctuations).

LINK

How changes in the money supply and the central bank's interest rate are used to influence the total demand in an economy are explored in Chapter 24.2 (Monetary policy measures).

ACTIVITY 15.5

The Central Bank of Nigeria (CBN) is based in Abuja. It has 37 branch offices across Nigeria.

One of its functions is to implement and monitor monetary policy. Another is to ensure that the country's commercial banks follow sound policies, including sensible lending policies.

Discuss the following questions with another student. Write down your answers.

1   Identify one way in which a central bank differs from a commercial bank.

2   What is the key feature of a sensible lending policy?

3   Explain one other function of a central bank.

Independence of central banks

A number of governments have given their central banks the authority to decide the rate of interest. The governments still decide the aims of their central banks and give them a target for inflation. The Bank of England, for example, is instructed to use the rate of interest to achieve an inflation target of 2%. If it thinks that there is a danger that the price level will increase by more than 2% it is likely to raise the rate of interest, whereas if it thinks it will fall below 2% it is likely to lower the rate of interest.

There are a number of advantages in allowing the central bank to decide the rate of interest for banking. Unlike a national government, a central bank is unlikely to be tempted to lower the rate of interest to win public support. Most central banks also have vast knowledge of the banking system and the appropriate rate of interest to set.

> ### TIP
>
> It is important to recognise the difference between a commercial bank and a central bank. It is, for example, for the central bank that acts as banker to the government whereas a commercial bank acts as a banker to households and firms.

> ### REFLECTION
>
> Are you clear about the difference between the role of central and commercial banks? What will you do to improve your understanding?

ECONOMICS IN ACTION

The risk of commercial banks getting into difficulties

Figure 15.5: Bank branches are becoming fewer, as many banking services are available online

In October 2023, a UK commercial bank got into difficulties. The bank was set up in 2010, aiming to compete with the older, established commercial banks in the country. By 2023, the new bank had nearly 3 million customers and $20 billion in deposits, partly as a result of offering long opening hours and being open seven days a week. The bank had 76 branches and was planning to open more. This was at a time when the older, established banks were closing branches because of the growth in online banking. As well as having a different approach to branches, the new bank also lent proportionally less than the older, established banks. Its higher costs and lower revenue resulted in a loss in 2022 and 2023. To try to stay in business, the bank announced that it was planning to reduce the number of staff, reduce its opening hours and seek more finance.

Economists were concerned that if the bank went out of business, it might worry other banks' customers, who could withdraw their deposits. Commercial banks play a key role in the economy. By allowing households and producers/firms to make and receive payments, they facilitate trade and increases in output. The key role commercial banks play in the economy is the reason why central banks will sometimes lend to those banks that get into financial difficulties.

1 Why might the length of bank opening hours become less important in the future?

2 Should a central bank always lend to a commercial bank that gets into difficulties?

SUMMARY

You should now know:

- The four functions of money are medium of exchange, store of value, unit of account and standard of deferred payments.

- To act as money, an item has to be generally acceptable, limited in supply, durable, portable, divisible, homogeneous and recognisable.

- The three main functions of commercial banks are to accept deposits, to lend and to enable their customers to make payments.

- A central bank is owned by the government.

- The functions of the central bank include acting as the banker to the government and commercial banks, managing the national debt, holding reserves of foreign currency, acting as lender of last resort, issuing banknotes, controlling the money supply, implementing interest rate changes, supervising the banking system and meeting with other central banks and international organisations.

Chapter 15 practice questions

1   Money enables people to save. Which function of money does this describe?

   A   medium of exchange

   B   standard for deferred payments

   C   store of value

   D   unit of account   [1]

2   What would make an item unsuitable to act as money?

   A   it is easy to carry

   B   it is generally acceptable

   C   it is perishable

   D   it is recognisable   [1]

3   What is a function of a central bank?

   A   controlling the money supply

   B   deciding on the amount of government expenditure

   C   issuing shares

   D   raising taxes   [1]

4   What is the main aim of a commercial bank?

   A   to act as banker to the government

   B   to issue banknotes

   C   to make a profit

   D   to manage the national debt   [1]

5 What would stop an item acting as money?

  A   it is divisible

  B   it is durable

  C   it is portable

  D   it is unlimited in supply   [1]

                                                           Total: [5]

6 a   Identify **two** characteristics of money.   [2]

  b   Explain **two** functions of a central bank.   [4]

  c   Analyse in what circumstances a commercial bank will increase
      its lending.   [6]

  d   Discuss whether or not gold rings can carry out the functions
      of money.   [8]

                                                          Total: [20]

CHECK YOUR PROGRESS

How well do you think you have achieved the learning intentions for this chapter?
Give yourself a score from 1 (still need a lot of practice) to 5 (feeling very confident)
for each learning intention. Provide an example to support your score.

Now I can...	Score	Example
explain the forms, functions and characteristics of money		
analyse the role and importance of central banks and commercial banks.		

Households

Introduction

Some households spend large sums of money, while others spend only a small amount each week. Some households save large sums of money, while others do not save any money. The amount that households and their members borrow also varies. The reasons for these differences are discussed in this chapter.

ECONOMICS IN ACTION

The wide gap between some households

Shu Ping and Zhang Yong opened their first hot pot restaurant in Sichuan, south-west China, in 1994. By 2023, they had more than 1 400 restaurants, operating under the name Haidilao in a number of countries, including not only China but also Japan, Singapore, the Republic of Korea, the UK and the USA. Also by 2023, the couple had a combined wealth of $10 billion. Their high income and wealth enables them to both spend and save large amounts of money. Banks are likely to be keen to lend to them and at a low rate of interest. In 2021, their only child, Zhang Hanzhi, bought a $42 million home next to his parent's home in Singapore.

In contrast, Barkhado and Abdi Ali, sheep farmers in the south of Somalia, have little wealth and income (see Figure 16.1). They and their five children live in a home without electricity. Their children are not in school, and the oldest two, aged eight and ten, help look after the sheep. Due to the household's low income, they have to borrow from local traders to buy some of their food and clothes. They have been turned down for a loan to buy more livestock by a bank in the nearby city of Kismayo.

Discuss in a pair or group:

1   What are the reasons why the children of the rich are likely to be able to spend a large amount when they are adults?

2   Why may a bank not want to lend to low-income households?

Figure 16.1: Sheep farmers in Somalia

16.1 Influences on households' spending

Households spend money to buy goods and services and to maintain a given standard of living. The main items of expenditure include food, clothing and footwear, housing, gas, electricity, water, **consumer durables** such as refrigerators, transport, entertainment, and leisure goods and services.

> **KEY TERM**
>
> **consumer durables:** goods purchased by households that last a relatively long time and are purchased infrequently.

The main influences on a household's spending are:

- **Income and wealth**. The main influence on the amount spent by a person or household is **disposable income**. As income rises, people usually spend more in total, but less as a percentage of their income (see 'Income and spending'). Wealth is linked to spending in four main ways. One is that wealth generates income, for example, dividends from shares, and this income can be spent. The second is that wealth can be cashed in by, for example, withdrawing money from a bank account or selling a car, and then spent. The third way is that people can use their wealth as security for loans. The fourth way is that wealth also affects confidence. If, for example, the value of people's housing rises, people will feel richer and are likely to spend more.

- **Rate of interest**. If the rate of interest rises, it will make borrowing more expensive, encourage saving and reduce the amount spent by people who have borrowed in the past. Of course, those people who have savings will gain more income and they may spend more. Their higher spending, however, will be more than offset by reduced expenditure of others. This is because savers tend to be richer than borrowers and tend to spend a smaller percentage of their income.

- **Confidence** is an important influence on consumption. If people feel more optimistic about their future career prospects and income, they are likely to spend more. In contrast, if they become anxious about economic prospects, they will tend to spend less.

- **Age.** People tend to spend a smaller proportion of their income as they age. For example, a household with parents in their 30s with young children are likely to spend a larger proportion of their income than a household with two adults in their early 60s. This is because the younger household may have more expenses and may still be adding consumer durables. However, when people reach a greater age, they may have to spend a higher proportion of their income. This is because their income may fall, they may need to spend money on care services and they may decide to use up their savings.

- **Culture.** Different groups of households may have different histories of spending. For example, households in Spain have traditionally spent a high proportion of their income. When people from Spain move to other countries where households spend a lower proportion of their income, such as Singapore, they tend to continue to spend at the same high rate for some years.

Other influences on a household's spending include:

- **Distribution of income.** The difference that exists between the proportion of income that high-income and low-income groups spend means that a more even distribution of income and transfer of income from the rich to the poor is likely to increase expenditure in a country.

- **Advances in technology** may increase expenditure because new products, such as smart TVs, encourage people to replace existing products.

Income and spending

Households can either spend or save their disposable income. When people are very poor, they cannot afford to save. All of their disposable income will be spent on buying basic necessities to survive. In fact, some may have to spend more of their income in order to be able to buy enough food and clothing and pay for housing.

When people spend more than their income, they are said to be *dissaving*. This is because they are either drawing on their past savings or, more likely, borrowing other people's savings.

As income rises, households are able to both spend and save more. As people become richer, they buy more and better-quality products. However, while the total amount spent rises with income, the proportion spent tends to fall. For example, a world-class footballer in Italy may earn a disposable income of $105 000 a week, while an unemployed person in Italy may live on state benefits of $140 a week. The unemployed person may spend all of the $140. The footballer can clearly afford to spend more and is likely to do so. However, even if the footballer has a very luxurious lifestyle, it is unlikely that they will spend all of the $105 000. If the footballer spends $63 000 (a huge amount) they will only be spending 75% of their disposable income, while the unemployed person is spending 100% of their income.

The proportion of income which people spend usually decreases as income rises. Table 16.1 shows that as income rises, expenditure (spending) increases, but the proportion of income spent falls. For example, at an income of $300 people spend 90% of their income.

Table 16.1: The relationship between disposable income and consumption

Disposable income ($)	Consumption ($)	Proportion of income spent (%)
100	120	120
200	200	100
300	270	90
400	320	80
500	350	70

The relationship between disposable income and **consumption** can also be shown graphically. Figure 16.2 shows that at very low levels of income there is dissaving. At Z level of income all income is spent. Then as income rises past Y, saving occurs. Over the complete range of income, expenditure continues to rise, but it rises at a slower rate.

> **KEY TERM**
>
> **consumption:** expenditure by households on consumer goods and services.

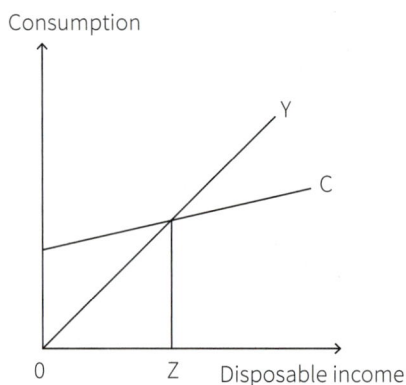

Figure 16.2: The relationship between disposable income and consumption

Pattern of expenditure

Households with different incomes tend to have different patterns of spending. Low-income households tend to spend a higher proportion of their income, and total expenditure, on food and clothing than high-income households. This is not because they eat more and or buy more clothing than those with a high income. High-income households are likely to spend more in total on food and clothing, as they tend to buy a greater variety and higher quality of food and more clothing of a higher quality. The amount high-income households spend is, however, usually a smaller proportion of their income and total expenditure. A high-income household may spend $400 a week on food and clothing out of a disposable income of $2000, and a low-income household may spend $40 out of a disposable income of $100. This would mean that 40% of the disposable income of the family living in poverty goes on food and clothing compared with 20% of the disposable income of the wealthier one.

High-income households spend more, both in total and as a proportion, on luxury items, consumer durables, entertainment and services. For example, high-income households spend more on cars, jewellery, theatre trips and foreign holidays. This difference in spending patterns also occurs between countries, with spending, as a proportion of disposable income and total expenditure on food and other necessities, being higher in low-income countries, while spending on luxuries forms a greater share of disposable income and total expenditure in high-income countries.

Spending patterns vary within income groups in a country, according to differences in who is living in the household, tastes and age. Households without children are likely to spend a higher proportion on leisure activities and eating out than households with children. Some households may value cultural activities more than others, while others may need to spend more on medical care. Retired people tend to spend a higher proportion than average on transport and entertainment. On the other hand, younger people often spend a higher proportion on clothing and entertainment.

> **TIP**
>
> It is important to distinguish between the amount of their income that households spend and the proportion of their income they spend. A low-income household is likely to spend less in total than a high-income household but a higher proportion.

ACTIVITY 16.1

Table 16.2 shows how three households spend their disposable income. In your group, place the three households in the most likely order of disposable income from the highest-income household to the lowest-income household.

Discuss how you decided on the order with your group.

Table 16.2

	Household A	Household B	Household C
Food and clothing	35%	45%	15%
Consumer durables	35%	35%	45%
Leisure goods and services	30%	20%	40%

16.2 Influences on households' saving

There are several ways of saving. Some ways are *contractual*. This means that an individual signs a contract, agreeing to save a certain amount on a regular basis. The main forms of contractual saving are insurance policies and pension schemes.

Non-contractual saving includes an individual depositing money in bank and building society accounts, and buying government securities, shares and property. By its very nature, non-contractual saving varies more with time and is more heavily influenced by changes in interest rates than contractual saving.

The main influences on a household's saving include:

- **Income and wealth.** As with household spending, the main influence on saving is disposable income. As disposable income rises, the total amount saved and the proportion saved (the **savings rate/ratio**) increases. The wealthier people are, the easier they will find it to save.

- **Rate of interest.** A rise in the rate of interest may reduce some target saving as people can now reach their target amounts by saving less. Overall, it is likely to increase non-contractual saving as it pushes up the reward for saving.

- **Confidence.** Households may save more if they are worried about the future. For example, if people think they may lose their job, they may save more now to help cover future expenses.

- **Age.** The young and the old tend to save less than middle-aged people. Older people, especially those who are very old, draw on their savings to ensure a reasonable living standard during retirement.

- **Cultural attitudes.** The attitude to saving varies between countries and cultures. In some countries and cultures, saving is considered to be very important. In others, people prefer to spend most of their income when they receive it.

> **KEY TERM**
>
> **savings rate/ratio:** the proportion of household disposable income that is saved.

ACTIVITY 16.2

Table 16.3 shows the relationship between disposable income, consumption and saving.

1 Copy and complete the table.

Table 16.3

Income ($)	Consumption ($)	Saving ($)
100	100	
200	180	
300	240	
400	280	
500	300	

2 Calculate what proportion of income is spent when income is:

   a $100

   b $300.

Other influences on a household's saving include:

- **Tax treatment of savings.** Tax concessions on the income earned from saving will encourage people to save. In a number of countries (e.g. Panama, Portugal and the UK) there are some tax-free savings schemes where no tax is charged on the interest earned.

- **Range and quality of financial institutions.** The greater the variety of saving opportunities on offer, the more likely people will find a scheme that will suit them. Confidence in the ability of institutions to pay interest and repay the amount saved is also important.

Reasons for saving

Households save for a variety of reasons. Some people are target savers (see Figure 16.3). Target savers want to buy something specific and save up the money to buy it, for example, a smartphone, a car or a deposit for a home.

Figure 16.3: A target saver saves up to buy a specific item such as a car

People also save for their retirement. When people retire, they usually no longer receive an income from work. Even if they receive a state pension and an occupational pension, income from savings can make their retirement more comfortable.

Some people save to help finance their children's education or to leave them an inheritance when they die. Most people like to have some savings to deal with emergencies and unexpected problems and to take advantage of any unforeseen opportunities. For example, people may lose their jobs, their drains may become blocked or they may see a car for sale (at what they regard to be a bargain price).

Some people also save to increase their current income. The more people save, the more interest they tend to receive, not only in total, but also per unit saved. This is because financial institutions usually reward, disproportionately, those who save large amounts. Those who hold their savings in the form of shares, government bonds or a property may also hope that they will benefit from a rise in the value of their assets.

Table 16.4 shows the household savings rates of selected countries in 2023. Discuss the table with another student, then answer the questions individually.

Table 16.4

Country	Household savings rate (%)
Germany	11.9
Japan	39.3
Portugal	5.9
South Africa	−0.2

1   Why do you think South Africa had a negative savings rate?

2   What was the rate of household spending in Japan?

3   What might Germany's and Portugal's savings rates suggest about the relative income levels in each of these countries?

4   Apart from differences in disposable income, what may be responsible for the savings rates of Germany being higher than that of Portugal?

Write down your answers in your notebook. Share them with your partner. Did you agree?

TIP

Remember that a rise in disposable income enables people to both spend and save more.

Income and savings

Savings is disposable income which is not spent. As already noted, it is not possible to save below a certain income level. As disposable income rises, both the total amount saved and the proportion of disposable income saved increases. Table 16.5, using the same disposable income and consumption figures as in Table 16.1, shows this. The proportion of income saved and the proportion of income spent must add up to 100.

Table 16.5: The relationship between disposable income and savings

Disposable income ($)	Consumption ($)	Savings ($)	Proportion of income saved (%)
100	120	−20	−20%
200	200	0	0%
300	270	30	10%
400	320	80	20%
500	350	150	30%

Figure 16. 4 shows the usual relationship between disposable income and savings.

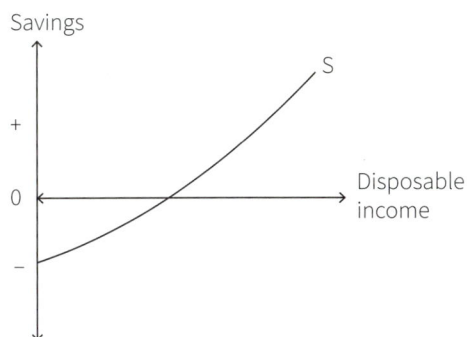

Figure 16.4: The relationship between disposable income and savings

ACTIVITY 16.4

The savings rate in Italy fell from 11% in 2000 to 7% in 2023. One reason given for this by Italian economists was the rise in the number of retired people in relation to the number of workers.

1   Define the term 'savings rate'.

2   Explain why the savings rate may fall due to a rise in the number of retired people in relation to the number of workers.

Write your answers in your notebook.

DISCUSSION

Discuss whether you might expect to save more when you are 25, 40 or 75 years old. In your discussion, you may want to consider what expenses you may have, what you might want to save for, what your expectations and what your incomes may be at the different ages.

Changes in saving and spending in Qatar

Economists study not only the amount households save but also the proportion of disposable income they save, that is the savings rate. Economists explore the reasons for changes in countries' savings rates and the effects such changes may have. Economists found that Qatar's household savings rate rose every year from 2018 to 2023.

It was not surprising that the savings rate rose during the COVID-19 pandemic in 2020–2021. Households in Qatar, as in other countries, were staying at home more than usual. They were not taking holidays, they were not eating out in restaurants and they were not engaging in other forms of entertainment. As a result, saving rose and spending fell.

After the pandemic, the savings rate continued to increase in Qatar. Analysing surveys of Qatari households, economists concluded that this was due to higher incomes and more attractive savings schemes. The total amount of household spending, however, also rose in Qatar, in part because of higher confidence in the future.

1 What items may Qataris have spent more on in 2023 than in 2021?

2 How might higher savings now be linked to higher spending in the future?

Figure 16.5: Doha, the capital of Qatar

16.3 Influences on households' borrowing

Borrowing moves income from people who do not want to spend it now to those who need more money than they currently have. Some people who run into financial difficulties borrow in a bid to maintain their living standards. These people hope that their income will soon rise, so that they can repay the loans and overdrafts. Other people may borrow in order to buy a car or go on a holiday. Most people who buy a house have to borrow some of the money to finance their purchase. The loan they take out is called a **mortgage**. People may also borrow to finance their own education or the education of their children or to cover healthcare costs.

Borrowing enables people to spend more than their current disposable income. However, it involves a cost in the form of interest which has to be paid. It is also usually a temporary situation as loans and overdrafts have to be repaid.

The main influences affecting the amount of money households may borrow includes:

- **Income.** Low-income households may sometimes have a greater need to borrow but are likely to experience greater difficulty in getting a loan. This is because low-income households will have less security to offer for any loan and lenders may be unsure about their ability to keep up interest payments and repay any loan.

KEY TERM

mortgage: a loan to help buy a house.

- **Availability of loans and overdrafts.** The easier it is to borrow, the more likely people are to borrow.

- **Rate of interest.** A rise in the rate of interest will increase the cost of borrowing, which is likely to reduce borrowing.

- **Confidence.** The more confident people are about the future, the more they will expect to earn in the future. They may adjust their spending patterns now, financing some of their extra expenses by borrowing with an expectation that their higher income will enable them to repay their loans.

- **Age.** People in their 20s and 30s may borrow relatively large amounts. Some may be paying university fees. A number may be buying a home and so may be spending more than their income now, in anticipation of their income rising in the future.

- **Cultural attitudes.** Some countries and some groups within countries are more concerned than others about the risks of people getting into debt by borrowing.

LINK

The influence of changes in the rate of interest on saving and borrowing are also considered in Chapter 24.2 (Monetary policy measures – Changes in the interest rate).

ACTIVITY 16.5

A household in your country earns an income which is close to the average for your country. In a small group, decide whether the household is likely to borrow to purchase each of the following items:

1 clothing

2 driving lessons

3 a hip replacement

4 a home

5 a university degree

6 a wedding.

Note down the reasons for the group's decision in each case.

REFLECTION

Do you feel confident that you understand the different influences on why households spend, save and borrow? If not, what can you do to gain a better understanding of them?

SUMMARY

You should now know:

• Disposable income can be spent or saved.

• As disposable income rises, people spend more in total, but less as a percentage.

• Saving rises in total and as a percentage of disposable income, as people get richer.

• Those with lower incomes spend a higher proportion of their total expenditure and disposable income on food and other basic necessities than the rich, but a smaller proportion on luxuries.

• The influences on households' spending include the level of disposable income, wealth, confidence, the rate of interest, the distribution of income and advances in technology.

• Some forms of saving are contractual and some are non-contractual.

• People save to buy certain products, to make their retirement more comfortable, to help their children, to cope with unexpected expenses and opportunities and to earn income.

• The influences on households' saving are income, wealth, the rate of interest, the tax treatment of savings, the range and quality of financial institutions, age structure and social attitudes.

• By borrowing, people can spend more than their disposable income.

• The influences on households' borrowing are the availability of loans, the rate of interest, confidence and cultural attitudes.

Chapter 16 practice questions

1   How would rising interest rates affect household savings and expenditure?

	Saving	Expenditure
A	rise	rise
B	rise	fall
C	fall	fall
D	fall	rise

[1]

2   What is most likely to cause a rise in expenditure in an economy?

A   a more uneven distribution of income

B   a reduction in wealth

C   a rise in confidence

D   a rise in income tax

[1]

3 What can cause a fall in saving?

   A a fall in the rate of interest

   B a fall in the rate of tax imposed on earnings from saving

   C a rise in disposable income

   D a rise in the range of financial institutions [1]

4 What must be occurring if consumption is less than disposable income?

   A borrowing

   B income levels are falling

   C income is being redistributed to those with lower incomes

   D saving [1]

5 Which change is most likely to increase household spending?

   A a decrease in the range of consumer goods available

   B an increase in the number of unemployed people

   C a reduction in both business and consumer confidence

   D a redistribution of income from high-income households to low-income households [1]

Total: [5]

6 a Identify the 'opportunity cost of saving'. [2]

   b Explain **two** reasons why young workers may save less than middle-aged workers. [4]

   c Analyse the causes of a reduction in borrowing by households. [6]

   d Discuss whether or not an increase in income will cause an increase in spending. [8]

Total: [20]

CHECK YOUR PROGRESS

How well do you think you have achieved the learning intentions for this chapter? Give yourself a score from 1 (still need a lot of practice) to 5 (feeling very confident) for each learning intention. Provide an example to support your score.

Now I can...	Score	Example
analyse the influences on households' spending: income, rate of interest, confidence, age and culture		
analyse the influences on households' saving: income, rate of interest, confidence, age and culture		
analyse the influences on households' borrowing: income, rate of interest, confidence, age and culture.		

> Chapter 17
Workers

LEARNING INTENTIONS

By the end of this chapter, you will be able to:

- analyse the wage and non-wage factors that influence an individual's choice of occupation
- discuss, using demand and supply diagrams, the influences on wage determination: demand and supply of labour, trade unions and their relative bargaining power, government policy
- explain the reasons for differences in wages
- discuss how the reasons for differences in wages influence the wages of workers
- explain the causes and consequences of changes in the occupational and geographical mobility of labour
- define the division of labour (worker specialisation)
- discuss the advantages and disadvantages of division of labour.

Introduction

Have you thought about what career you would like to follow? There is a range of factors that influence a person's choice of a career. One factor, although it is unlikely to be the only one, is the wages a person might expect. There are non-wage factors too that will influence a person's choice, such as the skills and qualifications required. Some careers get paid more than others, and jobs may be very specialised.

ECONOMICS IN CONTEXT

The Indian gig economy

The gig economy covers workers who are paid for an individual task or number of tasks. This is a way that traditionally musicians and singers have worked (see Figure 17.1). For example, Twice, the Republic of Korea's pop group, toured Europe with gigs in a number of stadiums including the O2 Arena in London.

The connection between the worker and the employer is temporary in the gig economy. It may be renewed but it is not permanent. This form of flexible working with no long-term contract between a worker and an employer is now increasing in a range of jobs throughout the world. Its growth has been particularly rapid in India. In 2023, there were 14 million Indian workers employed in the gig economy. It is predicted that by 2050 there will be 56 million Indian workers in the gig economy.

Figure 17.1: Musicians rehearsing for a gig

Some workers in the gig economy, such as taxi drivers, delivery drivers and cleaners, are medium- or low-skilled. Other workers in the gig economy, including educational consultants, legal advisers, financial consultants, data analysts and VFX (visual effects) artists, are highly skilled.

There are two main reasons for the increase in the gig economy. One is the growth and success of digital platforms. Digital platforms bring employers and workers into contact with each other. The other reason for the growth in the gig economy is the benefits this type of economy can bring to employers and workers. Employers may need less office or factory space, may need to carry out less training, may need to provide fewer non-wage benefits and may be able to match supply more closely to demand. Workers can decide the hours they want to work and when they want to work, and it may enable them to work from home. It can provide workers with a better work/life balance and may make it easier for some workers to care for children or elderly parents.

However, not having a permanent job and no guarantee of any hours of work can bring a number of disadvantages. It may create uncertainty for workers, may make it more difficult for them to obtain a loan to buy a house and may not provide any income when sick, on holiday or retired.

Discuss in a pair or group:

1   Would you want to work in the gig economy?

2   Why might a firm want to employ some workers on permanent contracts?

17.1 Factors affecting an individual's choice of occupation

A wide range of factors may influence a person's choice of occupation. The factors can be divided into wage factors (also called monetary or pecuniary factors) and non-wage factors (also known as non-monetary or non-pecuniary factors).

Wage factors

An important influence on what jobs a person decides to do is the pay on offer. The total pay a person receives is known as their **earnings**. As well as the basic wage, earnings may also include overtime pay, bonuses and commission.

Wages

Wages may also be referred to as pay or salaries. Generally, the higher the **wage rate** on offer, the more a person would want to do the job. Higher pay is one reason why more people would prefer to work as a doctor than a window cleaner.

The wages of many workers are based on a standard number of hours. Some workers' wages may vary according to the number of hours they work (a time rate system) or the amount they produce (a piece rate system). A time rate system benefits the employers as they can easily estimate their labour costs, and also the workers as they can negotiate about the rate paid. However, a time rate system does not reward hard work since it pays both industrious and less-productive workers the same.

This problem is overcome by a piece rate system, which pays workers according to their output. This system can only be used if a worker's output can be easily measured and the product is standardised. This is why the piece rate system is sometimes found in agriculture and manufacturing but is very uncommon in the services sector. For example, the piece rate system could not be applied to doctors. One doctor may carry out three operations in a day, while another may perform eight operations. The three operations, however, might have been more complex operations. Less supervision may be needed with a piece rate system, but workers may focus on quantity at the expense of quality. Also, the health of some workers may suffer if they feel pressurised to produce a high output.

Overtime pay

Overtime pay may be paid to the workers who work longer hours than the standard working week. Overtime is usually paid at a higher rate. Overtime can benefit both employees and employers. Workers with young families, for example, are often keen to increase their pay and may be attracted by jobs that offer regular overtime. It enables employers to respond to higher demand without taking on new workers, until the employers are sure that the higher demand will last. It is easier, less costly and less disruptive to reduce overtime than to dismiss workers if demand declines.

There is a risk that workers may become tired as a result of working for longer hours. If this does occur, the output they produce over the day may not increase and its quality may fall. In fact, some employers have found that when workers are aware that they are going to be working for longer hours, they pace themselves accordingly and put less effort into each hour.

> **KEY TERMS**
>
> **earnings:** the total pay received by a worker.
>
> **wage rate:** a payment which an employer contracts to pay a worker. It is the basic wage a worker receives per unit of time or unit of output.

Bonuses

A bonus is an extra payment. It can be paid to workers who produce above a standard amount, finish a project ahead of time, secure a profitable contract or contribute to higher profits in some other way. Bonuses can provide an incentive for workers to produce both a high and a good-quality output or to stay with a firm.

Employers need to award bonuses fairly to ensure the workers who do not receive a bonus do not become demotivated. Demotivated workers may result in a fall in the quantity or quality of output and some workers may resign.

Those people who welcome a challenge and have confidence in their own ability may be attracted to the jobs which pay bonuses. In recent years, there have been instances when very large bonuses have been paid to some workers in the financial sector, particularly in banking.

Commission

Commission is a payment often given to salespeople to reward them for the quantity of goods or services that they sell. Commission is a proportion of the value of the sales the salesperson makes. Sometimes, this is in addition to a standard wage and sometimes it makes up their total payment.

ACTIVITY 17.1

Chinese airlines are among the fastest growing, carrying more and more passengers. Between 2012 and 2023, the number of pilots employed by Chinese airlines doubled. The country's airline industry expanded more rapidly than the rate at which Chinese pilots could be trained. As a result, the airlines recruited some foreign pilots. In 2023, some Chinese airlines were offering pilots from other countries wages of $300 000 a year. This was four times the average wage of Brazilian pilots and approximately twice the average wage of US pilots.

1   How much were pilots paid, on average, in Brazil in 2023?

2   What would be likely to happen to pilots' pay in Brazil?

Share your answers with another student.

Non-wage factors

People do not always choose the highest paid job on offer. They consider a range of non-wage factors such as job satisfaction, type of work and career prospects.

Job satisfaction

Enjoying what you do is an important aspect of any job. Some people put job satisfaction above wage factors. Occupations such as nursing and teaching are not particularly well paid, and a number of nurses and teachers could earn more in other occupations. These jobs, however, can provide a high degree of job satisfaction. People who do them get satisfaction from helping people and serving their community (see Figure 17.2). Of course, some jobs provide both high pay and a high level of job satisfaction. Neurosurgeons, TV presenters and IT architects all have interesting, challenging and well paid jobs.

Figure 17.2: Caring roles may give a high degree of job satisfaction

Type of work

Most people would prefer non-manual to manual work. Non-manual work is physically less tiring and generally offers more mental stimulation. Non-manual work tends to be better paid. People also like to do jobs which enjoy a high status and most of these tend to be non-manual. For example, university professors tend to be held in higher regard than stonemasons. Some people are prepared to undertake dangerous work, for example deep-sea diving and bomb disposal, but most people prefer to work in a safe environment.

Working conditions and working hours

Working conditions are an important factor. People like to work in pleasant surroundings, with friendly colleagues and enjoying regular breaks.

Occupations vary in terms of the number of hours expected from workers and the timing of those hours. Managers and senior officials tend to work for longer hours than shop workers.

Some occupations offer workers the opportunity to work part-time, say 16 hours a week. A number of them also offer flexible working hours, where workers alter the hours they work from week to week. This is sometimes to suit the employer, with workers working longer hours when demand for the product is high, and sometimes to suit the worker, allowing them to undertake caring responsibilities.

Nurses, emergency plumbers and workers in the hospitality industry often work unsociable hours, for example, they often have to work at nights and in the evenings when other people are resting or enjoying themselves. Some nurses and other workers, including factory workers, work in shifts. This involves working at different periods of the day and night. There may be day and night shifts or three eight-hour shifts during the day.

Holidays

In a number of countries, the law sets a minimum length of holiday entitlement for full-time workers. Even in these countries, however, the length of holidays varies. Teaching is one occupation well known for the length of holidays on offer. In fact, one reason for people preferring to go for teaching is the benefit of long holidays. Having time off when their children are on holiday is an advantage for parents.

Pensions

With people living longer in most countries, pensions are becoming an important non-wage factor. Some jobs provide their workers with generous pensions, while others do not provide any financial help to retired workers. In many countries, for example, the police can retire relatively early on good pensions, whereas casual agricultural workers are unlikely to receive a pension. Generally, workers in the public (state) sector receive more generous pensions than those in the private sector.

Fringe benefits

Fringe benefits are the extra benefits provided to workers by their employers. Fringe benefits may include free or subsidised meals, private health insurance for the employee and their family, employee discounts and social and leisure facilities.

Job security

Many workers are attracted by occupations which offer a relatively high degree of job security. A high degree of job security means that workers are unlikely to be made redundant. Job security is more likely to exist in occupations where there is a high demand for the product and workers are given long-term contracts. High demand for the product would mean that employers would not want to get rid of the workers, and a contract would restrict their ability to do so. Civil servants often have a high degree of job security, but casual workers, including some agricultural and building workers, have little job security and can be dismissed at short notice.

Career prospects

People are often prepared to accept low wages at the start of their careers, if they think there is a good possibility that they will gain promotion to a well paid and interesting job. Trainee accountants, barristers and doctors are not usually highly paid and often work for long hours at the beginning of their careers. They will expect, however, that as they pass examinations and gain experience, their pay will rise to a relatively high level and their work will become more challenging.

Size of the firms and location

People are often attracted to jobs in large firms and organisations. This is because large firms and organisations often pay more and offer better career prospects, job security and fringe benefits than smaller ones. For example, a number of people are attracted to work for their country's civil service for such reasons. On the other hand, some people prefer to work for smaller firms. This is because they believe that the atmosphere will be more friendly than in a large firm. Studies have shown that labour relations are better in small factories and offices.

People may choose an occupation which is close to their home. This will mean that they do not have to spend much money or time on travelling to and from work.

Qualifications and skills

In practice, people's choice of occupation is limited by a number of factors, including the qualifications they have and the skills they possess. The more qualifications and skills an individual has, the more jobs will open to them.

ACTIVITY 17.2

Write the names of 20 occupations on cards. You could use the occupations suggested below or replace some of them with your own choices.

accountant	economist	optician
actor	engineer	police officer
architect	farmer	property developer
chef	hairdresser	software developer
clothing designer	journalist	teacher
dentist	lawyer	train driver
doctor	nutritionist	

In pairs, select one card. Research details about the selected occupation and then give a presentation to the class on the advantages and disadvantages of the occupation.

> **TIP**
>
> Remember, non-wage factors that may influence a person's choice of occupation do not include wages, overtime, pay, bonuses or commission.

DISCUSSION

What job would you like to do? What are the reasons for your choice?

17.2 Wage determination and the reasons for differences in wages

The key factors that determine the amount of pay received by workers and why some workers earn more than others are the demand for and supply of their labour. Other influencing factors include the relative bargaining strengths of employers and workers, discrimination in the workplace and government policies.

Demand for and supply of labour

The higher the demand for and the lower the supply of workers in an occupation, the higher the pay is likely to be. Figure 17.3 shows the markets for doctors and for cleaners.

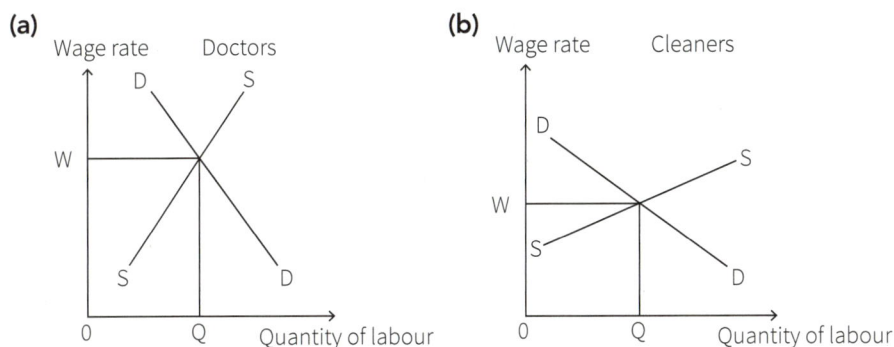

(a)

Wage rate   Doctors

(b)

Wage rate   Cleaners

Figure 17.3: The market for **(a)** doctors and **(b)** cleaners

The supply of doctors is low, relative to demand for their services. There is only a limited number of people with the necessary qualifications and the willingness and ability to undertake a long period of challenging training to become doctors.

It might also be expected that the supply of cleaners would be low and their pay high, as few people would want to work as cleaners. Cleaning is not a particularly interesting job as it can involve unsociable hours, not very pleasant working conditions and does not usually offer good career prospects. The supply of cleaners, nevertheless, is often high relative to their demand. This is because although some people may not be keen to work as cleaners, they do so because the job does not require any qualifications or special skills and only a minimum amount of training is necessary. This often results in the supply of cleaners being high relative to the demand.

Supply also explains why some workers who are involved in dangerous jobs are well paid. There is a limited supply of people who are willing to work as crane operators (see Figure 17.4). To try to overcome this reluctance, a number of employers pay workers undertaking this job a higher rate than that paid to other building workers.

Figure 17.4: A crane operator may expect better wages because of the dangers of working at height

Relative bargaining strengths of employers and workers

Wages are likely to be higher in occupations where workers have greater bargaining strength relative to employers. This is more likely to be the case if most of the workers are members of a **trade union** or professional body which can bargain collectively on the workers' behalf.

An individual worker may not have the skill, time or willingness to negotiate with their employer. A worker is also likely to have limited bargaining strength. If they ask for a wage rise or an improvement in working conditions, the employer may be able to dismiss them and recruit another worker as a replacement.

Trade unions and professional bodies enable workers to press their claims for higher wages and/or better working conditions through **collective bargaining**. Collective bargaining involves negotiations between trade union officials, representing a group of workers, and representatives of employers.

Most doctors and lawyers, for example, belong to their professional body which represents their interests. Their bargaining position is strengthened by the knowledge that they would be difficult to replace with other workers and any industrial action taken by them would have serious consequences. In contrast, most cleaners and workers in the hospitality industry do not belong to a workers' organisation. Their bargaining strength is further reduced by the fact that they are usually employed by different organisations, are not in the same workplace and so lack the opportunity to form a strong trade union. Such workers can be easily replaced by other workers.

The role of the trade unions

Trade unions carry out a number of functions. They negotiate on behalf of their members on wages, job security, working hours and working conditions. These areas can include basic pay, overtime payments, holidays, health and safety, promotion prospects, maternity and paternity rights, and job security. Depending on the circumstances, trade unions may be trying to protect or improve workers' rights.

Unions may also provide information on a range of issues for their members, for example on pensions. They help with education and training schemes and may also work to increase demand for the product produced and hence for labour. Some trade unions also provide a range of benefits to their members including strike pay,

KEY TERMS

trade union: an association which represents the interests of a group of workers.

collective bargaining: representatives of workers negotiating with employers' associations.

legal advice and sickness pay. In addition, many get involved in pressurising their governments to pass legislation that will benefit their members or workers in general, such as fixing a national minimum wage.

The basis of wage claims

There are a number of arguments a trade union can put forward when asking for a wage rise.

- Workers deserve to be paid more because they have been working harder and have increased productivity.

- An industry where profits have risen can afford to pay higher wages to its workers. This argument may be linked to the first one as the workers are likely to have contributed to the higher profits.

- The comparability argument. A union may argue that the workers it represents should receive a pay rise to keep their pay in line with similar workers. For example, a union representing nurses may press for a wage rise if doctors are awarded higher pay. The nurses' union is unlikely to ask for the same pay as doctors. What is more likely is that they will seek to maintain their **wage differential**. So, if before the increase in doctors' pay, nurses received a wage that was 60% of the doctors' earnings, they are likely to demand a rise that will restore this differential.

- Workers need a wage rise to meet the increased cost of living. If the price level is rising by 6%, workers will need a wage rise of at least 6% to maintain their wage's purchasing power. This is sometimes referred to as maintaining their **real income** (income adjusted for inflation).

> **KEY TERMS**
>
> **wage differential:** the difference in wages.
>
> **real income:** income adjusted for inflation.

ACTIVITY 17.4

In October 2023, the Bangladesh Garment and Industrial Workers' Federation called its members in the garment industry out on strike. The trade union had been negotiating with representatives of garment firms and the Bangladeshi government to raise the minimum wage paid to its members. The workers were offered a rise in their monthly wage from $75 to $113. However, the trade union was pressing for a rise to $208 to keep up with inflation and to move the wage closer to garment workers in other countries.

Discuss these questions with another student before writing your answers individually.

1. Calculate the percentage wage rise the garment workers were offered and the percentage wage rise they were seeking.

2. Which two arguments were the trade union using for a wage rise?

3. Explain one other change a trade union may ask for in their negotiations with an employer.

Factors affecting the strength of a trade union

Among the factors that gives a trade union bargaining strength are:

- **A high level of economic activity.** If output and income in a country are increasing, most industries are likely to be doing well, and so should be able to improve the pay and conditions of workers. When output reaches high levels and most people who want to work are employed, firms will be competing for workers. To keep their existing workers and to recruit more workers, firms are likely to be more willing to agree to union requests for higher pay and better working conditions.

- **A high number of members.** The more members a union has, the more funds it is likely to have to finance its activities. Also, the employers will find it difficult to replace union labour by non-union labour when so many workers belong to the union.

- **A high level of skill.** Unions representing skilled workers are in a relatively strong position, as it can be difficult to replace their workers with other skilled workers and expensive to train unskilled workers.

- **A consistent demand for the product produced by the workers.** Unions that represent workers making goods and services that are essential to consumers are in a strong position to bargain.

- **Favourable government legislation.** A union will be in a stronger position if laws allow trade unions to take industrial action.

Industrial action

If negotiations break down on wage claims, or disputes occur over working conditions, a trade union can take **industrial action** in support of its claim. Industrial action includes an overtime ban, with workers refusing to work longer than their contracted hours. Workers may also 'work to rule'. This involves workers undertaking the tasks required by their contracts only.

The most common form of industrial action is a **strike**. A strike involves workers withdrawing their labour. A strike can be official or unofficial. An official strike is one which is approved and organised by the union. In contrast, an unofficial strike is one which has not been approved by the union. This can occur when the strike is called by local union representatives and is over before the union has the time to approve it, or in the cases when the union does not agree with the action.

> **KEY TERMS**
>
> **industrial action:** when workers disrupt production to put pressure on employers to agree to their demands.
>
> **strike:** a group of workers stopping work to put pressure on an employer to agree to their demands.

Figure 17.5: If workers are unable to negotiate successfully with employers, they may take industrial action

ACTIVITY 17.5

In each case, decide which union is likely to be more successful, if it takes strike action.

1   A trade union representing firefighters or a union representing flower sellers.

2   A trade union representing skilled workers or a union representing unskilled workers.

3   A trade union striking during a period of high unemployment or a union striking during a period of low unemployment.

Discuss your decisions with the rest of the class.

Discrimination

Discrimination occurs when a group of workers is treated unfavourably in terms of employment, the wage rate, the training received and/or promotional opportunities. For example, some employers may be reluctant to employ workers approaching retirement age or workers beyond retirement age. The lower demand will result in lower pay, as shown in Figure 17.6.

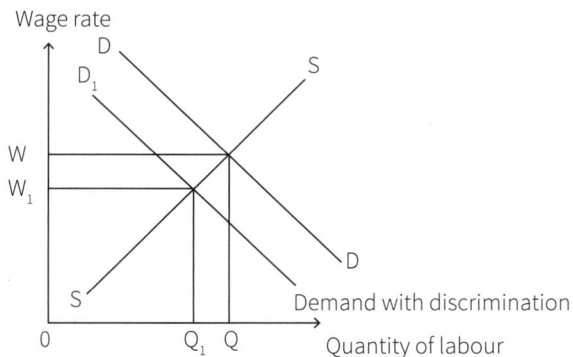

Figure 17.6: The effect of discrimination

Increasingly, governments are making such discrimination illegal. Nevertheless, throughout the world, some groups of workers, including female workers, continue to face discrimination in the workplace.

Government policy

Government policies affect wages in a variety of ways. A government clearly influences the wages of those workers whom it employs in the public sector. Its policies also influence wages in the private sector. Those policies, which promote economic growth, tend to push up wages throughout the economy as they increase demand for labour.

Specific government policies may have an impact on particular occupations. For example, if a government introduced a law requiring car drivers to take a driving test every ten years, demand for driving instructors would be likely to rise, pushing up their wages.

Government labour market policies, of course, directly affect wages. One of the best-known labour market policies is a **national minimum wage (NMW)**. Such a policy imposes a wage floor, making it illegal to pay a wage rate below that. The aims behind a national minimum wage are to raise the pay of low-paid workers and reduce poverty. To have any impact on wages, however, a NMW must be set above the market equilibrium wage rate. This has led some economists and politicians to argue that an NMW may cause unemployment.

Figure 17.7 shows a NMW raising the wage rate from W to W_1, but this causes unemployment since the supply of people wanting to work at this wage rate exceeds demand for workers' labour.

Other economists argue that a NMW can raise both the wage rate and employment. They think that paying a higher wage to workers will raise their motivation and hence their productivity. This, combined with higher demand for products arising from higher wages, can increase demand for labour.

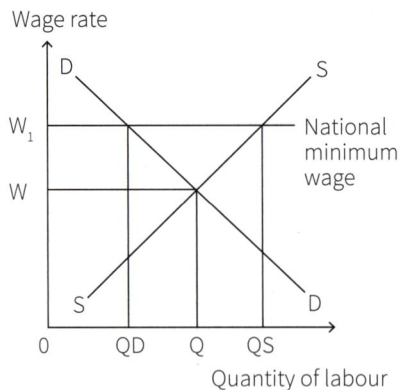

Figure 17.7: A national minimum wage causing unemployment

Figure 17.8 shows that if demand for labour does increase, the equilibrium wage rate may be equal to NMW. The introduction of a NMW may encourage some workers who were previously being paid a wage at or just above that level to press for a wage rise to maintain their wage differential.

> **KEY TERM**
>
> **national minimum wage (NMW):** a minimum rate of wage for an hour's work, fixed by the government for the whole economy.

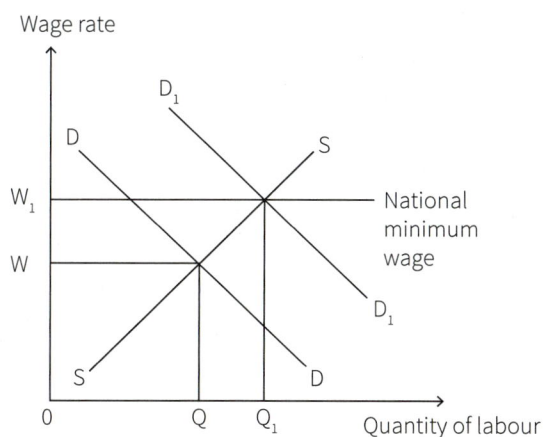

Figure 17.8: A national minimum wage with rising employment

LINK

A minimum wage is a minimum price of labour. Chapter 14.3 (Government interventions to address market failure – Maximum and minimum prices in product markets) examines the effects of setting a minimum price.

Differences in the wages of different groups of workers

Levels of skills of workers

Unskilled workers are generally paid less than skilled workers. Demand for skilled workers is high, while their supply is low. There are two main influences on the demand for workers. One is the amount of output they can produce and the other is the price for which that output can be sold. Skilled workers are usually highly productive, producing both a high quantity and a high quality of output per hour. Also, the supply of skilled workers is usually lower than that of unskilled workers.

Economic sector workers

The supply of workers in the primary and secondary sectors varies. In a number of countries, including some Asian and African countries, there is a surplus of **primary sector** workers which results in lower primary sector wages. The demand for and price of products made by **secondary sector** industries tend to increase at a more rapid rate than those made by primary sector industries. This helps to keep the demand for secondary sectors workers high, relative to primary sector workers. There are, of course, some highly paid primary sector workers. For example, in the oil industry some workers are paid high wages partly because of the high demand for oil.

The wages of workers in the **tertiary sector** vary. Some in the hospitality industry and the care industry are relatively low paid (see Figure 17.9). Those in tertiary sector jobs which require high skills, such as surgeons and lawyers, and those in jobs where demand for the service provided is expanding, such as sustainability managers and data analysts, are usually relatively highly paid.

KEY TERMS

primary sector: covers agriculture, fishing, forestry, mining and other industries which extract natural resources.

secondary sector: covers manufacturing and construction industries.

tertiary sector: covers industries which provide services.

Figure 17.9: Some workers in the hospitality industry are low-paid

Discrimination between workers

Female workers are (on average) still paid less than male workers. One reason for this is that females tend to work for fewer hours than males. Even when hourly wage rates are considered, female workers are paid less than males. The International Labour Organisation's Global Wage Report 2018/19 mentions that women are paid, on average, 20% less than men.

The gender pay gap varies between countries. The Organisation for Economic Co-operation and Development (OECD) reported that the gender pay gap in the Republic of Korea was 31.2% but only 1.2% in Belgium. There are a number of reasons why female workers may earn less than male workers:

- Female workers tend to be less well qualified than male workers, but this is changing in a number of countries with more females now going to university than males.

- Female workers tend to be more heavily concentrated in low-paid occupations.

- They are less likely to belong to trade unions and professional bodies.

- They are still more likely than men to take time out of the labour force to undertake caring responsibilities which can result in women losing out on promotion.

- In some countries, social attitudes make it harder for female workers to find employment.

Private or public sector workers

Demand and supply of workers in the private and public sectors vary among countries. In some countries the public sector is expanding, while in others it is contracting. A number of people like working in the public sector because there may be greater job security, longer holidays and better pensions than those offered in the private sector.

Public sector workers in many countries, including the UK and India, are more likely to belong to a trade union or professional organisation than private sector workers. In some cases, this can be attributed to the fact that the governments are more willing to negotiate with trade unions than private sector employers. In other cases, it is because public sector workers find it easier to get together to operate as one bargaining body.

Public sector workers also tend to be affected by government labour market policies more than private sector workers. Labour market policies may or may not raise wages. A government is, for example, likely to ensure that all its workers are paid at, or above, a national minimum wage (NMW), whereas some private sector firms may seek to find ways round such legislation. If, however, a government introduces a policy to hold down wage rises in an attempt to reduce inflationary pressure, it is in a stronger position to restrict the wage rises of its own workers.

ACTIVITY 17.6

In 2015, female workers in Chile earned 18% less than male workers. By 2022, the gender pay gap had narrowed to 12%. There had been improvements in the education of children, particularly the education of girls. In 2022, a higher proportion of females aged 25–34 had a university degree than males, 37% compared to 30%. Among all working age groups, however, a higher proportion of women were in low-paid jobs than men and fewer were in leadership roles.

1   Identify two possible reasons for a smaller proportion of working women than men in Chile being in leadership roles.

2   Explain why 'improvements in the education of children, particularly the education of girls' may reduce a gender pay gap.

Write your answers in your notebook.

17.3 Effects of changes in demand and supply in the labour market

Change in demand and supply of labour

The main reason for a rise or, less commonly, fall in earnings is a change in demand and/or supply of labour. Other reasons include changes in the stages of production, in bargaining power, in government policies and in public opinion.

Changes in the demand for labour

If demand for labour increases, earnings are likely to rise. The wage rate may be pushed up and bonuses increased. In addition, more overtime may become available, and it may be paid at a higher rate too. Figure 17.10 shows the wage rate for bricklayers being driven up by an increase in demand for their labour.

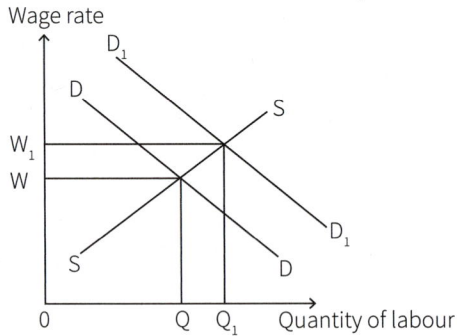

Figure 17.10: The effect of an increase in the demand for bricklayers' labour

What can cause demand for labour to increase? There are three main causes:

- **An increased demand for the product.** Demand for labour is a *derived demand*. The higher the demand for products, the greater is the number of workers employed.

- **A rise in labour productivity.** Higher productivity increases the return from hiring workers.

- **A rise in the price of capital.** In some occupations, it is possible to substitute labour for capital in the production process.

In recent years, the pay of airline pilots has been rising throughout the world. More and more people are travelling by plane for both business and leisure, and so the demand for the services of pilots is increasing. In contrast, in many countries the wages of agricultural workers have been falling relative to the wages of other workers. Demand for their labour has been declining, in part because it has become easier to replace agricultural workers with capital (machines).

Changes in the supply of labour

A decrease in the supply of labour for a particular occupation or sector would be expected to raise the wage rate. Among the factors that could cause a decrease in the supply of workers are:

- **A fall in the size of the labour force.** If there are fewer workers, in general it is likely that an individual business will find it more difficult to recruit workers.

- **A rise in the qualifications or length of training required to do the job.** This will reduce the number of people eligible for the job.

- **A reduction in the non-wage benefits of a job.** If, for example, the working hours or risks involved in doing a job increase, fewer people are likely to be willing to do it.

- **A rise in the wage or non-wage benefits in other jobs.** Such a change would encourage some workers to switch from one occupation to another.

Consider the situation shown in Figure 17.11. One of the reasons the wage for accountants, for example, has risen is that the qualifications to do the job have increased. The figure shows the wage rate of accountants being driven up by a decrease in the supply of their labour.

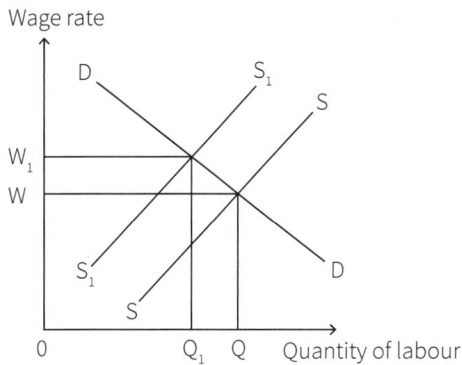

Figure 17.11: The effect of a decrease in the supply of accountants' labour

LINK

Changes in the supply of labour affect both the price of labour (wages) and the quantity of labour employed – see Chapter 17.2 (Wage determination and the reasons for differences in wages – Demand for and supply of labour).

The extent to which wages change

How much wage rates change due to a change in demand for, or supply of, labour is influenced not only by the size of the change, but also by the **elasticity of demand for labour** and the **elasticity of supply of labour**.

Figure 17.12 shows demand for labour increasing by the same amount in both cases, but the impact on the wage rate is much greater in (a) where both the demand for and supply of labour are inelastic.

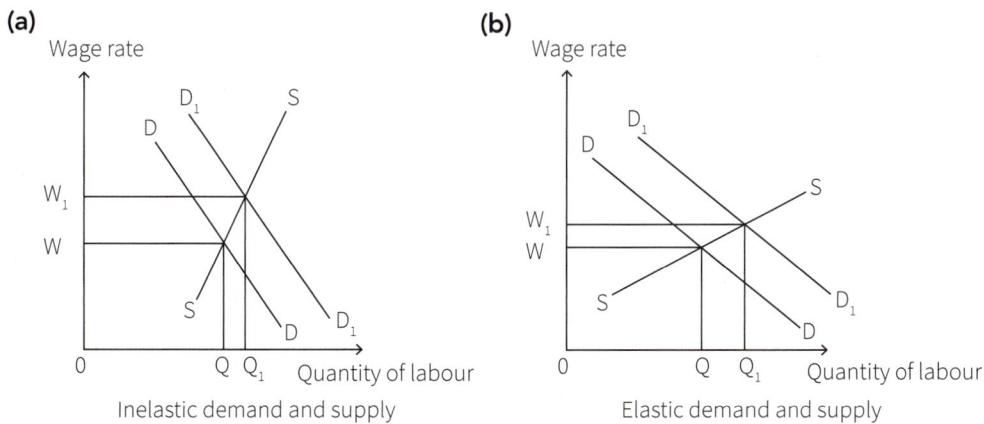

TIP

Always remember to use demand and supply analysis when analysing the differences in earnings between different occupations.

(a)

Inelastic demand and supply

(b)

Elastic demand and supply

Figure 17.12: The influence of elasticity on the effect of an increase in demand for labour

KEY TERMS

elasticity of demand for labour: a measure of the responsiveness of demand for labour to a change in the wage rate.

elasticity of supply of labour: a measure of the responsiveness of the supply of labour to a change in the wage rate.

The main determinants of elasticity of demand for and supply of labour are shown in Table 17.1.

Table 17.1: Main determinants of elasticity of demand for and supply of labour

Elasticity of demand for labour	Elasticity of supply of labour
The proportion of labour costs in total costs. If labour costs form a large proportion of total costs, a change in wages would have a significant impact on costs and so demand would be elastic.	**The qualifications and skills required.** The more qualifications and skills needed, the more inelastic supply will be. For example, a large increase in the wage paid to neurosurgeons will not have much effect on the supply of labour. This is especially true in the short run, as it will take years to gain the required qualifications and experience.
The ease with which labour can be substituted by capital. If it is easy to replace workers with machines, demand would again be elastic.	**The length of training period.** A long period of training may put some people off the occupation. It will also mean that there will be a delay before those who are willing to take it up are fully qualified to join the labour force. Both effects make the supply of labour inelastic.
The elasticity of demand for the product produced. A rise in wages increases costs of production which, in turn, raises the price of the product. This causes demand for the product to contract and demand for labour to fall. The more elastic the demand for the product is, the greater the fall in demand for it and so for workers, making demand for labour elastic.	**The level of employment.** If most workers are employed already, the supply of labour to any particular occupation is likely to be inelastic. An employer may have to raise the wage rate significantly to attract more workers and encourage the workers employed in other occupations to switch jobs.
The time period. Demand for labour is usually more elastic in the long run as there is more time for firms/producers to change their methods of production.	**The mobility of labour.** The easier workers find it to change jobs, or to move from one area to another, the easier it will be for an employer to recruit more labour by raising the wage rate. Thus, higher mobility makes the supply elastic.
	The degree of vocation. The stronger the attachment of workers to their jobs, the more inelastic supply tends to be in case of a decrease in wage rate.
	The time period. Supply of labour tends to become more elastic over time. This is because it gives workers more time to notice wage changes and to gain any qualifications or undertake any training needed for a new job.

KEY TERM

mobility of labour: the ability of labour to change where or in which occupation it works.

In which of the following occupations is the demand for labour likely to be elastic?

1   An occupation in which technical progress is continually developing inexpensive labour-saving techniques.

2   An occupation which produces a product with inelastic demand.

3   An occupation belonging to a labour-intensive industry.

4   An occupation where labour costs form a small proportion of total costs.

Share your answers with another student.

Changes in the stages of production

As previously noted, people working in the primary sector may be less well paid than those who work in secondary and tertiary sectors. This is because the workers in the primary sector tend to be less skilled and have fewer qualifications. In addition, as an economy develops, the demand for primary sector workers usually declines. Demand for workers in the secondary sector increases first, followed by demand for workers in the tertiary sector. Some of the best-paid workers are employed in the tertiary sector. For example, some judges and some surgeons receive high wages. Demand for a number of services rises with income and high qualifications needed to carry out a number of jobs in the tertiary sector. Of course, there are some high-paid workers in the primary sector and some low-paid workers in the tertiary sector. For example, an engineer working in the oil industry is likely to earn more than a shop assistant.

Changes in bargaining strength

A change in a trade union's bargaining power or willingness to take industrial action can affect earnings. If, for example, a government removes a ban on agricultural workers forming unions collectively, it would be expected that the wage rate of agricultural workers would rise. In recent years, the greater willingness of UK NHS workers to threaten industrial action is perceived as one reason why their pay has increased.

Changes in government policy

The pay of public sector workers is likely to rise if the government decides to expand the public sector. In contrast, a government decision to reduce road building may reduce the wages of those working for road construction firms in the private sector. Among the other ways governments can change wage rates are:

* Raising the national minimum wage will increase the pay of low-paid workers.

* Despite the rise in supply, improved education may actually raise the wages of skilled workers, as it may increase the demand more than the supply. This is because employing more skilled workers should reduce costs of production and increase international competitiveness. If this is the case, demand for products

produced by the country's firms should increase and more multinational companies (MNCs) may be attracted to set up their franchises in the country.

- Government policies on immigration can also affect wages. Making it easier for people from abroad to live and work in the country should increase the supply of labour. For example, if a country is short of information and communication technology (ICT) workers, giving more permits to foreign workers should increase the supply of ICT workers and may hold down wage rises too.

- The introduction of government anti-discrimination laws may help to increase the career prospects and wages of disadvantaged groups. Such legislation works, in part, by changing public opinion. In many countries, attitudes to female workers have become more favourable, and the capabilities and services of female workers are being valued more. This, combined with a rise in the education of women, has raised female workers' wages.

- Advances in technology can alter wage rates. In some cases, it can put downward pressure on wage rates by reducing demand for workers. For example, new technology in the banking industry has reduced the number of banking staff in a number of countries. In other cases, however, new technology can increase wages. For example, the development of online shopping in recent years has increased demand for the services of delivery drivers.

LINK

The role of multinational companies (MNCs) is covered in Chapter 34.3 (Multinational companies).

Changes in the earnings of individuals over time

The earnings of most individuals change over the course of their working life. For most workers, their earnings increase as they get older. This is because the longer people work, the more skilled and productive they tend to become. Their productivity increases because they gain experience and, in some cases, undertake training. Becoming more skilled increases a worker's chances of being promoted and achieving higher pay.

Some workers may switch employers to get higher pay. Others may agree to take on more responsibility for more pay. There is a chance, however, that earnings may fall with passage of time. Some older workers may decide to give up working overtime and some may switch to less demanding work. The firm or organisation that people work for, may experience financial difficulties, and as a result it may reduce wages and cut bonuses.

REFLECTION

Are you able to draw and interpret diagrams that show wage determination and how changes in the demand and supply in the labour market can affect wages? What will you do to increase your skill?

17.4 Mobility of labour

The mobility of labour influences wage differentials. The more mobile workers are, the more elastic the supply of labour is likely to be. The mobility of labour varies both in terms of workers changing where they work (**geographical mobility**) and changing what work they do (**occupational mobility**). Some workers may find it easier to move from one area of the country to another, or from one country to another

KEY TERMS

geographical mobility: the ability to move from one location to another.

occupational mobility: the ability to switch between occupations.

(geographical mobility), and some may find it easier to switch from one type of job to another type (occupational mobility).

Causes and consequences of changes in geographical and occupational mobility of labour

- **Differences in the price and availability of housing in different areas and countries.** Workers who lose their jobs in less affluent areas may not be able to take up jobs in rich areas because they cannot afford or find housing there.

- **Family ties.** People may be reluctant to leave the country they are currently living in because they do not want to move away from friends and relatives.

- **Differences in educational systems in different areas and countries.** People may not be willing to move to a job elsewhere if it disrupts their children's education.

- **Lack of information.** People without jobs, or those in lower-income jobs, may stay where they are because they are unaware of job opportunities elsewhere.

- **Restrictions on the movement of workers.** It is often necessary to obtain a work visa to work in another country and these can be limited in supply.

There are also a number of causes of occupational immobility. Again, there may be a lack of information about vacancies in other types of jobs. The main cause, however, is a lack of appropriate skills and qualifications. A shortage of doctors cannot be solved by hiring bus drivers!

The more mobile labour becomes, the quicker labour and product markets can change in response to changes in market conditions. For example, demand for train travel may increase while demand for bus travel decreases. If bus drivers can switch easily to become train drivers, the supply of train travel may be able to respond to the higher demand relatively quickly.

An increase in the mobility of labour is also likely to reduce unemployment as workers will be more able to move from declining to expanding industries.

LINK

Chapter 27.3 (Types and causes of unemployment – Structural unexmployment) explains how measures to increase labour mobility may reduce unemployment.

ECONOMICS IN ACTION

Changes in the wages of US plumbers and teachers

Figure 17.13: A plumber in the USA may earn more than a teacher

Economists analyse changes in wage differentials between different groups of workers and make predictions about future changes. Figure 17.14 shows the gap between some low-paid and some high-paid workers in the USA narrowed between 2012 and 2022. For example, the pay of US plumbers increased by more than the pay of US teachers (see Figure 17.13). The increase in demand for plumbers increased by more than the supply of plumbers, creating a shortage of plumbers. In contrast, the supply of some skilled workers, such as teachers, has increased by more than demand (see Figure 17.14).

CONTINUED

Some economists predict that the development of artificial intelligence (AI) may reduce the wage gap between occupations in related occupations. For example, the wage gap between doctors and nurses and doctors and pharmacists may narrow as AI may reduce the training needed to decide on the causes of medical problems, the treatment required and, in some cases, to carry out medical procedures.

1   Why may the supply of skilled workers increase?

2   Why may the development of AI increase worker satisfaction?

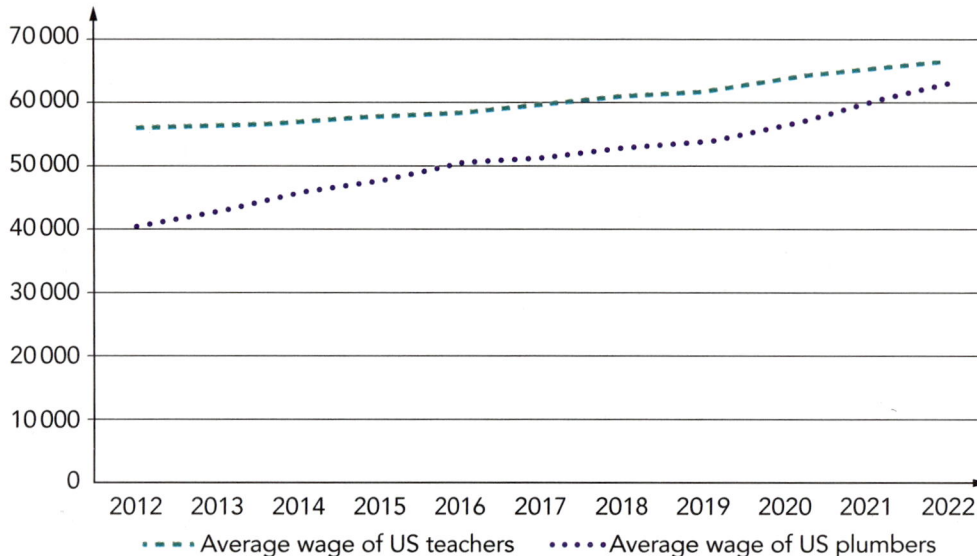

Figure 17.14: Average wages of US teachers and plumbers, 2012–2022

17.5 Division of labour

Division of labour occurs when workers specialise in one aspect of a role or task. Instead of producing the whole good or service, a worker carries out one particular task. There are a number of reasons why division of labour may occur.

One is that workers can specialise in the task they are best at, and by doing this task over and over again, they become very good at it – practice makes perfect. This should mean that output per worker increases. Concentrating on a particular task means that workers can be trained more quickly and providing training to handle a full range of equipment may not be necessary. Time may be saved as workers will not have to move from one job to another. Breaking down the production process into a number of tasks may also make it easier to design machinery, enabling the use of workers alongside.

Table 17.2 shows the advantages and disadvantages of division of labour.

KEY TERM

division of labour: workers specialising in particular tasks.

Table 17.2: Advantages and disadvantages of division of labour

Advantages	Disadvantages
Workers who specialise in particular tasks can become very skilled. Output per worker may increase, leading to lower cost per unit produced.	Workers may get bored repeating the same tasks day after day. This may lead to workers not taking care in their work and making mistakes. Output per work may fall, leading to higher cost per unit produced.
Workers with specialist skills may find they are in high demand. They may be able to earn high wages.	Workers may take more days off due to sickness and stay in jobs for shorter periods of time.
Concentrating on a particular task or job can enable workers to pursue their specific interests. For example, doctors who are interested in brain disorders and injuries may seek to specialise in neurology.	Where workers are absent, other workers may not have the training to cover their specialist tasks or jobs.
Specialising in less demanding jobs can reduce the pressure on workers. Some factory workers who have undertaken the same task for some years may be able to do it almost without thinking.	May not make full use of a worker's talents.
Total output and exports may increase.	If workers are only trained or practised in one job and demand for their skills falls, they may have problems finding another job.

There is no guarantee, however, that worker **specialisation** will reduce unit costs. In fact, there is a risk that specialisation may result in higher unit costs.

Whether division of labour will benefit an economy will depend on how it affects the cost of production and the quality of the products produced. If it does result in lower costs of production and higher quality, the economy may benefit from being able to produce and export more goods and services.

KEY TERM

specialisation: the concentration on particular products or tasks.

ACTIVITY 17.8

Rank the following educational workers, starting with the most specialised and finishing with the least specialised:

1 a teacher of 19th-century French history

2 a supply teacher who covers for absent teachers

3 a teacher of 19th-century history

4 a teacher of history

5 a teacher of history and geography.

Check your order with another student.

SUMMARY

You should now know:

- A person's choice of occupation is influenced by both wage and non-wage factors.

- The main reason for some occupations receiving higher earnings than others is because demand for their labour is higher, whilst supply of their labour is lower.

- A national minimum wage is likely to raise the wages of the low-paid, but its effect on unemployment are uncertain.

- Trade unions seek to protect and enhance workers' pay, working hours and working conditions through collective bargaining.

- Skilled workers are paid more than unskilled workers because they are more productive and are in shorter supply.

- Wages in the tertiary sector tend to rise more than in the secondary and primary sectors largely because of the expansion in the tertiary sector.

- The gender pay gap between male and female workers is declining.

- The extent of change in wage rates, as a result of a change in the demand for and supply of labour, is influenced by the elasticity of demand for and supply of labour.

- The quality and occupational mobility of labour can be increased by better education and training.

- The geographical mobility of labour may be increased by more housing and information about job vacancies.

- Division of labour influences the nature of work, cost per unit produced and output.

Chapter 17 practice questions

1   What is a non-wage factor that may influence a person's choice of occupation?

   A   bonuses

   B   fringe benefits

   C   overtime payments

   D   salary   [1]

2 Point x in the diagram shows the market for electricians in a country. There is an increase in the number of people who train as electricians. What is the new equilibrium point?

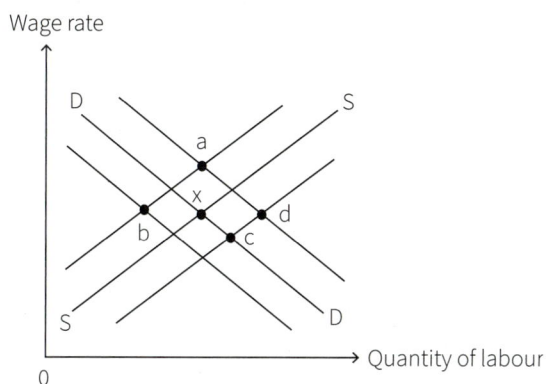

A a

B b

C c

D d   [1]

3 In which circumstance is a trade union most likely to be successful in raising the wages of its members?

A it is easy to replace workers with machines

B it is easy to replace unionised labour with non-unionised labour

C the profits of the firms in the industry are low

D the share of labour costs in total costs is low   [1]

4 What does the derived demand for labour depend on?

A demand for the product produced by workers

B government revenue from taxes on workers' wages

C productivity of workers

D wages paid to workers   [1]

5 What would reduce labour mobility?

A a decrease in house prices

B a decrease in labour market information

C an increase in labour flexibility

D an increase in the skills gained by workers   [1]

Total: [5]

6   a   Identify how wages are determined in a free market.   [2]

    b   Explain **two** benefits a chef may gain from specialising
        in cooking one type of food such as Thai food.   [4]

    c   Analyse, using a demand and supply diagram, how an increase
        in demand for restaurant meals may affect the wages that chefs are paid.   [6]

    d   Discuss whether or not an increase in the wage rate paid
        to chefs will encourage more people to become chefs.   [8]

        Total: [20]

CHECK YOUR PROGRESS

How well do you think you have achieved the learning intentions for this chapter?
Give yourself a score from 1 (still need a lot of practice) to 5 (feeling very confident)
for each learning intention. Provide an example to support your score.

Now I can...	Score	Example
analyse the wage and non-wage factors that influence an individual's choice of occupation		
discuss, using demand and supply diagrams, the influences on wage determination: demand and supply of labour, trade unions and their relative bargaining power, discrimination and government policy		
explain the reasons for differences in wages		
discuss how the reasons for differences in wages influence the wages of workers		
explain the causes and consequences of changes in the occupational and geographical mobility of labour		
define the division of labour (worker specialisation)		
discuss the advantages and disadvantages of division of labour (worker specialisation).		

Firms

Introduction

In every country, there are firms of different sizes, producing in different sectors of the economy. Each year new firms are set up. Some of these go out of business quickly, while others grow, sometimes by merging, to become large firms with names you are probably familiar with. Large firms can have significant advantages, but there are cases where small firms are still able to compete with them.

ECONOMICS IN CONTEXT

From the mine to the shop

Figure 18.1: A goldsmith makes jewellery in a small family-run business in Pakistan

In 2023, a group of firms, including a large foreign private sector firm and three state-owned enterprises, were planning to mine for copper and gold in Reko Diq, Balochistan, Pakistan. Most mining firms are large firms, often employing thousands of workers and making use of large quantities of capital equipment.

Some of the gold mined will be used by Pakistani firms to produce gold jewellery and gold watches (see Figure 18.1). Many jewellery firms are relatively small, employing less than 50 workers. Some jewellery-producing firms sell their jewellery to retail jewellers while others sell directly to consumers. One such firm is Hanif Jewellers. This firm was started in 1978 in Lahore. Over the years, the firm has grown in size, producing more high-quality jewellery and luxury watches and opening new stores in Lahore, Islamabad and Dubai.

Discuss in a pair or group:

1   Why do some firms grow in size over time?

2   Do you think you would prefer to be in charge of a small or a large firm?

18.1 Different types of firms

Industries consist of firms producing the same good or service. The car **industry**, for example, includes firms such as Geely, Tata Motors and Toyota. A firm is a business entity, also sometimes referred to as a business organisation. Firms can have a number of plants. A plant is a production unit or workplace such as a factory, farm, office or branch. A firm may own several plants. The major car firms have factories throughout the world and the major banks have branches throughout the world. Figure 18.2 shows the level of provision of services in the banking industry.

> **KEY TERM**
>
> **industry:** a group of firms producing the same product.

Banking industry

↓

Bank

↓

Branch

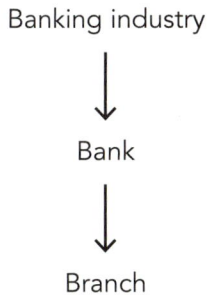

Figure 18.2: Production in the banking industry

Primary, secondary and tertiary sector firms

Industries and their firms and plants operate at different stages of production.

- The **primary sector** is the first stage of production. It includes firms in industries, such as agriculture, coal mining and forestry, involved in the extraction and collection of raw materials.

- The **secondary sector** is involved with the processing of raw materials into semi-finished and finished goods – both capital and consumer goods. It covers manufacturing and construction (see Figure 18.3). The building, clothing and steel industries are in this sector.

- The third stage of production is the **tertiary sector**. Firms in industries producing services such as banking, insurance and tourism are part of this sector. The tertiary sector also includes those service industries which are involved with the collection, processing and transmission of information – essentially information technology.

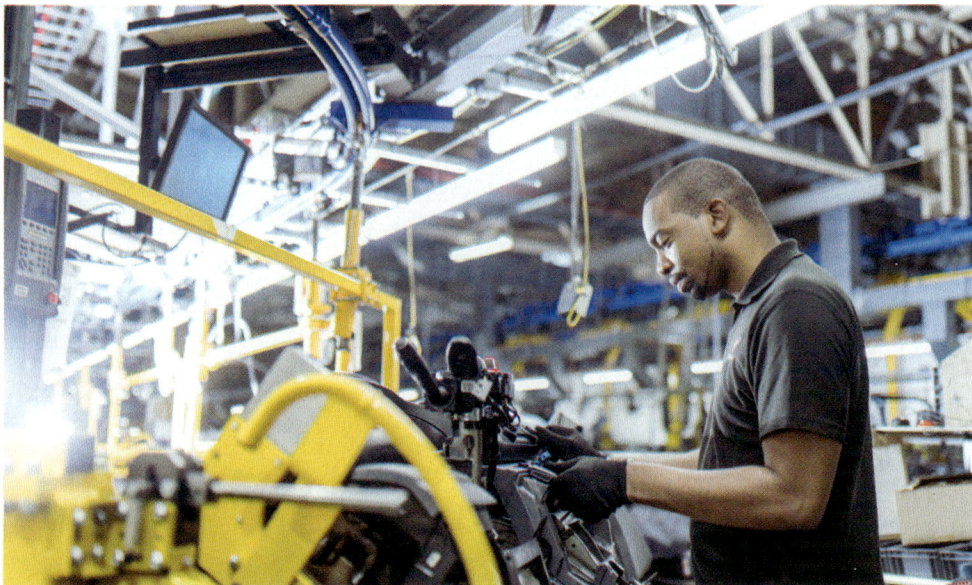

Figure 18.3: Car assembly is in the secondary sector

> **KEY TERMS**
>
> **primary sector:** covers agriculture, fishing, forestry, mining and other industries which extract natural resources.
>
> **secondary sector:** covers manufacturing and construction industries.
>
> **tertiary sector:** covers industries which provide services.

As the income of economies grow, their industrial structure usually changes. Low-income countries often have a large proportion of their output accounted for and the labour force employed in industries in the primary sector. As they develop, the secondary sector becomes more important, and gradually the tertiary sector accounts for most of their output and employment. Table 18.1 shows the contribution to output of the three sectors in five selected countries in 2023.

Table 18.1: Percentage contribution to selected countries' output by different industrial sectors in 2023

Country	Primary %	Secondary %	Tertiary %
Pakistan	20	21	59
India	15	25	60
China	7	40	53
USA	1	18	81
Luxembourg	1	11	87

ACTIVITY 18.1

Table 18.2 shows a list of industries. Decide the sector to which each industry belongs. Copy and complete the table.

Share your answers with another student.

Table 18.2

Industry	Sector
1 chemicals	
2 education	
3 fishing	
4 retailing	
5 telecommunications	
6 transport	

LINKS

The difference between the private sector and the public sector is discussed in Chapter 12.2 (Market economic system – Private and public sectors). Some firms move from the private to the public sector, and others move from the public sector to the private sector – see Chapter 14.3 (Government intervention to address market failure – Nationalisation and Privatisation).

Private sector and public sector firms

In a market economic system, most firms are in the private sector. These firms are owned by an entrepreneur or groups of entrepreneurs pursuing their own interests, including profit. In contrast, firms in the public sector (state-owned enterprises) are owned by the government and are run in the interest of the whole country. In a mixed economic system, firms are in both the private and public sectors.

Advantages and disadvantages of small and large firms

Small firms produce a lower output and employ fewer factors of production than large firms. A large firm will be likely to have a higher **total cost** than a small firm. How much it costs to produce each unit it produces (**average total cost**), however, may be lower. Indeed, a lower average total cost is one of the advantages often claimed for large firms. Table 18.3 shows some of the possible advantages and disadvantages of small firms and large firms.

KEY TERMS

total cost: the total amount spent on the factors of production used to produce a product.

average total cost: total cost divided by output.

Table 18.3: Advantages and disadvantages of small and large firms

Small firms	Large firms
Advantages	
• Able to cater for individual needs and provide personal services such as in hairdressing	• May be able to charge a low price due to low average total cost
• Relatively easy to manage	• May have access to large financial capital
• May be able to adjust quickly to changes in market conditions	• Banks tend to be more willing to lend to large firms than small firms
• May pick up on changes in demand quickly due to close contact with consumers	• May be able to employ specialist managers
• May be able to cooperate with other small firms, for example small farms may share combine harvesters	• May be able drive down the prices paid to suppliers
• May be able to specialise in part of the market, such as luxury soap	• May have a global reputation
• Can concentrate on handmade goods which do not require expensive capital equipment	• May be able to spread risks by producing a variety of products
• May be subsidised by the government as small firms provide jobs, develop skills of entrepreneurs and may have the potential to grow into large firms	• Can use large amounts of capital equipment
	• May be subsidised by the government to stop the firms going out of business which may cause a large increase in unemployment
• Workers employed may enjoy doing a variety of tasks	• Workers can engage in division of labour
Disadvantages	
• Price may be high due to high average total cost	• May be difficult to control
• Lack of financial capital. Banks may be reluctant to lend to small firms	• May not have a close relationship with workers
• Output may be too small to employ large, efficient capital equipment	• May be slow to respond to changes in market conditions
• Firm's name may not be well known	• If the firm gains control of the market, it may raise the price

ACTIVITY 18.2

Decide which of the following circumstances are likely to explain the existence of a number of small firms in an industry:

1   the need for high expenditure on research and development

2   low barriers to entry and exit

3   low start-up costs

4   a global market

5   discounts given for bulk buying.

Take turns to explain your answers to another student.

DISCUSSION

Discuss whether you would prefer to buy a coffee from a small coffee shop or a branch of a large firm with coffee shops throughout the world.

18.2 Mergers of firms

There are two ways a firm can increase in size. Internal growth involves a firm increasing the market for its current products or diversifying into other products. This type of growth may occur through increasing the size of existing plants or by opening new ones. For example, Starbucks, the speciality coffee retailer, has grown to a large size by opening more and more stores throughout the world.

External growth involves the firm joining with another firm or firms to form one firm through a merger or a takeover. The three main types of merger are:

1   A **horizontal merger** is the merger of two firms at the same stage of production, producing the same product, for example, the merger of two car producers or two TV companies.

2   A **vertical merger** occurs when a firm merges with another firm involved with the production of the same product, but at a different stage of production. It can take the form of vertical merger backwards or vertical merger forwards.

- **Vertical merger backwards** is when a firm merges with a firm that is the source of its supply of raw materials, components or the products it sells. For example, a supermarket chain may take over a bakery and a tyre manufacturer merge with a producer of rubber.

- **Vertical merger forwards** is when a firm merges with, or takes over, a market outlet. For instance, a wind farm buying an electricity supplier, and an airline merging with a tour operator.

3   A **conglomerate merger** involves the merger of two firms making different products. For example, an electricity company may merge with a travel company and an insurance company may merge with a chocolate producer.

KEY TERMS

horizontal merger: the merger of firms producing the same product and at the same stage of production.

vertical merger: the merger of one firm with another firm that either provides an outlet for its products or supplies it with raw materials, components or the products it sells.

vertical merger backwards: a merger with a firm at an earlier stage of the supply chain.

vertical merger forwards: a merger with a firm at a later stage of the supply chain.

conglomerate merger: a merger between firms producing different products.

The advantages and disadvantages of the different types of mergers are summarised in Table 18.4.

Table 18.4: Advantages and disadvantages of horizontal, vertical and conglomerate mergers

Type of merger	Advantages	Disadvantages
Horizontal	• Merger may lead to greater economies of scale enabling the firm to produce at lower average cost – consumer may benefit from reduced prices • Increases the merged firm's market share • Merger with another firm producing the same product may remove direct competitor from the market • If both firms are not using their resources fully, merging could result in **rationalisation**. Redundant resources, such as one office could be sold and expenditure could be saved by reducing the number of managerial staff	• May lead to reduced choice for consumers • Merged firm may use greater market power to push up prices • Merged firm may experience diseconomies of scale – consumers may experience higher prices and poorer quality • Difficult to control a large firm • Difficult to integrate the merged firms if their management structures are different or they are located some distance apart

Vertical	• Backwards merger:
	  • ensures adequate supply of good-quality raw materials at a reasonable price
	  • restricts access of rival firms to supplies
	• Forwards merger:
	  • ensures there are sufficient outlets for the products and the products are stored and displayed well in high-quality outlets
	  • may lead to development and marketing of new products
		• Managers of merged firms may not be familiar with, for example, running a market outlet
		
		• Merged firms may be of different sizes which may require the buying in of some supplies from other firms or the selling of supplies to other firms

Conglomerate	• Allows merged firm to diversify • Spreads a firm's risk and may enable it to continue its growth even if the market of one of its products is declining	• Managing a firm producing a range of products can be very challenging • Some merged firms may decide to demerge, that is divide into two or more firms

KEY TERM

rationalisation: eliminating unnecessary equipment and plant to make a firm more efficient.

LINK

How average total cost is calculated is explained in Chapter 20.1 (Calculating the costs of production – Total cost and average total cost).

ACTIVITY 18.3

There are proposed mergers between:

1   a carpet-producing firm and an insurance firm

2   a chocolate producer and a large cocoa firm.

Produce a leaflet explaining in both cases what type of merger would be involved, one advantage and one disadvantage for consumers and one advantage and one disadvantage for the firms of the proposed mergers.

REFLECTION

Consider how you might evaluate arguments for and against different economic decisions and outcomes. What ways could you use to reinforce your understanding of the advantages and disadvantages of different aspects of economics? Did the leaflet you produced in Activity 18.3 help you to understand the possible effects of a decision, in this case a merger?

18.3 Economies and diseconomies of scale

Economies of scale are the advantages, in the form of lower average total cost (ATC) in the **long run** of producing on a larger scale. When economists and entrepreneurs talk about economies of scale, they are usually referring to **internal economies of scale**. These are the advantages gained by an individual firm from increasing its size, that is having larger or more plants. **External economies of scale** are the advantages available to all the firms in an industry, resulting from the growth of the industry.

Diseconomies of scale are essentially the disadvantages of 'being too large'. A firm that increases its scale of operation to a point where it encounters rising long run average total cost is said to be experiencing **internal diseconomies of scale**. **External diseconomies of scale** arise from an industry being too large, causing the firms within the industry to experience higher long run average total cost.

Using diagrams to illustrate economies and diseconomies of scale

Internal economies and diseconomies of scale

As a firm or industry changes its scale of production, its average costs are likely to change. Figure 18.4 shows the usual U-shaped average total costs (ATC) curve. Average total costs fall at first, reach an optimum point and then rise.

KEY TERMS

long run: the time period when all factors of production can be changed and all costs are variable.

internal economies of scale: lower average total cost resulting from a firm growing in size.

external economies of scale: lower average total cost resulting from an industry growing in size.

internal diseconomies of scale: higher average total cost arising from a firm growing too large.

external diseconomies of scale: higher average total cost arising from an industry growing too large.

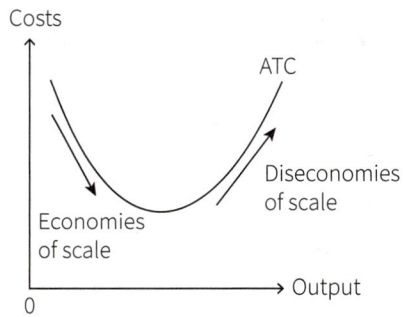

Figure 18.4: Internal economies and diseconomies of scale

In very capital-intensive industries, such as oil refining, ATC may fall over a considerable range of output, as shown in Figure 18.5.

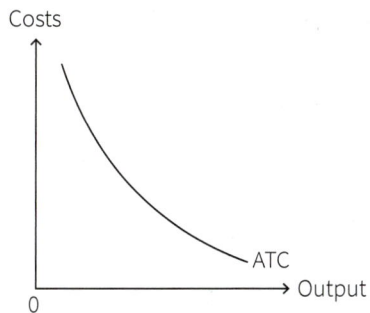

Figure 18.5: Downward-sloping ATC curve

In other cases, average total costs may fall relatively quickly to their lowest point (the minimum efficient scale) and then remain constant over a large range of output. This would give an L-shaped ATC curve, as shown in Figure 18.6.

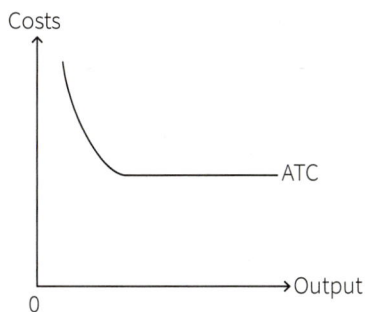

Figure 18.6: L-shaped ATC curve

External economies and diseconomies of scale

External economies and diseconomies of scale have a different effect on a firm's ATC curve. In the case of external economies of scale, a firm's average total cost will be reduced not by changes in the firm's output, but by changes in its industry's output. Figure 18.7 shows how external economies of scale result in a downward shift of a firm's ATC curve.

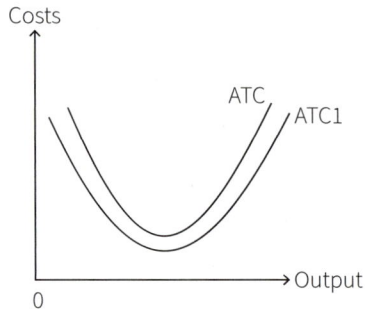

Figure 18.7: The effect of external economies of scale

In contrast, external diseconomies of scale will raise a firm's ATC curve at each and every level of output, as shown in Figure 18.8.

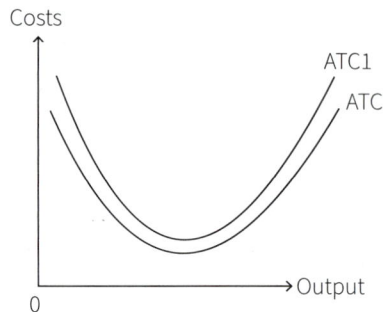

Figure 18.8: The effect of external diseconomies of scale

How economies of scale may affect a firm or industry

Types of internal economies of scale

As a firm increases its scale of production, different types of internal economies will cause the average total cost to fall. These include:

- **Purchasing economies.** These are probably the best-known type and are also called buying economies. Large firms that buy raw materials in bulk and place large orders for capital equipment usually receive a discount. This means that they pay less for each item purchased. They may also receive better treatment than small firms in terms of quality of the raw materials and capital equipment sold and the speed of delivery. This is because the suppliers will be anxious to keep such large customers.

- **Selling economies.** The total cost of processing orders, packing the goods and transporting them does not rise in line with the number of orders. For instance, it costs less than twice as much to send 10 000 washing machines to customers than it does to send 5 000 washing machines. A lorry that can transport 40 washing machines does not cost four times as much to operate as four vans which can carry 10 washing machines each.

- **Marketing economies.** A large volume of output can reduce the cost of finding out about consumer demand and advertising costs. The total cost of an advertising campaign can be spread over more units and, again, discounts may be secured. A full-page advertisement in a newspaper or magazine is usually less than twice the cost of a half-page advertisement.

- **Managerial economies.** Large firms can afford to employ specialist staff in key posts as they can spread their pay over a higher number of units. Employing specialist buyers, accountants, human resource managers and designers can increase the firm's efficiency, reduce costs of production, and raise demand and revenue.

- **Labour economies.** Large firms can take advantage of division of labour by enabling their workers to specialise in different aspects of the production process.

- **Financial economies.** Large firms usually find it easier and cheaper to raise finance. Banks tend to be more willing to lend to large firms because such firms are well known and have valuable assets to offer as collateral. Banks often charge large borrowers less per pound or dollar (any unit of currency) borrowed in order to attract them and because they know that the administrative costs of operating and processing large loans are not significantly higher than the costs of dealing with small loans. Large firms can also raise finance through selling shares, which is not an available option for sole traders and partnerships. Public limited companies can sell to the general public. The larger and better known the companies are, the more willing people are to buy their shares.

- **Technical economies.** The larger the output of a firm, the more viable it becomes to use large, technologically advanced machinery. Such machinery is likely to be efficient, producing output at a lower average cost than small firms can.

- **Research and development economies.** A large firm can have a research and development department, since running such a department can reduce average costs by developing more efficient methods of production and raise total revenue by developing new products.

- **Risk-bearing economies.** Larger firms usually produce a range of products. This enables them to spread the risks of trading. If the profitability of one of the products it produces falls, it can shift its resources to the production of more profitable products.

ACTIVITY 18.4

In a small group, decide the type of internal economies each of the following may be an example of:

1   A farmer using a combine harvester.

2   A pharmaceutical company setting up a laboratory to develop anti-AIDS drugs.

3   A supermarket chain employing an expert in chocolate to place its orders with suppliers.

4   A book publisher buying a large quantity of paper.

5   A soap manufacturer buying a two-minute advertisement on national television.

6   A car manufacturer borrowing from a bank at a low rate of interest.

Write down the type of internal economies in each case.

Internal diseconomies of scale

Growing beyond a certain output can cause a firm's average total cost to rise. Internal diseconomies may result from:

- **Difficulties controlling the firm.** Those managing a large firm may have difficulties supervising everything that is happening in the business. Management becomes more complex. A number of layers of management may be needed and there may be a need for more meetings. This can increase administrative costs and make the firm slower in responding to changes in market conditions.

- **Communication problems.** It can be difficult to ensure that everyone in a large firm has full knowledge about their duties and available opportunities, such as training. Also, they may not get the opportunity to effectively communicate their views and ideas to the management team.

- **Poor industrial relations.** Large firms may be at a greater risk from a lack of motivation of workers and industrial action. This is because workers may have less sense of belonging, longer time may be required to solve problems and poor employee relations may lead to conflict.

External economies of scale

A larger industry can enable the firms in that industry to reduce their average total cost in a number of ways including developing:

- **A skilled labour force.** A firm can recruit workers who have been trained by other firms in the industry.

- **A good reputation.** An area can gain a reputation for a high-quality production. For example, the Netherlands is well known for its high-quality Gouda cheese (see Figure 18.9) and the Maldives has a reputation of being a popular holiday destination.

Figure 18.9: Dutch Gouda cheese made in the Netherlands is famous around the world

- **Specialist suppliers of raw materials and capital goods.** When an industry becomes large enough, it can become worthwhile for other industries, called ancillary industries, to set up to provide for the needs of the industry. For instance, the tyre industry supplies tyres to the car industry.

- **Specialist services.** Universities and colleges may run courses for workers in large industries and banks, and transport firms may provide services specially designed to meet the particular needs of firms in the industry.

- **Specialist markets.** Some large industries have specialist selling places and arrangements, such as corn exchanges and insurance markets.

- **Improved infrastructure.** The growth of an industry may encourage a government and private sector firms to provide better road links and electricity supplies, build new airports and develop dock facilities.

External economies of scale are more likely to arise if the firms in the industry are located in one area. This is why they are sometimes referred to as 'economies of concentration'.

External diseconomies of scale

Just as a firm can grow too large, so can an industry. With more and larger firms in an area, there will be an increase in transport with more vehicles bringing in workers and raw materials and taking out workers and finished products. This may cause congestion, increased journey times, higher transport costs for firms and possibly reduced worker productivity. The growth of an industry may also result in increased competition for resources, pushing up the price of key sites, capital equipment and labour.

> **TIP**
>
> Economies of scale result from the growth of a firm or industry – they do not cause it. The type of economy of scale that is defined incorrectly by students most frequently is financial economies.

ACTIVITY 18.5

In 2023, the US firm Newmont, was the largest gold mining firm in the world, employing nearly 15 000 workers. It has gold mines in North America, South America, Australia and a number of African countries. It also mines copper, lead, silver and zinc in a number of countries (e.g., the Dominican Republic and Mexico). In 2019, it bought out Goldcorp, a large Canadian mining firm.

1   Explain two types of internal economies of scale that can be enjoyed by a mining company.

2   Explain two types of external economies that may be experienced by firms in the mining industry.

Write your answers in your notebook.

ECONOMICS IN ACTION

The possible effects of firms growing in size

Figure 18.10: Larger supermarket chains may be able to lower prices

Quickmart is supermarket firm in Kenya. It was started in 2006 by entrepreneur John Kinuthia with one supermarket in Nakuru. While some other Kenyan supermarket firms, including Nakumatt and Tuskys, have gone out of business since 2006, Quickmart has expanded. It has opened more supermarkets and, in 2019, merged with Tumaini Self Service, with the new merged firm keeping the name Quickmart. By 2024, Quickmart had supermarkets in most parts of Kenya.

Economists assess whether mergers and growth in the size of firms benefit consumers, firms and the economy. They examine a range of factors including the effect on average total cost, competition, revenue, price, choice, innovation, quality and employment. Some effects, such as a rise in quality, would be likely to benefit consumers, firms and the economy. Other effects, such as a lower average total cost, would benefit firms, but whether they would benefit consumers depends on how firms react. If firms respond to the lower average total cost by lowering their prices, this would benefit consumers. It is also possible that some effects, such as lower competition, may benefit firms but may harm consumers.

1   Why may Quickmart experience internal diseconomies of scale if it expands further?

2   Why may a large firm innovate more than a small firm?

SUMMARY

You should now know:

- Industries consist of many firms producing the same products, and firms may have a number of plants.

- The three main stages of production are primary (collecting and extracting raw materials), secondary (manufacturing and construction) and tertiary (services).

- Firms in the private sector are owned by an entrepreneur or groups of entrepreneurs whereas firms in the public sector are owned by the government.

- The three main types of merger are horizontal, vertical and conglomerate.

- Horizontal merger increases market share and may enable the new firm to take greater advantage of economies of scale.

- Vertical merger backwards secures supplies whilst vertical merger forwards secures outlets.

- The key motive behind a conglomerate merger is diversification.

- The main benefit of a small firm may be personal service and the main advantage of a large firm may be lower average total cost.

- Increasing output can reduce average total cost. The savings made are referred to as economies of scale.

- Internal economies of scale are falling average total cost resulting from the growth of a firm.

- Internal diseconomies of scale are rising average total cost, resulting from a firm growing too large.

- External economies arise from the growth of the industry while external diseconomies of scale are caused by an industry growing too large.

- Internal economies and diseconomies of scale explain the usual U-shape of the long run average total cost curve.

- If the increasing size of the industry gives rise to external economies of scale, a firm's average total cost curve will shift downwards. The creation of external diseconomies of scale will cause the average total cost curve to move upwards.

Chapter 18 practice questions

1   What is most likely to be supplied by small firms?

    A   banking

    B   film production

    C   shoe repair

    D   steel   [1]

2   A toy manufacturer merges with a chemical company. What type of merger is this?

    A   conglomerate

    B   horizontal

    C   vertical merger backwards

    D   vertical merger forwards   [1]

3   What is meant by 'financial economies of scale'?

    A   lower average total cost arising from a large firm operating its finance department more efficiently

    B   lower average total cost due to the ability of large firms to borrow more cheaply

    C   lower average total cost experienced by large banks and other financial institutions

    D   lower average total cost occurring because of the use of larger capital equipment   [1]

4   Why might the growth of an industry reduce a firm's average total cost of production?

    A   it may cause a decrease in subsidiary industries

    B   it may create greater competition for resources

    C   it may lead to the development of specialist markets

    D   it may reduce the supply of infrastructure   [1]

5   In which sectors are silver mining and insurance?

	Silver mining	Insurance
A	primary	primary
B	secondary	tertiary
C	tertiary	secondary
D	primary	tertiary

           [1]

Total: [5]

6   a   Define 'state-owned enterprise'.   [2]

    b   Explain why a firm may decide to stay small.   [4]

    c   Analyse **two** internal economies of scale.   [6]

    d   Discuss whether or not a merger between two book publishing
        firms will benefit consumers.   [8]

                                                                 Total: [20]

CHECK YOUR PROGRESS

How well do you think you have achieved the learning intentions for this chapter?
Give yourself a score from 1 (still need a lot of practice) to 5 (feeling very confident)
for each learning intention. Provide an example to support your score.

Now I can...	Score	Example
explain the difference between primary, secondary and tertiary sector firms		
explain the difference between private sector firms and public sector firms		
discuss the advantages and disadvantages of small and large firms		
define different types of mergers: horizontal, vertical and conglomerate		
discuss the advantages and disadvantages of horizontal, vertical and conglomerate mergers		
discuss how internal and external economies and diseconomies of scale can affect a firm/industry as the scale of production changes		
draw and interpret average total cost (ATC) diagrams to illustrate economies and diseconomies of scale.		

Firms and production

LEARNING INTENTIONS

By the end of this chapter, you will be able to:

- analyse the influences on the demand for factors of production
- analyse the reasons for adopting labour-intensive production or capital-intensive production
- discuss the advantages and disadvantages of different forms of production
- explain the difference between production and productivity
- explain the influences on production and productivity
- analyse the effects of changes in investment on productivity.

Introduction

Some industries employ many workers but use little capital equipment, while others use a high proportion of capital and also employ many workers. It is also the case that the same industries in different countries use different combinations of factors of production. For example, the number of farm workers per unit of land is much lower in the USA than in Mali. In any country, varying the combination of labour and capital may affect production and productivity.

ECONOMICS IN CONTEXT

The winds of change

Figure 19.1: The demand for wind turbine technicians is growing

The wind energy industry is one of the fastest-growing sectors in the world. More wind turbines are being installed and used in most countries. In 2022, the five countries which had the largest number of new installations were China, the USA, Brazil, Germany and Sweden.

The increased use of wind turbines is increasing the demand for wind turbine technicians (see Figure 19.1). These workers install, maintain and repair wind turbines. It is estimated that the number of wind turbine technicians will increase by more than 40% between 2024 and 2034 in the USA. It is expected that the wage of wind turbine technicians will rise in the USA from an average of $55 000 to $60 000 over this period.

Wind turbine technicians need a set of technical skills and the willingness to work outside, sometimes in confined spaces and often at significant heights. With advances in education and training, the skills of those applying to be wind turbine technicians is increasing. As a result, on average, new wind turbine technicians tend to complete their tasks efficiently.

Discuss in a pair or group:

1   What is the likely relationship between the demand for wind power and the demand for the resources used to produce wind power?

2   Do you think the supply of wind turbine technicians is likely to increase in the future?

19.1 Demand for factors of production

The demand for factors of production is influenced by demand for the product, the price of the different factors of production, their availability and their productivity. A firm producing a standardised model of car is likely to be very capital-intensive, whereas a beauty salon is likely to be labour-intensive.

When factors of production are substitutes, a rise in the productivity or a fall in the cost of one of them, may result in a change in the combination of resources being used. A fall in the price of capital goods, for example, might lead to the replacement of some workers with machines. In other cases, where factors of production are complements, a fall in the price of one or a rise in its productivity, may increase the employment of all factors in a firm. For example, a fall in the price of aircraft may make it possible for an airline to buy more planes to fly to more destinations. If so, they will also employ more pilots, more cabin crew and obtain more take-off and landing slots at airports.

Changing factors of production

If a firm wants to change the quantity of resources it uses, the firm will find it easier to do this with some factors than others. In the short run, there is likely to be at least one fixed factor of production. This means the quantity cannot be changed quickly. The most obvious example is the physical size of the factory or office. It will take time for a firm wanting to expand to extend its buildings or build new ones. Similarly, a firm that wants to reduce output is unlikely to be able to stop renting or sell off its buildings quickly.

In contrast, it is likely to be easier to change the quantity of labour. Even in the very short run, it may be possible to alter the quantity of labour by changing the amount of overtime available. It may also be possible to change orders for raw materials and capital equipment, but it will depend on the length of contracts and, in the case of increasing demand, the availability of spare capacity in firms producing them.

Combining the factors of production

It is important to achieve the right combination of factors of production. For example, it would not make sense for a hairdressing salon to have ten hairdryers and two hairdressers, or a farmer to have a large amount of land and only a few cattle. In the first case, labour would be underutilised and in the second case, there would be an insufficient number of livestock to make full use of the land. While deciding the combination of resources, firms seek to achieve the highest possible productivity. For example, Table 19.1 shows that the most appropriate number of workers to be employed (in terms of productivity) with five machines is seven, since this is where output per worker is highest. The combination is not always one machine per worker. This is because workers may work in shifts, some workers may be undertaking training and in some cases one worker may use more than one piece of machinery.

Table 19.1: Combining labour with machines

No. of machines	No. of workers	Total output (units)	Output per worker (average product) (units)
5	1	50	50
5	2	120	60
5	3	210	70
5	4	320	80
5	5	450	90
5	6	600	100
5	7	770	110
5	8	800	100
5	9	810	90

LINK

There are three main reasons why the demand for labour may increase – see Chapter 17.3 (Effects of changes in demand and supply in the labour market – Change in demand and supply of labour).

TIP

Remember that while production is output, productivity is output per worker or output per factor of production.

ACTIVITY 19.1

Using the information in Table 19.2, calculate the output per worker. Decide the most efficient combination of workers and machines.

Check your answers with another student.

Table 19.2

No. of machines	No. of workers	Total output (units)
4	1	10
4	2	24
4	3	45
4	4	72
4	5	100
4	6	108
4	7	112

Factors influencing demand for capital goods

Among the key factors influencing demand for capital goods are the price of capital goods, price of other factors of production, profit levels, **corporate income (corporation) tax**, income, interest rates, confidence levels and advances in technology.

- A rise in the price of capital goods will cause a contraction in demand for capital goods, whereas an increase in the price of another factor of production, particularly labour, may increase the demand for capital goods. This will occur if the factors are substitutes and the rise in price of another factor makes the production of a unit of output more expensive than that involving a rise in capital. If another factor is a complement, an increase in its price would cause a decrease in demand for capital.

- If profit levels are high, firms will have both the ability and the incentive to buy capital goods.

- A cut in corporation tax would also mean that firms would have more profit available to invest in the business and a greater incentive to invest.

- Rising real disposable income will lead to an increase in consumption. This, in turn, is likely to encourage firms to invest as they will expect to sell a higher output in the future.

- A cut in interest rates would also tend to raise consumption and so encourage firms to expand their capacity. In addition, lower interest rates would increase investment because they would reduce the opportunity cost of investing and lower the cost of borrowing. Firms can use profits to buy more capital goods instead of depositing the profits in bank accounts. With low interest rates, firms would be sacrificing less interest by buying capital goods. Borrowing to buy capital goods would also be less costly.

KEY TERM

corporate income (corporation) tax: a tax on profits of a company.

- Another key influence on investment is firms' expectations about the future. If firms are confident that sales will rise, they will invest now. In contrast, if firms are pessimistic about the future, there will be decline in investment.

- Advances in technology will increase the productivity of capital goods. If new and more efficient machinery is developed, firms are likely to invest more.

Demand for land

Productivity is a key factor influencing demand for land. In terms of agricultural land, the most fertile land will be in highest demand and receive the highest rent. City centre sites are also very productive as firms have the potential to attract a high number of customers. If a shop in the centre of New York becomes vacant, it is likely that a number of retail firms would compete for it in the expectation that they could earn a high revenue there. The competition pushes up the rent that can be charged for a favourable site.

One natural resource which is experiencing an increasing global demand is water. Water is used for domestic, agricultural, industrial and energy production purposes (see Figure 19.2). As countries become richer, they make heavier demands on scarce water supplies. The global use of water has increased six times in the last 100 years and is predicted to double again by 2050.

Figure 19.2: Domestic use of water is increasing as consumers can afford to buy labour-saving devices such as washing machines and dishwashers

---

ACTIVITY 19.2

Rising living standards throughout the world are increasing the demand for water, which in turn is affecting the price of water.

Produce a short presentation to explain how improving living standards are likely to increase the global demand for water. Include a demand and supply diagram to explain what may happen to the price of water in the future.

Factors of production and sectors of production

The demand for factors of production can alter as an economy changes its industrial structure. As mentioned in Chapter 18 (Firms), the distribution of resources among different sectors changes with economic development. In most cases, agricultural reform allows resources to move to low-cost manufacturing. Then, resources move to higher value-added manufacturing and finally the service sector becomes the most important one. Not all economies, however, fit this pattern. For example, India's service sector has expanded before it has built up a sizeable manufacturing sector. Now, in most countries, the service sector makes the largest contribution to output. In 2022, the service (tertiary) sector accounted for 65% of global output.

Different industries make use of different factors of production. The chemical industry, for example, is very capital-intensive and agriculture is land-intensive (as well as being water-intensive).

> **LINK**
>
> The difference between the primary, secondary and tertiary sectors is described in Chapter 18.1 (Different types of firms).

ACTIVITY 19.3

Advances in technology are revolutionising the way many people work. Technology allows more people to work from home and effectively introduces a new work model. The more flexible a country is in creating new employment relationships, the better it may be at getting the most from the new technologies.

In a pair, produce a table showing the advantages and disadvantages a firm may experience as a result of allowing workers to work from home.

19.2 Labour-intensive and capital-intensive production

Some producers choose to use labour-intensive methods of production. The reasons for this may include:

- There may be a large supply of labour in the country, making labour relatively cheap.

- Some producers may be too small to take advantage of capital equipment. If, for example, a machine could produce 3 000 pairs of shoes a day, but a producer could only sell 50, they would not consider it worthwhile to buy the machine.

- Some producers may choose to make handmade products as consumers may think that handmade products are of a higher quality and are more likely to meet their individual needs than mass-produced products. This may make consumers willing to pay a higher price for handmade shoes, for example. Custom-made products can also provide greater status and some consumers like the personalised attention that labour-intensive production may make possible.

- Workers can be more flexible in terms of what they do, and the size of the labour force can be adjusted by small amounts.

- Labour can also provide feedback on how to improve production methods and the quality of products.

- Firms may switch from capital-intensive production to labour-intensive production if the price of capital increases and labour can carry out the same functions with the same level of productivity as the machines they replace.

In practice, however, firms tend to switch from labour-intensive production to capital-intensive production. This is because advances in technology tend to make capital goods more affordable and more productive. Education, for example, is becoming more capital-intensive with developments such as online university degrees. As well as often having the capacity to produce more products at a lower average total cost (technical economies), capital goods produce products of a uniform standard unaffected by human error. Production is not affected by industrial action, illness or tiredness, although machinery does need to be maintained and can break down.

> **TIP**
>
> Employing capital goods does not involve just a one-off cost. As well as the cost of buying or renting capital goods, firms have the cost of regularly maintaining the capital goods and sometimes may need to repair them.

ACTIVITY 19.4

In a small group, discuss and decide which of the following should be placed in each of the categories in the bulleted list below.

You could put the points on a poster, under the four categories.

1 no need for holidays

2 may be high maintenance costs

3 risk of human error

4 products can be standardised

5 relatively easy to meet individual customer requirements

6 can be used to carry out dangerous tasks

7 may become outdated due to advances in technology

8 may be more flexible

9 risk of break-down

10 more suited to low-scale production.

- advantages of capital-intensive production

- disadvantages of capital-intensive production

- advantages of labour-intensive production

- disadvantages of labour-intensive production

19.3 Production and productivity

There are clear links between production and productivity, but they are not the same thing. If output per worker hour increases and the number of working hours stays the same, production will increase. It is possible, however, that productivity could rise and production could fall. This could occur if unemployment increases. Indeed, a rise in unemployment may increase productivity as it is the most skilled workers who are likely to keep their jobs.

As economies develop, both production and productivity tend to increase due to advances in technology and improvements in education. These developments can result in productivity rising so much that total output can increase while the number of working hours declines.

DISCUSSION

Discuss whether you expect productivity to increase in your country in the next ten years.

The influences on production and productivity

What is produced and the total amount produced are influenced by what goods and services are in demand and the quality and quantity of resources to produce them. For example, an increase in demand for video games has resulted in a rise in their profitability. This has encouraged an increase in the production of video games. A flood may damage the quality of land and reduce the output of some agricultural products. A larger labour force will enable more of most products to be produced.

There are a number of reasons why productivity may increase. These are linked to improvements in the quality of resources. For example, better irrigation systems may increase the output that can be produced from a given quantity of land. Improvements in education can mean that the productivity of future workers will increase. Advances in technology are also likely to increase the output per hour that workers can produce.

The effect of changes in productivity on investment

Increases in investment is one of the main causes of an increase in productivity. This is because new capital equipment is often of a higher quality incorporating advances in technology. For example, a printer bought today is likely to print more pages per minute and may enable more ink to be extracted from an ink cartridge than older models.

However, for new capital equipment to increase productivity, it is important that workers have the skills to make best use of it. Equipping agricultural workers with the latest in drone technology to spray crops may not be effective if they do not know how to operate the drones.

REFLECTION

Do you understand the difference between production and productivity? What could you do to improve your understanding?

ECONOMICS IN ACTION

How robots are changing fruit picking

Figure 19.3: Fruit-picking robots are able to harvest delicate fruit such as raspberries

Some economists are assessing the effects of changes in how fruit and vegetables are being harvested. In 2023, there were approximately 840 million tonnes of fruit harvested. A proportion of this fruit was sold past its peak at a lower price than it could have been sold for at its peak. An even larger quantity of fruit was not picked. It was left to rot. This was, because, in a large number of countries, there was a shortage of fruit pickers.

It is difficult to recruit fruit pickers. Fruit picking is physically hard work and it is seasonal work. However, the nature of fruit picking is changing. Some farmers have already started to use robots to pick fruit and vegetables. There are a number of different types of robots, including articulated robots and drones. These can be programmed to identify and pick ripe fruit, even soft fruit such as raspberries. Robots can work long hours and can work instead of, or alongside, human fruit pickers.

1   Why might the price of fruit-picking robots fall in the future?

2   What effect may the introduction of fruit-picking robots have on the price of fruit?

SUMMARY

You should now know:

- The demand for factors of production is influenced by demand for the product, the price of different factors of production, their availability and their productivity.

- In the short run, there is likely to be at least one fixed factor of production, most commonly capital.

- Demand for capital goods is influenced by the price of capital goods, the price of other factors of production, profit levels, income, interest rates, confidence and advances in technology.

- The factors of production used in an economy are influenced by the economy's industrial structure.

- Capital-intensive production can result in higher output at a lower average total cost, and avoids human error and disruptions caused by strikes, tiredness and sickness.

- Labour-intensive production may be appropriate where there is a good supply of low-wage labour, personal attention is important, consumers want custom-made products and where workers' ideas can make significant improvements to production methods.

- Improvements in the quality of resources are likely to increase production and productivity.

Chapter 19 practice questions

1   The table shows the distribution of the labour force of a country between two years.

	Employment in millions	
	Year 1	Year 2
Agriculture	10	8
Mining	4	5
Manufacturing	20	20
Retailing	10	12
Education	5	5

How did the distribution of employment change between Year 1 and Year 2?

	Primary industry	Secondary industry	Tertiary industry
A	fell	unchanged	rose
B	rose	fell	unchanged
C	unchanged	rose	fell
D	rose	unchanged	fell

[1]

2   What are a doctor and operating theatre?

   A   an example of enterprise and capital

   B   an example of labour and land

   C   complementary factors of production

   D   substitute factors of production   [1]

3   Which scenario would cause an increase in demand for capital goods?

   A   a decrease in corporate tax

   B   a fall in disposable income

   C   a rise in interest rates

   D   a rise in pessimism   [1]

4   Twenty-five workers produce a total output of 300 units. What is output per worker?

   A   12

   B   25

   C   300

   D   7 500   [1]

5   What would increase the demand for aeroplane pilots?

   A   a decrease in business travel

   B   a decrease in the price of sea travel

   C   an increase in air passenger numbers

   D   an increase in the size of aeroplanes   [1]

Total: [5]

6   a   Define 'investment'.   [2]

     b   Explain why the production of cars may increase whilst the productivity of car workers may fall.   [4]

     c   Analyse the reasons why car production has become more capital-intensive.   [6]

     d   Discuss whether or not industries becoming more capital-intensive will increase unemployment.   [8]

Total: [20]

CHECK YOUR PROGRESS

How well do you think you have achieved the learning intentions for this chapter? Give yourself a score from 1 (still need a lot of practice) to 5 (feeling very confident) for each learning intention. Provide an example to support your score.

Now I can...	Score	Example
analyse the influences on the demand for factors of production		
analyse the reasons for adopting labour-intensive production or capital-intensive production		
discuss the advantages and disadvantages of labour-intensive production and capital-intensive production		
explain the difference between production and productivity		
explain the influences on production and productivity		
analyse the effects of changes in investment on productivity.		

Chapter 20

Firms' costs, revenue and objectives

LEARNING INTENTIONS

By the end of this chapter, you will be able to:

- define key terms: total cost (TC), average total cost (ATC), fixed cost (FC), average fixed cost (AFC), variable cost (VC), and average variable cost (AVC)
- calculate total cost, average total cost, fixed cost, average fixed cost, variable cost and average variable cost
- draw and interpret diagrams that show how changes in output can affect costs of production
- define total revenue (TR) and average revenue (AR)
- calculate total revenue and average revenue
- explain the influence of sales on revenue
- discuss the objectives of firms including survival, social welfare, profit maximisation and growth.

Introduction

In 2023, Alphabet, the US-based technology firm, earned $307bn from selling its products. To produce those products cost the firm $223bn. This gave the firm a profit of $84bn. As firms change their output, their costs change. Their revenue can also change, this time influenced by the price they charge and the quantity they sell.

ECONOMICS IN CONTEXT

Manchester City reaches new heights

Figure 20.1: Football fans celebrating their team winning

Manchester City Football Club had a very successful season in 2022/2023. It was one of the top football team in terms of revenue, earning $890m. Sales of Manchester City merchandise, including shirts and scarves, increased.

Broadcasting and advertising revenue also rose as did revenue from ticket sales.

Manchester City achieved considerable success in winning a treble of trophies: the UEFA Champions League, the Premier League and the FA Cup. This resulted in the club playing more matches, attracting more supporters and more matches being televised, and each televised match earning more revenue.

As well as revenue increasing, Manchester City's costs also increased. The club's wage bill rose, with 23 of its players earning more than $1m and two of these earning more than $24m. As the club's revenue rose by more than its costs, its profit increased. It rose to $100m, nearly double the $52m profit earned the year before.

Discuss in a pair or group:

1 Why might paying high wages have increased Manchester City's profits?

2 What might cause Manchester City to make a loss in the future?

20.1 Calculating the costs of production

Total cost and average total cost

Total cost (TC) is the total cost of producing a given output. The more the output is produced, the higher the total cost of production. Producing more units requires the use of more resources. **Average total cost** (ATC) is also referred to as average cost (AC) or unit cost, and is given as total cost divided by output. Table 20.1 shows the relationship between output, total cost and average cost.

KEY TERMS

total cost: the total amount spent on the factors of production used to produce a product.

average total cost: total cost divided by output.

Table 20.1: Total and average cost

Output	Total cost ($)	Average total cost ($)
0	10	–
1	30	30
2	48	24
3	60	20
4	88	22
5	125	25

Fixed cost

Table 20.1 indicates that there is a cost even when output is zero. In the **short run**, some factors of production are in fixed supply. When a firm changes its output, the costs of these factors remain unchanged – they are **fixed costs** (FC) (see Figure 20.2). For instance, if a firm raised its output, the interest it pays on past loans would remain unchanged. If the firm closes during a holiday period, it may still have to pay for security and rent for buildings.

Figure 20.2: The steel industry has high fixed costs

Figure 20.3 shows that total fixed cost (TFC) remains unchanged as output changes. Fixed costs are also sometimes referred to as overheads or indirect costs.

KEY TERMS

short run: the time period when the quantity of at least one factor of production is fixed/ cannot be changed.

fixed costs: costs which do not change with output in the short run.

TIP

Remember that while total cost rises with output, average total cost may rise, remain the same or fall.

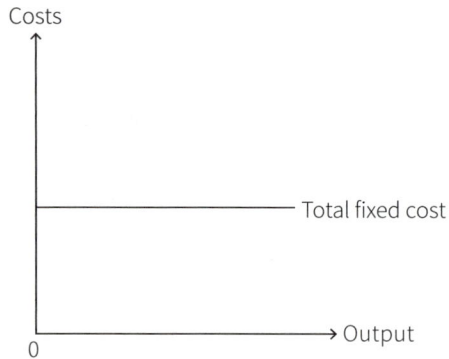

Figure 20.3: Total fixed cost

Average fixed cost

Average fixed cost (AFC) is total fixed cost divided by output. As total fixed cost is constant, a higher output will reduce average fixed cost. Table 20.2 and Figure 20.4 show how the average fixed cost falls as output increases.

Table 20.2: Average fixed cost

Output	Total fixed cost ($)	Average fixed cost ($)
0	10	–
1	10	10
2	10	5
3	10	3.33
4	10	2.5
5	10	2

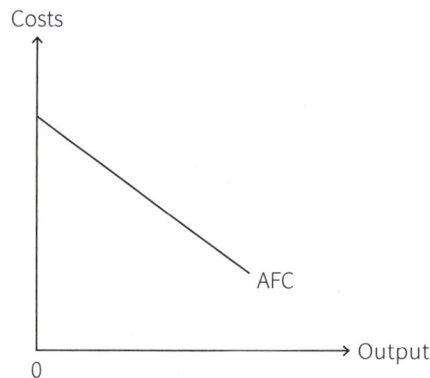

Figure 20.4: Average fixed cost

> **KEY TERM**
>
> **average fixed cost:** total fixed cost divided by output.

> **TIP**
>
> Remember that while total fixed cost remains unchanged as output rises, average fixed cost falls.

Variable cost

Variable costs (VC), also sometimes called direct costs, are the costs of the variable factors. Variable costs vary directly as output changes. Production and sale of more cars will involve an increased expenditure on component parts, electricity, wages and transport for a car firm. As output increases, total variable cost rises. Total variable cost usually tends to rise slowly at first and then rise more rapidly. This is because productivity often rises at first and then begins to decline after a certain output. Figure 20.5 shows the change of total variable cost (TVC) with output.

> **KEY TERM**
>
> **variable costs:** costs that change with output.

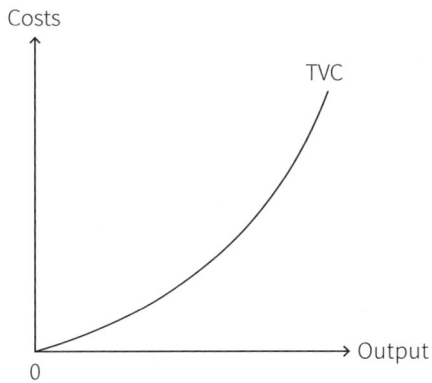

Figure 20.5: Total variable cost

Average variable cost

Average variable cost (AVC) is total variable cost divided by output. As output increases in the short run, average variable cost tends to fall and then rise. This is for the same reason that accounts for an increase in total variable cost at different rates with increase in output. Table 20.3 and Figure 20.6 show the change in average variable cost with output.

KEY TERM

average variable cost: total variable cost divided by output.

Table 20.3: Average variable cost

Output	Total variable cost ($)	Average variable cost ($)
1	40	40
2	70	35
3	90	30
4	120	30
5	175	35

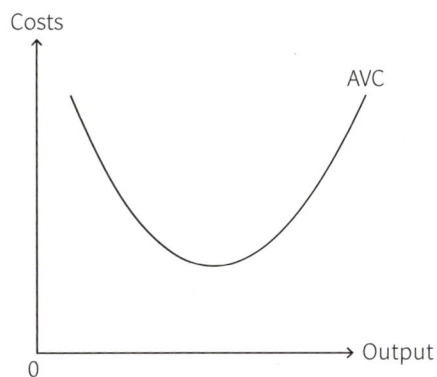

Figure 20.6: Average variable cost

ACTIVITY 20.1

Table 20.4 shows the costs of a bakery. Decide which are fixed and which are variable costs. Copy and complete the table.

Table 20.4

Costs	Fixed or variable costs?
1 flour	
2 yeast	
3 rent	
4 business rates	
5 insurance	
6 overtime pay	
7 depreciation	
8 energy costs	

Fixed and variable costs

In practice, it is not always easy to decide whether a cost is fixed or variable. This is particularly true of payments to workers. Overtime payments and the wages of temporary workers are clearly variable costs as they vary directly with output. The basic wage or salary paid to workers, however, may be considered a fixed cost since it has to be paid whatever the amount of output.

The sum of total fixed cost and total variable cost equals total cost. For instance, if fixed costs are $800 and variable costs are $4 200 a week, the total cost of production would be $5 000 a week. Figure 20.7 shows how total cost is made up of fixed and variable costs.

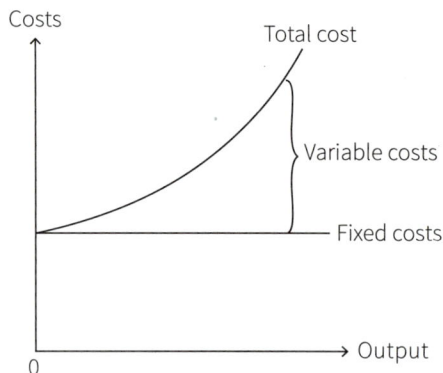

Figure 20.7: The composition of total cost

ACTIVITY 20.2

Copy and complete Table 20.5 about fixed and variable costs.

Table 20.5

	Fixed cost	Variable cost
Effect of a rise in output in the short run		Increase
Example		
Average	Fixed cost divided by output	
Effect of a strike		Fall

REFLECTION

How much of Table 20.5 were you able to fill out? Would you be able to produce a table on AFC and AVC?

In the **long run**, however, all costs are variable. This is because all factors of production can be altered if there is sufficient time to change them. For instance, a firm can increase the size of its factory, office or farm. Therefore, its rent and business rates would rise, and it can hire more workers, so increasing the wage bill. Figure 20.8 shows total cost in the long run.

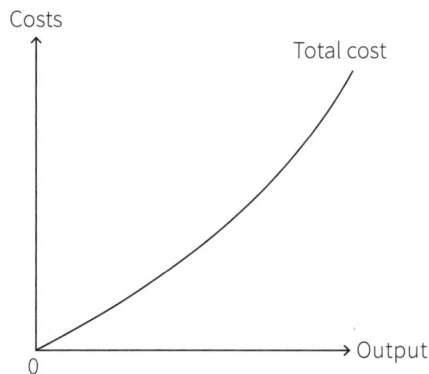

Figure 20.8: Long-term total cost

Average total cost

In the short run, average total cost consists of average fixed cost and average variable cost. The shape of the short-run average total cost curve is usually U-shaped. The long run average total cost curve is also usually U-shaped. This can be explained as follows: as a firm alters its scale of production, it first experiences economies of scale, and then, after reaching a certain output, it may encounter diseconomies of scale.

KEY TERM

long run: the time period when all factors of production can be changed and all costs are variable.

LINK

A key reason why average total cost may vary in the long run is due to changes in the scale of production – see Chapter 18.3 (Economies and diseconomies of scale).

TIP

When deciding whether costs are fixed or variable, remember to consider whether the costs will change with output in the short run. Remember that **all** costs change with output in the long run.

ACTIVITY 20.3

Copy and complete Table 20.6 with the costs of production.

Check your answers with another student.

Table 20.6

Output	TC	TFC	TVC	ATC	AFC	AVC
0	60					
1	110					
2	150					
3	180					
4	200					
5	230					
6	300					

20.2 Calculating revenue and the influence of sales on revenue

The money received by firms from selling their products is referred to as revenue. Total revenue is the total amount of money received by firms through the sale of their products. Average revenue is found by dividing total revenue by the quantity sold and is the same as **price**.

In very competitive markets each firm's output may have no effect on price. In this case, total revenue rises consistently as more quantity is sold. Table 20.7 shows the change of total revenue with sales.

> **KEY TERM**
>
> **price:** the amount of money that has to be given to obtain a product.

Table 20.7: Average and total revenue of a highly competitive firm

Quantity sold	Average revenue (price per unit) ($)	Total revenue ($)
1	10	10
2	10	20
3	10	30
4	10	40
5	10	50
6	10	60
7	10	70

Figure 20.9 illustrates the information shown in Table 20.4 graphically.

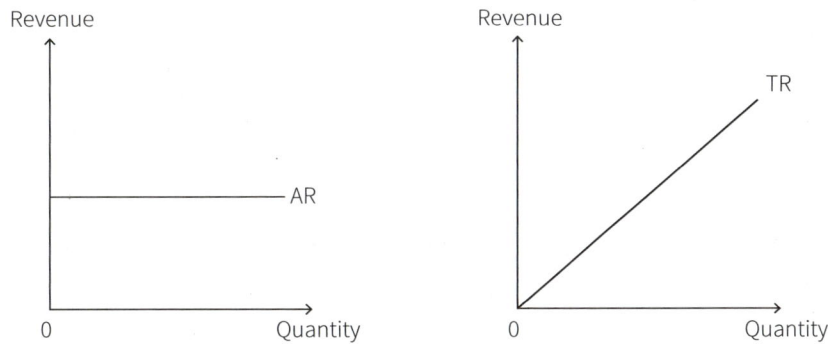

Figure 20.9: The average and total revenue curves of a perfectly competitive firm

In most markets, however, firms are price makers and need to lower price to sell more.

Table 20.8 and Figure 20.10 illustrate the change in **total revenue** and **average revenue** in a market with only one firm. In this case, to sell more, the firm has to lower price.

Table 20.8: Average and total revenue in a market with one firm

Quantity sold	Average revenue (price per unit) ($)	Total revenue ($)
1	10	10
2	9	18
3	8	24
4	7	28
5	6	30
6	5	30
7	4	28

> **KEY TERMS**
>
> **total revenue:** the total amount of money received from selling a product.
>
> **average revenue:** the total revenue divided by the quantity sold.

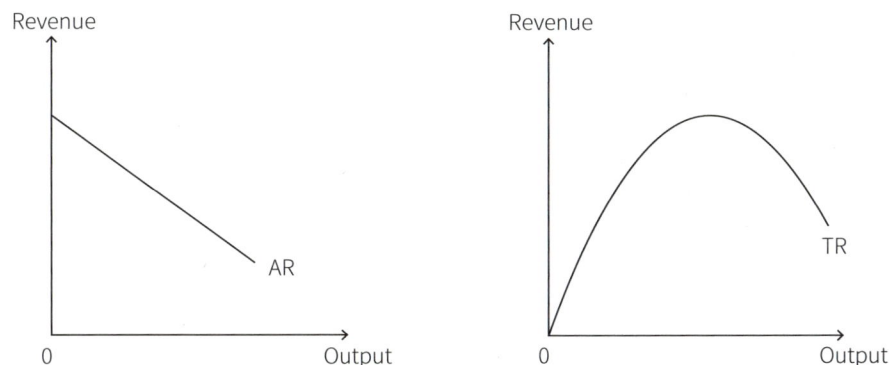

Figure 20.10: The average and total revenue curves of a firm which has 100% share of the market

Average revenue falls as the quantity sold rises. Total revenue rises at first, reaches a peak and then falls beyond a certain level of sales.

20.3 Objectives of firms

Firms may pursue a range of objectives including survival, growth, social welfare, and **profit maximisation**.

KEY TERM

profit maximisation: making as much profit as possible.

Survival

A start-up firm's initial objective may be just to survive in what may be a very competitive market. A firm may be content simply to cover its costs until it becomes better known. During difficult times when demand is falling, even large firms may have survival as their key objective. They will try to stay in the market in the hope that conditions will improve.

Growth

Some firms may have the objective of growth. Increasing the size of the firm may bring a number of advantages. High and increasing sales tend to enable firms to take advantage of a number of internal economies of scale, for instance, to raise finance more easily and to buy raw materials at a discounted rate. Those who run firms, the managers, directors and chief executives, may have the growth of the firm as their key objective because their pay and status may be more closely linked to the size of the firm they run. Those in charge of large firms are usually paid more than those running smaller firms and also tend to be held in higher esteem. They may also have greater job security as the larger the firm they run, the more difficult it will be for any other firm to take it over and replace them with their own managerial team. If growth is achieved by merging with other firms, competition will be reduced and the firm will gain a larger market share.

Social welfare

The government may give state-owned enterprises the objective of improving social welfare. They may, for instance, charge a relatively low price for their products to ensure they are affordable to even people living in poverty. They are more likely than private sector firms to base their production decisions on social costs and benefits.

In recent years, some private sector firms have also been showing a greater concern about the environmental and social effects of their actions. A number of firms have sought to clean up their production processes and ensure that they source their raw materials from firms that do not employ child labour.

Profit maximisation

Traditional theory suggests that firms seek to maximise profits. This means that they try to earn the largest profit possible over a period of time. Although some of the other objectives may appear to conflict with profit maximisation, objectives such as growth and social welfare may actually increase profits in the longer term. For instance, growth may involve reducing the number of competitors. This would reduce the price elasticity of demand (PED) for its product and so its ability to raise price and revenue. In addition, increasing the scale of operation may reduce average costs. Both of these outcomes would increase profits.

Social welfare objectives may also increase profits in the long run. For example, a firm that has environmentally friendly policies and aims to be socially responsible may find that to follow its objectives the costs of production will rise. At the same time, it may find demand and revenue increase as consumers opt to buy from firms that act in an environmentally sustainable way (see Figure 20.11). Treating workers better may help retain workers, which would reduce the costs of recruiting and training workers.

Figure 20.11: A zero-waste shop where customers refill their own jars and containers. The firm may have environmental sustainability as its main objective, but the business' popularity with consumers may allow it to make a profit

DISCUSSION

Discuss if you were setting up a business what would be your objective.

When profit maximisation is achieved

Profit is made when the revenue earned by a firm is greater than the costs incurred by it. Profit maximisation is an objective pursued by most private sector firms. Total profit is the positive difference between total revenue and total cost. Profit per unit (sometimes referred to as the profit margin) is the positive difference between average revenue (revenue per unit) and average total cost (unit cost). Profit is maximised when the positive gap between revenue and cost is greatest. Table 20.9 shows that profit would be maximised at 40 units of output.

Table 20.9: The relationship between total revenue, total cost and total profit

Output	Total revenue ($)	Total cost ($)	Total profit ($)
10	200	220	–20
20	380	380	0
30	500	480	20
40	600	540	60
50	660	620	40
60	700	710	–10

Besides calculating total profit, the profit per unit can be found by deducting average total cost from average revenue, as shown in Table 20.10. In this case, profit is maximised at three units.

Table 20.10: The relationship between average revenue, average total cost and total profit

Output	Average revenue ($)	Average total cost ($)	Total profit ($)
1	15	15	0
2	14	12	2
3	12	9	3
4	9	8	1
5	5	10	−5

From the information in Table 20.10, it is possible to calculate total revenue (by multiplying average revenue with output), total cost (by multiplying average total cost with output) and total profit (by multiplying profit per unit with output). These figures are shown in Table 20.11.

Table 20.11: Total revenue, total cost and total profit

Output	Total revenue ($)	Total cost ($)	Total profit ($)
1	15	15	0
2	28	24	4
3	36	27	9
4	36	32	4
5	25	50	−25

If information is given on output, costs and revenue, it is possible to work out revenue, as shown in Table 20.12. This is because it is known that

$$profit = revenue - cost$$

So, revenue = profit + cost. Similarly, from information on output, revenue and profit, cost can be calculated.

$$cost = revenue - profit$$

Table 20.12: The relationship between total profit, total revenue and total cost

Output	Total profit ($)	Total revenue ($)	Total cost ($)
10	0	400	400
20	100	800	700
30	300	1 200	900
40	400	1 600	1 200
50	300	2 000	1 700

ACTIVITY 20.4

1 Using the information in Table 20.13, calculate the profit maximising output.

Table 20.13

Output	Total revenue ($)	Total cost ($)
10	80	90
20	150	150
30	210	190
40	260	210
50	300	260

2 Copy Table 20.14 and complete the total cost for each level of output.

Table 20.14

Output	Total revenue ($)	Total profit ($)	Total cost ($)
10	80	−20	
20	150	0	
30	210	30	
40	260	20	
50	300	−40	

Effects of changes in profits

Profits provide an incentive for entrepreneurs to undertake production. An increase in profit will encourage more firms to enter a competitive market. It will also provide firms with more finance to update their capital equipment and expand their business.

A profitable firm will also find it easier to obtain external finance. Shareholders are more likely to want to buy shares in profitable firms and banks are usually willing to give them loans. These firms may also find it easier to recruit top managers and directors who are attracted by their success.

The effect of a fall in profit may vary with time. At first it may have little impact on the behaviour of firms if they think that it will only be short lived. After a while, if profits remain low, or fall further, some firms will cut back on production and others will cease production.

Ways of increasing profit

The two main ways of increasing profit are to

- reduce costs of production, and

- raise revenue.

There are a number of ways of reducing costs of production. One is by reducing any wastages and inefficiency. Another is by increasing the productivity of factors of production. In the short run the second strategy may actually raise costs, but in the long run it may lower average total costs and raise revenue by improving quality. For instance, a firm may spend more on training workers and may replace existing equipment with a more technologically advanced version. In the longer run, these measures should increase output per worker and per machine and therefore reduce average total cost. A third way is by increasing the size of the firm through merger or takeover. A larger firm may be able to take advantage of economies of scale. The firm will be likely to have higher total revenue. It may also have a higher total profit and profit per unit, due to its greater market share. Firms with considerable market power often have inelastic demand for their products. When demand is inelastic, a firm can increase its revenue by raising price. In contrast, if demand is elastic, the revenue may be raised by reducing price.

Besides trying to raise revenue by changing price, firms may seek to increase demand for the products. They may seek to improve the quality of their products, diversify and be more responsive to changes in consumer demand by improving their market research. Another method that firms may employ is advertising. A successful advertising campaign is one which increases revenue by more than the cost and so raises profit.

LINK

Having growth as its objective may enable a firm to take greater advantage of economies of scale – see Chapter 18.3 (Economies and diseconomies of scale).

ACTIVITY 20.5

In 2022, the US retailer Walmart experienced a rise in total revenue, and an even greater percentage rise in profit. A company spokesperson said the firm was seeking to reduce stock levels and expected the demand to continue to increase. Imagine you are the company's spokesperson. Write a short press release explaining:

1 how profit could rise by a greater percentage than revenue

2 how a reduction in stock levels could increase the company's profit

3 one way a large retailer like Walmart might increase demand.

TIP

Remember that profit is not the same as revenue. Revenue might increase, but profit would fall if costs rise by more than revenue.

ECONOMICS IN ACTION

Surge pricing

Economists have noticed that there has been an increase in what is sometimes called surge pricing or dynamic pricing. This involves changing the price frequently, perhaps several times a day. Changing prices so often, in response to changes in demand and supply, can increase firms' profits.

For example, if a firm selling home-delivered pizzas finds that more people are ordering paneer pizza, it may decide to raise the price of paneer pizza.

Similarly, if the firm finds that the price of durians in the local market increases, raising the cost of making durian pizzas, it may decide to increase the price of its durian pizzas this evening.

CONTINUED

Figure 20.12: Would they be charged a different price if they had ordered an hour earlier?

What is making it easier for firms to respond more quickly and more flexibly to changes in market conditions are advances in technology. Firms have more access to data on changes in market conditions, have closer contact with consumers and can communicate price changes relatively easily.

Those firms that are engaging in surge pricing, including some hotels, some restaurants, some sports firms and some concert promoters, recognise that there is a risk that frequent price changes may annoy consumers. To try to avoid this, firms tend to emphasise price reductions rather than price rises.

1 What is likely to be the main objective of firms that engage in surge pricing?

2 How may flexible resources influence whether a firm engages in surge pricing?

SUMMARY

You should now know:

- Total cost rises with output.
- Fixed costs do not change with output in the short run.
- Average fixed costs fall as output rises.
- Variable costs increase as output rises.
- Average variable cost tends to fall and then rise as output increases.
- In the long run, all costs are variable.
- The shape of the long run average variable cost is influenced by economies and diseconomies of scale.
- Average revenue (price) is total revenue divided by the quantity sold.
- Firms may seek to survive, grow, promote social welfare or make as much profit as possible.
- Profits are maximised when the positive gap between revenue and cost is greatest.
- Profit can be increased by raising revenue or cutting costs.
- Costs can be cut by reducing wastages and inefficiency, raising productivity and increasing the scale of operation.
- Revenue can be raised by altering price, improving the product, adapting more quickly to changes in consumer demand and advertising.

Chapter 20 practice questions

1   Which is a fixed cost to a manufacturing firm?

    A   insurance on buildings

    B   overtime payments to workers

    C   the cost of energy

    D   the cost of raw materials   **[1]**

2   A firm produces 50 units of output. The total variable cost of this output is $200 and the total fixed cost is $300. What is the average total cost of production?

    A $2

    B $4

    C $6

    D $10   **[1]**

3   A firm sells 100 units at a price of $4 per product. Using this information, what is the firm's total revenue (TR) and average revenue (AR)?

	Total revenue ($)	Average revenue ($)
A	100	4
B	100	25
C	400	4
D	400	25

    [1]

4   A firm achieves profit maximisation. What does this mean?

    A   it cannot increase its profit by changing its output

    B   it makes more profit than the other firms in the industry

    C   it maximises its total revenue

    D   it produces at the lowest possible cost   **[1]**

5   A firm has total fixed cost of $20 000. Its average variable cost is $6 and its average fixed cost is $2. What is its output?

    A   2 500

    B   3 333

    C   5 000

    D   10 000   **[1]**

                      Total: [5]

6 **a**   Define 'variable cost'. [2]

  b   Explain **two** causes of an increase in a firm's profit. [4]

  c   Analyse, using diagrams, how a rise in output affects total fixed cost and average fixed cost. [6]

  d   Discuss whether or not firms try to maximise profits. [8]

Total: [20]

CHECK YOUR PROGRESS

How well do you think you have achieved the learning intentions for this chapter? Give yourself a score from 1 (still need a lot of practice) to 5 (feeling very confident) for each learning intention. Provide an example to support your score.

Now I can...	Score	Example
define total cost, average total cost, fixed cost, average fixed cost, variable cost and average variable cost		
calculate total cost, average total cost, fixed cost, average fixed cost, variable cost and average variable cost		
draw and interpret diagrams to show how changes in output can affect costs of production		
define total revenue and average revenue		
calculate total revenue and average revenue		
explain the influence of sales on revenue		
discuss the objectives of firms including survival, social welfare, profit maximisation and growth.		

Chapter 21

Types of markets

LEARNING INTENTIONS

By the end of this chapter, you will be able to:

- explain the characteristics of a competitive market
- discuss the advantages and disadvantages of competitive markets
- explain the effect of having a high number of firms on price, quantity, choice and profit
- explain the characteristics of a monopoly market
- discuss the advantages and disadvantages of a monopoly market
- explain the effect of having only one firm on price, quantity, choice and profit.

Introduction

There can be a large difference in the number of firms in a market. For example, there may be 40 taxi firms and four bus firms operating in a city and one train firm operating a service into and out of the city.

ECONOMICS IN CONTEXT

Hairdressing salons are booming in Mumbai

Figure 21.1: One of many hairdressing salons in India

In the Indian city of Mumbai, the number of hairdressing salons continues to increase. Rises in income and extensive advertising on television and social media are increasing the demand for the services of hairdressers.

In 2023, there were nearly 3 500 hairdressing salons in Mumbai. All of the salons offer haircutting and most also offer hairstyling. Their other services vary, with some offering hair colouring and a number offer hair-loss treatments. A number also provide related services such as eyebrow threading and makeup services.

Some of the hairdressing salons are part of a chain of salons owned by large Indian firms and a few chains are owned by foreign multinational companies. However, most are independent salons owned by individual hairdressers.

Discuss in a pair or group:

1   Why might a hairdressing salon in Mumbai find it difficult to charge a high price?

2   What may attract consumers to a particular hair salon?

21.1 Competitive markets

Market structure is a term for the conditions which exist in a market. There are a number of categories of market structure, from very competitive to a monopoly which does not face any direct competition.

The more competitive a market is, the more sellers and buyers there are. With a high number of sellers, each firm will have a small share of the market, accounting for a small amount of the total market supply. This means that the change in the output of one firm has little or no effect on price. The existence of a number of firms means that consumers can switch between the products of the rival firms.

Characteristics of competitive markets

In **competitive markets**, there is usually relatively free entry into and exit from the market. This means that there must not be anything which makes it difficult for the firms to enter or leave the industry, that is to start or stop producing the product.

KEY TERMS

market structure: the conditions which exist in a market, including the number of firms.

competitive market: a market with a number of firms that compete with each other.

ACTIVITY 21.1

The soft drinks market is an important and growing global market. The market consists of carbonated (fizzy) soft drinks, non-carbonated soft drinks and sports and energy drinks. Some consumers are prepared to pay a higher price for brands containing ingredients, such as vitamins and minerals, that may offer health benefits.

In a small group:

1 Identify three reasons why consumers may prefer one firm's products over that of rival firms.

2 If a firm's products become more popular than those of its rivals, what will happen to its market share?

Make notes of the main points.

Advantages and disadvantages of competitive markets

There are a number of possible advantages and disadvantages of competitive markets, as shown in Table 21.1.

Table 21.1: Advantages and disadvantages of a competitive market

Advantages of a competitive market	Disadvantages of a competitive market
Consumers will have a choice of which firm to buy from.	There may not be much difference between the products produced.
Price may be low. A firm will be reluctant to raise its price for fear of losing consumers.	Price may be high as the firms may have high costs of production.
Cost may be low due to competition and the firms may be too small to experience diseconomies of scale.	Cost may be high if the scale of production is too low to take advantage of economies of scale.
Quality may be high as firms compete for consumers.	Quality may not be high if firms do not have enough profit to spend on investment.
It is usually easy for firms to enter the market, and so supply can adjust quickly to higher demand.	Firms may not stay in the market for long and so may not spend much on investment.

DISCUSSION

Discuss whether you think the level of competition between universities in your country to attract students is high or low.

The effect of competitive markets on price, quality, choice and profit

Competitive markets provide choice of sellers (see Figure 21.2). It is often claimed that price will be lower in a competitive market. This is because in such a market there is pressure for firms to keep prices low. If an individual firm charges a higher price, it runs the risk of losing all of its sales to its rivals as the products are likely to be close substitutes. Firms may seek to gain a competitive advantage by improving their products. They are likely to respond quickly and fully to any changes in demand.

A high level of competition is usually expected to promote efficiency. It provides firms with both an incentive and a threat to produce according to consumers' wants at the lowest possible cost. Any firm that can respond more quickly to consumers' demands, produce a higher quality product or can cut its costs should gain a competitive advantage and earn higher profits. The threat arises because any firm that is not efficient, that is produces at a higher cost or does not respond to changes in consumer tastes, will be driven out of the market. A high level of competition may drive the price down to a level which just covers the cost. That price, however, may not be that low. This is because competitive firms are likely to be small and often production on a larger scale reduces average total cost. Consequently, it may mean that costs and prices may be high in a competitive market.

A competitive market is likely to result in a low level of profit. Easy entry and exit will mean that in the long run, firms will probably earn relatively low profits. In some cases, this may be just enough profit to keep them producing the product. In the short run, they may earn more, or less, than this level of profit.

If firms do start to earn higher profits, other firms will come into the market to drive profits down. For example, if there is a major sports event or a festival held in the city, taxi firms from elsewhere may send more of their vehicles into the city to meet the higher demand.

Figure 21.2: Consumers have a wide range of washing machines to choose from produced by a variety of manufacturers

ACTIVITY 21.2

Find out how competitive the market for bookshops is in your town/city or a nearby city/town.

Write a report of your findings. You may want to cover the number of bookshops, their opening hours, the size of the shops, the range of books they sell, the price charged for the same book and other services they offer.

21.2 Monopoly markets

The usual meaning of a **monopoly** is a sole supplier of a product having 100% share of the market. This is often referred to as a pure monopoly, and we will concentrate on this definition. Some governments define a monopoly as a firm that has 25% or more share of the market, and a dominant monopoly when a firm has a 40% share of the market.

The number of firms that can be defined as monopolies depends, in part, on the way markets have been defined. The narrower the definition, in terms of the product and geographical area, the more examples will be found. For example, a country may have only one firm supplying gas, but several firms in its energy industry. There may be a relatively high number of food retailers in a town, but only one food shop in a neighbourhood, making it a local monopoly.

Characteristics of monopoly markets

The main characteristics of a monopoly firm include:

- The firm is the industry. It has a 100% share of the market.

- There are high **barriers to entry and exit**, making it difficult for other firms to enter the market.

- A monopoly is a price maker. Its output is the industry's output, and so changes in its supply affect the market price.

Why do monopoly firms arise?

What causes a firm to have total control of a market? In some cases, a monopoly may develop over time. One firm may have been so successful in cutting its costs and responding to changes in consumer trends in the past that it has driven out rival firms and captured the whole of the market. Also, mergers and takeovers may result in the number of firms being reduced to one.

Alternatively, a monopoly may exist from the start. One firm may own, for example, all the gold mines in a country or it may have been granted monopolistic powers by a government which makes it illegal for other firms to enter the market. A patent (the legal right to make or sell an invention) would also stop other firms from producing the product.

> ## KEY TERMS
>
> **monopoly:** a market with a single supplier.
>
> **barrier to entry:** anything that makes it difficult for a firm to start producing the product.
>
> **barrier to exit:** anything that makes it difficult for a firm to stop making the product.

> ## TIP
>
> You may find it useful to research a monopoly in your country and evaluate its performance. A real-world example may help to reinforce your understanding of monopoly markets.

Why do monopoly firms continue?

Another important question to be asked is: What stops new firms from entering the market and providing competition to a monopoly? It is the existence of barriers to entry and exit. One type of barrier is a 'legal barrier'. As mentioned above, this may be in the form of a patent or a government act.

Another important barrier to entry is the **scale of production**. If the monopoly is producing on a large scale, it may be able to produce at a low unit cost. Any new firm, unable to produce as much, is likely to face higher unit costs and therefore will be unable to compete. It can also be expensive to set up a new firm if large capital equipment is required. Other barriers to entry include the creation of brand loyalty through branding and advertising, and the monopoly's access to resources and retail outlets.

Barriers to exit can also stop new firms from entering the market. One barrier to exit may be a long-term contract to provide a product. Some firms may be reluctant to undertake such a commitment. **Sunk costs** are a significant barrier to exit. These are the costs, such as advertising and industry-specific equipment, which cannot be recovered if the firm leaves the industry.

> **KEY TERMS**
>
> **scale of production:** the size of production units and the methods of production used.
>
> **sunk costs:** cost that cannot be recovered if the firm leaves the industry.

> ### ACTIVITY 21.3
>
> In each case, what type of barriers to entry and exit may exist in each market below?
>
> 1   airlines
>
> 2   movie production
>
> 3   steel production
>
> 4   window cleaning
>
> Produce a poster from your answer.

Advantages and disadvantages of monopoly markets

The existence of barriers to entry means that a monopoly can earn high profits in the long run. Firms outside the industry may not be aware of the high profits being earned. Even if they do know about the high profits and want to enter the industry, they are kept out by the high barriers to entry and exit.

A monopoly has control over the supply of the product, but although it can seek to influence the demand, it does not have control over it. In fact, a monopoly has to make a choice. It can set the price, but then it has to accept the level of units that consumers are prepared to buy at that price. If, on the other hand, it chooses to sell a given quantity, the price will be determined by what consumers are prepared to pay for this quantity. Figure 21.3 shows that if a firm sets a price P, the demand curve determines that it will sell amount Q. If it decides to sell amount Q_1, it will have to accept a price of P_1.

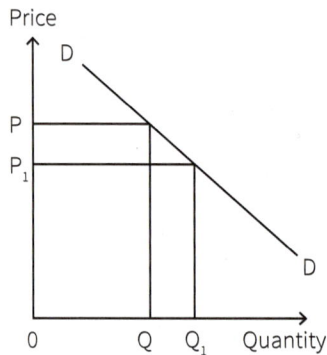

Figure 21.3: The choice facing a monopolist

Monopolies are often viewed negatively, but monopoly firms also have advantages for market and consumers alike – see Table 21.2.

Table 21.2: Advantages and disadvantages of monopoly markets

Advantages	Disadvantages
Average total cost may be low. This is because it may be able to take advantage of economies of scale.	Average total cost may be high if the monopoly grows too large and experiences diseconomies of scale.
Price may low due to low average total cost.	Price may be high as lack of competition may enable a firm to restrict supply to push up prices.
Avoids wasteful purchase of duplicate capital equipment by several firms. For example, it would be expensive to have a number of different firms laying and operating rail tracks.	May not update capital equipment if the firm is complacent about the lack of competition.
High profits may be spent on research and development, allowing the introduction of new and improved types of products. No direct competitive pressure means all profits resulting from new methods and products will benefit the monopoly firm.	May produce poor quality product, knowing that consumers will not be able to switch to rival products.
The need to overcome barriers to entry and break the monopoly may encourage firms outside the industry to try and develop a better product.	May fail to develop new products that respond to changes in consumer trends and tastes.

LINK

The risk of monopoly power reducing the pressure on the firm to keep costs and price low and some measures a government may take to reduce monopoly power is discussed in Chapter 13.2 (Causes and consequences of market failure – Abuse of monopoly power).

ACTIVITY 21.4

Table 21.3 compares a competitive market and a monopoly market. Copy and complete the table.

Table 21.3

	Competitive market	Monopoly market
Level of competition		None
Number of producers	Many	
Barriers to entry		High
Influence on price	Limited or none	
Number of substitutes		None

REFLECTION

Did completing the table in Activity 21.4 help you understand the difference between a competitive market and a monopoly market? Or would a different approach such as a mind map help reinforce your understanding?

The effect of having only one firm on price, quality, choice and profit

As a monopoly firm will have market power, it may charge a high price, not be concerned about improving the quality of the product and will not provide consumers with a choice of which firm to buy from. This, however, may not always be true. If a monopoly produces a large output, it may be able to take advantage of economies of scale and may have the funds to spend on improving the product.

A monopoly may be able to earn a high profit, but there is still a risk that if it does not take notice of changes in market conditions it might make a loss. For example, a firm may have had a monopoly in shops renting videos and games in a country. However, the emergence of online streaming is likely to have resulted in the firm making a loss and going out of business.

ECONOMICS IN ACTION

Competition in the markets for board and video games

Figure 21.4: A family plays a popular board game

Economists study a variety of real-world markets to assess how firms perform under different market structures. They examine how the number of firms in a market can influence the behaviour of firms, but what they first have to do is to define the market. There are, for example, many firms that produce board games, a relatively high number of firms that produce chess sets, but only one firm that owns the right to produce the board game Monopoly. An owner of a board game is likely to protect its exclusive right to produce and sell the game by taking legal action against any firm that seeks to copy its game.

A number of board games are very profitable. This is also the case for some video games. The video game Minecraft, now owned by Microsoft, earns significant profits. In 2023, more than 240 million units of the game were sold. Related merchandise, including lunchboxes and T-shirts, also earned profits for Microsoft.

Legal barriers and other barriers to selling established board games and video games can encourage firms to develop new board and video games. To attract consumers away from the established firms' games, they are likely to try to produce games of a higher quality.

1   Why might other firms wish to produce and sell video games like Minecraft?

2   Why may consumers benefit from a firm stopping other firms producing the same product?

SUMMARY

You should now know:

- The key characteristics of competitive markets are the presence of many buyers and sellers and entry to and exit from the market.

- Competitive firms usually earn relatively low profits in the long run.

- Competitive markets may promote efficiency, keep prices low and quality high. However, low-scale production may mean that prices are not as low as possible and also there may be a lack of choice of types of products.

- The key characteristics of a monopoly market are dominance of the market by one firm and high barriers to entry and exit.

- A monopoly market can arise because one firm captures the market, one firm is formed by mergers and takeovers or the law protects a firm's monopolistic power.

- A monopoly can determine price or the quantity it sells, but not both.

- A monopoly may raise price, reduce quality and fail to innovate. However, it is also possible that it may produce at a low cost and charge a low price. It may also innovate due to the availability of finance and sense of security.

Chapter 21 practice questions

1   Which is a feature of a competitive market?

   A   easy entry and exit

   B   firms with a high market share

   C   small number of buyers

   D   small number of sellers   [1]

2   Indian Railways is a monopoly firm. What does this mean?

   A   the firm has a small share of the market

   B   the firm has no competitors

   C   the firm is a price taker

   D   the firm is not protected by barriers to entry   [1]

3   In which type of market structure can high profits be earned in the short run?

   A   competitive market

   B   monopoly

   C   monopoly and competitive market

   D   neither monopoly nor competitive market   [1]

4   Which is a barrier to entry?

   A   brand loyalty

   B   lack of advertising

   C   low set-up costs

   D   perfect information   [1]

5   More firms enter a market. What **must** occur as a result of their entry?

   A   better-quality product

   B   greater choice of sellers

   C   higher profit for each producer

   D   lower price   [1]

                                                           Total: [5]

6   a   Define 'barrier to entry'.   [2]

   b   Explain **two** characteristics of a competitive market.   [4]

   c   Analyse how a change in the number of firms in a market can
       affect the profits that are earned.   [6]

   d   Discuss whether or not a monopoly benefits consumers.   [8]

                                                          Total: [20]

CHECK YOUR PROGRESS

How well do you think you have achieved the learning intentions for this chapter?
Give yourself a score from 1 (still need a lot of practice) to 5 (feeling very confident)
for each learning intention. Provide an example to support your score.

Now I can...	Score	Example
explain the characteristics of a competitive market		
discuss the advantages and disadvantages of competitive markets		
explain the effect of having a high number of firms on price, quantity, choice and profit		
explain the characteristics of a monopoly market		
discuss the advantages and disadvantages of a monopoly market		
explain the effect of having only one firm on price, quantity, choice and profit.		

Section 3 practice questions

1   Read the source material carefully before answering all parts of the question.

CASE STUDY: CORPORATE LAWYERS

Corporate lawyers specialise in advising firms on their legal rights and undertake legal work in drawing up contracts. They work in law firms and in large companies including commercial banks. In a commercial bank, a corporate lawyer may undertake legal work on, for example, the setting up of a new saving scheme, a merger with another bank or on the rights of the bank's shareholders.

US corporate lawyers' wages are high in comparison to the wages paid in most other countries. In 2023, the average wage received by a US corporate lawyer was $142 000 a year. This compared with an average of $50 000 a year in India, for example. Some experienced US corporate lawyers working for top law firms and for multinational companies may earn in excess of $400 000. Most corporate lawyers enjoy relatively high job security and good working conditions. This is one reason why the number of law school graduates has been increasing in the country for some time. In recent years, there has also been an increase in corporate legal work with more mergers taking place and more legal cases being brought against firms.

In recent years, the bonuses paid to corporate lawyers has increased by a greater percentage than their wages. Bonuses paid to US corporate lawyers can vary significantly from year to year. They rise when firms' profits are increasing and when it is considered that the productivity of the corporate lawyers is increasing.

The average wage of a corporate lawyer in the UK in 2023 was $89 000. In the UK, as in other countries, the average wage a worker receives is influenced by the qualifications they possess. Figure 1 shows the average hourly wage rate for workers with different qualifications in the UK in 2023.

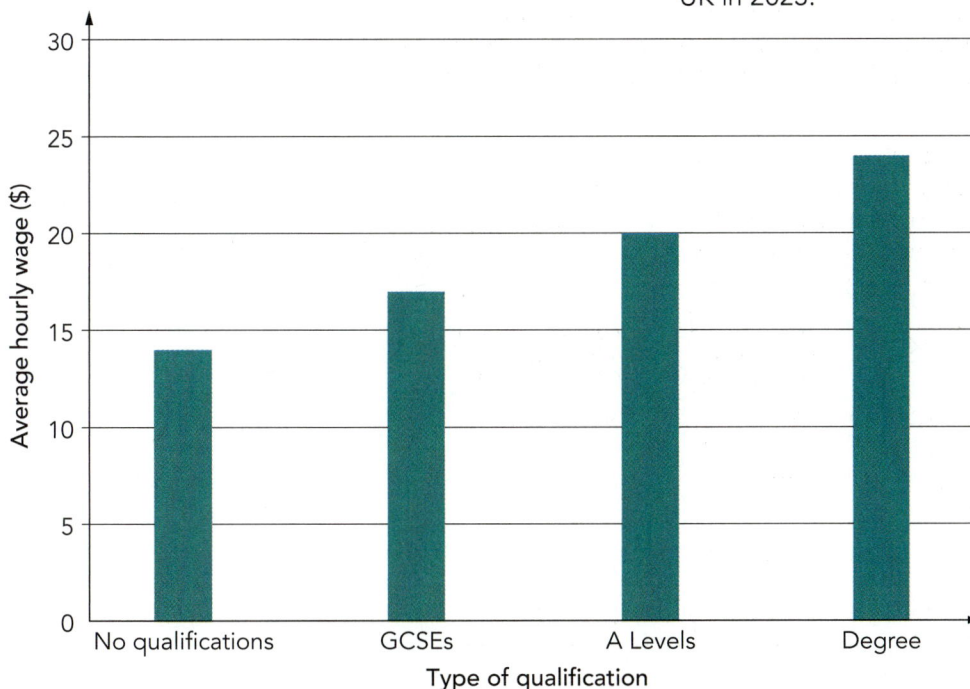

Figure 1: Average hourly wage rate by qualification, the UK, 2023

Refer to the information in the source material in your answers.

    a   Calculate, in percentage terms, how much more on average corporate lawyers earned in the USA than in India in 2023.   **[2]**

    b   Identify **two** reasons, other than high wages, why someone may want to work as a corporate lawyer.   **[2]**

    c   Explain **one** reason why US firms may prefer to pay bonuses rather than raise the wages of corporate lawyers.   **[2]**

    d   Draw a demand and supply diagram to show why the average wage of US corporate lawyers has increased in recent years.   **[4]**

    e   Analyse the relationship between qualifications and the average hourly wage rate.   **[4]**

    f   Discuss whether or not higher wages in the USA will result in Indian corporate lawyers moving to the USA.   **[6]**

                                                              Total: [20]

2   Read the source material carefully before answering all parts of the question.

CASE STUDY: E-COMMERCE IN CHINA

The e-commerce delivery business is expanding rapidly in China and throughout the world. More and more people are ordering products online, and a number of firms are delivering these products to people's doors. These delivery firms are investing in advanced IT systems and new methods of delivery. Some firms are using drone deliveries to speed up their deliveries, which reduces the number of workers and the amount of warehouse space needed, and so reduces the wages and rent paid.

One Chinese e-commerce delivery firm, Cainiao, is increasing its market share by buying out other e-commerce delivery firms. Its growth in size has enabled it to process orders and to use larger delivery vehicles more efficiently. It decreased its average cost of delivery to $1.40 in 2023 and is now delivering to more than 2 800 districts in China. The firm might be able to reduce its average total cost further by employing a greater proportion of capital. It currently makes good use of a supply of skilled workers and employs some temporary workers to deal with peaks in demand. The average delivery price it charged was 30% higher than its unit cost in 2023. This profit margin is below that of some of its competitors. To widen the gap between revenue and cost, the e-commerce delivery firms are seeking to be more responsive to changes in consumer demand and to be more productively efficient.

Foreign firms are also building up delivery networks in China, attracted by the rise in consumer spending in China. Figure 2 shows how household disposable income and consumer spending changed over the period 2010–2022.

CONTINUED

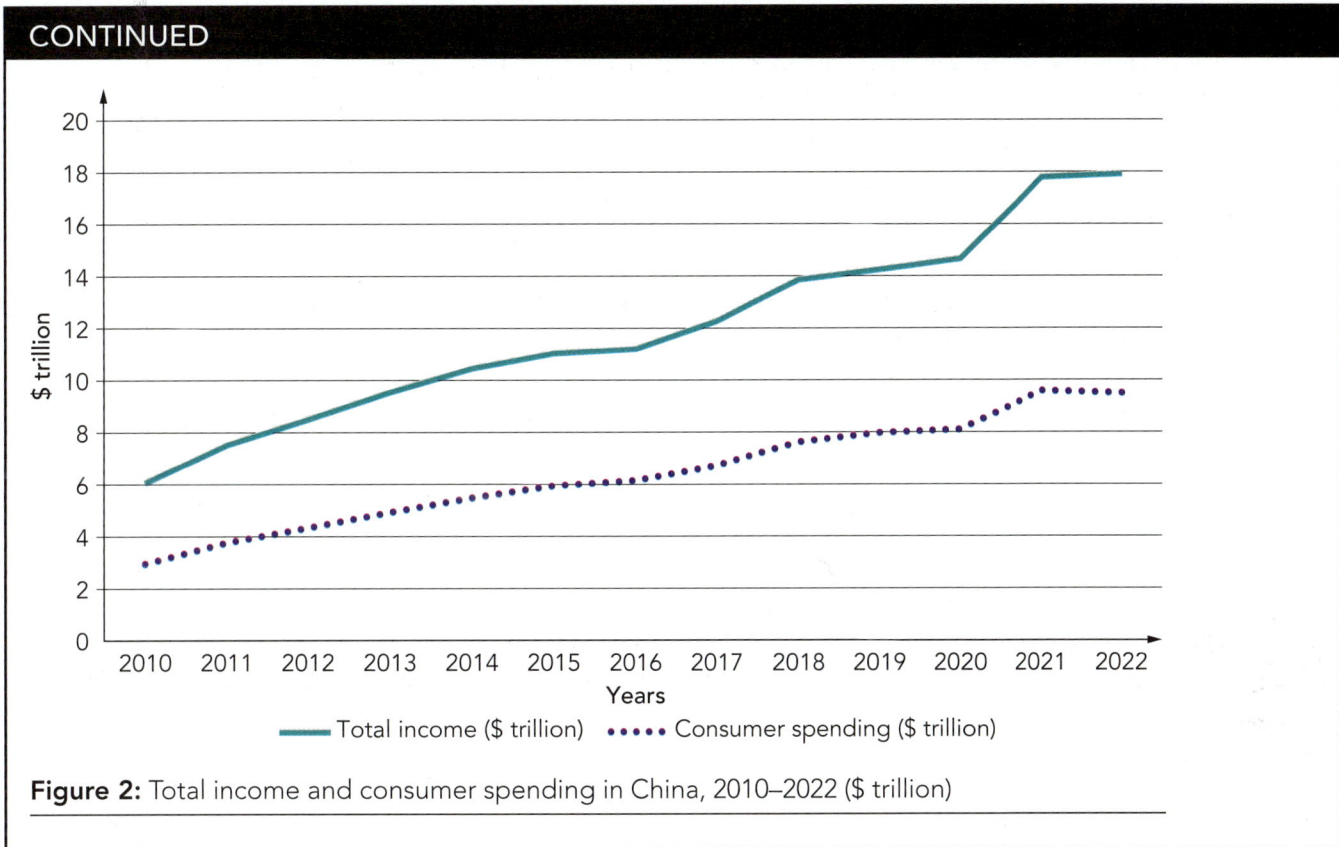

Figure 2: Total income and consumer spending in China, 2010–2022 ($ trillion)

Refer to the information in the source material in your answers.

a   Calculate how much Cainiao charged, on average, for a delivery in 2023.   **[2]**

b   Explain **one** type of economy of scale that Cainiao is able to enjoy.   **[2]**

c   Explain **one** advantage of capital-intensive production.   **[2]**

d   Analyse how firms following the objective of profit maximisation may benefit consumers.   **[4]**

e   Analyse the relationship between total income and consumer spending over the period shown.   **[4]**

f   Discuss whether or not small e-commerce delivery firms can compete against large e-commerce delivery firms.   **[6]**

Total: [20]

3 In 2023, teachers in England took industrial action. In that year, the average wage of a teacher in England was $52 000 a year with a starting salary of $38 000, and a national average wage of $48 260, compared to the national average for all workers of $39 950. Of course, some workers in England were paid less than teachers who were starting their careers. For example, some farm workers were paid only $19 500. A number of other workers experienced a fall in pay which took some into poverty and affected their spending.

    a   Define 'industrial action'. [2]

    b   Explain how the spending of people living in poverty is likely to differ from that of the rich. [4]

    c   Analyse the reasons why someone may continue to work in a job despite a fall in pay. [6]

    d   Discuss whether or not teachers will always earn more than farm workers. [8]

Total: [20]

4 Recent years have seen a number of mergers in food processing firms throughout the world. At the end of 2022, two food processing firms, the Italian Ferrero Group and the US Wells Enterprise, merged. It was hoped that the merger would reduce average fixed cost. The food processing industry is growing at a rapid rate and becoming more capital-intensive. These changes are having an impact on the profits of the firms in the industry.

    a   Define 'average fixed cost'. [2]

    b   Distinguish between a horizontal merger and a vertical merger, and give an example of each. [4]

    c   Analyse **three** causes of an increase in demand for capital goods. [6]

    d   Discuss whether or not the growth of an industry will increase the profit earned by the firms in the industry. [8]

Total: [20]

> Section 4

Government and the macroeconomy

Government macroeconomic intervention

Introduction

Each government has aims for the economy of its country. At the start of 2023, the Chinese government announced that it was aiming for its economy to produce a minimum of 5% more output than in 2022. Also in 2023, the Indian government said it would try to ensure that the price level would not rise by more than 6% above that for 2022. Do you know what your government is trying to achieve for the macroeconomy?

ECONOMICS IN CONTEXT

Sweden's economic problems

In 2023, the Swedish economy was facing three main problems. One was the rate at which prices were increasing. On average, prices were 9% higher than they had been a year before. This was the highest percentage rise for 30 years.

The country's unemployment rate was also high at 8% and was on an upward trend. A connected problem was that the country's output was 1% lower than in the previous year.

Higher prices mean that households will enjoy fewer goods and services unless their incomes rise in line with the increase in prices. Higher unemployment will mean that the income of those who lose their jobs is likely to fall. Lower output will reduce the goods and services available to households and is likely to lead to higher unemployment in the future.

Governments need to determine what their aims for the economy are. They have to think carefully how to tackle a number of problems that are occurring at the same time. They have to ensure that in trying to solve one problem they will not make one of the other problems worse.

Discuss in a pair or group:

1   What do you think is the main economic problem facing your economy?

2   How could you judge whether the Swedish government was successful in improving the Swedish economy?

Figure 22.1: Malmö in Sweden, a country that was facing a number of economic problems

22.1 Macroeconomic aims of government

The main government aims for the economy are economic growth, full unemployment / low unemployment, stable prices / low inflation, balance of payments stability, redistribution of income and environmental sustainability. A government can operate a range of policy measures to achieve these macroeconomic aims, and it will be judged on the success or otherwise of the measures.

Performance of the economy, however, is influenced not just by government policies. In a market that is becoming increasingly global, one economy's macroeconomic performance is being affected more and more by what is happening in other economies.

Economic growth

When an economy experiences **economic growth** there is an increase in its output in the short run. This is sometimes referred to as **actual economic growth**. In the long run, for an economy to sustain its growth, the productive potential of the economy has to be increased. Such an increase can be achieved as a result of a rise in the quantity and/or quality of factors of production.

The difference between actual and **potential economic growth** can be shown on a production possibilities curve (PPC) diagram. In Figure 22.2, the movement from point A to point B represents actual economic growth – more capital and consumer goods are made. The shift outwards of the PPC from YY to ZZ represents potential economic growth – the economy is capable of producing more.

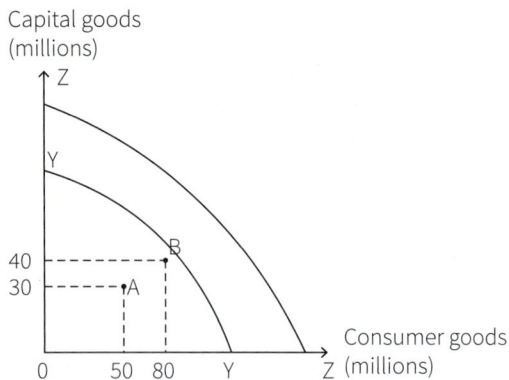

Figure 22.2: Actual and potential economic growth

In analysing economic growth and other macroeconomic issues, economists also make use of aggregate demand and aggregate supply diagrams.

Aggregate demand (AD) consists of consumer expenditure (household spending), investment, government spending and net exports (exports minus imports):

$$C + I + G + (X - M)$$

There are a number of causes of an increase in aggregate demand, and a shift to the right of the AD curve. These include an increase in population, a cut in the rate of interest, a lower exchange rate and greater confidence.

Aggregate supply (AS) is the total supply of a country's products. It is perfectly elastic if the economy has a significant number of unemployed resources, as then more can be produced without a contingent rise in costs of production and prices. The curve becomes more inelastic as the economy approaches full employment, since then the firms will be competing for resources, and this will push up their costs and, as a result, the price level. At full employment of resources, aggregate supply becomes perfectly inelastic, since at this point a further increase in output is not possible. Aggregate supply will increase, and the AS curve shifts to the right, if costs of production fall and if the quantity or quality of resources increases.

Changes in AD and AS affect the macroeconomy. Figure 22.3 shows actual economic growth. The rise in AD has resulted in a rise in the country's output and a small rise in the price level.

Figure 22.4 shows potential economic growth. The maximum amount that the economy can produce has increased. In this case, the rise in the quantity and/or quality of resources has no impact on output.

KEY TERMS

economic growth: an increase in the output of an economy and, in the long run, an increase in the economy's productive potential.

actual economic growth: an increase in the output of an economy.

potential economic growth: an increase in an economy's productive capacity.

aggregate demand (AD): the total demand for a country's product at a given price level. It consists of consumer expenditure, investment, government spending and net exports (exports – imports).

aggregate supply (AS): the total amount of goods and services that domestic (local) firms are willing to supply at a given price level.

If, however, an increase in productive potential occurs when an economy is operating close to full employment, it can cause a rise in the country's output and a fall in the price level, as shown in Figure 22.5.

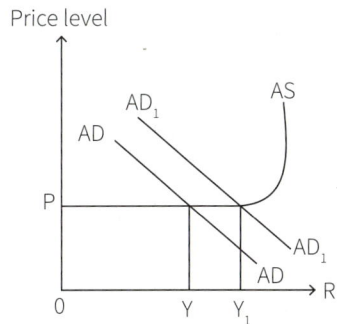

Figure 22.3: Actual economic growth

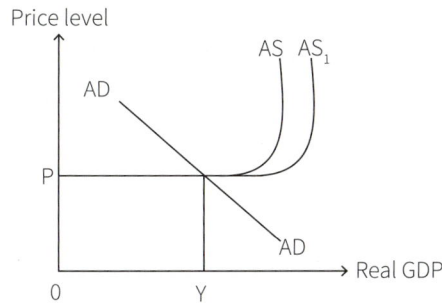

Figure 22.4: Potential economic growth

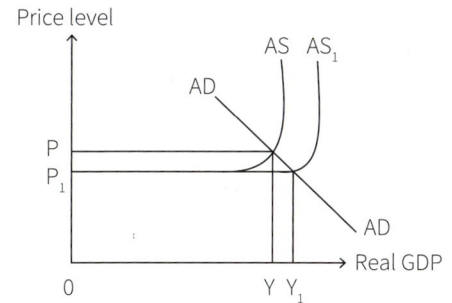

Figure 22.5: Potential economic growth causing a rise in national output

Reasons why governments aim for economic growth

Governments want to achieve economic growth because producing more goods and services can raise people's living standards. Economic growth can indeed transform people's lives and enable them to live longer because of better nutrition, housing and healthcare.

Economic growth can also help a government achieve its other economic aims. As output increases, employment is likely to rise. If output increases to match higher demand, upward pressure on the price level can be avoided. A country's trade position may be improved if some of the extra output is exported. Some of the poor may gain jobs and some may be helped by the extra tax revenue generated.

Criteria that governments may set for economic growth

The determinant of a country's possible economic growth rate is its level of output in relation to its current maximum possible output and its growth in productive capacity. If, for instance, an economy is growing at 2% below its maximum possible output and its productive capacity is expected to increase by 3% this year, its possible economic growth rate is 5%. Most governments would like their economies to be working at full capacity. Some governments set a target for the economic growth rate of their economies based on their assessment of the possible economic growth rate.

> ### DISCUSSION
>
> Discuss the reasons why a country may produce a lower output this year than last year.

Full employment / low unemployment

Most governments try to achieve as low a level and rate of unemployment as possible. This is sometimes expressed as **full employment**. Those people who are willing and able to work at the going wage rate can find employment when there is full

LINK

There are a number of possible causes of economic growth – see Chapter 26.2 (Causes and consequences of economic growth – Causes of economic growth).

KEY TERM

full employment: the lowest level of unemployment possible.

employment. Of course, not everyone wants to work or is able to work. These people are not in the labour force. They are said to be economically inactive and are dependent on those in the labour force. The **economically inactive** includes children, the retired, students in full-time education, homemakers and those who are too sick or disabled to work. People who are in work or are unemployed but actively seeking work form the labour force and are said to be **economically active**. The unemployment rate is the percentage of the labour force who are willing and able to work but are unemployed.

Reasons why governments aim for full employment / low unemployment

Unemployment is a waste of resources. Those unemployed can suffer a number of disadvantages, including low income. Government tax revenue may have to be spent supporting the unemployed.

Criteria that governments may set for unemployment

Most governments and economists think that it is not possible to achieve 0% unemployment. This is because they think that even in a strong economy with demand for labour equalling the supply of labour, there will always be some workers changing jobs and being unemployed for short periods. As a result, governments aim for a low rate of unemployment. This rate can vary from country to country depending on their economic circumstances, with what is regarded as the full employment rate varying between countries and over time. In most countries, it is thought to be difficult to get unemployment below 3%.

KEY TERMS

economically inactive: people of working age who are not in the labour force.

economically active: being a member of the labour force.

LINK

How the unemployment rate is calculated is shown in Chapter 27.2, (Measurement of unemployment), with an example.

LINK

Unemployment has a number of effects – see Chapter 27.4 (Consequences of unemployment).

ACTIVITY 22.1

In 2023, Mexico had an economic growth rate of 3.2%, an unemployment rate of 3% and an underemployment rate of 29%. Table 22.1 shows Mexico's industrial structure by output and employment in 2023.

Table 22.1

	% share of output	% share of employment
Agriculture	3	12
Manufacturing	32	25
Services	65	63

Discuss these questions with another student.

1   What do you think is meant by underemployment?

2   In which sector is underemployment likely to have been the highest in 2023? Explain your answer.

3   From the information given, explain whether Mexico had the potential to grow at a faster rate than 3.2% in 2023.

Write your answers in your notebook.

Stable prices / low inflation

Stable prices means that the price level in the economy is not changing significantly over time. The price of some products may be falling while the price of others may be rising, but generally the amount households are paying for the products they are buying is relatively stable. This will mean that the value of money will largely retain its value. So the purchasing power of wages and savings will not noticeably change.

Reasons why governments aim for stable prices

Governments aim for stable prices because these ensure greater economic certainty and prevent the country's products from losing international competitiveness. If firms/ producers, households and workers have an idea about future level of prices, they can plan with greater confidence. It also means that they will not act in a way that will cause prices to rise in the future. Firms/producers will not raise their prices because they expect their costs to be higher, households will not bring forward purchases for fear that items will be more expensive in the future, and workers will not press for wage increases just to maintain their real disposable income.

KEY TERMS

stable prices: the price level in the economy not changing significantly over time.

inflation rate: the percentage rise in the price level of goods and services over time.

inflation: a rise in the average price of goods and services over time.

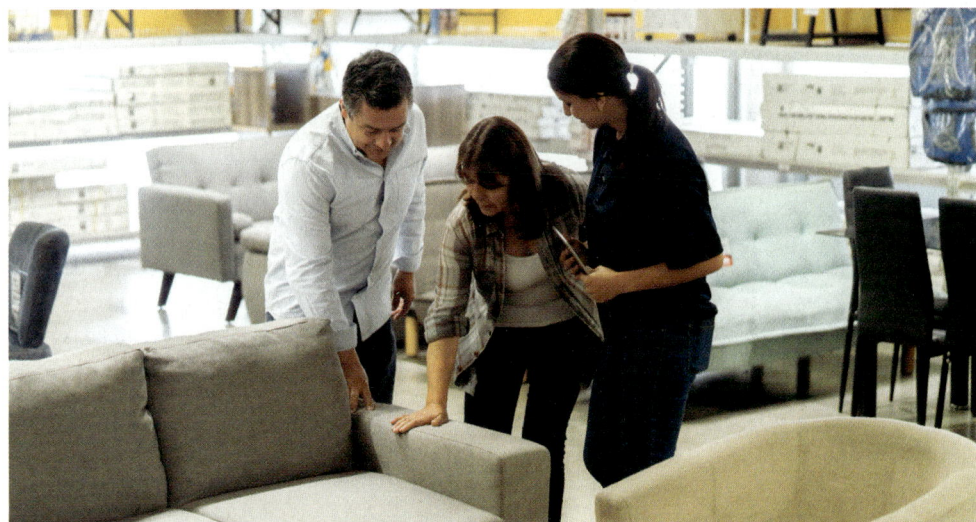

Figure 22.6: Stable prices make it easier for households to calculate how much they will need to save for expensive items such as furniture

Criteria that governments may set for low inflation

In seeking to achieve stable prices, most governments are not aiming for a 0% change in price. Some governments, for instance, have set a target **inflation rate** of 2%. Others have a higher rate. They do not aim for unchanged prices for two main reasons. One is that measures of **inflation** tend to overstate rises in prices. A price index, for instance, might indicate that the general price level has risen by 1%, but in practice, prices might not have changed and might have even fallen slightly. Some of the prices paid by people are lower than those appearing in the official price level indices, as people buy some products at reduced prices in sales and also make second-hand purchases. Price rises can also hide the improvements in products. A car may cost $100 more this year than last year, but it may include a number of new features, such as front and rear parking sensors. So the question arises, is the car actually more expensive or is it a different car?

A second reason is that a slight rise in prices can provide some benefits. It can encourage producers to increase their output, as they may think that higher prices will lead to higher profits. It can also enable firms to cut their wage costs by not raising wages in line with inflation. The alternative to such a move might be a cut in employment.

Governments also try to avoid a fall in the price level if it is caused by a fall in aggregate demand. This is because it could result in a decline in output and a rise in unemployment.

LINK

Inflation is measured using the consumer price index – see Chapter 28.2 (Measurement of inflation and deflation – Constructing a price index).

ACTIVITY 22.2

In 2009, the South African government set its central bank, the South African Reserve Bank, an inflation rate target of between 3% and 6%. This target range was still in force in 2023. Figure 22.7 shows the country's inflation rate for the period from 2016 to 2023.

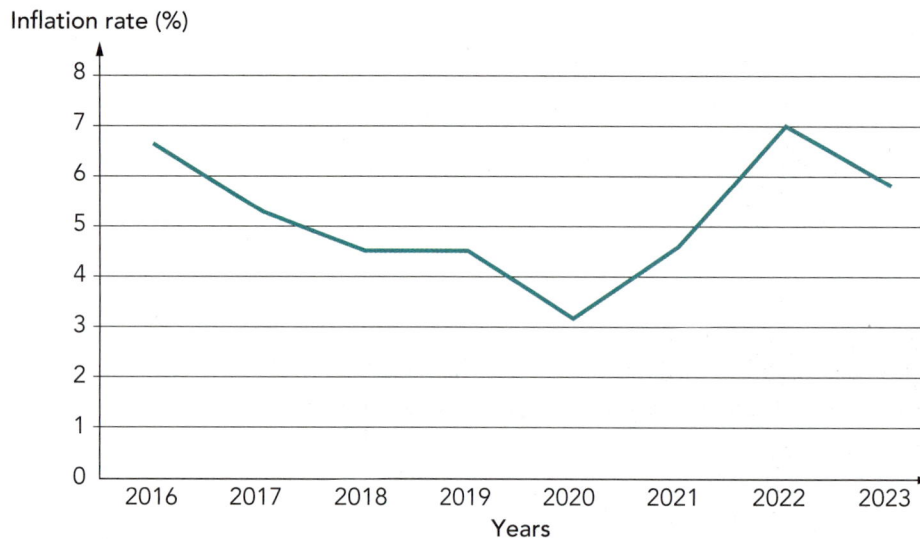

Figure 22.7: South Africa's inflation rate, 2016–2023

Discuss what the graph shows with another student. Individually, write your answers to the questions. Then share your answers.

1   Identify one function of a central bank other than controlling the inflation rate.

2   How successful do you think the South African Reserve Bank was in achieving the government's inflation rate target over the period shown? Explain your answer.

Balance of payments stability

A key part of a country's **balance of payments** is its record of revenue received from selling exports and its expenditure on imports. Over the long run, most governments want the value of their country's exports to equal the value of their country's imports, so that what the country earns from exports equals what it spends on imports. It does not want large fluctuations in the difference between the revenue coming into the country and the spending going out of the country.

KEY TERM

balance of payments: the record of a country's economic transactions with other countries.

Reasons why governments aim for balance of payments stability

If expenditure on imports exceeds revenue from exports for a long period of time, the country will be living beyond its means and will get into debt. If export revenue is greater than import expenditure, the population of the country will not be enjoying as many products as possible.

Criteria that governments may set for balance of payments stability

While governments usually aim for export revenue to equal import expenditure, they may not be concerned if there is a surplus of export revenue over import expenditure or a deficit of export revenue, provided this is of a small amount or if it lasts a short period of time. A deficit may occur caused by an increase in the import of raw materials and capital goods. This is unlikely to be a cause for concern as the products purchased may increase the economy's ability to produce more goods and services to sell at home and abroad. Short-term deficits and surpluses may also arise from fluctuations in income at home and abroad.

ACTIVITY 22.3

Table 22.2 shows selected economic indicators in 2023.

Table 22.2

Economy	Economic growth rate %	Unemployment %	Inflation rate %
Greece	2.4	10.0	4.0
India	6.5	8.0	5.6
Japan	2.0	2.6	3.2
Pakistan	1.7	6.3	31.8
Venezuela	5.5	5.4	360.0

In a group of five, each select a country from Table 22.2. Look at the data for your chosen country.

1   Explain to the rest of the group whether you think your country achieved all of its macroeconomic aims in 2023. Do you all agree?

2   Now, discuss whether the information will allow you to decide which country is likely to have had the highest number of unemployed workers in 2023.

Redistribution of income

A government may seek to redistribute income from the rich to those living in poverty. The more money someone has, the less they tend to appreciate each unit. A rich person with an income of $10 000 a week is unlikely to miss $10, but that sum would make a huge difference to someone currently struggling on $20 a week.

Governments redistribute income by taxing and spending. The rich are taxed more than those living in poverty. Some of the money raised is spent directly on those living in poverty by means of benefits such as housing benefit and unemployment benefit. Other forms of government expenditure, such as that on education and health, particularly benefit those living in poverty. Without the government providing these services free of charge or at subsidised prices, those living in poverty may not be able to access them.

Reasons why governments aim to redistribute income

Inequality of income and wealth may mean that some people are experiencing poverty. Governments try to reduce poverty because of the hardships it causes. Inequality can grow without government intervention. The rich tend to marry the rich and benefit from better education and have more opportunity to save. A significant gap between the rich and those experiencing poverty can also cause social unrest as those experiencing poverty may feel a sense of social injustice.

Criteria that governments may set for income redistribution

Governments are unlikely to aim for a perfectly equal distribution of income. This is because people have different needs. It is also because taxing the rich too heavily and providing too generous benefits may act as a disincentive to effort and enterprise.

Environmental sustainability

Environmental sustainability aims to conserve the natural world in a healthy state. Sustainability involves not depleting non-renewable resources, reducing the loss of biodiversity and cutting levels of pollution. There is now greater awareness of the damage being done to the environment by greenhouse gas emissions. The term 'greenhouse gases' cover the emission of carbon dioxide, methane and nitrous oxide. Such emissions arise from the burning of fossil fuels, coal, oil and gas, for industrial and domestic use and from agriculture, particularly livestock agriculture. Greenhouse gas emissions can trap the sun's heat and cause a rise in average temperature (global warming). Most governments are now taking measures to both offset the effects of climate change and to try to stop the global temperature rising further by reducing greenhouse gas emissions.

Reasons why governments aim for environmental sustainability

Governments may aim for environmental sustainability to protect their country and others from the impacts of a decline in the quality of the environment. For example, global warming is thought to cause more severe weather, including heat waves, storms, floods and droughts and rising sea levels. Such severe weather can cause loss of life, loss of infrastructure, destruction of crops and can spread diseases.

Governments may also aim to protect the environment to ensure that it is available in a healthy state for future generations. As well as reducing global warming, this would reduce the use and depletion of non-renewable resources by making greater use of renewable resources.

Criteria that governments may set for environmental sustainability

At a United Nations climate change conference held in 2015, 196 countries signed the Paris Agreement. This commits them to prevent the global temperature rising above pre-industrial levels by 1.5°C by 2100. To achieve this, it is thought that there needs to be global net zero greenhouse gas emissions by 2050.

Net zero greenhouse emissions does not mean that there are no greenhouse gas emissions. What it does mean is that any greenhouse gas emissions are matched by the capture of such emissions by natural means and technology. Trees, soil and the sea absorb some greenhouse gas emissions naturally and advances in technology are allowing some collection of the emissions before they enter the atmosphere, so that they can be stored underground and, in some cases, reused. Most countries have set targets for when they want to achieve net zero greenhouse gas emissions.

ACTIVITY 22.4

Saudi Arabia has stated that it will achieve net zero greenhouse gas emissions by 2060. It intends to plant 10 million trees between 2023 and 2060. Many of these trees will be planted in cities. They will increase the tree canopy cover, which will directly reduce temperature in towns and cities, and they will capture more carbon emissions. Despite its large reserves of oil, the Saudi Arabian government is encouraging the development of renewable energy. It is also investing in the development of carbon capture and reuse technology.

Produce a short presentation on environmental sustainability. Include two examples of renewable energy. Explain how other countries would benefit if Saudi Arabia achieves net zero greenhouse gas emissions by 2060.

22.2 Possible conflicts between macroeconomic aims

- **There is the risk that full employment may conflict with stable prices.** When there is a low level of unemployment, it will be difficult to increase output to match increases in aggregate demand. In this case, higher aggregate demand is likely to lead to higher prices. A low level of unemployment is likely to push up wages as firms compete for workers. The resulting higher costs of production are likely to result in inflation.

- **Full employment may conflict with balance of payments stability.** Producing a higher output may be partly the result of higher exports. The resulting rise in employment is likely to increase incomes, however, and spending on imports may increase by more than export revenue. To produce a higher output, firms may also import more imported raw materials and capital goods.

- **Economic growth and environmental sustainability are sometimes in conflict.** Countries may grow by simply increasing output without considering the impact of their actions on the environment. They may use fossil fuels to produce electricity for firms and to heat homes, some of which may be built in areas which were previously rich in biodiversity. Firms may do little to cut waste, save energy or reduce the pollution they may cause through the discharge of chemicals into rivers, for example. Households may not take part in environmental sustainability initiatives such as reducing energy use, conserving water, reusing and recycling items. However, it is possible that economic growth and environmental sustainability may be combined. For example, greater output of solar panels may contribute to both economic growth and environmental sustainability.

If the aims appear to conflict, a government may have to decide between, for instance, reducing inflation and reducing unemployment. Its choice will be influenced by the scale of the problem, the consequences of the problem and which problem the country's citizens are most concerned about.

ACTIVITY 22.5

In a group of six, write each of the six macroeconomic aims of government described in this chapter on a small piece of paper, fold the papers and place in a bag. Each take a macroeconomic aim from the bag. You have 3–5 minutes to put forward arguments for your macroeconomic aim to be given priority. At the end of the arguments, vote anonymously for what aim should be given priority. You cannot vote for the aim you argued for.

REFLECTION

What did you learn from presenting your case and from the cases put forward by the others in the group? Did it help you understand why governments have macroeconomic aims and why some may conflict while others may not?

TIP

When considering macroeconomic performance, it is important to show that you are aware of the events in your economy and other economies. To help you, find out and make a note of the unemployment rate, inflation rate, economic growth rate and current account position of your country, and compare them with the figures for three major economies.

ECONOMICS IN ACTION

The increase in awareness of the importance of the environment

Figure 22.8: During annual Earth Hour, people around the world switch off their lights

Economists have studied the link between the environment and the economy for a long time. Recently, economists have increased their focus on the environment. This reflects the increased awareness of the general public and governments of the dangers posed to the environment by human activity.

In 2007, Earth Hour was started to promote a sustainable environment. On the last Saturday in March, people in a large number of countries switch off their lights between 8.30 p.m. and 9.30 p.m.

Governments now meet each year at UN climate change conferences to assess their progress in cutting net carbon emissions to zero. A number of economists provide advice to governments on the measures they could adopt to achieve this objective. Some also write articles, blogs and books on the environment. Kate Raworth, an economist, has written a book titled *Doughnut Economics*, in which she emphasises how countries should aim to meet the needs of their populations for goods and services and social justice without exceeding environmental ceilings on, for example, loss of biodiversity and pollution.

1   Why do you think concern about the environment is increasing?

2   How may loss of animal and plant species reduce countries' ability to meet consumer needs?

SUMMARY

You should now know:

- The main macroeconomic aims of government are economic growth, full employment / low unemployment, stable prices / low inflation, balance of payments stability, redistribution of income and environmental stability.

- Economic growth can improve people's living standards by increasing the availability of goods and services.

- Full employment is usually considered to be the lowest rate of unemployment possible.

- Low and stable inflation creates certainty and avoids a loss of international competitiveness.

- Most governments aim for a match between export revenue and import expenditure in the long run.

- Governments redistribute income from the rich to those living with poverty by means of taxation and government expenditure.

- Environmental sustainability aims to conserve the quality of the natural world by avoiding the depletion of non-renewable resources, reducing the loss of biodiversity and cutting levels of pollution.

- There is the possibility that full employment may conflict with stable prices and economic growth, full employment may conflict with balance of payments stability and economic growth may conflict with environmental sustainability.

Chapter 22 practice questions

1   Which of the following is a macroeconomic aim of the government?

   A   a fall in national output

   B   high unemployment

   C   imports exceeding exports

   D   stable prices   [1]

2   A country has a population of 120 million and a labour force of 50 million, of which 46 million of its labour force are employed. How many people are unemployed?

   A   4 million

   B   24 million

   C   70 million

   D   74 million   [1]

3   Which could increase a country's productive potential?

   A   an improvement in education

   B   a reduction in the retirement age

   C   retention of worn-out machinery by firms

   D   migration of workers to other countries   [1]

4   What is meant by potential economic growth?

    A   an increase in productive capacity of an economy

    B   an increase in the total demand in the economy

    C   the economy's export revenue being greater than its import expenditure

    D   the economy operating at full employment   [1]

5   What is a government macroeconomic aim?

    A   an objective for all consumers in a market

    B   an objective for all firms in an industry

    C   an objective for the whole economy

    D   an objective for the whole labour force   [1]

                                                Total: [5]

6   **a**   Identify **two** macroeconomic aims apart from full employment.   [2]

    b   Explain what is meant by full employment.   [4]

    c   Analyse why governments want to achieve full employment.   [6]

    d   Discuss whether or not all governments will have the same economic aims.   [8]

                                                Total: [20]

CHECK YOUR PROGRESS

How well do you think you have achieved the learning intentions for this chapter? Give yourself a score from 1 (still need a lot of practice) to 5 (feeling very confident) for each learning intention. Provide an example to support your score.

Now I can...	Score	Example
explain the macroeconomic aims of government: economic growth, full employment / low employment, stable prices / lower inflation, balance of payments stability, redistribution of income, environmental sustainability		
analyse the reasons behind this choice of aims		
explain the criteria that governments may set for meeting each aim		
discuss the possible conflicts between macroeconomic aims: full employment and stable prices, economic growth and environmental sustainability, full employment and balance of payments stability.		

Fiscal policy

LEARNING INTENTIONS

By the end of this chapter, you will be able to:

- define the government budget, deficit and surplus
- calculate the size of a government budget deficit or surplus
- explain the main areas of government spending
- analyse the reasons for and effects of government spending
- analyse the reasons for taxation: raising revenue, discouraging consumption of demerit goods, reducing imports, redistributing income, influencing total demand, encouraging environmental sustainability
- explain the different classifications of tax: progressive, regressive, proportional, direct and indirect
- analyse the impact of taxation on consumers, workers, firms/producers, government and the economy
- define fiscal policy
- analyse taxes and government spending changes in the form of fiscal policy measures
- discuss how fiscal policy measures may enable a government to achieve its macroeconomic aims.

Introduction

Many of the products you buy will have a tax on them. When you start working, some of your income will be taken in tax. The firm you work with will also pay tax on the income it earns. Governments use the tax revenue they collect to spend on a range of items.

ECONOMICS IN CONTEXT

Will Denmark introduce a cow flatulence tax?

In 2009, the Danish Tax Commission suggested introducing what became known as a cow flatulence tax of $110 per cow per year. There were two main reasons given for such a tax. One was to reduce the number of cows kept by farmers as cows emit 60% of livestock emissions of methane per year (see Figure 23.1). The other reason was to raise revenue to finance research on carbon emissions. However, due to the strong opposition of farmers, the tax was not introduced.

Seven years later, in 2016, the Danish Ethics Council recommended a greenhouse tax on livestock carbon dioxide emissions. A further seven years later, in 2023, the Danish government reconsidered imposing a greenhouse tax on livestock carbon dioxide emissions, hoping that farmers might switch to arable production. In both cases, the proposed measure was strongly opposed by farmers. They argued that a better measure would be to develop livestock feed additives that can reduce the amount of methane emitted from livestock.

Discuss in a pair or a group:

1 Do you think a tax should be imposed on the emissions of methane that come from livestock?

2 On what would you spend the revenue from such a tax?

Figure 23.1: Cows are a major contributor to greenhouse gases

23.1 Government budget

A government sets out the amount it plans to spend and raise in revenue in a **government budget** statement. The budget statement shows the relationship between government revenue and government spending. A **government budget deficit** is when the government's spending, also sometimes called public expenditure, is higher than its revenue. In this case, the government will have to borrow to finance some of its spending. In contrast, a **government budget surplus** occurs when government revenue is greater than government spending. A balanced government budget, which occurs less frequently, is when government spending and revenue are equal.

LINKS

The reasons for government spending and taxation include to correct market failure and to increase the income of people living in poverty – see Chapter 14.3 (Government intervention to address market failure) and Chapter 30.3 (Policies to alleviate poverty and redistribute income).

KEY TERMS

government budget: the relationship between government revenue and government spending.

government budget deficit: government spending is higher than government revenue.

government budget surplus: government revenue is higher than government spending.

23.2 Reasons for government spending

One of the main areas that governments spend money on is social security benefits. These are also known as state benefits or welfare benefits and include state pensions, unemployment benefits, child benefits and housing benefits. Other main areas of government spending are health, education, law and order, defence and interest rate payments on past borrowing.

Governments spend for a number of reasons. These are:

- **To influence economic activity.** A government may, for example, increase its spending in order to increase aggregate demand in the hope that the higher aggregate demand will stimulate higher output and so result in economic growth.

- **To reduce market failure.** Governments spend on public goods as this would not be financed by the private sector. They spend on merit goods, particularly education and healthcare, as market forces would not allocate sufficient resources to their production. In addition, they spend money regulating markets where there is a difference between social and private costs and benefits and abuse of market power.

- **Government spending can be a powerful government measure.** This is because of the **multiplier effect** whereby any initial increase in spending will eventually cause a greater increase in aggregate demand. For example, if a government raised its spending by $20m, the final rise in the country's income, expenditure and output would be greater. This is because those who benefit from the $20m extra spending, may themselves spend $16m (saving $4m). In turn, those who receive the $16m may spend $13m, and so on. If expenditure continues to rise at this rate, total spending, income and output will rise by $100m. In this case, the final increase in expenditure is five times greater than the initial rise.

- **To promote equity (fairness).** Governments provide benefits and products to vulnerable groups and the unemployed. For example, some governments provide state pensions to the retired, subsidised housing for those living in poverty and free education to children.

- **To pay interest on national debt.** If a government has borrowed in the past to finance a gap between its spending and its tax revenue, it will have to pay interest on the loans.

- **To encourage environmental sustainability.** Governments are spending an increasing amount on promoting environmental sustainability. A number of governments, for example, subsidise renewable energy and subsidise home insulation to reduce energy use.

> **KEY TERMS**
>
> **multiplier effect:** the final impact on total (aggregate) demand being greater than the initial change.
>
> **national debt:** the total amount the government has borrowed over time.

ACTIVITY 23.1

Write a one-paragraph report for the Maldives Ministry of Tourism explaining how a decline in tourism would be expected to affect the government budget position of the Maldives. Start your report by stating how much the Maldives government raised in tax revenue in 2023.

23.3 Taxation

Reasons for taxation

Most people think that taxes are used to raise revenue for government spending. This is, indeed, a key aim of taxation, and in a number of countries tax revenue is the main source of government revenue. There are, however, other aims as well, including:

- **To redistribute income from the rich to low-income groups.** Higher-income groups usually pay more in tax than lower-income groups, and some of the revenue raised is used to pay benefits to those on low incomes.

- **To discourage the consumption of demerit goods.** Demerit goods are products the government considers more harmful to consumers than they realise, for example, cigarettes and sugary drinks.

- **To reduce imports** and so protect domestic industries. By placing tariffs on rival imported products, the country's inhabitants may buy fewer foreign and more domestic products.

- **To influence total (aggregate) demand.** As with government spending, changes in taxation can be used to change total demand. If an economy is experiencing rising unemployment, its government may cut taxes to stimulate an increase in consumption and investment.

- **To encourage environmental sustainability** by raising the costs of firms that impose costs on others by, for example, causing pollution.

The different classifications of tax

Taxes are either direct or indirect and progressive, proportional or regressive. Direct taxes are taxes levied on a person's or a firm's income or wealth. They are called direct taxes because the people or firms responsible for paying the tax have to bear the burden of the tax. Indirect taxes, which can also be called expenditure or outlay taxes, differ from direct taxes in two key ways. One is that they are levied on spending. The other is that the firms that actually make the tax payment to the government may pass on at least some of the burden of the tax to other people. For example, most of the tax that governments impose on petrol is passed on by petrol companies to the customers in the form of higher prices.

A **progressive tax** is one which takes a higher percentage of the income or wealth of the rich. As taxable income or wealth rises, so does the rate of taxation. In the case of a **proportional tax**, the percentage paid in tax stays the same as income or wealth changes. With a **regressive tax**, the percentage paid in tax falls as income or wealth rises. So, in this case, people with higher incomes pay a smaller percentage of their income in tax than those with low incomes do.

In the case of all three types of tax, the total amount of tax paid usually rises with income or wealth, but what differs is the percentage paid (see Table 23.1). For example, a rich person and a person with a low income pay the same excise duty per litre of petrol bought. The rich person is likely to buy more petrol and so will pay more tax in total. The amount paid, however, is likely to form a smaller percentage of their income, making this a regressive tax.

> **KEY TERMS**
>
> **progressive tax:** tax that takes a larger percentage of the income or wealth of the rich.
>
> **proportional tax:** tax that takes the same percentage of the income or wealth of all taxpayers.
>
> **regressive tax:** tax tax that a larger percentage of the income or wealth of those living in poverty.

Table 23.1: Progressive, proportional and regressive taxes

Progressive tax		
Income ($)	Tax paid ($)	Tax rate (%)
100	10	10
500	100	20
1 000	400	40
Proportional tax		
Income ($)	Tax paid ($)	Tax rate (%)
100	25	25
500	125	25
1 000	250	25
Regressive tax		
Income ($)	Tax paid ($)	Tax rate (%)
100	40	40
500	150	30
1 000	200	20

ACTIVITY 23.2

Some countries, including Bangladesh, Canada and Rwanda have banned plastic carrier bags. Other countries, including Ireland, the UK and the USA, impose taxes on plastic bags. The main reason for this is to cut their use and so reduce litter.

Produce a presentation on 'Government measures to reduce the use of plastic bags'. Your presentation should include:

1   reasons for imposing a tax on plastic carrier bags

2   whether a tax on plastic carrier bags is a direct or indirect tax

3   a demand and supply diagram to explain the effect of imposing a tax on plastic carrier bags on the market.

The main types of tax

The types of taxes imposed vary from country to country. There are some taxes, however, which are levied in most countries. Among the most common type of direct taxes are:

- **Income tax.** This is a tax on income that people receive from their employment and investment income. It is also known as personal income tax. People are given a tax allowance, which is an amount of income they earn free of tax. Income above this level is referred to as taxable income.

- **Corporate tax.** This is also referred to as corporate income tax or corporation tax. It is a tax on the profits of firms.

- **Capital gains tax.** This is a tax on the profit made on assets when they are sold for a higher price than what they were bought for. For example, a capital gain may be made by shareholders selling shares for more than what they paid for them. When a capital gains tax is imposed, there are usually some exemptions where capital gains tax is not payable. Exemptions normally include any money made on the sale of a person's main residence.

- **Inheritance tax.** This is a tax on wealth above a certain amount which is passed on to other people when a person dies.

Common types of indirect taxes are:

- A sales tax is a tax imposed when products are sold. The main examples of sales tax are GST (general sales tax) and VAT (value added tax).

- Excise duties are taxes charged on certain domestically produced goods, most commonly on petrol and tobacco. They are charged in addition to VAT.

- Customs duties are taxes on imports and are also called tariffs.

- A licence needed to use a range of products including a television and a car.

Local taxes

Most taxes are levied on a national basis, but some are levied on a local basis. Local taxes are used to pay for local services such as education, fire services, libraries, roads and refuse collection (see Figure 23.2). There are two main types of local taxes. One is based on the property of local firms and the other is based largely on the value of household property.

Figure 23.2: Fire services are usually paid for out of local taxation

In a number of countries, business rates are levied on local firms. The government collects the revenue and then distributes it to local authorities on the basis of the number of people living in each area. Municipal tax is based on the value of people's housing and expenditure of each municipality. It is collected directly by the municipal authority. Some countries also use local sales tax.

ACTIVITY 23.3

In Egypt, in 2023, the standard rate of corporate tax was 22.5%. Oil exploration and production firms were charged a higher rate of 40.55%. After a tax-free allowance, the rate of personal income tax in 2023 increased from 2.5% to 10%, then from 10% to 15%, then 15% to 20%, then 20% to 22.5%, then 22.5% to 25% and finally 25% to 27.5% as income rose.

Discuss these questions with another student. Write your answers in your notebook.

1   Explain why a government may charge oil firms a higher corporate tax rate than other firms.

2   Explain whether Egypt was operating a progressive or regressive income tax system in 2023.

The impact of taxation on consumers, workers, producers/firms, the government and the economy

The tax base is the source of tax revenue, that is what is taxed. A wide tax base means that a large range of items and people are taxed. The tax burden relates to the amount of tax paid by people and firms. It is sometimes expressed as a percentage of the country's total income (gross domestic product, or GDP). The higher the tax burden, the greater the percentage of people's and firms' income taken through tax.

There can be a link between the tax base and tax rates. A wide tax base may enable tax rates to be relatively low. High tax rates, particularly corporate tax rates, can reduce the tax base. This is because they may cause firms to move out of the country.

Impact of taxation on consumers

Some of the goods and services that consumers buy will have an indirect tax, such as GST, imposed on them. It is the legal responsibility of firms to pay the tax to the government. However, firms can pass some of the tax on to consumers in the form of a higher price. The incidence of taxation refers to the distribution of an indirect tax shared between consumers and firms.

In the case of products with inelastic demand, consumers bear most of the tax. This is because the firms can pass on a high proportion of the tax in the form of a higher price as they know it will not reduce the demand significantly. In contrast, if products have elastic demand, it is the firms who bear most of the tax. This is because they know that they cannot pass on much of the tax to consumers as such a move would bring down the sales significantly. Figure 23.3 shows the contrasting impact of a tax on a product with inelastic demand and a product with elastic demand.

(a)

Inelastic demand

(b)

Elastic demand

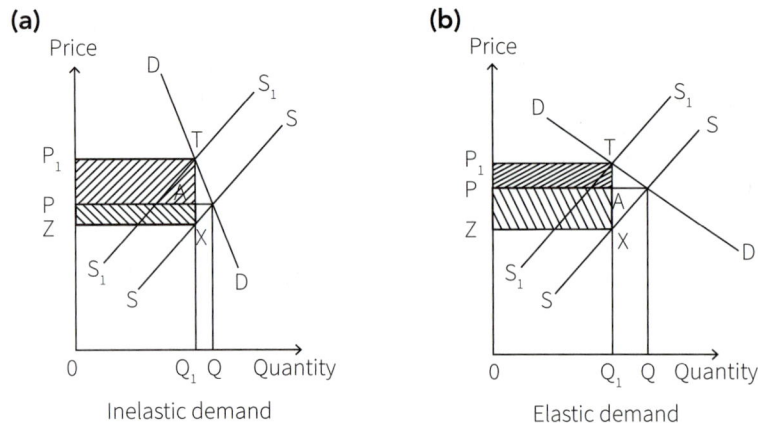

Figure 23.3: The proportion of tax paid by consumers and producers in (a) a market with inelastic demand and (b) a market with elastic demand

In both (a) and (b) in Figure 23.3 the tax shifts the supply curve to the left by the amount of the tax (TAX). The total tax revenue is P_1TXZ. The proportion of tax borne by consumers is represented by the change in price multiplied by the quantity sold, that is PP_1TA. The proportion borne by the firms is the amount by which the price producers receive after tax is below the original market price, multiplied by the quantity sold, that is PAXZ. Elasticity of supply also influences the incidence of taxation. The more inelastic supply is, the more the tax will be borne by the firms. In contrast, if supply is elastic, more of the tax will be borne by consumers.

Impact of taxation on workers

Workers pay personal income tax on their wages. The higher personal income tax rates are, the larger will be the gap between workers pre-tax income and their disposable income. A rise in personal income tax rates, by reducing disposable income, will reduce workers' purchasing power. High rates of income tax may stop some people from working overtime and taking promotion and prevent some people from entering the labour force. On the other hand, high tax rates may encourage some people to work harder. This is particularly likely to be the case with workers who have fixed financial commitments, such as mortgages. In addition, a number of workers cannot alter the hours they work because they are contracted for a fixed number of hours per week.

Impact of taxation on firms

As mentioned earlier, firms are responsible for paying indirect revenue to the government. Firms also have corporate income tax imposed on them. This is based on the profits they earn. High rates of corporation tax may discourage entrepreneurs from expanding their firms and investing in new markets. They may also encourage some firms to move to countries with low rates of corporate income tax. However, high rates of corporate income tax may not discourage firms from investing if after-tax profits are high. This may be the case if there is high demand in the country and if the government spends high amounts on areas, such as training and infrastructure, which can reduce firms' costs of production.

The firms in the country which compete with imports may welcome the government imposing taxes on imports. If the tax is high enough, it may give the domestic firms a competitive price advantage.

Impact of taxation on the government

Most governments get most of their revenue from taxation. The more tax revenue it receives, the more it can spend on, for example, healthcare and education (see Figure 23.4). Taxation can also help a government to influence total demand and to reduce market failure. In the case of reducing market failure, taxes on demerit goods may reduce their consumption. If consumption reduces, it could reduce pressure on government spending on healthcare.

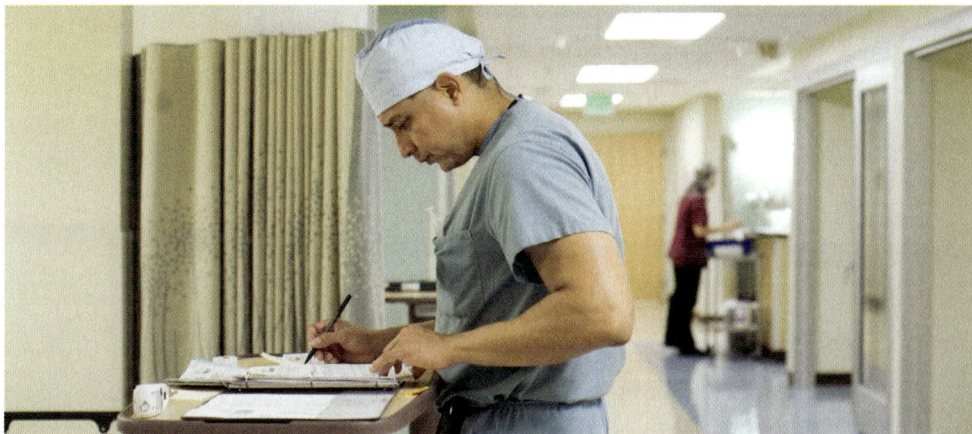

Figure 23.4: Taxation may be used to fund healthcare

Impact of taxation on the economy

One way taxation can influence total demand is by affecting saving. High taxes on income earned from saving reduce the return from saving, and may cause some people to save less, but they may encourage target savers to save more. A tax on saving is a direct tax. There is a risk that direct taxes, if set too high, may discourage effort, enterprise and saving. However, direct taxes have the benefits of being able to redistribute income and wealth and being a good source of income.

While direct taxes tend to be progressive, indirect taxes are regressive and therefore proportionately fall more heavily on those living with poverty. Increasing indirect taxes will also raise prices. This increase may stimulate workers to press for wage increases and set off a trend of rising prices, that is, inflation.

Indirect taxes do, however, have a number of benefits. They are relatively easy and cheap to collect as firms do some of the work. It is believed that they act as less of a disincentive to effort and enterprise than direct taxes. They can be used selectively to achieve particular aims, such as reducing the consumption of alcohol. They tend to be harder to evade than direct taxes and easier to adjust. To a certain extent, people also have more choice with indirect taxes. The amount of tax paid by them depends on what they buy. They may decide not to buy products which are highly taxed.

DISCUSSION

Discuss whether you think the money and assets people inherit should be taxed. You may want to consider how the tax revenue could be used, the issue of fairness and whether the measure will affect effort and enterprise.

23.4 Fiscal policy and policy measures

Fiscal policy refers to decisions on government spending and taxation taken to influence total (aggregate) demand in the economy.

Changes in taxes and government spending

Fiscal policy has a direct effect on the budget balance. To calculate a government's budget balance, as indicated above government spending is deducted from its revenue. The size of any budget deficit or budget surplus can be expressed in absolute amounts, for example $10bn, or as a percentage of GDP.

If government spending equals government revenue, and then the government increases its spending or cuts taxes, it will cause a budget deficit in the short run. It is possible, however, that the effects of these changes may be different in the long run. For example, an increase in government spending on education may increase productivity and output, which would be expected to raise tax revenue. Similarly, a cut in corporate tax may attract firms from overseas to set up in the country and for domestic firms to expand, and so increase revenue from corporate tax.

Since 2000, in a number of countries (such as Brazil and Nigeria), governments have become more reliant on indirect taxes and less on direct taxes. This move has been designed to reduce disincentive effects and tax evasion. More recently, some countries (such as Estonia and Kazakhstan) have been adopting what are called **flat taxes**. A pure flat rate tax system would involve income tax, corporate tax and sales tax being set at the same rate with no exceptions. A number of advantages are claimed for flat taxes. They are simple to administer for governments and firms, there is less incentive to evade paying tax and more incentive for workers and entrepreneurs to earn and produce more. However, concerns have been expressed about the regressive nature of flat taxes.

KEY TERMS

fiscal policy: decisions on government spending and taxation designed to influence aggregate demand.

flat taxes: taxes with a single rate.

ACTIVITY 23.4

Table 23.2 shows government spending and revenue in the UK in 2023.

Table 23.2

Government spending ($bn)		Government revenue ($bn)	
Social security benefits	434	Personal income tax	560
Healthcare	312	VAT (sales tax)	242
Education	168	Corporate tax	104
Interest payments	147	Excise duty	64
Defence	86	Other taxes	254
Transport	76	Other revenue	122
Law and order	64		
Other	224		

CONTINUED

1   Calculate the UK's government budget deficit in 2023.

2   Identify one form of government spending in the table which is spending on a merit good.

3   What proportion of the UK's government revenue was accounted for by personal income tax?

Discuss your answers with another student.

REFLECTION

How did carrying out the calculations increase your understanding of budget imbalances? Would you find it useful to write down on cards how economic figures can be calculated with examples?

23.5 Effects of fiscal policy on government macroeconomic aims

If a government wants to raise total (aggregate) demand in order to increase economic growth and employment, it will increase its spending and/or cut taxation by lowering tax rates, reducing the items taxed or raising tax thresholds. For example, a government may cut income tax rates. This will raise people's disposable income which will enable them to spend more. Higher consumption is also likely to raise investment. Figure 23.5 shows the effect of an **expansionary fiscal policy**.

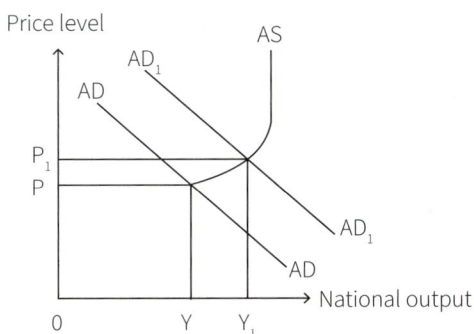

Figure 23.5: The effect of an expansionary fiscal policy

In this case, the higher aggregate demand causes economic growth. With more goods and services being produced, employment is likely to rise. A government may implement a **contractionary fiscal policy** to reduce inflationary pressure. A cut in government spending on education, for example, would reduce aggregate demand. Such a reduction may lower the rise in the general price level. It may also reduce an excess of import spending over export revenue. This is because spending is likely to fall, including spending on imports. Domestic firms, facing lower demand at home, may also put more effort into exporting.

KEY TERMS

expansionary fiscal policy: rises in government expenditure and/or cuts in taxation designed to increase aggregate demand.

contractionary fiscal policy: cuts in government expenditure and/or rises in taxation designed to reduce aggregate demand.

LINKS

How fiscal policy can be used to influence government macroeconomic aims is discussed in a number of chapters – see Chapter 26.4 (Policies to promote economic growth), Chapter 27.5 (Policies to reduce unemployment), Chapter 28.5 (Policies to control inflation) and Chapter 30.3 (Policies to alleviate poverty and redistribute income).

ACTIVITY 23.5

Table 23.3 shows the budget balance GDP for six countries in 2023.

Table 23.3

Country	Budget balance as a % of GDP	GDP ($ billions)
Germany	–2.4	4 082
Indonesia	–2.5	1 320
Malaysia	–5.0	407
Norway	10.8	375
Pakistan	–7.6	580
Saudi Arabia	–1.9	1 103

1   Calculate Norway's government budget surplus in dollars.

2   Which country came closest to matching government spending and revenue?

3   Which country had the largest budget deficit in terms of dollars?

Discuss your answers with another student.

ECONOMICS IN ACTION

Taxation and government spending in Finland

Figure 23.6: Helsinki, the capital of Finland

Economists advise governments on their spending and taxation plans and interpret the likely effects of these for firms and news media. In 2023, the Government of Finland announced in its budget that it was not planning to change the country's personal income tax rates. Figure 23.7 shows the type of personal income tax system Finland was operating in 2023.

CONTINUED

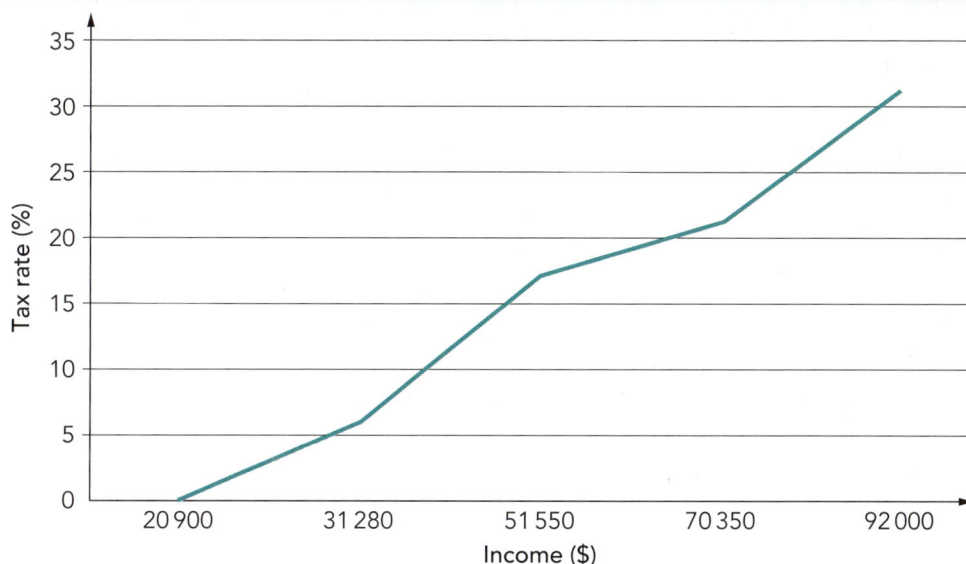

Figure 23.7: Finland's personal income tax system in 2023

Finland had a standardised rate of VAT of 24%. In its 2023 budget, the Finnish government announced that the rate of VAT on electricity would be reduced from the standard rate to 10%. There was already a reduced VAT rate of 14% on food and a reduced rate of 18% on books.

The government announced an increase in spending on education, partly to cover the continued increase in the cost of raising the minimum school-leaving age from 16 to 18 years old two years before. It also announced an increase in spending on environmental protection. This included more spending on improving waterways and processing food waste into energy in the form of biogas.

1 What type of personal income tax system was used in Finland in 2023?

2 Do you think books should be taxed at a lower rate than most products?

SUMMARY

You should now know:

- The government budget shows the relationship between government spending and government revenue.

- Governments spend money to influence economic activity, to reduce market failure, to promote equity and to pay interest on the national debt.

- The reasons for taxation are to raise revenue, redistribute income, discourage the consumption of demerit goods, raise the costs of firms that impose these costs on others, discourage the consumption of imports, influence total demand and encourage environmental sustainability.

- Direct taxes are levied on income and wealth and include income tax, corporate income tax, capital gains tax and inheritance tax.

CONTINUED

- Indirect taxes are levied on expenditure and include sales tax, excise duties, customs duties and licences.

- Progressive taxes take a higher percentage as income or wealth rises, a proportional tax takes the same percentage and a regressive tax takes a smaller percentage.

- If demand is inelastic, most of an indirect tax will be borne by the consumers, whereas if demand is elastic, it will be borne mainly by the firm.

- Direct taxes may discourage effort, enterprise and saving, but they can help to redistribute income and wealth, and raise a significant amount of revenue.

- Indirect taxes tend to be regressive and may raise prices, but these are relatively easy and cheap to collect, do not tend to act as a disincentive to effort, enterprise and saving and are harder to evade.

- Consumers may pay high prices due to indirect taxes, personal income reduces workers' disposable income, firms pay both direct and indirect taxes, and taxation provides the main source of most governments' revenue.

- Fiscal policy influences total (aggregate) demand in the economy by changing taxes and government expenditure.

Chapter 23 practice questions

1   What is a regressive tax?

   A   a tax that falls in line with inflation

   B   a tax that is replaced by one which generates more income

   C   a tax that places a greater burden on those experiencing poverty than the rich

   D   a tax that reduces government revenue over time   [1]

2   A government wants to redistribute income from the rich to those experiencing poverty. Which changes in taxation would help it to achieve this objective?

   A   a cut in capital gains tax and inheritance tax

   B   a cut in corporate tax and a rise in sales tax

   C   a rise in customs duties and excise duties

   D   a cut in VAT and a rise in income tax   [1]

3   In which circumstance will the greatest amount of the tax be borne by the consumer?

	PED	PES
A	elastic	inelastic
B	inelastic	inelastic
C	inelastic	elastic
D	elastic	inelastic

                                                                          [1]

4   The diagram shows the effect of introducing a tax (TAX). What is the producer's revenue now?

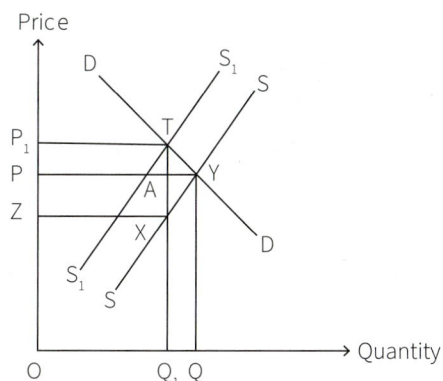

A $OPAQ_1$

B $OPYQ$

C OP_1TQ_1

D $OZXQ_1$ [1]

5   A government increases its spending from \$360bn to \$420bn and experiences an increase in its income from \$295bn to \$310bn. What is the change in its government budget?

A   a decrease in its budget deficit of \$65bn

B   a decrease in its budget surplus of \$110bn

C   an increase in its budget deficit of \$45bn

D   an increase in its budget surplus of \$15bn   [1]

                                                                Total: [5]

6   a   Define 'progressive tax'.   [2]

    b   Explain the difference between a direct tax and an indirect tax, giving an example of each.   [4]

    c   Analyse the reasons why governments impose taxes.   [6]

    d   Discuss whether or not an increase in income tax rates will improve economic performance.   [8]

                                                                Total: [20]

CHECK YOUR PROGRESS

How well do you think you have achieved the learning intentions for this chapter? Give yourself a score from 1 (still need a lot of practice) to 5 (feeling very confident) for each learning intention. Provide an example to support your score.

Now I can...	Score	Example
define the government budget, deficit and surplus		
calculate the size of a government budget deficit or surplus		
explain the main areas of government spending		
analyse the reasons for and effects of government spending		
analyse the reasons for taxation: raising revenue, discouraging consumption of demerit goods, reducing imports, redistributing income and influencing total demand encouraging environmental sustainability		
explain the different classifications of tax: progressive, regressive, proportional, direct and indirect		
analyse the impact of taxation on consumers, producers, government and the economy		
define fiscal policy		
analyse taxes and government spending changes in the form of fiscal policy measures		
discuss how fiscal policy measures may enable a government to achieve its macroeconomic aims.		

> # Chapter 24
Monetary policy

LEARNING INTENTIONS

By the end of this chapter, you will be able to:

- define money supply and monetary policy
- explain monetary policy measures: changes in money supply, interest rate and foreign exchange rate
- discuss the effect of monetary policy on government macroeconomic aims.

Introduction

Monetary policy plays a key role in most economies. In recent years, there have been frequent changes in interest rates throughout the world. Interest rate changes can have significant effects on economies. By influencing total (aggregate) demand, they and changes in other monetary policy measures can affect not only inflation but also economic growth, unemployment and the balance of payments.

> **KEY TERM**
>
> **foreign exchange rate:** the price of one currency in terms of another currency or currencies.

ECONOMICS IN CONTEXT

What should be the aims of a central bank?

Central banks play a key role in implementing monetary policy. They are given an aim or aims by their governments that they are required to meet. To achieve their aim or aims, they make decisions about the interest rate they charge commercial banks and the money supply. They may also influence the country's **foreign exchange rate**. For example, the US government has set its central bank, the Federal Reserve, the task of achieving an inflation rate of 2%. It also requires the Federal Reserve to help it achieve the lowest rate of unemployment that is consistent with the inflation target. The Bank of England has also been set an inflation target of 2% as its main aim, while recognising that it may sometimes have to balance low inflation with economic growth and low unemployment.

In 2020, the Saudi Arabian government changed its instructions to its central bank to make achieving stable prices and promoting economic growth equally important. The Central Bank of Nigeria is required to maintain stable prices and promote economic growth. Its mission statement also refers to improving living standards and achieving sustainable economic development.

Discuss in a pair or group:

1   What would you include in the instructions for the central bank of your country?

2   How easy is it likely to be to achieve both stable prices and economic growth?

Figure 24.1: In Nigeria, the country's central bank is tasked with keeping prices stable and promoting economic growth

24.1 Money supply and monetary policy

Monetary policy covers decisions on the money supply, the interest rate and the foreign exchange rate, although some economists regard changes in the foreign exchange rate as a separate policy. Monetary policy influences the supply and/or price of money. The money supply is the total amount of money in circulation in a country. It includes notes, coins and bank accounts. The price of money is the interest rate. The aim of monetary policy is to influence total (aggregate) demand. In most countries monetary policy measures are carried out by central banks on behalf of governments (see Figure 24.2).

> **KEY TERM**
>
> **monetary policy:** decisions on the money supply, the rate of interest and the foreign exchange rate taken to influence aggregate demand.

Figure 24.2: The People's Bank of China

ACTIVITY 24.1

In its meeting in December 2023, the Monetary Policy Committee (MPC) of the State Bank of Pakistan (SBP) stated that it was going to keep its interest rate unchanged at 22%. This was despite expectations that total (aggregate) demand and inflation would increase and despite rising imports which were increasing the deficit on the current account balance of payments.

Write a press release on behalf of the bank's monetary policy committee, announcing that the interest rate is to stay unchanged. Explain the main reason behind the MPC's decision and why the MPC thinks its decision will encourage investment.

24.2 Monetary policy measures

Changes in the money supply

A central bank can increase the money supply by printing more money, buying back government bonds or encouraging commercial banks to lend more. Printing more money is a straightforward way of increasing the money supply. It is sometimes referred to as 'resorting to the printing press'. Buying government bonds gives commercial banks more money to lend to their customers. Encouraging commercial banks to lend or removing any restrictions on bank lending may also result in more borrowing to spend on consumer and capital goods. So, if the money supply is increased, there is likely to be an increase in consumer spending and investment. Such a rise in aggregate demand is likely to increase output.

TIP

The word 'monetary' should help you remember that monetary policy is involved with money – both its supply and its price (the interest rate).

ACTIVITY 24.2

Follow the monetary policy changes of the central bank of your country as well as those of another central bank. Consider why their monetary policy measures may be similar and why they may be different. Discuss your findings with another student.

Changes in the interest rate

The main monetary policy measure currently used in most countries is changes in the interest rate. Central banks set the interest rate. This interest rate is used as the basis for the interest rate it pays to commercial banks on their deposits with it and the interest rate it would charge for lending to the commercial banks. If a central bank raises its interest rate, commercial banks are likely to raise the rate they charge to their customers. Such a rise in the interest rate is likely to reduce aggregate demand by lowering consumer expenditure and investment. It will do this in three main ways:

- Any households or firms who have borrowed in the past will have to pay more interest on their loans. This will reduce the amount of money they have to spend.

- It will make it more expensive for households and firms to borrow to finance their spending. Borrowers will now have to pay more for any new loans they take out.

- A higher interest rate will increase the incentive to save. Households and firms will earn more from saving than before. This means that for households the opportunity cost of spending will have increased and for firms the opportunity cost of investment will have increased. Firms may also have less incentive to invest as they will expect consumption to be lower.

Some households and firms that are savers will now earn more interest, and so they may spend more. However, those people who save are less likely to spend any extra money than borrowers are, and so the net effect will probably be a reduction in consumer expenditure. A higher interest rate may also reduce aggregate demand by encouraging a rise in the foreign exchange rate. Such a rise may lower net exports by causing a rise in the price of exports and a fall in the price of imports.

There may be times when a central bank decides to keep the rate of interest unchanged for a relatively long period of time. It may do this to promote certainty which can make planning easier. This, in turn, may encourage investment.

LINK

Central banks can influence the foreign exchange rate by changing the interest rate and by buying and selling the currency – see Chapter 35.3 (Determination of a foreign exchange rate in foreign exchange markets – Causes of foreign exchange rate fluctuations).

LINKS

Monetary policy may be used to try to achieve the government's macroeconomic aims – see Chapter (Policies to promote economic growth), Chapter 27.5 (Policies to reduce unemployment) and Chapter 28.5 (Policies to control inflation).

ACTIVITY 24.3

In October 2023, the Central Bank of Argentina raised the interest rate from the very high rate of 118% to 133%.

A local business owner knows you are studying economics. They have messaged you their concern about the bank's decision to raise the interest rate. Write a message explaining the most likely reason why the central bank has raised the rate of interest. Explain also whether the business owner should be concerned about the increase.

Changes in the foreign exchange rate

A government may instruct its central bank to change the country's foreign exchange rate or to try to influence it to move in a particular direction. A government may want the price of the foreign exchange rate to fall to encourage a rise in exports, for example.

24.3 Effects of monetary policy on government macroeconomic aims

Monetary policy is used to increase total (aggregate) demand. If a government wants to increase the economic growth rate and reduce unemployment it may use **expansionary monetary policy**, reducing the interest rate or increasing the money supply.

Monetary policy is often used to control changes in the price level in the economy. If the price level is rising too quickly, the central bank may use **contractionary monetary policy**, increasing the interest rate or reducing the growth in the money supply. The aim of contractionary monetary policy would be to reduce total (aggregate) demand and the upward pressure on prices.

> ### KEY TERMS
>
> **expansionary monetary policy:** increases in the money supply and/or the rate of interest designed to increase aggregate demand.
>
> **contractionary monetary policy:** cuts in the money supply or growth of the money supply and/or rises in the rate of interest designed to reduce aggregate demand.

DISCUSSION

Discuss whether you think your country's central bank is following a contractionary or expansionary monetary policy.

ACTIVITY 24.4

Copy and complete the following flowchart.

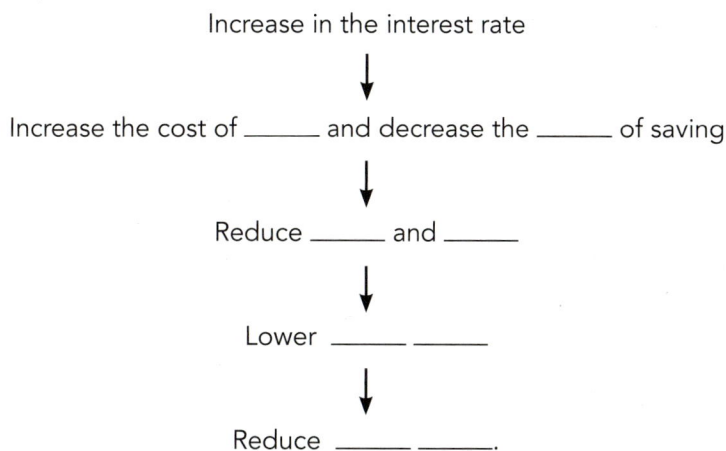

Increase in the interest rate

↓

Increase the cost of _____ and decrease the _____ of saving

↓

Reduce _____ and _____

↓

Lower _____ _____

↓

Reduce _____ _____.

REFLECTION

How did completing the flowchart help you understand the important links between a change in the interest rate and the effects on the economy? What action did you take if you were not able to fill out some of the chart?

ECONOMICS IN ACTION

Influences on central banks' decisions on interest rates

Figure 24.3: The Monetary Policy Committee of the Bank of Japan makes an important decision

Committees of central banks meet regularly to decide whether to leave the bank's interest rate unchanged or whether to raise or lower it. In making their decision, they take into account that any change may take up to two years to have an effect.

In making their decisions, the committees are provided with a range of information by economists. This includes data on changes in wages, investment, consumer expenditure and energy prices. Some of the bank's economists are likely to go to different parts of the country, visiting firms and regional governments to assess if the conditions are different in the rest of the country. Economists also conduct surveys for the bank on consumer and business confidence.

The committees are also influenced by their government's fiscal policy. It is likely that both the government and the central bank will follow similar policy approaches. In deciding their fiscal policy and monetary policy, the government and the central bank consider what all the information they receive indicates about the future growth in total demand. If it is thought that total demand will grow too fast, causing a rise in the inflation rate, it is likely that both contractionary fiscal policy and contractionary monetary policy will be used.

1   What are two pieces of information that might cause a central bank to raise its interest rate?

2   In what circumstances might expansionary fiscal policy and expansionary monetary policy be used?

SUMMARY

You should now know:

- Monetary policy seeks to influence aggregate demand.

- Monetary policy measures are decisions on the money supply, the interest rate and the foreign exchange rate.

- An increase in the money supply would be expected to increase aggregate demand.

- A reduction in the interest rate may increase aggregate demand as it reduces the cost of borrowing and reduces the reward for saving.

- A fall in the foreign exchange rate is likely to increase net exports.

- To increase economic growth and reduce the unemployment rate, a central bank may reduce theinterest rate.

- A central bank may increase the interest rate to reduce upward pressure on the price level.

Chapter 24 practice questions

1   Which one of the following is a monetary policy measure?

   A   a decrease in government regulations on labour markets

   B   a decrease in government spending on education

   C   an increase in the interest rate

   D   an increase in sales tax   [1]

2   What would increase the money supply?

   A   a decrease in consumer expenditure

   B   a decrease in investment

   C   an increase in bank lending

   D   an increase in the interest rate   [1]

3   Which type of institution is responsible for conducting monetary policy?

   A   a central bank

   B   a commercial bank

   C   a multinational company

   D   a trade union   [1]

4   What is most likely to increase demand in the economy?

   A   a reduction in government spending

   B   a reduction in the rate of interest

   C   a rise in a budget surplus

   D   a rise in income tax   [1]

5   What is **not** included in monetary policy?

    A   foreign exchange rate

    B   government spending

    C   interest rates

    D   money supply   **[1]**

                          Total: [5]

6   **a**   Define 'monetary policy'.   **[2]**

    b   Explain one similarity and one difference between monetary policy and fiscal policy.   **[4]**

    c   Analyse why trade unions are likely to welcome an expansionary monetary policy.   **[6]**

    d   Discuss whether or not an increase in the interest rate will reduce consumer expenditure.   **[8]**

                          Total: [20]

CHECK YOUR PROGRESS

How well do you think you have achieved the learning intentions for this chapter? Give yourself a score from 1 (still need a lot of practice) to 5 (feeling very confident) for each learning intention. Provide an example to support your score.

Now I can...	Score	Example
define money supply and monetary policy		
explain the effect of monetary policy measures on the money supply, interest rate and foreign exchange rate		
discuss whether monetary policy measures may enable a government to achieve its macroeconomic aims.		

Chapter 25
Supply-side policy

Introduction

Governments try to increase both firms' and workers' ability to produce more. They do this in a variety of ways, including improving education and training, spending on infrastructure projects and introducing labour market reforms. They may also lower direct taxes and improve the incentives to work and invest in other ways. They may transfer some industries from the public sector to the private sector. There is the potential for these measures to improve a government's macroeconomic aims, but they are not always successful.

ECONOMICS IN CONTEXT

Rising Vietnamese educational standards

Figure 25.1: Students in Vietnam aim for full marks

The Vietnamese government has set a target of spending a minimum of 20% of total government spending on education.

By 2023, it had not achieved the target, but it had come close. There have been improvements in school attendance and student achievement (see Figure 25.1). In international comparisons of student performance, Vietnamese students do well, particularly in science subjects.

As well as seeking to raise the quality of primary and secondary education, the Vietnamese government is investing more in university education, including developing the research facilities at the country's universities. Educated school leavers and university graduates tend to be more productive, innovative and occupationally mobile workers.

Over time, as in many countries, adult literacy and output have increased in Vietnam. Figure 25.2 compares Vietnam's rise in adult literacy and the global rise in adult literacy, and Figure 25.3 compares the Vietnam's rise in total output and the global rise in total output.

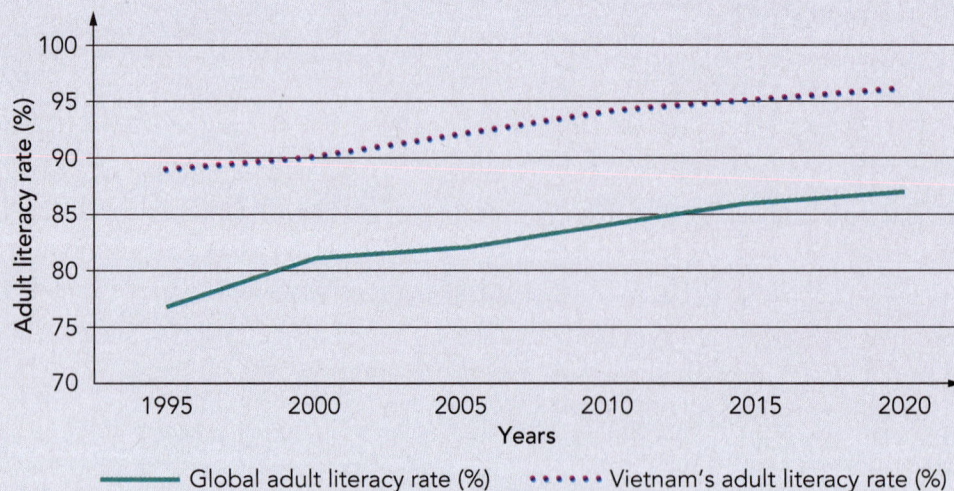

Figure 25.2: Global and Vietnamese adult literacy rates, 1995–2020

CONTINUED

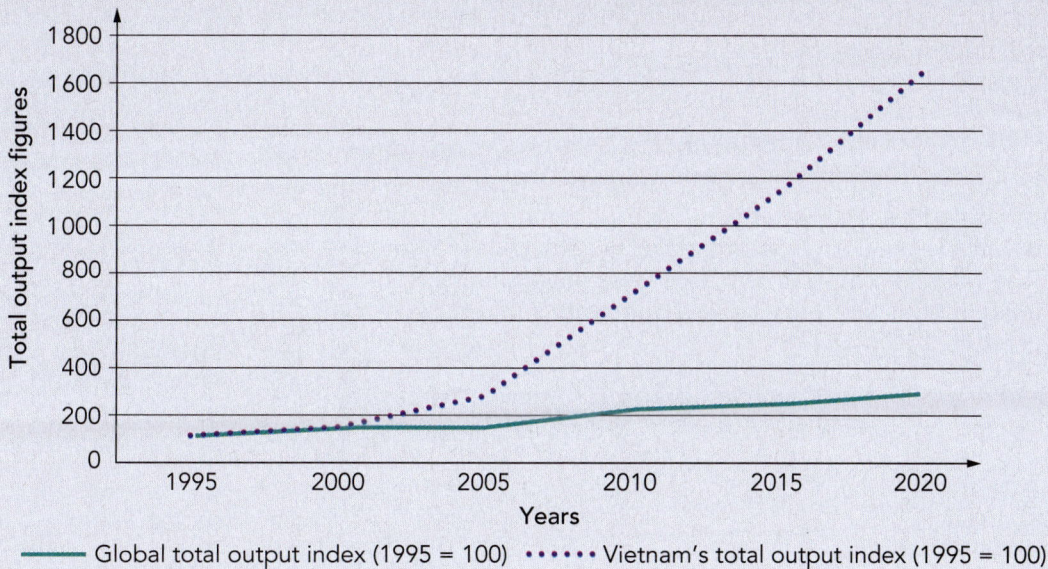

Figure 25.3: Global total output and Vietnam's total output index figures, 1995–2020

Discuss in a pair or group:

1   Why is a more educated labour force likely to be more occupationally mobile?

2   Why may more money need to be spent on education in the future even if a 100% adult literacy rate is achieved?

25.1 What is supply-side policy?

Supply-side policy measures are designed to increase aggregate supply and so increase productive potential. Such policy measures seek to increase the quantity and quality of resources and raise the efficiency of product and factor markets. Supply-side policy measures include improving education and training, infrastructure spending, labour market reforms, cutting direct taxes, improving incentives to work and invest, deregulation, privatisation and subsidies.

25.2 Supply-side policy measures

Education and training

Improving education and training is designed to increase the skills of workers. If successful, this would make workers more productive. Higher labour productivity can reduce costs of production and raise the quality of the products produced. Both effects can result in the country's firms being able to sell more and so are likely to encourage them to expand. Workers with higher skills are also likely to be more occupationally mobile. This should mean that supply would adjust more quickly to changes in demand.

KEY TERM

supply-side policy: measures designed to increase aggregate supply.

TIP

Supply-side policy measures always seek to increase aggregate supply. They never try to reduce it.

There is, however, the possibility that the education and training may not be in the right areas. For example, providing resources to teach children flower arranging may be less useful than providing more resources to teach them mathematics. Training people to work as taxi drivers will also serve little purpose if driverless cars are about to be widely used. Improved education, particularly primary education, will also take time to have an effect.

ACTIVITY 25.1

In the 2020s, Mauritius has had a skills shortage in a number of areas. These include skill shortages in hotel and tourism management, cybersecurity and data processing. The Mauritian government, like most governments, spends money on training. It does this to increase productivity and reduce skill shortages.

In a pair, produce a brief report for the Mauritian government on whether it should increase its spending on training.

Infrastructure spending

Government spending on infrastructure and incentives for the private sector to spend more on infrastructure are expected to raise the quality of the structures and systems that support production (see Figure 25.4). Better transport, energy, water and telecommunication systems increase productivity and reduce costs of production. For example, government spending on a country's road system may reduce congestion, allowing workers to arrive at work on time and not stressed. This is likely to increase the quantity and quality of their output. A better road system is also likely to reduce the time it takes to transport goods, enabling firms to use their lorries and vans for more journeys each day.

Figure 25.4: The construction of a sustainable power station

The Chinese government is spending large amounts on developing its railway infrastructure. It is upgrading existing rail lines and extending its rail network. It now has the world's largest high-speed network, with fast, reliable links between most of the country's cities.

1   How may a faster and more efficient rail network benefit employed workers?

2   Explain how infrastructure spending could reduce unemployment.

Discuss your answers with a partner.

Labour market reforms

Labour market reforms are designed to make labour markets work more efficiently. The aim is to increase the quality, quantity and flexibility of labour. There is some overlap between labour market reforms and other supply-side policy measures. For example, the reforms can include better training and the removal of barriers to entry, such as unnecessary qualifications, and barriers to exit from labour markets, such as long contracts.

Changes in employment law

Making it easier for employers to hire and fire workers, is one way that some governments seek to increase the efficiency of labour markets. This is likely to make it easier for firms to adjust their supply to changing market conditions. It may also encourage firms to employ more workers, as they will know that they will not have to continue to pay them should demand for their products fall. There is a risk, however, that firms may not spend as much on training their workers if they think the workers may not be with them for very long.

Reform of trade unions

Reform of trade unions may make labour more productive. If the power of trade unions is reduced, there may be less chance of industrial action. There may be less disruption to production, and trade union members may be more willing to be flexible in what tasks they do and the hours they work. If trade unions have been intimidating their members into taking industrial action, there may be a case for reducing their power. In some cases, though, reducing trade union power may reduce the benefits that trade unions may provide not only for their members, but also for employers and the economy. It is also possible that trade union reforms may give too much power to employers, which could lower the pay of workers and increase their working hours. Being paid less and working more hours may reduce the motivation of workers and make them tired, which would be likely to reduce their productivity.

National minimum wage

Governments may remove or introduce a national minimum wage. They may also increase or lower an existing national minimum wage. If a national minimum wage discourages employers from recruiting workers, its removal may increase employment and output. However, if the introduction of a national minimum wage or a rise in a national minimum wage increases the incentive for the unemployed to accept job offers and more people to enter the labour force, and if it increases total demand, it may increase employment, output and productive potential.

Lower direct taxes and improving incentives to work and invest

The reason for cutting direct taxes is to increase the incentive to work and invest. Reducing personal income tax rates will increase the reward from working, especially if combined with a cut in unemployment benefit. Such measures may make the unemployed search for work more actively and may increase the labour force by encouraging more people to seek employment.

Of course, some workers may respond to lower income tax by working fewer hours. This may be because they were happy with their pay and may prefer to have more leisure time rather than higher wages. In addition, increasing the incentive to work will not be effective if there are no jobs available for the unemployed and those currently inactive. Indeed, cutting unemployment benefit and other benefits could make unemployment worse. This is because the unemployed and, for example, people with disabilities, will have less income to spend. This may result in a fall in aggregate demand and so in output and employment.

Cutting corporate tax may increase the incentive to invest. This is because it is likely to make firms more willing and able to invest. The greater willingness will come from them being able to keep more of the profits they earn. The greater ability will come from the rise in funds they will have to invest.

If, however, firms lack confidence in the future, they may not invest even with lower corporate tax. If firms do not think they will be able to sell more goods and services in the future, they will not want to expand. When deciding whether to invest, a firm does not only take the rate of corporate tax into account. It also takes confidence in the future into account and things like advances in technology.

> **LINK**
>
> Trade unions can increase the bargaining power of workers – see Chapter 17.2 (Wage determination and the reasons for differences in wages – Relative bargaining strengths of employers and workers: The role of trade unions).

ACTIVITY 25.3

In 2023, the Malaysian government cut the lower rates of personal income tax. It also reduced the number of tax bands from 12 to 10.

1   What is a possible disadvantage of cutting personal income tax rates?

2   Why may reducing the number of tax bands encourage work and effort?

Write your answers in your notebook.

Deregulation

KEY TERM

deregulation: the removal of rules and regulations.

Deregulation involves reducing or removing rules and regulations that have been enforced by laws. The reasons for deregulation are to remove barriers to entry to markets and to reduce the costs of complying with the rules and regulations. It will also reduce the cost to the government of regulating the industries and occupations affected.

If deregulation does increase competition, it may increase efficiency and so lower costs of production and prices. Removing rules and regulations, however, does not guarantee that a monopoly will not develop. There are arguments for regulating monopolies, given their market power. Imposing restrictions on who can undertake particular occupations may also protect consumers. For example, most people would not want the government to remove the requirement that surgeons have to possess medical qualifications. There are, however, debates in some cases about what qualifications are needed for particular occupations.

ACTIVITY 25.4

In recent years, the Indonesian government has engaged in deregulation including reducing bureaucratic red tape. For example, the government reduced the time foreign multinational companies had to spend on getting the permits and licences needed to produce in the country. The key aims of Indonesia's deregulation programme are to increase investment and promote economic growth.

In a pair, produce a presentation on why reducing bureaucratic red tape is likely to increase private sector investment and an alternative way a government could increase private sector investment.

Privatisation

LINK

Privatisation can increase productive capacity by improving the efficiency of markets – see Chapter 14.3 (Government intervention to address market failure – Privatisation).

As with deregulation, privatisation seeks to increase competition and efficiency by increasing the role of market forces. Moving industries into the private sector may put more pressure on them and provide them with a greater incentive to respond to changes in consumer demand, and to provide them with high quality products at low prices. If they do not, they will go out of business, but if they do, they could make high profits. Privatisation will increase productive capacity, if private sector firms invest more and work more efficiently than state-owned enterprises.

Again, as with deregulation, privatisation will not necessarily ensure greater competition. Especially as over time a monopoly may develop. A private sector firm may be less inclined to take into account social costs and social benefits than a state-owned enterprise and may be more willing to make workers redundant.

Privatising state-owned enterprises will raise revenue which could be spent on education, for example. However, if privatised firms were profitable, it may reduce the revenue the government has to spend in the long run.

Subsidies

A government may provide subsidies to firms, in particular industries, for a number of reasons connected to increasing the performance of markets. For example, new small firms might be subsidised to increase competition in markets. Firms may also be subsidised to encourage them to buy new capital equipment. Of course, a government needs to consider whether this is the best use of its spending. There is also the risk that the firms may become dependent on the subsidies.

LINK

Subsidies can encourage firms to increase output to expand their output – see Chapter 14.3 (Government measures intervention to address market failure – Indirect taxation and subsidies).

25.3 Effects of supply-side policy measures on government macroeconomic aims

In the long run, all the government's macroeconomic aims have the potential to benefit from supply-side policy. Increasing aggregate supply enables an economy to continue to grow in a non-inflationary way. Figure 25.5 shows aggregate supply rising in line with aggregate demand. Such a combination enables output and employment to increase without inflation.

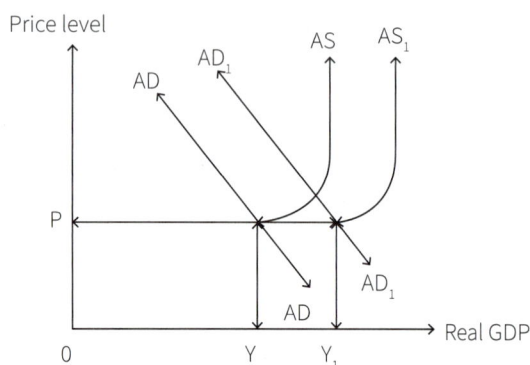

Figure 25.5: Aggregate supply increasing with aggregate demand

Increasing productive potential and efficiency can improve an economy's balance of payments position. Producing better-quality, and cheaper, products can increase exports and reduce imports.

In the case of some supply-side policy measures there is a time lag involved. For example, it can take some time before the effects of improved education and privatisation are experienced. In addition, some supply-side measures can be expensive.

DISCUSSION

Discuss whether government spending on health could be considered a supply-side policy measure.

TIP

You may find it useful to draw up a table comparing the effects of particular policy measures such as a cut in income tax on unemployment, inflation, economic growth and the balance of payments.

Increasing the effectiveness of macroeconomic policies

Besides using supply-side policy measures in the long run to improve macroeconomic performance, there are a number of other ways a government can try to ensure that it achieves all its macroeconomic aims.

- The government may use a number of policies. A Nobel Prize winning economist, Jan Tinbergen, suggested that a government needs to use one policy measure for each of its objectives. So, for example, if a government wants to stimulate economic growth and reduce imports, it may provide investment grants to firms and place a tax on imports.

- A government will benefit from accurate forecasts of future aggregate demand. Increasing productive capacity by means of supply-side policies will not be effective if there is going to be a lack of aggregate demand.

- Governments also try to decide and implement their policies relatively quickly. If there is a delay in introducing policies, there is a danger that economic activity undergoes a change and the policy measures may actually harm the economy. For example, a period of high unemployment may lead the government to cut income tax and to raise aggregate demand and employment. If, however, by the time the measure is introduced, aggregate demand is increasing anyway, it may increase inflationary pressure.

ECONOMICS IN ACTION

How the popularity of supply-side policy measures can vary

Figure 25.6: Not everyone is happy with supply-side policy

Economists have had a number of opportunities in recent years to study the effects of supply-side policy and how people react to it. In the early 2020s, the French government used a number of supply-side policy measures aimed at increasing work incentives and labour reforms.

In 2020, the government cut the starting rate of personal income tax from 14% to 11% and was three years through a training scheme for the long-term and young unemployed. These were popular measures with French workers. However, they did not like the other measures the government introduced. The government put a limit on the amount that has to be paid to workers who have been unfairly dismissed. It also required workers to have a longer work history before they could claim unemployment benefit and made it more difficult for workers who turn down job offers and offers of training to receive unemployment benefit.

The most unpopular measure, however, was to raise the state pension age from 62 to 64 years (see Figure 25.6).

1 At what level, compared to the average wage rate, do you think unemployment benefit should be set?

2 Explain whether you think the retirement age should be raised in your country.

ACTIVITY 25.5

Copy and complete Table 25.1 on the three main types of government policy.

Table 25.1

	Fiscal policy	Monetary policy	Supply-side policy
Definition			
Implemented by			
Aim			
Example of a measure			

REFLECTION

When filling out the table, did you recall the information on all three policies? If this was not the case, did you review some of them again?

SUMMARY

You should now know:

- Supply-side policy measures are designed to increase aggregate supply.

- Improved education and training can increase labour productivity and so the productive potential of the economy.

- Infrastructure spending can increase productivity and reduce costs of production.

- Cutting income tax rates and unemployment benefits may be designed to make work more attractive than living off state benefits.

- Lowering corporate tax may increase investment.

- Deregulation and privatisation may increase competition and efficiency.

- Labour market reforms may increase the efficiency of labour markets.

- Subsidies may allow small firms to grow and compete and may be used to encourage firms to invest.

- All government macroeconomic aims may be helped by supply-side policy measures in the long run.

- The effectiveness of macroeconomic policy measures can be increased by using a number of policies, accurate information and implementing measures promptly.

Chapter 25 practice questions

1   Which is a supply-side policy measure?

   A   a decrease in government spending on education

   B   a decrease in government spending on healthcare

   C   an increase in corporate tax

   D   an increase in the threshold at which people pay income tax   **[1]**

2   What is most likely to conflict with a government's aim of full employment?

   A   higher government expenditure

   B   higher interest rates

   C   lower income tax

   D   lower spending on imports

3   What combination of macroeconomic aims is most likely to benefit from a decrease in government spending?

   A   a fall in imports and stable prices

   B   economic growth and full employment

   C   full employment and a fall in imports

   D   stable prices and economic growth   **[1]**

4   What might reduce the effectiveness of a government policy measure?

   A   a time lag

   B   accurate information

   C   an absence of economic problems in other economies

   D   an absence of policy conflicts   **[1]**

5   What determines whether a government policy measure is a supply-side policy measure?

   A   whether it aims to increase or reduce total supply

   B   whether it aims to increase total supply

   C   whether it aims to leave total supply unchanged

   D   whether it aims to reduce total supply   **[1]**

Total: [5]

6 a   Define 'deregulation'.   [2]

   b   Explain whether a cut in income tax is a fiscal policy measure or
       supply-side policy measure.   [4]

   c   Analyse, using a production possibility curve, the intended outcome
       of a supply-side policy measure.   [6]

   d   Discuss whether or not supply-side policy measures always reduce
       unemployment.   [8]

                                                                   Total: [20]

CHECK YOUR PROGRESS

How well do you think you have achieved the learning intentions for this chapter?
Give yourself a score from 1 (still need a lot of practice) to 5 (feeling very confident)
for each learning intention. Provide an example to support your score.

Now I can...	Score	Example
define supply-side policy		
explain supply-side policy measures: education and training, infrastructure spending, labour market reforms, lower direct taxes and improving incentives to work and invest, deregulation, privatisation and subsidies		
discuss the effects of supply-side policy on government macroeconomic aims.		

> Chapter 26
Economic growth

LEARNING INTENTIONS

By the end of this chapter, you will be able to:

- define economic growth
- explain how economic growth is measured: real gross domestic product (GDP)
- analyse the causes of economic growth: an increase in total demand, an increase in the quantity of resources or an increase in the quality of resources
- discuss the advantages and disadvantages of economic growth
- define a recession
- analyse the causes of a recession: a decrease in total demand, a decrease in the quantity of resources or a decrease in the quality of resources
- discuss the consequences of a recession for consumers, workers, producers/firms and the government
- discuss the range of policies available to promote economic growth and their effectiveness.

Introduction

Most governments have economic growth as one of their main macroeconomic aims. This is because economic growth can give many benefits to households, workers, firms and the government. However, depending on how it is achieved, it can have some disadvantages. It is commonly recognised that producing a lower output can have disadvantages for each of the above groups. Understanding the causes and consequences of economic growth can help a government decide on the policies it may use to increase its country's output.

ECONOMICS IN CONTEXT

China speeding ahead

In 1990, Japan, the UK and the USA each produced a higher total output than China. By 2010, China's output of goods and services had overtaken that of Japan's and the UK's output of goods and services. China's total output had also moved closer to the total output of the USA and continued to do so in 2020 (see Figure 26.2).

Over the whole period, each country increased its total output, but China's output increased at the fastest rate. China has benefited from an increase in the quality and quantity of its resources. It has experienced an increase in its labour force, an increase in investment, advances in technology and a rise in educational standards.

Figure 26.1: Rapid changes in China include more investment in solar power

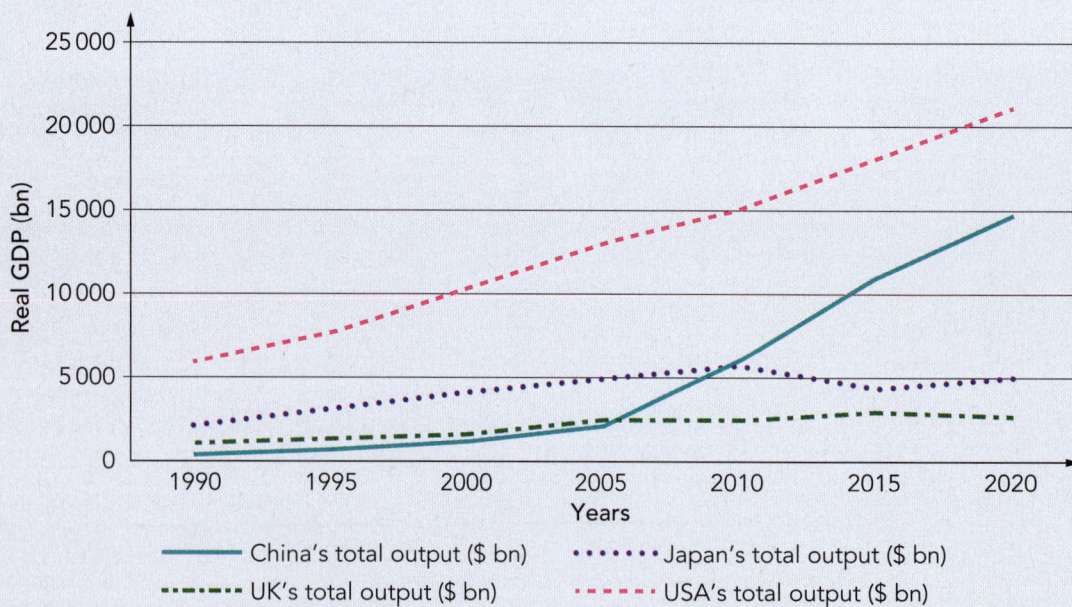

Figure 26.2: Total output of China and selected countries, 1990–2020

26.1 How economic growth is measured

Gross domestic product (GDP)

Economic growth occurs when real gross domestic product increases, that is more total output is produced. 'Gross' means total, 'domestic' refers to the home country, and 'product' means output. So **gross domestic product (GDP)** means the total output produced in a country.

There are three methods of measuring this output. These are the output, income and expenditure methods. All three methods should give the same figure. This is because an output of $20bn will give rise to an income of $20bn which, in turn, will be spent on the output. This relationship is referred to as the **circular flow of income** and is illustrated in two diagrams in Figure 26.3.

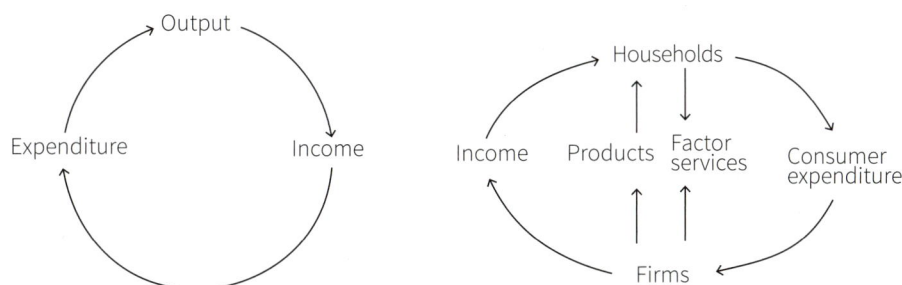

Figure 26.3: The circular flow of income

Methods of calculating GDP

The *output method* measures GDP by adding up the output produced by all the industries in the country. When using the output method, it is important to ensure that output is not counted twice. For example, the value of the output of the car industry includes output produced by the steel and tyre industries. To avoid this problem, economists include the '**value added**' by each firm at each stage of production.

The *income method* includes all the incomes which have been earned in producing the country's output. **Transfer payments**, such as pensions and unemployment benefit, are not included. This is because there is no corresponding output of goods and services.

KEY TERMS

gross domestic product (GDP): the total output of a country.

circular flow of income: the movement of expenditure, income and output around the economy.

value added: the difference between the sales revenue received and the cost of raw materials used.

transfer payments: transfers of income from one group to another not in return for providing a good or service.

The *expenditure method* calculates GDP by adding up all the expenditure on the country's finished output. Some of this comes from foreigners when they buy the country's *exports*. Some of the expenditure in the country goes on *imports* which are not produced in the country and which do not generate income for the country's citizens. So, in the expenditure method, it is necessary to add exports and deduct imports. Total expenditure on a country's output, and hence its GDP, includes consumption, investment, government expenditure and exports minus imports.

Nominal and real GDP

When governments calculate GDP, they usually first measure it in terms of **nominal GDP**, which is also referred to as money GDP or GDP at current prices. Nominal GDP is GDP valued in terms of the prices operative at that time. Nominal GDP has not been adjusted for inflation. For this reason, nominal GDP figures may give a misleading impression of what is happening to the output of a country over time. For example, if prices rise by 20% in a year, there will be a 20% rise in nominal GDP even if output does not change.

To get the real picture of a country's output and assess its economic growth, economists adjust nominal GDP by taking out the effects of inflation. They do this by multiplying nominal GDP with the price index in the base year, divided by the price index in the current year. This gives a figure for GDP at constant prices referred to as **real GDP**. A rise in real GDP of 5% would mean that the country's output has increased by 5%.

For example, in 2025, the nominal GDP of a country may be $800bn and its price index may be 100 (base year). In 2026, nominal GDP may increase to $900bn, giving the impression that output has risen by $\frac{\$100bn}{\$800bn} \times 100 = 12.5\%$.

If, however, the price index rises to 110, the real GDP in 2026 will be $\frac{\$900bn \times 100}{110} = \$818.18bn$.
So, the increase in output is $\frac{\$18.18bn}{\$800bn} \times 100 = 2.27\%$, which is considerably below the 12.5% increase in nominal GDP.

Real GDP per head

A rise in real GDP means that more goods and services have been produced. Its impact on the goods and services available to people will depend on what may have happened to the size of population. If real GDP increases by 5% but the population increases by 8%, there will actually be fewer goods and services per head of the population, and people's living standards may fall.

To find out what is happening to people's living standards, economists calculate real GDP per head, which is also referred to as real GDP per capita. It is found by dividing real GDP by population.

If, for example, real GDP is $80bn and the population is 20m, real GDP per head is $\frac{\$80bn}{20m} = \$4\,000$. If real GDP rises to $90bn and population rises to 30m, real GDP per head will fall to $\frac{\$90bn}{30m} = \$3\,000$. In most countries, however, real GDP grows more rapidly than population, causing real GDP per head to rise.

Changes in population size can make a significant contribution to changes in real GDP. This has led some economists to suggest that a country's economic growth rate should be measured in terms of changes in real GDP per head. The international conventional measure, nevertheless, is currently changes in real GDP.

ACTIVITY 26.1

1   In 2024, a country's nominal GDP is $375bn. In 2025, it rises to $500bn. Between the two years, the price index rises from 100 to 125. What was the percentage increase in real GDP?

2   Table 26.1 shows a country's real GDP and population over a period of three years, 2024–2026. Calculate the real GDP per head in each year.

Table 26.1

Year	Real GDP ($bn)	Population (millions)	Real GDP per head
2024	100	20	
2025	110	22	
2026	90	15	

The difficulty of measuring real GDP

GDP figures tend to understate the true level of output. This is because of the existence of unrecorded economic activity, both legal and illegal, and non-marketed goods and services (see Figure 26.4).

There are a number of reasons why economic activity goes unrecorded. One is that the activity is on a small scale, and there are relatively high costs of registering a business. Another reason is that the activity is illegal, such as selling smuggled goods, and work undertaken by immigrants who have not been given permission to work in the country. The activity may be legal, but the person undertaking it does not want to pay a tax on it. In the UK, it is thought that some workers in building, electrical installation, plumbing and car repairs do not declare all their earnings to the tax authorities. Some employers may want their businesses to be in the **informal economy**, so they can avoid government regulations such as having to pay the national minimum wage.

The size of undeclared economic activity is influenced by a number of factors. These include the number of activities that are declared to be illegal, tax rates, penalties for tax evasion and government regulations.

The existence of undeclared economic activity, besides understating the output produced through GDP figures, has a number of other effects on an economy. It means that tax revenue is below what could be collected. It can also mean that the official inflation rate overstates the rate at which the general price level is rising. This is because prices charged in undeclared economic activity tend to rise less quickly than in the formal economy.

There are also non-marketed goods and services. These are products which are not bought or sold. Family members who produce food for their own use, including in **subsistence agriculture**, people who clean their own houses and repair their own cars, are all providing products, but these are not counted in GDP.

KEY TERMS

informal economy: that part of the economy that is not regulated, protected or taxed by the government.

subsistence agriculture: the output of agricultural goods for farmers' personal use.

Figure 26.4: Economic activity, which may be formal or informal activity

TIP

In economics, the word 'real' refers to something that has been adjusted for inflation. This includes real GDP, real wages and real disposable income.

LINK

Economic growth is a key macroeconomic aim for governments – see Chapter 22.1 (Macroeconomic aims of government – Economic growth).

26.2 Causes and consequences of economic growth

Causes of economic growth

In the short run, an increase in aggregate demand may stimulate a rise in output if the economy has unused resources. For example, a rise in consumption resulting from increased consumer confidence, or a cut in income tax, may encourage firms to increase their output. This would cause a movement from inside toward the production possibility curve (PPC). In the long run, an economy can continue to experience economic growth only if the quantity or quality of resources increases. The quantity of resources may rise as a result of an increase in net investment or the size of the labour force, for example. The quality of resources may increase due to an improvement in education and training and advances in technology. In this case, there would be a shift to the right of the PPC.

Advantages and disadvantages of economic growth

An increase in output can improve living standards of people. Access to more goods and services can improve living conditions and increase life expectancy. In high-income economies, people are likely to consume luxury products, have better healthcare and access better education than in low-income economies. In very low-income countries, economic growth is essential to ensure that people have access to basic necessities.

Higher output and incomes increase government tax revenue, making it easier for governments to finance measures to reduce poverty, increase healthcare provision and raise educational standards without having to raise tax rates. Poverty can be reduced in a number of ways. Some of the extra tax revenue raised can be used to increase benefits for those living in poverty, to improve schools in lower income areas and provide training to the unemployed.

As an economy grows, its political and economic standing and influence usually increases. Voting power at the International Monetary Fund (IMF), for example, is influenced by the size of an economy's GDP. Economic growth, however, can involve costs. If the economy is working at full capacity, it may be necessary to shift resources from making consumer goods to capital goods in order for it to grow. Such a shift will reduce living standards, as fewer goods and services will be available for households. This will be only a short-term cost, as in the longer term, the extra capital goods will enable manufacture of more consumer goods. Figure 26.5 shows the output of consumer goods initially falling due to the reallocation of resources but then increasing due to the resulting economic growth.

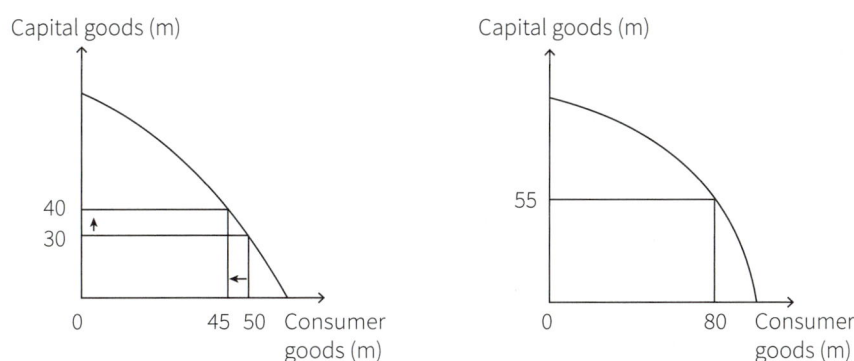

Figure 26.5: The short-term and long-term effects of devoting more resources to capital goods

Higher output can increase pollution, lead to depletion of non-renewable resources and damage the natural environment. More factories and cars may increase carbon dioxide emissions. Rapid expansion of the furniture and fishing industries, for example, may result in deforestation and depletion of fish stocks, respectively. Construction of more factories, offices, roads and other infrastructure can also destroy wildlife habitats. Due to these risks, economists are increasingly emphasising the need for sustainable economic growth. Economic growth may also lead to greater stress on workers. An increase of output may require some people to work for longer hours, some to learn new skills and some to change their job.

The net impact of economic growth is influenced by its rate, means adopted to achieve it and distribution of its benefits. A very high rate of economic growth may not be sustainable. It may involve non-renewable resources being used up too quickly before the development of alternative resources.

If productive capacity can be increased in line with increases in aggregate demand, more goods and services can be enjoyed without an increase in prices. Stable economic growth is better than a high economic growth rate which fluctuates. This is because it makes it easier for firms and households to plan for the future and so encourages investment. Some of the extra resources which develop when productive potential increases can also be used to reduce levels of pollution. Although there is a risk that economic growth can generate pollution and cause environmental damage, it can lead to improved education and information, pressure the government and society to care

KEY TERMS

International Monetary Fund (IMF): an international organisation which promotes international cooperation and helps countries with balance of payments problems.

sustainable economic growth: economic growth that does not endanger the country's ability to grow in the future.

LINK

Not everyone is affected by economic growth in the same way – see Chapter 29.2 (Comparing living standards and income distribution).

for the environment and provide the resources to do so. Economic growth has the potential to raise living standards, but the extent to which it does so is influenced by the type of products produced and the equality of distribution of extra income.

ACTIVITY 26.2

It is proposed to build a coal power station close to a tourist area of natural beauty near to where you live. It is estimated that 2000 jobs will be created to construct the power station and 400 employees will be required to operate it. The provision of more electricity is expected to reduce the price of energy in the country.

However, the power station is also expected to increase the emission of greenhouse gases, which could cause breathing difficulties and other health problems and could reduce the fertility of farmland. Its disposal of wastewater might also pollute rivers and the sea, killing marine life and damaging fishing. The building of the power station would also destroy wildlife habitats.

In a group of six, you are going to consider whether you would support approval of the power station from the viewpoint of different local people. Write the numbers 1–6 on folded pieces of paper, and put them into a bag. Each person picks a number from the bag. The number corresponds to the roles below:

1   the owner of a local paper-producing firm that uses a large amount of electricity

2   the owner of a local coffee shop

3   the owner of a local hotel that is popular with tourists from abroad

4   a local farmer

5   a local unemployed worker

6   a local family who have a child with asthma.

Before you begin the discussion, individually write down some points you will put forward in support of your view. Then, in your group, debate the arguments for and against the proposal.

REFLECTION

Did you find that the role-play activity helped you recognise that economic growth can have different effects on different groups?

Economic growth rate

It is important to avoid the confusion between a fall in the economic growth rate and a fall in national output. If a country's economic growth rate falls from 5% to 3%, output will still be rising although it may be rising at a slower rate. If output reduces, the economic growth rate would be negative. For example, an economic growth rate of –2% would mean that a country has produced 2% less this year than last year.

Table 26.2 shows the change in GDP of Pakistan over a six-year period.

Table 26.2: Pakistan's economic growth rate, 2018–2023

Year	Economic growth rate (percentage change in GDP on a year earlier)
2018	6.0
2019	3.1
2020	−1.5
2021	6.8
2022	6.1
2023	1.5

From 2018 to 2023, Pakistan's output grew. Each year except 2020, it produced more than the previous year. Between 2018 and 2019, the rate at which its output was increasing slowed down, though it did produce more in 2019 than it did in 2018. In 2020, Pakistan produced 1.5% less than it had the year before. In 2021, the country returned to positive economic growth. It achieved its highest economic growth rate in 2021 but continued to produce more in both 2022 and 2023.

ACTIVITY 26.3

Figure 26.6 shows the economic growth rate of Venezuela from 2018 to 2023.

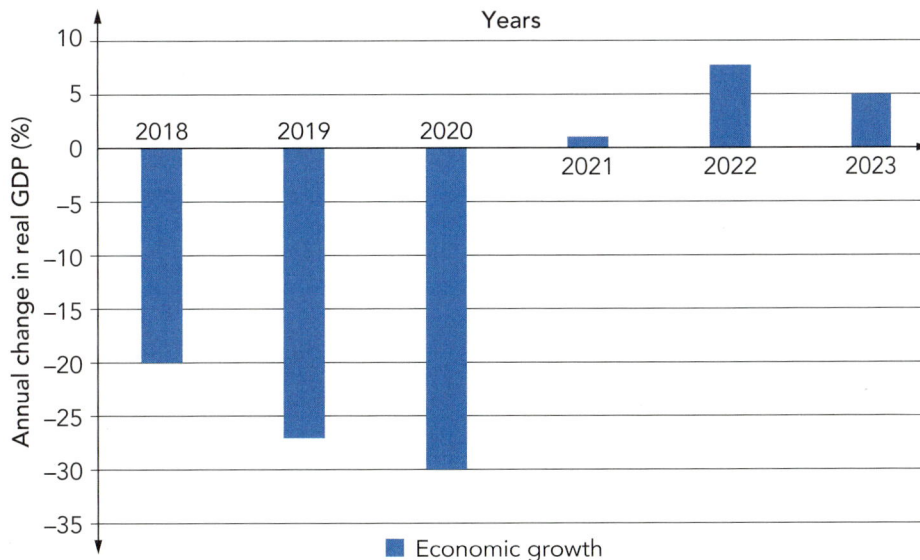

Figure 26.6: Venezuela's economic growth rate, 2018–2023

Discuss these questions with another student.

1   Did Venezuela experience a period of stable economic growth between 2018 and 2023? Explain your answer.

2   What happened to the output in 2020 and in 2023?

Write your answers in your notebook.

A new island in the Maldives

Figure 26.7: Hulhumalé, an island in the Maldives, is intended to provide sustainable living for its residents

---

Economists are concerned not only with examining countries' economic growth rates but also with the quality of the economic growth. The economists in the Maldives, for example, advise the country's firms and its government on how sustainable economic growth might be achieved.

The Maldives, a country consisting of over 1 000 small islands, is facing a number of challenges. The Maldives is the world's lowest-lying country, with more than three-quarters of its inhabited islands being only a metre above sea level. With global warming, it is at risk from rising sea levels. Its capital city island, Malé, is also very densely populated with very little space per person and the country is heavily dependent on one industry, tourism.

To help with these challenges, a new island known as Hulhumalé, or 'City of Hope', was created close to Malé (see Figure 26.7). The island's construction was completed in 2002 but is still being developed. Hulhumalé has been designed to promote sustainable economic growth. To date, a third of its energy comes from solar power. Streets are built to make the best use of wind in order to reduce the need for air conditioning. Car use is discouraged by the easy access to electric buses, the provision of cycle lanes and the building of schools and other social amenities close to people's homes. However, it is not certain the extent to which the land reclamation may have damaged the coral reefs in the area.

1   How might an increase in global economic growth affect the Maldives?

2   To what extent do you think the other inhabited islands of the Maldives would benefit from adopting the transport and energy approaches of Hulhumalé?

26.3 Causes and consequences of recession

A **recession** occurs when real GDP declines over a period of six months or more. This time period is also sometimes referred to as two successive quarters. It is a period of negative output with less being produced than in the previous period.

Causes of a recession

Just as economic growth can be caused by an increase in aggregate demand and/or an increase in aggregate supply, a recession is caused by a decrease in aggregate demand and/or a decrease in aggregate supply.

There are a number of reasons why aggregate demand may fall. These reasons are sometimes referred to as negative demand-side shocks. For example, consumer expenditure and investment could decline due to a fall in business and consumer confidence arising from a global financial crisis or falling house prices in the domestic economy. The government may cut back its spending too much, and net exports could fall as a result of a rise in the exchange rate.

A decrease in aggregate supply, a negative supply-side shock, could result from a rise in fuel or raw material costs. Such effects would increase firms' costs of production, which may cause them to produce less. Figure 26.8 shows a recession caused by a decrease in aggregate demand and a recession caused by a decrease in aggregate supply.

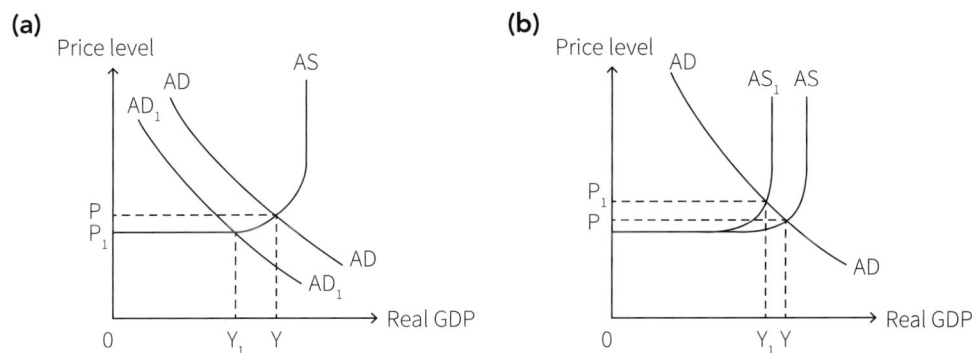

TIP

The causes and consequences of a recession are the opposite of the causes and consequences of economic growth.

(a)

(b)

Figure 26.8: (a) A recession caused by a decrease in aggregate demand **(b)** A recession caused by a decrease in aggregate supply

Consequences of a recession

Consequences for consumers

A recession may change the prices that consumers pay. The effect on the price level will depend on whether the recession has been caused by a decrease in aggregate demand or a decrease in aggregate supply. Figure 26.8 shows that if it is due to a decrease in aggregate demand, it would be expected that the price level would fall. If, on the other hand, it was caused by a decrease in aggregate supply, it would be expected to be accompanied by inflation.

LINK

Inflation is influenced by changes in the aggregate demand and aggregate supply in an economy – see Chapter 28.3 (Causes of inflation).

Consequences for workers

With lower output, unemployment is likely to rise. Less-skilled workers are most likely to lose their jobs as they will be the least productive. Workers who stay in employment may feel less secure. Their ability to get wage rises is likely to be reduced as firms are likely to be earning lower profits and because there will be more competition for jobs. Some workers may have to accept pay cuts to stay in employment. Workers whose wages fall by more than any fall in the price level and those who lose their jobs will experience a fall in living standards. However, workers whose wages stay unchanged during a recession where prices fall will experience a rise in their purchasing power.

Consequences for producers/firms

A recession involves a fall in output. This is very likely to be harmful for many firms. They will be likely to lose revenue and some may go out of business.

A recession is likely to discourage investment and even those firms that may want to update or replace worn-out equipment may find it difficult to get loans. This is because commercial banks tend to reduce their lending during a recession.

A small number of firms may gain. These are the firms that produce goods and services that compete with higher priced, higher quality products. Consumers may switch some of their purchases to these firms.

Consequences for government and the economy

A recession would obviously mean that a government would not achieve the macroeconomic aim of economic growth and would be unlikely to achieve full employment/low unemployment. Tax revenue will also decline while government spending on benefits may be increased. This would increase any budget deficit or reduce any budget surplus.

DISCUSSION

Discuss whether a recession would have a beneficial effect on the environment.

26.4 Policies to promote economic growth

If an economy is operating with spare capacity, a government may use expansionary fiscal and/or monetary policy to promote economic growth. A reduction in income tax rates or a cut in the rate of interest, for example, would be expected to increase consumer expenditure and investment. The resulting rise in aggregate demand is likely to encourage firms to increase their output. They will be able to do this as they will be able to take on unemployed workers and buy more capital equipment to expand their production.

The effectiveness of fiscal and monetary policy measures will be influenced by a number of factors. For example, households and firms may not spend more, despite a lower rate of interest and lower taxes, if they lack confidence. If the rate of interest is already very low, there may not be much room to cut it further, and a very small reduction may have little impact.

As aggregate demand tends to increase over time, it means that without any change in aggregate supply the maximum level of output will be reached. So, in the long run, an economy can continue to increase the output it produces only if it gets more resources or higher quality resources. This means that to help achieve long-run economic growth, a government needs to use both demand-side and supply-side policy measures. To increase productive potential, for example, a government may seek to improve education and training. If successful, this measure will raise labour productivity and so productive capacity. There is, of course, no guarantee that supply-side policy measures will work.

LINKS

Governments may use a range of policies to promote economic growth – see Chapter 23.5 (Effects of fiscal policy on government macroeconomic aims), Chapter 24.3 (Effects of monetary policy on government macroeconomic aims), Chapter 25.3 (Effects of supply-side policy on government macroeconomic aims).

ACTIVITY 26.4

Thailand's economic growth rate rose from 2.5% in 2022 to 2.8% in 2023. However, the government was concerned at the start of 2024 that, without government and central bank intervention, it would decline. As a result, the government encouraged the Bank of Thailand to cut the rate of interest. A lower interest rate might encourage the country's commercial banks to lend more to households, farmers and small firms. The government was planning to increase its spending. Some of its spending would go on infrastructure projects, including building light railways, in a bid to extend the benefits of its programme to stimulate the economy.

1   Identify a monetary policy measure mentioned in the information.

2   Why might an increase in commercial bank lending cause economic growth?

3   Explain why spending on infrastructure projects may promote economic growth in the long run.

In a pair, discuss the answers to these questions. Then, on the basis of your answers, produce a 5-minute presentation on how the monetary policy measure you have identified may promote economic growth in the long run.

SUMMARY

You should now know:

- GDP can be measured by adding up all output produced, all incomes earned from producing that output or the total amount spent on the output.

- Real GDP is adjusted for inflation.

- Changes in real GDP show changes in output.

- If real GDP per head increases, there will be more goods and services available for people.

- In the short run, increases in aggregate demand can lead to an increase in output, but in the long run, aggregate supply must also increase for output to continue to rise.

- Economic growth can improve living standards, reduce poverty, raise government expenditure on healthcare and education and increase the influence of an economy. Economic growth may involve a short-run opportunity cost, can cause pollution and damage to the environment and may put stress on people.

- A recession involves a fall in real GDP over two quarters of a year or more.

- A recession may reduce prices for consumers, cause some workers to lose their jobs, result in some firms going out of business and reduce tax revenue.

- A recession will be likely to cause unemployment and a decline in living standards.

- Countries aim for stable and sustainable economic growth.

Chapter 26 practice questions

1   What is economic growth?

   A   an increase in exports

   B   an increase in population

   C   an increase in real GDP

   D   an increase in the price level   [1]

2   The diagram shows a country's economic growth over the period 2023–2027. What can be concluded from the diagram?

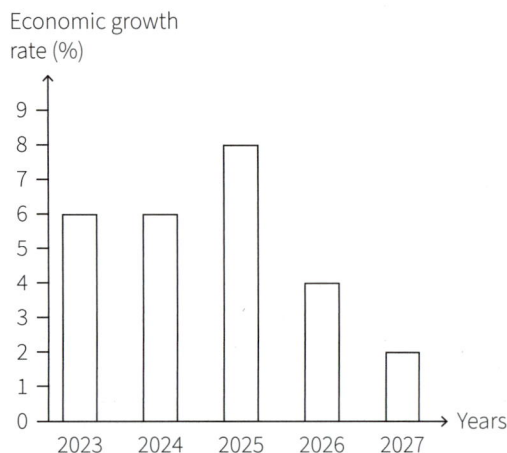

Economic growth rate (%)

   A   output was highest in 2023

   B   output was highest in 2027

   C   output fell from 2023 to 2027

   D   output was unchanged between 2023 and 2027   [1]

3   If consumer expenditure is $30bn, government expenditure is $10bn, investment is $20bn, exports are $16bn and imports are $20bn, what is GDP?

   A $56bn

   B $76bn

   C $80bn

   D $96bn   [1]

4   What is most likely to cause economic growth?

   A   an increase in capital depreciation

   B   an increase in education and training of workers

   C   an increase in taxation

   D   an increase in unemployment   [1]

5   If an economy has spare capacity, what could cause economic growth?

   A   a decrease in consumer expenditure

   B   a decrease in investment

   C   an increase in government spending

   D   an increase in imports   [1]

                                                        Total: [5]

6   a   Define 'real GDP'.   [2]

   b   Explain **two** consequences of a recession.   [4]

   c   Analyse the relationship between economic growth and the
       government budget balance.   [6]

   d   Discuss whether or not an increase in government spending will lead
       to economic growth.   [8]

                                                        Total: [20]

CHECK YOUR PROGRESS

How well do you think you have achieved the learning intentions for this chapter?
Give yourself a score from 1 (still need a lot of practice) to 5 (feeling very confident)
for each learning intention. Provide an example to support your score.

Now I can...	Score	Example
define economic growth		
explain how economic growth is measured: real GDP		
analyse the causes of economic growth: increase in total demand, an increase in the quantity of resources or an increase in the quality of resources		
discuss the advantages and disadvantages of economic growth		
define a recession		
analyse how a recession may be caused by a decrease in total demand, a decrease in the quantity of resources or a decrease in the quality of resources		
explain the consequences of recession for consumers, workers, producers/firms and the government		
discuss the range of the policies available to promote economic growth and their effectiveness.		

> Chapter 27

Employment and unemployment

LEARNING INTENTIONS

By the end of this chapter, you will be able to:

- define employment, unemployment and full employment
- explain how unemployment is measured
- analyse the causes and types of unemployment: frictional, structural, cyclical and seasonal
- discuss the consequences of unemployment for the individual, producers/firms, the government and the economy
- discuss policies to reduce unemployment and their effectiveness [syllabus revision].

Introduction

Most people would like to have more goods and services. So, why are people who could produce some of those products unemployed? Why are some machines and some factories lying idle? Leaving capital goods unused can cause them to become outdated and, in some cases, to rust and fall apart. Not employing workers can have even more significant costs for not only the unemployed workers, but also their families, firms and the economy as a whole.

ECONOMICS IN CONTEXT

Can unemployment be too low?

Figure 27.1: Electricians were in short supply

In 2023, the unemployment rate in the European country of Czechia fell to 2.3%, one of the lowest rates in the world. The unemployment rate was higher in the north and east of the country, and in the autumn and winter than in the spring and summer. Czechia is a high-income country, with high levels of consumer expenditure and investment. The country's school curriculum emphasises digital learning and its universities make use of advanced technology in delivering their courses.

Governments aim for low unemployment, but it is possible that a government may think that unemployment has fallen too low. In Czechia, in 2023, there were more vacancies than unemployed people. For every one vacancy, there were only 0.6 applicants. There were shortages of a number groups of workers, including electricians, pipefitters and plumbers. These shortages were making it difficult for some firms to expand. For example, some firms producing and selling heat pumps to replace gas boilers could not meet consumer demand because of a shortage of plumbers.

Discuss in a pair or group:

1   Why might unemployment be high at particular times of the year?

2   In what ways could workers benefit from low unemployment?

27.1 Employment, unemployment and full employment

People are in employment if they are paid employees or self-employed. In contrast, people are unemployed if they are willing and able to work but cannot find a job. The labour force consists of both the employed and the unemployed – these two groups make up the country's available workers. Full **employment** occurs when **unemployment** is at its lowest possible rate.

As well as looking at the proportion of the labour force who are employed, economists also examine the quality of the employment and how flexible the labour force is.

High-quality employment is skilled work which is interesting and provides workers with the opportunity to progress, access to training, good working conditions and a relatively high degree of job security. In contrast, low-quality employment is unskilled work, which often does not require or provide training and does not provide good working conditions. As an economy develops, the proportion of high-quality jobs tends to increase.

Global competition is putting pressure on firms to ensure that their labour force is flexible. A **flexible labour force** is one which adjusts quickly and smoothly to changes in market conditions. This flexibility can take a number of different forms, including what jobs workers do, the hours they work and where they work.

Changes in employment and unemployment

A rise in employment may reduce unemployment if it is the unemployed who fill at least some of the extra jobs. It is, however, possible that both employment and unemployment increase. This will occur if the labour force grows faster than the number of jobs available. It is also possible for unemployment to fall without an increase in employment. This is because finding a job is not the only reason why people stop being unemployed. Some unemployed people may reach retirement age, some may go into full-time education and some may emigrate, while some may just stop searching for work.

> ### ACTIVITY 27.1
>
> Some economists suggest that to encourage the long-term unemployed to seek work more actively, governments should cut income tax rates and tighten up the requirements people have to fulfil to receive unemployment benefit. Another approach to make work more attractive and to make employers more willing to employ workers is to increase the quality of jobs and raise labour productivity.
>
> In a pair, produce a podcast on 'Getting the long-term unemployed back to work'.

> ### TIP
>
> Remember that the unemployed are included in the labour force and that the unemployment rate is the unemployed as a percentage of the labour force and not of the total population.

27.2 Measurement of unemployment

One way to measure the number or workers who are unemployed is to use the **Labour Force Survey** method.

LINK

Full employment is one of the aims that governments try to achieve – see Chapter 22.1 (Macroeconomic aims of government).

KEY TERMS

flexible labour force: a labour force which adjusts quickly and smoothly to changes in market conditions.

Labour Force Survey: a measure of employment and unemployment in the country's population by means of a survey.

TIP

Take care to note whether information on unemployment and employment shows numbers of people unemployed and employed, or percentages.

Labour Force Survey

The Labour Force Survey is also sometimes called the ILO measure as it makes use of the International Labour Organization's definition of unemployment. This measure involves conducting regular surveys of a proportion of households and asking adults about their employment status. It counts people as unemployed if they are without a job and have been actively searching for employment in the past month. This method has the advantage that it can be used to make international comparisons. It also tends to identify the unemployed population more accurately.

The accuracy of the survey depends on how the questions are asked and interpreted, and whether the sample selected is representative of the labour force as a whole. This method also takes some time to gather the information. In addition, the information has to be examined carefully. For instance, it counts people as employed if they do any work, even just an hour's work. This means that a country may have a relatively low number of unemployed workers but a relatively high number of workers who are underemployed. This means that a relatively high proportion of workers may be working fewer hours than they wish, or in some cases, they may be in jobs that do not make full use of their skills.

Unemployment rate

Once the number of workers who are unemployed is found, the unemployment rate can be calculated.

The **unemployment rate** is the number of unemployed as a percentage of the labour force:

$$\frac{\text{Unemployment}}{\text{Labour force}} \times 100$$

So, if 5 million workers are unemployed out of a labour force of 40 million, the unemployment rate is:

$$\frac{5\,\text{m}}{40\,\text{m}} \times 100 = 12.5\%$$

> **KEY TERM**
>
> **unemployment rate:** the percentage of the labour force who are willing and able to work but are without jobs.

ACTIVITY 27.2

In 2023, Brunei had a labour force of 250 000 and an unemployment rate of 7.5%. In the same year, Bulgaria had a labour force of 3 200 000 and an unemployment rate of 4%.

1   What is the main reason why a country may have a larger labour force than another country?

2   What was the difference in the number of unemployed workers in the two countries in 2023?

Write your answers in your notebook.

27.3 Types and causes of unemployment

Frictional unemployment

Workers who have been fired or voluntarily left their job may have to wait for some time before finding another job. This type of unemployment, when workers are in between jobs, is called **frictional unemployment**.

One form of frictional unemployment is **search unemployment**. This arises when workers do not accept the first job offered but spend time looking around for what they regard as an 'acceptable job'.

Another form of frictional unemployment is **casual employment**. Casual unemployment occurs when people are out of work between periods of employment. Actors and migrant farm workers are particularly likely to undertake casual unemployment (see Figure 27.2).

Figure 27.2: Casual work, such as serving in a restaurant, is popular with actors during periods of casual unemployment

Structural unemployment

Structural unemployment is caused by the decline of industries and particular occupations arising from long-term changes in demand and supply. These can result in a mismatch between the skills workers have and the skills demanded, and between where the workers are and where the jobs are.

Industries and occupations can become smaller or cease to exist as a result of another country (or countries) becoming better at producing the product, a substitute being found for the product or capital being substituted for labour. Structural unemployment, which is concentrated in one area, can cause particular problems. Such unemployment can be referred to as **regional unemployment**.

Another form of structural unemployment is **technological unemployment**. This occurs when workers are made redundant as a result of advances in ICT.

KEY TERMS

frictional unemployment: temporary unemployment arising from workers being in between jobs.

search unemployment: unemployment arising from workers who have lost their jobs looking for a job they are willing to accept.

casual unemployment: unemployment arising from workers regularly being between periods of employment.

structural unemployment: unemployment caused by long-term changes in the pattern of demand and methods of production.

regional unemployment: unemployment caused by a decline in job opportunities in a particular area of the country.

technological unemployment: unemployment caused by workers being replaced by capital equipment.

For instance, airlines are currently reducing the number of backroom staff they employ, as more people are booking their flights online.

Structural unemployment is more serious than frictional unemployment, as it lasts for longer periods and usually affects more workers. In both cases, however, labour immobility plays a key role. If workers are more geographically and occupationally immobile, frictional and structural unemployment will be greater and last for a longer time. Measures to reduce frictional unemployment include those which seek to increase labour mobility (including education and training) and those which increase the incentive to work (including cutting income tax and benefits). Measures to reduce structural unemployment also include those which aim to increase labour mobility and encourage firms to move to areas of high unemployment.

Cyclical unemployment

Cyclical unemployment may be even more serious than structural unemployment as it can potentially affect more workers and is spread throughout the country. It arises from a lack of aggregate demand. It is also sometimes referred to as demand-deficient unemployment. If an economy goes through a recession, demand for labour is likely to fall and cyclical unemployment will occur. Figure 27.3 shows an economy operating below the full employment level of national output. In such a situation, unemployment is likely to be high. To tackle cyclical unemployment, a government will seek to raise aggregate demand by, for instance, reducing income tax or increasing its expenditure.

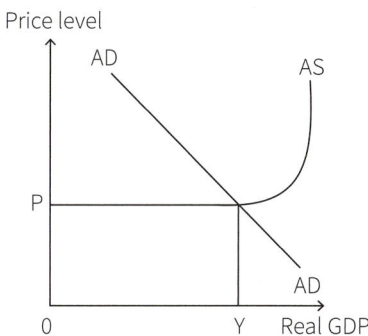

Figure 27.3: An economy producing below full capacity

Seasonal unemployment

Seasonal unemployment is a form of frictional employment. It affects workers, including those working in the building and tourist industries and whose labour is not in demand at certain periods of the year and during periods of bad weather (see Figure 27.4).

KEY TERMS

cyclical unemployment: unemployment caused by a lack of aggregate demand.

seasonal unemployment: unemployment caused by a fall in demand at particular times of the year.

Figure 27.4: A worker who harvests grapes may be affected by seasonal unemployment

Stocks and flows of unemployment

The number of people unemployed at any one time is a stock. It is influenced by two factors: the rate of flow of people into unemployment and the time period for which they are unemployed. So the number of people unemployed may be higher than in a previous period in three circumstances:

- more workers have been dismissed from their jobs

- more people have entered the labour force without finding a job

- people have been unemployed for a longer period of time.

DISCUSSION

Discuss what type/types of unemployment you think your country is experiencing.

ACTIVITY 27.3

In 2022, unemployment in Egypt was 7.1%, and in Saudi Arabia, it was 5.6%. Produce a leaflet explaining what measures the Egyptian government could take to reduce unemployment in the country. Include in the leaflet one way unemployment may have been measured in the two countries, and explain why unemployment may be higher in one country than another.

27.4 Consequences of unemployment

The existence of unemployed workers makes it easier for firms wishing to expand to recruit new workers. It can also keep down inflationary pressure by lowering wage rises. However, it is generally agreed that the costs of unemployment exceed any benefits.

The extent and seriousness of these costs are influenced by the numbers unemployed and the length of time for which they are unemployed. An unemployment rate of 9% with people being unemployed, on an average, for three months is less serious than an unemployment rate of 6% with the average length of unemployment being a year. Those who bear the main burden of unemployment are the unemployed themselves. But there are also costs for the wider economy.

Consequences for the individual

Most people who are unemployed suffer a fall in income. In some countries the unemployed do not receive any financial assistance when they are out of work. In countries where unemployment benefits are paid, these are usually noticeably lower than what most of the unemployed were previously earning. Having a job also provides a person with a sense of worth. So losing a job can result in a loss of self-worth. Lower income and the stress of being unemployed can result in a decline in the mental and physical health of the unemployed and may also lead to relationship break-ups in some cases. Lower income may have an adverse effect on the education of the children of the unemployed and subsequently their employment chances. Those who are unemployed may not be able to afford the education of their children past the school-leaving age.

Being unemployed can also reduce a person's chances of gaining another job. The longer people are unemployed, the more they lose out on training in new methods and technology. They may also lose the work habit and their confidence may fall.

Consequences for producers/firms

As mentioned earlier, firms may benefit from unemployment. They can employ unemployed workers in order to expand production. The existence of unemployment may put downward pressure on wage rises, as workers may be more concerned that if they press for significant wage rises they may be replaced by some of the unemployed. For the same reason, workers may be prepared to be more flexible in terms of the tasks they perform and the hours they work. Greater flexibility of workers would enable firms to adjust more quickly to changes in market conditions.

Unemployment, however, may bring a significant disadvantage for firms. A high rate of unemployment is likely to mean a low demand for most firms' products. In such a situation, firms will be reducing rather than expanding production.

Consequences for the government and the economy

Unemployment imposes an opportunity cost on an economy. Having unemployed workers means that the economy is not using all of its resources. The economy will not be making as many goods and services as possible. Figure 27.5 shows that unemployment causes an economy to produce at point A. Producing at this point involves the economy forgoing the opportunity to produce more capital and consumer goods. Producing at point B would mean that the economy would be making more products and living standards would potentially be higher.

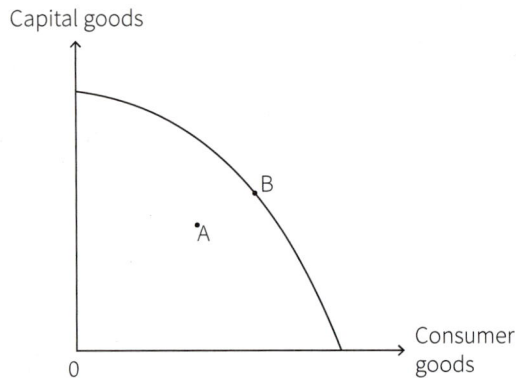

Figure 27.5: The opportunity cost of unemployment

Unemployment also means that government tax revenue will be lower than otherwise possible. When people lose their jobs, their expenditure falls, and as a result, indirect tax revenue declines. Income and firms' profits fall and, therefore, revenue from income tax and corporate tax decreases.

Besides lowering tax revenue, unemployment also puts pressure on government expenditure. Expenditure on unemployment benefits will automatically rise with unemployment. If the unemployed suffer from bad health, the government may have to spend more on healthcare. There is a risk that rising unemployment may lead to rising levels of crime, as some of the unemployed may turn to criminal activities to gain a higher income. If crime does rise, the government may have to spend more to tackle the problem and ensure the security of its citizens.

Higher government expenditure, resulting from unemployment, involves an opportunity cost. The money spent on benefits, for instance, could have been spent on higher education. Spending on the treatment of unemployed people for depression might mean that the government has to spend less on treating people with cancer.

ACTIVITY 27.4

In 2019, the unemployment rate in South Africa was 26%. In 2023, the rate had increased to 32%. During this time, the South African government had tried a number of policy measures to try to boost aggregate demand in a bid to create jobs and reduce poverty. These measures included increased government spending on infrastructure.

In a pair, discuss the answers to these questions.

1   What type of unemployment did South Africa appear to be suffering from in 2019 and in 2023?

2   Explain how expenditure on infrastructure may reduce unemployment.

3   Explain how a decrease in unemployment may reduce poverty.

Write the answers in your notebook.

27.5 Policies to reduce unemployment

The policies a government will adopt to reduce unemployment will be determined by what it thinks are the causes, or cause, of unemployment. If it believes that most of the unemployment is frictional unemployment, it may seek to improve the working of the labour market by using supply-side policy measures. For instance, it may seek to increase the gap between pay and unemployment benefit by cutting income tax rates and reducing unemployment benefit. This may reduce the time that people spend searching for a new job. The government may also increase information on job vacancies so that people are made more aware of the jobs on offer (see Figure 27.6).

Figure 27.6: How could a government help this person find a job?

To tackle structural unemployment a government would also use supply-side policy measures. In particular, it is likely to try to improve the quality of education and training. If workers are more skilled and qualified, they will be more occupationally mobile. A government may increase training in specific skills needed in particular industries. For example, if a country's coal industry is declining, while its tourism industry is increasing, it may offer special courses in, for example, hotel management and catering. A government may also give subsidies to new industries in areas of high unemployment to speed up their expansion.

To reduce cyclical unemployment, a government will use expansionary fiscal and monetary policy. An increase in government spending, a reduction in tax rates and a cut in the rate of interest, for instance, may be used to raise aggregate demand. With higher aggregate demand, firms would expand and take on more workers.

Effectiveness of policies

How effective government policy measures are in tackling unemployment will be determined by a number of factors. One is whether the government has identified the cause of unemployment correctly. For example, increasing the skills of the unemployed will not help to solve the problem if there is no demand for goods and services they could produce. In the case of structural unemployment, a government would also have to be able to accurately identify which industries will expand in the future and what skills will be needed. A government may decide to use privatisation and deregulation in a bid to increase the efficiency and expansion of industries, but there is no guarantee these measures will work. Indeed, privatisation may increase unemployment. Reducing cyclical unemployment requires a government to judge accurately the gap between the current level of real GDP and the full employment level. If it injects too much spending into the economy, it could cause inflation.

ACTIVITY 27.5

Table 27.1 lists policy measures that governments use to try to reduce unemployment. Copy and complete the table with the type of unemployment each policy measure is most likely to target.

Table 27.1

Policy measure	Type of unemployment
1 Encouragement of an increase in commercial bank lending.	
2 Government spending on a new university in an area of high unemployment.	
3 Increase in the government's budget deficit.	
4 Movement of government offices to an area of high unemployment.	
5 Online provision to employers of details of the qualifications and skills of the unemployed.	
6 Reduction of sales tax.	
7 Removal of unemployment benefit when a worker turns down their third job offer.	

REFLECTION

Were you able to decide on the type of unemployment each policy measure would be most suitable to tackle? If you were unsure of any, what will you do to increase your understanding?

LINKS

There are a range of policies a government may use to reduce unemployment – see Chapter 23.5 (Effects of fiscal policy on government macroeconomic aims), Chapter 24.3 (Effects of monetary policy on government macroeconomic aims), Chapter 25.3 (Effects of supply-side policy on government macroeconomic aims). Lowering unemployment is an important way of reducing poverty – see Chapter 30.3 (Policies to alleviate poverty and redistribute income).

ECONOMICS IN ACTION

Unemployment in Eswatini

Figure 27.7: Fruit and vegetable market in Eswatini

The government is looking for solutions to the high unemployment rate in Eswatini.

Economists examine the causes, consequences and possible solutions to unemployment and explore why unemployment rates differ between countries.

Eswatini, a small low-income country surrounded by South Africa, has one of the highest unemployment rates in the world. In 2022, the country had an unemployment rate of 30% and an unemployment rate of 57% for young workers aged 20–24. In that year, only 60% of children completed their primary school education. As they lack qualifications and skills, it is likely that these children will be able to do only low-skilled jobs when they enter the labour market, and there may be a shortage of these. In 2023, even the country's 4 000 graduates were finding it difficult to find employment.

To try to reduce unemployment, the Eswatini government proposed an internship scheme where unemployed graduates would be placed with government organisations or private sector firms to gain work experience.

1   What might explain the causes of the shortage of jobs in Eswatini?

2   How successful do you think the proposed internship scheme would be in reducing unemployment in Eswatini?

SUMMARY

You should now know:

- Unemployment consists of people willing and able to work who cannot find employment.

- A rise in employment may be accompanied by a rise or fall in unemployment.

- Unemployment can be measured by undertaking a labour force survey.

- Frictional unemployment arises when workers are finding new jobs after leaving the old one.

- Structural unemployment is caused by long-term changes in demand and supply.

- Cyclical unemployment results from a lack of aggregate demand.

- The unemployed suffer from lower income and possibly from lower self-esteem and bad health.

- The longer people are out of work, the harder it can be for them to find employment.

CONTINUED

- Unemployment is a waste of resources. It results in output and living standards being lower than possible, lower tax revenue and increased government expenditure on benefits and on other costs arising from unemployment.

- To reduce frictional and structural unemployment, a government will use supply-side policy measures.

- To reduce cyclical unemployment, a government will use demand-side policy measures.

Chapter 27 practice questions

1   Which group of people are of working age, but do not form a part of the labour force?

   A   people past the age of retirement

   B   people who are in full-time education

   C   the self-employed

   D   the unemployed   [1]

2   A country's steel industry is closed down as buyers switched their purchases of steel to another country. What type of unemployment will occur as a result of this?

   A   cyclical

   B   frictional

   C   seasonal

   D   structural   [1]

3   What is a cost of unemployment?

   A   higher tax revenue

   B   lost output

   C   lower productivity

   D   reduced inflationary pressure   [1]

4   Which policy is most likely to reduce cyclical unemployment?

   A   a reduction in government expenditure

   B   a reduction in interest rates

   C   an increase in direct taxes

   D   an increase in indirect taxes   [1]

5   What is a cause of structural unemployment?

   A   a fall in wages causing some workers to go back into education

   B   a recession which lasts for more than a year

   C   a short-term gap between leaving one job and gaining another

   D   job skills becoming outdated   [1]

                                                              Total: [5]

6   a   Define 'cyclical unemployment'.   [2]

   b   Explain how the unemployment rate may fall while the number of
       people employed declines.   [4]

   c   Analyse how a cut in the interest rate could reduce unemployment. [6]

   d   Discuss whether or not unemployment is harmful.   [8]

                                                             Total: [20]

CHECK YOUR PROGRESS

How well do you think you have achieved the learning intentions for this chapter?
Give yourself a score from 1 (still need a lot of practice) to 5 (feeling very confident)
for each learning intention. Provide an example to support your score.

Now I can...	Score	Example
define employment, unemployment and full employment		
explain how unemployment is measured: Labour Force Survey and the formula for the unemployment rate		
analyse the causes/types of unemployment: frictional unemployment, structural unemployment, cyclical unemployment and seasonal unemployment		
discuss the consequences of unemployment for the individual, producers/firms and the government and the economy		
discuss the range of policies to reduce unemployment and their effectiveness.		

> Chapter 28
Inflation

LEARNING INTENTIONS

By the end of this chapter, you will be able to:

- define inflation and deflation
- explain how inflation is measured using the consumer price index (CPI)
- analyse the causes of inflation: demand-pull and cost-push
- discuss the consequences of inflation for consumers, workers, producers/firms and the economy
- discuss the range of policies available to control inflation and their effectiveness.

Introduction

The money you are spending may buy you fewer goods this month than it did a few months ago. It is very likely to be buying less than 10, 20 or 30 years ago. For example, the price of a basket of foodstuffs in the UK was the equivalent of $0.31 in 1914. The price of the same basket increased to $1.12 in 1964, $21.93 in 2017 and is forecast to rise to $88.79 in 2064. There are a number of reasons why the prices of goods and services change. Higher prices can have both advantages and disadvantages. A large rise, however, is likely to bring more disadvantages than advantages. This why governments aim for stable prices and why they and their central banks use a range of policy measures to achieve stable prices.

ECONOMICS IN CONTEXT

Low inflation makes consumers happy

In the period 1997–2020, the UK had a low and stable inflation rate. The inflation rate averaged 1.9%, very close to the Bank of England's (the country's central bank) central target of 2%. It was also within the central bank's target range of 2% with a 1% point margin either side except in 2011. It was also lower than the global inflation rate until the end of the period.

Low inflation means that people's purchasing power will not be significantly affected. People may even experience a rise in real income if their wages rise by more than inflation. Low and stable inflation may mean that people may not realise the price level has risen. For example, workers are less likely to ask for wage rises just to match higher prices. This can keep rises in costs of production low.

Figure 28.1: When inflation is low, consumers benefit from stable prices

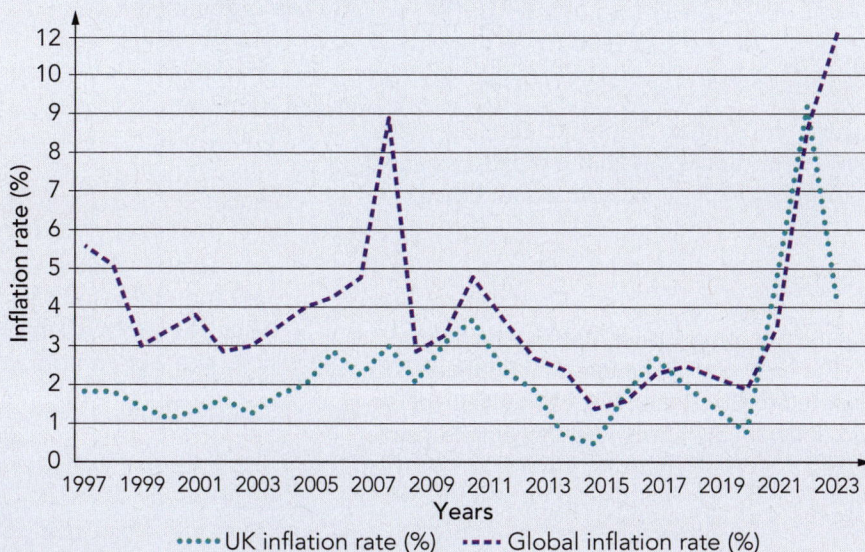

Figure 28.2: The UK and global inflation rates, 1997–2023

In 2021, the UK's inflation rate rose, largely due to higher energy and food prices (see Figure 28.2). The rise in the price level particularly harmed those experiencing poverty. People living on some state benefits and those earning low wages found they were not able to buy as many goods and services. Some had to go to food banks, which provide food free to those in need.

Discuss in a pair or group:

1 Have you been aware of price rises in your country?

2 What effect might a low and stable inflation rate have on a central bank's interest rate?

28.1 What are inflation and deflation?

Inflation is a rise in the average price of goods and services, also known as a rise in the price level or general price level. In contrast, deflation is a fall in the average price of goods and services. **Deflation** is, in effect, negative inflation. The rate at which the average prices of goods and services rise or fall changes over time. An increase in the rate of inflation means that prices are increasing more rapidly. A fall in the inflation rate from, for example, 10% to 7%, can be described as **disinflation**.

28.2 Measurement of inflation and deflation

To measure rises and falls in the price level, governments construct price indices (also referred to as price indexes). These show the change in general price level in percentage terms over time. One of the main price indices used is the **consumer price index (CPI)**.

Constructing a price index

There are a number of stages in constructing a price index. These include selecting a base year, finding out how households spend their money, attaching weights to items of expenditure, finding out price changes from a range of trade outlets and then constructing a weighted price index.

Selecting a base year

Government statisticians try to select a relatively standard year, one in which there were no dramatic changes, as a base year. The base year is then given a figure of 100 and the price levels in other years are compared to this figure. For example, if the base year is 2025, it would mean that if the price index in 2028 was 123, the general price level had risen by 23% between 2025 and 2028.

KEY TERMS

inflation: a rise in the average price of goods and services over time.

deflation: a fall in the average price of goods and services over time.

disinflation: a fall in the rate of inflation.

consumer price index (CPI): a measure of the weighted average of the prices of a representative basket of goods and services.

TIP

Remember that if inflation falls, for example from 8% to 6%, the general price level is still rising.

Finding out how households spend their money

In calculating the average rise in prices, it is important to know how people spend their money. This is because a price change in an item on which people spend a large proportion of their total expenditure will have more impact on the cost of living than an item on which they spend a relatively small proportion. If, for example, the price of water rose, it would affect most of the population much more than a rise in the price of a trip in an air balloon, something most people will not buy and those who do, will do so infrequently.

To find out the spending patterns of people, government officials carry out surveys of household expenditure. In New Zealand, a sample of approximately 3 000 households is used. These households are asked to keep a record of their expenditures. From the information collected, government officials work out the main commodities being bought by the households. This enables them to decide which items to include in the price index and what weights to attach to each of them. If people stop buying a product or their expenditure on it falls to a very small figure, it will be removed from the index. The weights reflect the proportion spent on the items. For example, if on an average, households spend $120 of their total expenditure of $600 on food, food will be given a weightage of 1/5 or 20%. Table 28.1 shows the categories of products in the UK's CPI in 2024 and their respective weights with, for example, 9.1% of UK households' expenditure going on food and soft drinks.

Table 28.1: The weights in the UK's CPI in 2024

Category	Weight (%)
1 Food and non-alcoholic beverages (soft drinks)	9.1
2 Alcohol and tobacco	3.2
3 Clothing and footwear	4.7
4 Housing and household services	29.9
5 Furniture and household goods	5.0
6 Health	2.1
7 Transport	10.9
8 Communication	1.9
9 Recreation and culture	11.5
10 Education	2.4
11 Restaurants and hotels	11.7
12 Miscellaneous goods and services	7.5

Household spending patterns are reviewed each year with new family expenditure surveys. If these reveal, for example, that people are spending a greater percentage on recreation and culture, and a lower percentage on food and non-alcoholic beverages, the weights of these items in price index will be altered to reflect these changes (see Figure 28.3).

Figure 28.3: In 2024, air fryers were added to the UK CPI's shopping basket to reflect consumers' buying habits

Finding out price changes

Each month, government officials find out information about prices. In the UK, about 130 000 price quotations are found for 650 different items. These are obtained from shops, post offices, power companies, train companies and a range of other outlets. From this information, the government estimates the change in prices.

ACTIVITY 28.1

India's consumer price index (CPI) covers 260 items. It draws on about 160 000 price quotes from more than 16 500 outlets and selected markets. Most price quotes are collected every week. In the case of products which experience a change in price less frequently, the price quotes are collected every month or every six months.

1 What does a CPI measure?

2 How will the Indian government select the 260 items included in its CPI?

Write your answers in your notebook.

Constructing a weighted price index

Once weights have been given to different items included in the index and the change in their prices measured over time, the final stage is to multiply the weights by the new price index for each category of products and to calculate the change in general price level. For example, consumers may spend $40 on food, $10 on housing, $25 on transport and $25 on entertainment. This gives a total expenditure of $100. The price of food may have risen by 10%, the price of housing may have fallen by 5%, the price of transport may not have changed and entertainment may have risen in price by 8%. The information would then be used to perform the calculation shown in Table 28.2.

Table 28.2: Weighted price index

Category	Weight		Price index		Weighted price index
Food	$\frac{4}{10}$	×	110	=	44.0
Housing	$\frac{1}{10}$	×	95	=	9.5
Transport	$\frac{1}{4}$	×	100	=	25.0
Entertainment	$\frac{1}{4}$	×	108	=	27.0
					105.5

The price index has risen by 5.5%. The change in the price level could also have been calculated rather more directly, as shown in Table 28.3.

Table 28.3: Weighted price change

Category	Weight		Price change (%)		Weighted price change (%)
Food	$\frac{4}{10}$	×	10	=	4
Housing	$\frac{1}{10}$	×	−5	=	−0.5
Transport	$\frac{1}{4}$	×	0	=	0
Entertainment	$\frac{1}{4}$	×	8	=	2
					5.5

ACTIVITY 28.2

In each case, calculate the inflation rate using the information given.

1   Consumers spend $20 on food, $20 on clothing, $10 on heating and $50 on entertainment. The price of food rises by 5%, the price of clothing falls by 10%, the price of heating rises by 30% and the price of entertainment rises by 20%.

2   Consumers spend $50 on food, $20 on clothing, $60 on transport and $70 on leisure goods and services. The price of food rises by 8%, the price of clothing rises by 10%, the price of transport falls by 10% and the price of leisure goods rises by 5%.

Share your answers with another student.

Different impact of price changes

A consumer price index (CPI) measures the price of goods and services consumed by the average household. Of course, the expenditure of particular households is likely to differ from the average in some way. For example, families with no or young children will experience lower inflation than some other households due to no expenditure on university fees if such fees increase at a greater rate than the inflation rate.

28.3 Causes of inflation

Inflation is not a one-off increase in the general price level. While examining the causes of inflation, therefore, it is necessary to consider the reasons for a rise in the price level over a period of time. Economists divide the causes into two main categories: **cost-push inflation** and **demand-pull inflation**.

Cost-push inflation

Cost-push inflation occurs when the price level is pushed up by increases in the costs of production. If firms face higher costs, they will usually raise their prices to maintain their profit margins.

There are a number of reasons for an increase in costs. One is wages increasing more than labour productivity. This will increase labour costs. As labour costs form the highest proportion of total costs in many firms, such a rise can have a significant impact on the price level. It will also not be a one-off increase. The initial rise in the price level is likely to cause workers to ask for even higher wages, leading to a **wage-price spiral**.

Another important reason is increase in the cost of raw materials. Some raw materials, most notably oil, can change in price by large amounts. If raw materials have to be bought from other countries, a country may import inflation from those countries. Other causes of cost-push inflation are increases in indirect taxes, higher cost of capital goods and increase in profit margins by firms.

Cost-push inflation can be illustrated on an aggregate demand and aggregate supply diagram. Higher costs of production shift the AS curve to the left, and this movement forces up the price level, as shown in Figure 28.4.

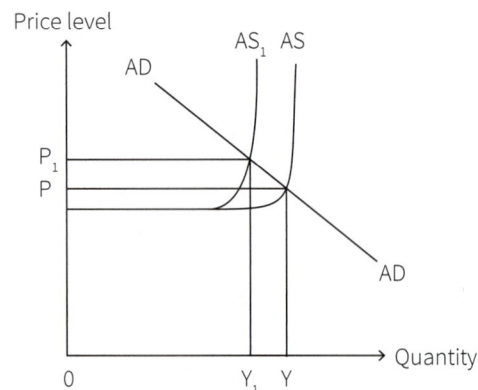

Figure 28.4: Cost-push inflation

TIP

In explaining the idea of a consumer price index, it is often useful to give a numerical example, such as shown in Table 28.3.

KEY TERMS

cost-push inflation: rises in the price level caused by higher costs of production.

demand-pull inflation: rises in the price level caused by excess demand.

wage-price spiral: wage rises leading to higher prices which, in turn, lead to further wage claims and price rises.

Demand-pull inflation

Demand-pull inflation occurs when the price level is pulled up by an excess demand. Aggregate demand can increase due to higher consumer expenditure, higher investment, higher government spending or higher net exports. Such an increase in aggregate demand will not necessarily cause inflation, for example if aggregate supply can extend to match it. When the economy has plenty of spare capacity, with unemployed workers and unused machines, higher aggregate demand will result in higher output but no increase in the price level. If, however, the economy is experiencing a shortage of some resources, for example skilled workers, then aggregate supply may not be able to rise in line with aggregate demand and inflation occurs. In a situation of full employment of resources it would not be possible to produce any more output. As a result, any rise in demand will be purely inflationary, as shown in Figure 28.5.

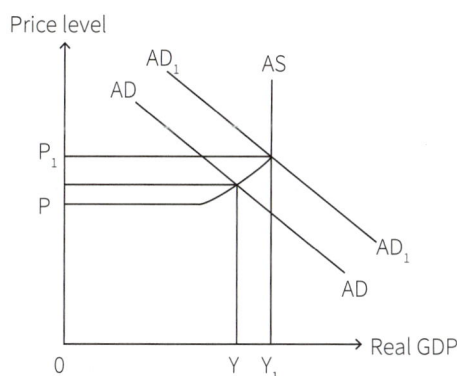

Figure 28.5: Demand-pull inflation

Monetary inflation is a form of demand-pull inflation. In this case, excess demand is created by an excessive growth of the money supply. A group of economists, known as **monetarists**, believe that the only cause of inflation is the money supply increasing faster than output. They argue that if the money supply increases, people will spend more and this will lead to an increase in prices.

KEY TERMS

monetary inflation: rises in the price level caused by an excessive growth of the money supply.

monetarists: a group of economists who think that inflation is caused by the money supply growing more rapidly than output.

TIP

It is a common mistake to say that inflation is caused by a rise in prices. Inflation is a rise in prices. So, the reasons for the rise in the general price level need to be considered.

ACTIVITY 28.3

Cambodia's inflation rose to 5.3% in 2022 from 2.9% in 2021. The price level was driven up mainly by rising energy prices, transport prices and wages. Economists were forecasting that wage rises would increase above inflation in 2023 and 2024, and that if inflation were to rise even higher, it could have a harmful effect on the country's exports, making them less internationally competitive.

In a pair, produce a report on whether Cambodia was experiencing demand-pull inflation or cost-push inflation in 2022, and how the inflation might have affected the demand for its exports. In considering the impact on demand for its exports, there is a range of information you might mention that would be useful. This information includes other countries' inflation rates, the price elasticity of demand for Cambodia's exports, changes in incomes in other countries and whether exports are subsidised. For example, a rise in the price of Cambodia's exports will have less of an effect if demand is inelastic. In this case, demand will fall by a smaller percentage than the rise in price.

28.4 Consequences of inflation

Most of the consequences of inflation are thought to be harmful, but some consequences may be beneficial. The impact that inflation has depends on a number of factors. The key ones are the rate of inflation, how stable the inflation rate is, its rate relative to the inflation rates of other countries and the reaction of the government. For example, inflation is less likely to be a problem and may be beneficial if the inflation is of a demand-pull, low and stable nature and is below that of rival countries.

Consequences for consumers

Inflation causes a fall in the value of money. If prices are rising, each unit of money (for example, each dollar) will buy fewer products. The higher the inflation rate, the greater will be the fall in the purchasing power of money. In a situation of **hyperinflation**, the value of money may be falling so rapidly that consumers may lose confidence in using the country's currency as money (see Figure 28.6). The minimum rate to qualify as hyperinflation is usually taken to be 50%.

Figure 28.6: Hyperinflation may result in supermarket shelves being stripped bare

The government can seek to protect some vulnerable groups from inflation by **index-linking** state benefit payments and interest rates on government securities.

Normally, borrowers benefit from inflation. If the interest rate is below the inflation rate, borrowers pay back less in real terms than what they borrowed. For example, an individual may borrow $100. If the inflation rate is 12%, they would have to repay $112 to the lender to just gain back the same amount of purchasing power. If the rate of interest is 8%, the borrower will repay only $108, which has less purchasing power than what they borrowed.

Inflation reduces the real burden of any debt that consumers and firms have built up. This may mean that some households and firms will avoid going bankrupt.

While borrowers are likely to benefit, savers and lenders are likely to lose, as they may be repaid less in real terms than what they have put into savings accounts and what they have lent.

KEY TERMS

hyperinflation: a very rapid and large rise in the price level.

index-linking: changing payments in line with changes in the inflation rate.

Consequences for workers

Some workers gain from inflation, while others lose. Workers with strong bargaining power tend to gain, as their income usually rises more than the inflation rate. Workers with low bargaining power may suffer during a period of inflation.

Inflation can prevent some workers being made redundant in a declining industry or region. This is because while workers are likely to oppose any cut in their money wages, they may accept their money wages rising by less than inflation. In such a case, firms' real wage costs will fall without having to make any workers redundant.

Consequences for producers/firms

The existence of inflation imposes extra costs on firms. Some additional staff time will be taken up estimating future costs of raw material. There will also be **menu costs** and **shoe-leather costs**. Menu costs are the costs involved in changing prices in catalogues, price lists and online. Shoe-leather costs arise because money paid to firms will be losing its value as soon as it is received. Even if the firms plan to pay out the money relatively soon, for example on wages or raw materials, they would need to protect the value of the money by placing it in a bank or other financial institution, which will pay an interest rate above the inflation rate. Seeking out good financial returns will involve the time and effort of firms.

However, inflation may encourage firms to expand. This is because a low and stable level of demand-pull inflation may make entrepreneurs optimistic about future sales.

Consequences for the economy

Inflation creates uncertainty. Inflation can make it hard for consumers and firms to judge the right price to be paid for products now. It can also make it difficult to plan ahead, as households and firms will be uncertain about future prices. This is a particularly serious problem with a high, fluctuating inflation rate. In such an unstable situation, firms may be discouraged from investing which will be harmful for the economy.

Inflation can harm the country's balance of payments position. If a country's inflation rate is above that of its rivals, its products will become less price competitive. This may result in a fall in export revenue and a rise in import expenditure. Such an effect would cause a deterioration in the current account balance. The fall in demand for the country's products may also result in a rise in unemployment.

Inflation can cause fiscal drag. Fiscal drag occurs when governments do not adjust tax brackets in line with inflation. As a result, people's incomes are dragged into higher tax brackets and they are left with lower real disposable income. Governments may also benefit from inflation as most governments are borrowers. Inflation can reduce the burden of national debt.

ACTIVITY 28.4

In a pair, copy and complete Table 28.4 on the effects of inflation.
The last one has been partially completed for you.

Table 28.4

	Which is likely to be the more harmful?	Reason why
Cost-push inflation or demand-pull inflation		
Fluctuating inflation rate or stable inflation rate		
Inflation rate above or below rival countries		
5% or 50% inflation rate		
Predicted or unpredicted	Unpredicted	

DISCUSSION

Discuss whether the effects of inflation impact in different ways on older people and younger people.

LINKS

Inflation may be controlled by using a range of policy measures – see Chapter 23.5 (Effects of fiscal policy on government macroeconomic aims), Chapter 24.3 (Effects of monetary policy on government macroeconomic aims) and Chapter 25.3 (Effects of supply-side policy on government macroeconomic aims).

28.5 Policies to control inflation

A policy measure that is becoming increasingly used throughout the world is the setting by a government of an inflation rate target for its central bank to achieve. The aim of an inflation rate target is to make the central bank accountable to the government and to influence the behaviour of consumers and firms. If a central bank does not achieve its target, it has to explain why and what measures it is going to take to get the inflation rate back on target. If a central bank can convince consumers and firms that there will be stable prices, the consumers and firms may behave in a way that reduces the chance of significant movements in the price level. Consumers will not rush to buy products, expecting them to be much more expensive in the future, and firms will not raise their prices just to cover expected increases in costs of production.

If the country is experiencing demand-pull inflation, the appropriate policy approach would be to use contractionary fiscal and/or monetary policy. Aggregate demand could be reduced by increasing tax rates, lowering government spending, raising the rate of interest and/or reducing the money supply. The effectiveness of such measures will be influenced by how consumers and firms react. If they are very confident about future economic prospects, they may continue to spend increasing amounts despite these measures. They may also react in a way that turns demand-pull inflation into cost-push inflation. For example, workers may respond to higher income rates by demanding higher wages or they may opt out of the labour force. Contractionary fiscal and monetary policy measures can have a number of adverse side effects, including reducing economic growth and possibly causing unemployment.

To reduce cost-push inflation, a government will use supply-side policy measures such as improved education and training and privatisation. These measures may be effective but, as noted before, they make take some time. They may also be relatively costly and may, at least in the short run, add to aggregate demand. In addition, rises in firms' costs of production are not just influenced by what is happening in the domestic economy. Rises in the price of imported raw materials and fuel may put significant upward pressure on prices. In this case, a government may try to lower inflation by subsidising firms, but this might need relatively large amounts of government revenue and so a high opportunity cost.

ACTIVITY 28.5

Research the inflation rate in your country over the last ten years, and decide how successful you think your central bank and government have been in controlling inflation.

REFLECTION

Did you find the concepts of demand-pull and cost-push inflation difficult to understand? If so, what can you do to gain a better understanding of them?

ECONOMICS IN ACTION

Inflation in Argentina

Figure 28.7: As the person withdraws cash from the machine, high inflation is causing its value to fall

A recent case of high inflation studied by economists is that experienced in Argentina. Between 2018 and 2022, Argentina's inflation rate averaged 50%. Prices rose by more than wages, and the proportion of the population living in poverty rose from 25% to 40%. The country's unemployment rate fell, but rose among unskilled workers.

In 2023, Argentina's inflation rate increased to 211%. Economists pointed to several causes of this rapid rise in the price level. One was the increase in government spending financed by borrowing. The government's budget deficit increased from 2.4% of GDP in 2022 to 4.8% of GDP in 2023. Import prices also increased because of a fall in the country's exchange rate.

In November 2023, a new government was elected. The new president proposed a number of radical policy measures to reduce inflation. He said that he would cut government spending by a large amount. He also said that the number of people employed by the government would be reduced, that all public sector projects would be stopped and government subsidies on food and transport would be reduced. The president had not been impressed by the performance of the central bank in controlling inflation. He said he was going to close the central bank and replace the country's currency, the peso, with the US dollar. This would involve relying on the monetary policy of the USA. Some economists suggested that this would not work, as economic activity in the two countries might be very different.

1   Why may people living in poverty have suffered both from inflation in Argentina and the policy measures proposed in 2023 to reduce it?

2   Would the proposed policy measures be likely to have reduced inflation?

Policy conflicts

Some of the policy measures designed to reduce unemployment may increase inflation. For example, an increase in government spending on pensions would raise consumer expenditure. This rise would encourage firms to expand their output and take on more workers. The higher aggregate demand may, however, raise the price level.

Policy measures to reduce expenditure on imports may reduce economic growth. A rise in income tax, designed to reduce households' expenditure on imports, would also reduce spending on domestically produced products. This fall in demand will reduce the country's output or at least slow down the economic growth.

Unemployment and economic growth both tend to benefit from expansionary fiscal and monetary policies. In contrast, contractionary fiscal and monetary policies are more likely to be used to reduce inflation and expenditure on imports.

SUMMARY

You should now know:

- The consumer price index (CPI) is a weighted measure of consumer prices.

- A rise in a consumer price index indicates inflation.

- Inflation may be caused by increases in the costs of production (cost-push) or excess demand (demand-pull).

- Among the causes of cost-push inflation are rises in wages and raw material costs.

- Demand-pull inflation is more likely to occur when the economy is at or approaching full employment.

- The effects of inflation will depend on its rate, stability of price rises, its rate relative to other countries and response of the government.

- Inflation will cause a fall in the purchasing power of money. Among the other possible harmful effects are an unplanned redistribution of income, menu costs, shoe-leather costs, uncertainty and a worsened position of the balance of payments.

- The possible beneficial effects of inflation include a stimulus to production, a reduction in debt and reduction of unemployment.

- Economic growth and employment are likely to benefit from measures designed to increase aggregate demand, but these measures may result in higher inflation and a rise in imports.

Chapter 28 practice questions

1   The price of a product rises by 8% in 2025 and its weighted price change is 2%.
    In 2026, the rise in the product's price is 5% and its weighted price change is 2.5%.
    What was the weight of the product in 2025 and 2026?

	2025	2026
A	$\frac{1}{4}$	$\frac{1}{2}$
B	$\frac{1}{4}$	$\frac{1}{4}$
C	4	2
D	2	4

[1]

2   Who, among the following, is most likely to benefit during a period of
    rapid inflation?

    A   borrowers

    B   pensioners

    C   savers

    D   workers in strong unions   [1]

3   What is a possible cause of demand-pull inflation?

    A   an increase in government expenditure, not matched by a rise in taxation

    B   an increase in the price of oil, not matched by a fall in the price of other
        raw materials

    C   a rise in imports, not matched by a rise in exports

    D   a rise in wages, not matched by an increase in productivity   [1]

4   What must happen as a result of inflation?

    A   a decline in uncertainty

    B   a fall in the value of money

    C   an improvement in the balance of payments

    D   an increase in savings   [1]

5   If the consumer price index rises from 125 to 140, what is the inflation rate?

    A   10.7%

    B   12%

    C   15%

    D   40%   [1]

                                                        Total: [5]

6 a   Define 'inflation'.   [2]

   b   Explain how an increase in consumer expenditure could cause inflation.   [4]

   c   Analyse how inflation is measured.   [6]

   d   Discuss whether or not workers suffer as a result of inflation.   [8]

                                                                    Total: [20]

CHECK YOUR PROGRESS

How well do you think you have achieved the learning intentions for this chapter?
Give yourself a score from 1 (still need a lot of practice) to 5 (feeling very confident)
for each learning intention. Provide an example to support your score.

Now I can...	Score	Example
define inflation and deflation		
explain how inflation is measured using the consumer price index (CPI)		
analyse the causes of inflation: demand-pull and cost-push		
discuss the consequences of inflation for consumers, workers, producers/firms and the economy		
discuss the range of policies to available to control inflation and their effectiveness.		

Section 4 practice questions

1   Read the source material carefully before answering all parts of the question.

CASE STUDY: BRAZIL, IMPROVING PERFORMANCE

Brazil fact file		
	2022	**2023**
GDP	$1 960bn	$2 200bn
Government budget deficit (as % of GDP)	4.6%	7.6%
Inflation rate	5.7%	4.8%
Unemployment rate	5.8%	7.7%

In 2015 and 2016, Brazil, one of the world's largest economies, experienced a recession. The country's negative economic growth was reversed in 2017, and between 2017 and 2023, there was positive economic growth averaging 2.6% a year.

Over the period 2017–2023, the government increased its spending, including on education and health, and the number of public sector workers rose to 7.5 million. In 2023, the government's budget deficit increased.

At the start of 2023, the Central Bank of Brazil announced that its inflation rate target for the year would be 3.25% with a margin of 1.5% points either side. The country's central bank lowered its interest rate during 2023, estimating that it would meet its inflation target. It did this as the inflation rate for 2023 was just within the upper margin of the inflation target. Inflation can affect households in different ways, depending on whether they are borrowers or savers and the pattern of their spending and how much bargaining power they may have as workers.

The Brazilian government was concerned about the rise in unemployment in 2023. One influence on the unemployment rate is consumer spending, which actually rose in Brazil in 2023. Consumer spending, in turn, can be influenced by changes in GDP. Table 1 shows GDP and consumer spending for Brazil and six of the other largest economies in 2023.

Table 1: GDP and consumer spending of seven large economies in 2023

Country	GDP ($bn)	Consumer spending ($bn)
Brazil	2 200	1 460
China	18 700	8 420
France	3 040	1 672
Germany	4 086	2 288
Japan	4 200	2 352
UK	2 800	1 876
USA	26 240	18 105

Refer to the information in the source material in your answers.

a	Calculate Brazil's government budget deficit in dollars in 2023.	[2]
b	Identify what type of fiscal policy and what type of monetary policy were operating in Brazil in 2023.	[2]
c	Explain the type of inflation experienced in Brazil in 2023.	[2]
d	Explain **two** possible reasons why the central bank lowered the interest rate in 2023.	[4]
e	Analyse the relationship between a country's GDP and its consumer spending.	[4]
f	Discuss whether or not inflation harms all households.	[6]

Total: [20]

2   Read the source material carefully before answering all parts of the question.

CASE STUDY: THE GOVERNMENT OF BANGLADESH TACKLES INFLATION

Bangladesh fact file

	2022	2023
Inflation rate	7.7%	9.0%
Inflation rate target	6.0%	7.5%
Population	171m	172m
Unemployment rate	5.0%	4.8%

Bangladesh's inflation rate rose in 2023. The country's government increased its inflation rate target for its central bank to meet from 6.0% to 7.5%. The prices of different goods and services rose at different rates. For example, the price of clothing rose by less than 9%, while the price of food and non-alcoholic drinks rose by more than 9%. The weight given to food and non-alcoholic drinks varies in different countries' CPIs, as shown in the table.

Bangladesh's government had an economic growth rate target of 6.5%. It did not have a specific target for the country's unemployment rate, but it wanted it to be as low as possible. Its unemployment rate fell in 2023. Youth unemployment nevertheless remained high and there was considerable underemployment. This was despite a relatively high rate of job vacancies. Employers said they could not fill them because the job applicants lacked the appropriate skills.

The Central Bank of Bangladesh raised the interest rate, but some economists suggested that it should be cut to stimulate investment and increase employment. Both changes in the interest rate and employment, as well as confidence, influence how much households save.

CONTINUED

Table 2: The weight given to food and non-alcoholic drinks and GDP per head in selected countries in 2023

Country	GDP per head ($)	Weight given to food and non-alcoholic drinks (%)
Bangladesh	2 720	56.2
Malta	35 000	16.5
The Philippines	3 520	35.0
South Africa	6 820	17.1
Sweden	57 000	14.0
Türkiye	10 710	23.7
UK	47 100	11.9

Refer to the information in the source material in your answers.

a Calculate Bangladesh's GDP in 2023. [2]

b Identify **two** categories of products in a country's CPI. [2]

c Explain what type of unemployment Bangladesh was experiencing in 2023. [2]

d Explain **two** policy measures that could be used to reduce unemployment in Bangladesh. [4]

e Analyse the relationship between GDP per head and the weight given to food and non-alcoholic drinks. [4]

f Discuss whether or not saving is likely to increase in Bangladesh. [6]

Total: [20]

3 In 2021, the Greek economy returned to economic growth after experiencing a period of recession. It was hoped that the economic growth would reduce the country's high rate of unemployment, restore confidence in the country's economic prospects and produce revenue from direct and indirect taxation.

a Define a 'direct tax'. [2]

b Explain how changes in resources affect economic growth. [4]

c Analyse how a fall in confidence in the economic prospects of a country could cause that country to experience a recession. [6]

d Discuss whether or not economic growth will always result in lower unemployment. [8]

Total: [20]

4 The unemployment rate, as measured by the Labour Force Survey method, in Sri Lanka rose between 2022 and 2023, while its inflation rate fell. Government spending increased over the period, and the government introduced a number of policy measures designed to increase the incentive to work.

    a Define 'the Labour Force Survey method' of measuring unemployment. **[2]**

    b Explain how a government could increase the incentive to work. **[4]**

    c Analyse why a fall in unemployment may be accompanied by a rise in inflation. **[6]**

    d Discuss whether or not an increase in government spending will reduce inflation. **[8]**

Total: [20]

Economic development

> # Chapter 29
> # Living standards

LEARNING INTENTIONS

By the end of this chapter, you will be able to:

* explain indicators of living standards: real gross domestic product (GDP) per head and the Human Development Index (HDI) and its components

* discuss the advantages and disadvantages of real GDP per head and HDI as indicators of living standards

* analyse the reasons for differences in living standards and income distribution within and between countries.

Introduction

One of the key roles of an economist can be seen to be to raise people's living standards. By helping to improve the performance of firms and advising governments on increasing macroeconomic performance, economists can make a significant difference to the quality of people's lives. In most countries living standards have increased over the last 50 years. There are, however, still significant differences in living standards within and between countries. Two main indicators of living standards used by economists are real GDP per head and the Human Development Index (HDI).

ECONOMICS IN CONTEXT

How people's lives can change

Figure 29.1: A Swedish family enjoys a high standard of living

Most people in Sweden now enjoy a high living standard and one which is higher than that experienced both in the past and in other countries. With a high income per head, the average Swede can enjoy a high quantity and quality of goods and services. With a good provision of high-quality healthcare, Swedes have a life expectancy of 83 years, ten years higher than the global average. They can also expect to have nearly 20 years of education between the ages of 5 and 39, higher than most countries in the world.

Every home in Sweden has an indoor flushing toilet, and most homes are stylish and spacious. Childcare is provided free by the government for every child aged between 1 and 5 years. The country has high-speed broadband connection, and ownership of electronic devices is widespread.

Every year people from other countries come to settle in Sweden, many attracted by Sweden's high living standards. In 2023, 20% of the country's population of 10.6m had been born outside the country.

Life has not always been so good in Sweden as it is today. Between 1840 and 1910, 1.1m Swedes, 20% of the population at the time, left Sweden for the USA in search of a better life. At the time, it was thought that higher incomes could be earned and better working conditions achieved by farm workers in the USA than in Sweden and that there were more opportunities for other types of work and better business opportunities in the USA.

Discuss in a pair or group:

1   What would influence which country you would like to live in?

2   How do you think education can increase people's living standards?

29.1 Indicators of living standards

There are a variety of indicators that can be used to assess the living standards in a country. Indicators of living standards include the number of people or households that own a given consumer good, such as cars and who have internet connection (see Table 29.1 and Figure 29.2). The number of patients per doctor, enrolment in tertiary education, the adult literacy rate and the average food intake per person can also be used as an indicator. A main measure of living standards is real gross domestic product (GDP) per head.

There are also composite indicators of living standards such as the **Human Development Index (HDI)**. Composite indicators like the Human Development Index consist of several measures of living standards including life expectancy at birth.

KEY TERM

Human Development Index (HDI): a measure of living standards which takes into account income, education and life expectancy.

Table 29.1: The top ten countries in terms of highest car ownership and internet access

Cars per 1 000 population		Percentage of households that have internet access	
San Marino	1100	Bahrain	100
Finland	950	Iceland	100
Monaco	900	Qatar	100
Iceland	890	United Arab Emirates	100
USA	880	Kuwait	100
Canada	870	Bermuda	98
New Zealand	805	Luxembourg	98
Malta	790	Saudi Arabia	98
Italy	770	Aruba	97
Australia	760	Denmark	97
		Republic of Korea	97

Figure 29.2: Households that have internet connection is an indicator of living standards

Real GDP per head

An increase in real GDP per head would suggest that living standards have risen, but it may not necessarily indicate the real situation for a number of reasons. One is that real GDP is an average. Not everyone may benefit from a rise in the average income level. The extra income may be unevenly spread, with a few receiving much higher income and some not receiving any extra income.

Higher output will mean that more goods and services are being produced, but not all of these may add to people's living standards. For example, an increase in the output and consumption of high-sugar foods may reduce the quality of people's lives by affecting their health and reducing their life expectancy. A rise in police services due to a higher crime rate is also unlikely to improve most people's living standards.

Due to undeclared economic activity and non-marketed output, increases in real GDP per head figures may understate the products available to people. It may, however, overstate it if the quality of output is falling. Living standards are also influenced by other factors besides the material goods and services produced. If output rises but working conditions deteriorate, the number of working hours increases or pollution increases, people may not feel better off.

Human Development Index

The Human Development Index (HDI) was developed by a team of economists at the United Nations Development Programme (UNDP). The Human Development Index has been published every year since 1990.

The HDI is a wider measure than real GDP per head. Besides including GDP per head (see Tip, right), the HDI considers two other indicators of living standards. One is the length of time for which people can enjoy life, measured as life expectancy at birth. The second is education. This is measured by mean years of schooling and expected years of schooling.

On the basis of their HDI values, countries are categorised into their level of human development. The HDI shows that economic growth and human progress may not always match. Some countries, such as Namibia and South Africa, have recently enjoyed a higher ranking in terms of GDP per head than HDI, while others, including Costa Rica and Cuba, usually score more highly in terms of HDI than GDP per head.

Although the HDI takes into account other factors that influence people's living standards, the index has been criticised for what it leaves out. In fact, it has been stated that the index would be high for someone who has been well educated and living in a prison for a long time. Among the factors it does not take into account are political freedom and the environment. It also does not consider differences in life expectancy, education and differences in income between males and females and between those living in rural and urban areas, among other groups.

In the Human Development Report of 2021/22, the United Nations (UN) divided countries into four categories: very high human development (HDI: 0.800 and above), high human development (HDI: 0.700–0.799), medium human development (0.550–06.999) and low human development (HDI: 0.001–0.499). In 2021, the three countries with the highest HDI value were Switzerland, Norway and Iceland. Table 29.2 gives examples of countries at the four different levels.

TIP

The HDI now uses gross national income per head rather than GDP per head. This is very similar to GDP per head, but it includes workers' remittances (people living and working in another country sending money home to help relatives). For consistency, GDP per head is used here.

Table 29.2: HDI rankings in 2021

Level of development	HDI value	HDI rank
Very high human development		
Switzerland	0.962	1
Chile	0.855	42
Mauritius	0.803	62
High human development		
Sri Lanka	0.782	73
Maldives	0.747	90
Indonesia	0.703	115
Medium human development		
Philippines	0.699	116
Ghana	0.632	133
Cambodia	0.593	146

(Continued)

Table 29.2: Continued

Level of development	HDI value	HDI rank
Low human development		
Tanzania	0.549	160
Sierra Leone	0.477	181
South Sudan	0.385	191

ACTIVITY 29.3

Figure 29.3 shows how the HDI value has changed over time for four countries and the world over a period of time.

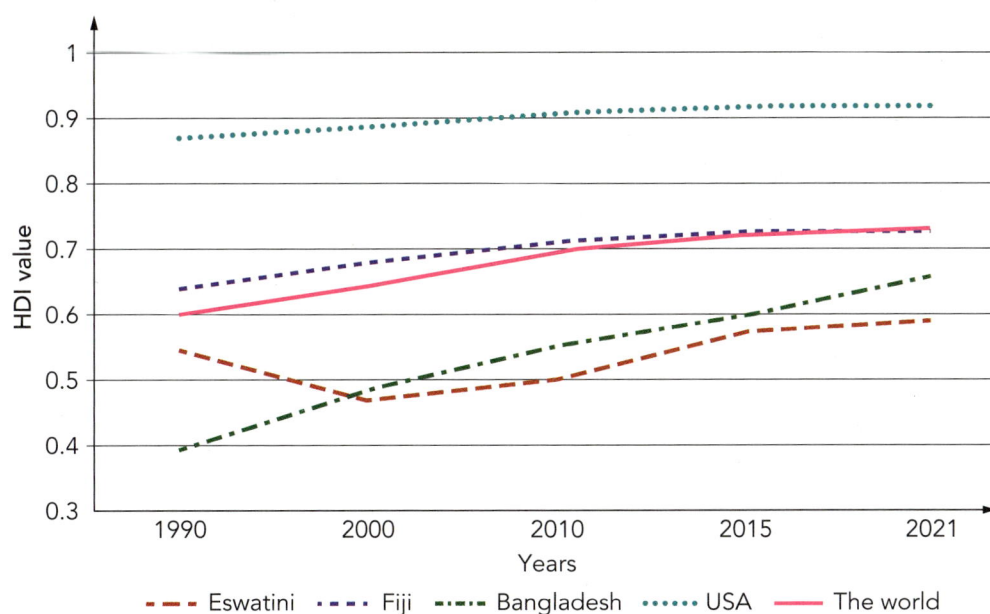

Figure 29.3: How the HDI value has changed over time for four countries and the world, 1990–2021

1   From the information in the graph:

   a   Which country may have experienced a fall in their living standards at one point over the period?

   b   Which country appears to have achieved the highest relative increase in their living standards over the period?

2   Why may the income per head of a country fall but its HDI value rise?

Write your answers in your notebook.

ECONOMICS IN ACTION

Living standards in the Seychelles

Figure 29.4: The Seychelles, the African country with the highest real GDP per head

Economists study how living standards change over time and the causes of these changes. One country that has seen a significant rise in living standards in recent years is the Seychelles. This is a small country made up of 115 islands. In 2015, it achieved high income status as measured by the World Bank. This made it the first African country to achieve this level of real GDP per head. In 2020, Mauritius became the second African country to achieve the status, but it moved back to middle-income status in 2022. This left the Seychelles as the only African country in the high-income category in 2023.

Both Mauritius and the Seychelles have a high HDI value. In the case of the Seychelles, all children in the country have access to education at primary and secondary levels, and the country has a good health system.

As well as examining current living standards, economists also consider how living standards may change in the future. There are some possible threats to living standards in the Seychelles in the future. The country is heavily dependent on tourism, and the number of tourists the country attracts may change significantly if, for example, there is a global recession. The living standards of the people in the Seychelles may also be threatened by climate change. Rising sea levels could put most of the low-lying islands under water. The increase in the temperature of the sea around the Seychelles is already damaging the country's coral reefs.

1   How may high living standards now increase the possibility of people enjoying higher living standards in the future?

2   Apart from a global recession and climate change, what else may reduce a country's living standards in the future?

Advantages and disadvantages of indicators of living standards

Table 29.3 summarises the main advantages and disadvantages of real GDP per head and HDI as indicators of living standards.

Table 29.3: Advantages and disadvantages of real GDP per head and HDI as indicators of living standards

	Real GDP per head	**HDI**
Advantages	Already measured to calculate economic growth rate.	Based on more than one influence on living standards.
	Widely understood throughout the world.	Includes three of the most important influences on living standards.

(Continued)

Table 29.2: Continued

	Real GDP per head	HDI
Disadvantages	Narrow – only considers income, that is, the goods and services we can buy.	Does not include some important influences, for example distribution of income, quality of the environment.
	May not include all the output produced.	Considers quantity of education but not quality of education or its distribution.
	Does not take into account the quality of what is produced.	Considers how long, on average, people live, but not whether those years are lived in good health or differences in life expectancy between different groups.

TIP

Remember that as HDI includes real GDP per head, the disadvantages of real GDP as an indicator of living standards can be considered as included in the disadvantages of HDI as an indicator.

ACTIVITY 29.4

In 2023, the Ugandan economy grew by 5.3% and the country's population increased by 3.0%. In its annual budget, the government increased its spending on education and defence. Property prices rose and sales of cars increased. Some of the country's richest citizens extended their mansions and bought expensive cars, including Porsches. However, more than a quarter of the country still lived in poverty.

In a pair, give a five-minute presentation on how living standards in Uganda may have changed in 2023. Include the points below in your presentation:

- two different indicators which would indicate that living standards rose in Uganda in 2023

- whether all Ugandans would have enjoyed a 5.3% rise in living standards in 2023

- whether all the extra government expenditure would have increased living standards.

29.2 Comparing living standards and income distribution

Income is unevenly distributed between households in every country, but to different extents. Wealth is even more unevenly distributed. Wealth is a stock of assets which have a financial value. Some of these assets, such as shares and government bonds, give rise to income. Some people have a considerable amount of wealth, while others have none.

To assess the distribution of income and wealth in a country, economists calculate the percentages of income earned and wealth owned by given proportions of the population. Two common proportions used are deciles (tenths) and quintiles (fifths).

Reasons for differences in living standards and income distribution

Living standards vary between countries and between regions within a country for a large number of reasons. These include, for example, differences in income, wealth, education and healthcare systems, levels of pollution and working hours.

Income may be unevenly distributed between households within and between countries due to uneven holdings of wealth, differences in the composition of households and differences in the opportunity and ability to earn an income. Some wealthy households can live off the income their wealth generates. In more cases, the income from wealth adds to earned income.

Households with a number of workers are likely to have a higher income than those with one or no workers and many dependants.

The wages received by workers are influenced by their skills, qualifications and the number of hours they work. High-skilled workers with better qualifications are likely to be in high demand and so are likely to receive high wages. Full-time workers usually earn more than part-time workers. Some people may be dependent on state benefits or help from relatives, and their income is likely to be relatively low.

Wealth is unevenly distributed because there are differences in the assets inherited by people, their savings and entrepreneurial skills. In fact, inheritance is a major reason for some people being wealthy. The more a person can save, the wealthier they will become. Of course, in this sense, wealth creates wealth. Wealthy people can afford to save more and this makes them wealthier. Entrepreneurs may be able to set up a business and become wealthy.

Comparing living standards between countries

Real GDP per head has the advantage that it takes into account differences in population size and also includes adjustments for inflation.

But real GDP per head on its own cannot be relied on to determine the quality of living standards of people in a country. In fact, some of the citizens of some countries enjoy a better quality of life than some of those in richer countries. This is because there can be differences in the distribution of income, the size of the informal economy, working hours and conditions, the composition and quality of output and environmental conditions between countries.

There is also a potential problem in comparing different countries' real GDP per head because countries measure their output in terms of their own currency initially. The comparison, on the other hand, needs to be done in a common unit. There is a risk that if an unadjusted currency is used, the comparison may be misleading. This is because the value of a currency can change from hour to hour. For example, US dollars may be used. If the real GDP of Kenya was KES1 200bn and the exchange rate was initially $1 = 100 Kenyan shillings (KES), the GDP of Kenya would be valued at $12bn. If the exchange rate changed to $1 = KES80 the next day, the value of its output in dollars would change to $15bn, even though Kenya would not have increased its output by 25% in that period (see Figure 29.5).

Figure 29.5: A Kenyan family living in Nairobi. In 2021, Kenya had an HDI value of 0.575, with an HDI ranking of 152

LINK

Economic growth can have a significant impact on living standards – see Chapter 26.3 (Causes and consequences of recession).

DISCUSSION

Discuss whether you think income should be more evenly distributed in your country. You may want to consider, for example, how those living in poverty may gain by a redistribution of income, but also the possible disincentive effects of redistributing income.

ACTIVITY 29.5

More than half of the world's wealth is owned by 2% of adults, while the least wealthy 50% of the world's adults own only 1% of global wealth. Wealth is heavily concentrated in North America, Europe and rich Asia-Pacific countries. People living in these countries together hold almost 90% of total world wealth. Wealth is also unevenly distributed within countries. The USA has one of the highest levels of inequality and Iceland one of the lowest.

Discuss these questions with another student. Write down the main points in your notebook.

1   How much of the world's wealth is owned by the wealthiest 50% of adults?

2   Iceland has one of the lowest levels of wealth inequality. What does this mean?

SUMMARY

You should now know:

- There are a number of possible indicators of living standards, including consumer goods per head, real GDP per head and the Human Development Index (HDI).

- Real GDP per head gives an indication of material living standards, but a rise in average income does not translate into a benefit for everyone.

- One country can have a higher real GDP per head than another, but its citizens may still have lower living standards, if they have less leisure time, worse working conditions, lower quality products, worse environmental conditions and a smaller informal economy.

- The Human Development Index is based on life expectancy and education, as well as GDP per head.

- Some households are rich because they earn high incomes and own assets which generate income.

- The main reasons accounting for why some people are wealthy are inheritance of wealth, accumulated savings or money earned in business.

Chapter 29 practice questions

1 What is the most popular measure of the difference in living standards between countries?

   A   average price level

   B   real GDP per head

   C   the size of the population

   D   the value of the currency   [1]

2 What is most likely to cause an increase in a country's standard of living?

   A   a fall in the school leaving age

   B   a fall in the size of the labour force

   C   a rise in the level of pollution

   D   a rise in the number of doctors per head of the population   [1]

3 Under which circumstance would the standard of living of a country be most likely to fall?

   A   a fall of 3% in real GDP and a fall of 6% in population

   B   a rise of 2% in real GDP and no change in population

   C   a rise of 5% in real GDP and a rise of 8% in population

   D   no change in real GDP and a fall of 3% in population   [1]

4   In what circumstance would a fall in working hours be most likely to increase
      the standard of living?

    A   the average income falls

    B   the level of output remains unchanged

    C   the rate of unemployment rises

    D   the standard of working conditions falls   [1]

5   Why may the population of Country X with a lower GDP per head than
      Country Y enjoy a higher living standard?

    A   consumption of demerit goods is higher in Country X

    B   health and safety standards are higher in Country Y

    C   traffic congestion is higher in Country X

    D   working hours are longer in Country Y   [1]

    Total: [5]

6   **a**   Identify **two** influences on living standards.   [2]

   b   Explain why real GDP per head is a better measure of the
standard of living in a country than nominal GDP.   [4]

   c   Analyse how a rise in labour productivity can increase
living standards.   [6]

   d   Discuss whether or not HDI is a good measure of
living standards.   [8]

    Total: [20]

CHECK YOUR PROGRESS

How well do you think you have achieved the learning intentions for this chapter?
Give yourself a score from 1 (still need a lot of practice) to 5 (feeling very confident)
for each learning intention. Provide an example to support your score.

Now I can...	Score	Example
explain indicators of living standards: real GDP per head and HDI		
discuss the advantages and disadvantages of real GDP per head and HDI as indicators of living standards		
analyse the reasons for differences in living standards and income distribution within and between countries.		

> Chapter 30
Poverty

LEARNING INTENTIONS

By the end of this chapter, you will be able to:

- define and explain the difference between absolute poverty and relative poverty
- analyse the causes of poverty: unemployment, low wages, illness, age and environmental factors
- discuss the policies to alleviate poverty and redistribute income: promoting economic growth, improved education, improved healthcare provision, more generous state benefits, progressive taxation and national minimum wage.

Introduction

No one wants to live in poverty. We all want to have sufficient income to enable us to enjoy a good standard of living. However, poverty exists in every country. Some people live in absolute poverty and some others live in relative poverty. There are several reasons why people experience poverty. There are also a number of policies governments use to try to reduce poverty and redistribute income towards those on low incomes.

ECONOMICS IN CONTEXT

What does it mean to live in poverty?

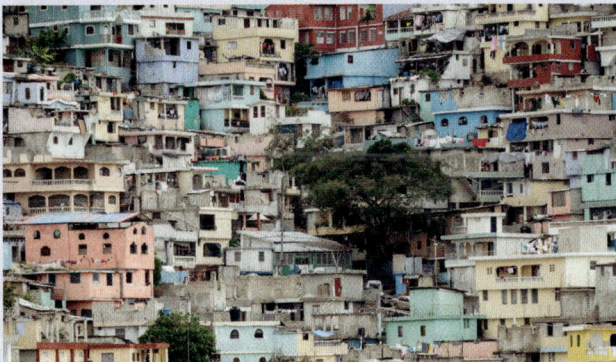

Figure 30.1: Low-quality housing in Haiti

Haiti has one of the lowest GDP per head in the world. More than half of its 11.5 million population struggle to meet their basic needs. Many of these people live in poor-quality housing which lack adequate sanitation and do not have electricity. Their homes are particularly vulnerable to the earthquakes, hurricanes and floods that often affect Haiti. They also lack access to nutritious food. Some families are permanently hungry. Other families eat cheap, high-fat food which is filling but does not provide them with the necessary vitamins and minerals. The children

of these families often miss school because of illness, inability to afford school fees and the need for the children to work to help support their families.

Those living in poverty have little access to good-quality healthcare. This, combined with poor nutrition, poor housing and limited education, results in a life expectancy for them being lower than the national average of 65 years.

Poverty is not restricted to low-income countries. There are some people living in poverty in high-income countries. In a number of cities in high-income countries, people are sleeping on the streets because they are homeless. In every country there are also people who, though they can afford basic necessities, do not have enough income to fully take part in the activities of their country. For example, they may not be able to buy tickets to a music festival because they do not have access to the internet.

Discuss in a pair or group:

1   Why might people in Haiti find it difficult to escape poverty?

2   Why do you think some people in high-income cities are homeless?

30.1 The difference between absolute poverty and relative poverty

Absolute poverty occurs when people do not have enough income to pay for their basic needs. They may lack access to adequate food, clothing, shelter, sanitation and healthcare. People experience **relative poverty** when they are poor relative to other people in the country. People who live in relative poverty are unable to participate fully in the normal activities of the society they live in. People who are regarded as living in relative poverty in a rich country may not be seen as such if they had the same income in a low-income country.

KEY TERM

absolute poverty: a condition where people's income is too low to enable them to meet their basic needs.

30.2 Causes of poverty

There are a number of reasons why people live in poverty. These include being unemployed, being in low-paid work, falling ill and growing old. In all of these cases, people may lack the income to ensure that they do not experience poverty. Once in poverty, it can become difficult to get out of it. People can become trapped in a **vicious circle of poverty**. Those who live in poverty are likely to have worse than average education and healthcare. This will reduce their productivity, employment opportunities and income and will also affect the prospects of their children.

Environmental factors contribute to poverty in a number of countries. Poverty is high among some farmers, some farm workers and some workers employed in tourism. Floods, cyclones and typhoons or droughts caused by global warming damage crops, kill livestock and may destroy buildings and equipment (see Figure 30.2).

Figure 30.2: Natural disasters may worsen poverty

> ## KEY TERMS
>
> **relative poverty:** a condition where people are poor in comparison to others in the country. Their income is too low to enable them to enjoy the average standard of living in their country.
>
> **vicious circle of poverty:** a situation where people become trapped in poverty.

ACTIVITY 30.1

The following are circumstances people may experience. In a group, identify which circumstances would indicate that people are living in absolute poverty. For each circumstance, give reasons why it would or would not indicate that people are living in poverty.

1 high car ownership

2 high internet use

3 homelessness

4 longevity (lifespan)

5 limited access to electricity

6 malnutrition.

Write a note of the main points in each case in your notebook.

30.3 Policies to alleviate poverty and redistribute income

Policies to alleviate poverty

There are a number of measures a government may take in an attempt to reduce poverty. The choice of measures may be restricted by the tax revenue the government has raised to fund them. Among the possible measures are:

- **Improving the quantity and quality of education.** In the long term this can be a very effective policy as it can increase the job prospects and earning potential of those experiencing poverty and their children.

- **Improving the quantity and quality of healthcare.** In the long term this can be a very effective policy. People will be less likely to fall into poverty due to illnesses, and workers are likely to be more productive and so may earn higher wages.

- **Promoting economic growth.** For example, increasing government expenditure or reducing the rate of interest will increase aggregate demand. This can increase output and create jobs. Unemployment is a major cause of poverty. A country with many unemployed and underemployed workers not only lowers the living standards of the unemployed and underemployed but also the living standards of others since output will be below potential.

- **Introducing or raising a national minimum wage (NMW).** This is designed to tackle the problem of people experiencing low living standards due to low wages.

- **Providing more generous state benefits.** The elderly, and some sick and disabled people, may not be able to work and may not have any savings to support them. Giving them benefits, such as housing benefit, or raising the benefits they receive, may enable them to avoid absolute poverty. What is more debatable is the effect that raising unemployment benefit will have on poverty. If there is a lack of jobs, it may help in the short run, as it will not only raise the living standards of the unemployed, but may also reduce unemployment by increasing aggregate demand. If, however, jobs are available and the unemployed are not filling them because they receive a higher income on benefits, raising benefits will reduce the incentive to work.

> **LINK**
>
> The ways a national minimum wage may affect wages and employment is explored in Chapter 17.2 National minimum wage (Wage determination and the reasons for differences in wages – Government policy).

ACTIVITY 30.2

Individually, rank the following according to the children's chances of experiencing poverty as adults. Start with the child that you think is most likely to experience poverty (1) and finish with the one you expect to be least likely to experience poverty (6).

1 the child of two farm workers

2 the child of two economics professors

3 the child of a doctor and a homemaker

4 the child of a journalist and a homemaker

CONTINUED

5   the child of a top division footballer and a supermodel

6   the child of two unemployed street cleaners.

Then, in a group, compare your rankings. Give two reasons why the child you think is least likely to experience poverty is likely to be able to earn a high income. Also give two reasons why it may be possible that the child you have selected as being the most likely to experience poverty may actually avoid it. Write down the reasons for your decisions.

REFLECTION

Were you able to agree? Were you able to bring out the influences on poverty in your answers? If not, what did you do to strengthen your understanding?

Measures to raise living standards

Measures to reduce poverty should also raise general living standards. Improving education and training will increase the knowledge and earning potential of the people and their ability to take part in the political system of the country. Reducing unemployment, as already mentioned, also raises living standards by increasing the quantity of available goods and services.

Other ways of improving living standards include improving healthcare, increasing and improving the housing stock, improving the working conditions and reducing pollution (see Figure 30.3).

Economists debate the extent to which government intervention is needed to achieve these objectives. Some economists argue that government policies, such as legislation, will be needed to give workers holiday entitlement and government provision of housing. Other economists argue that the private sector is better at providing improved living standards. If this is the case, living standards might be increased by reducing government regulation and taxation. For example, if corporate tax is reduced, firms may be encouraged to expand, taking on more workers and providing more training.

Figure 30.3: New housing construction may help to raise living standards

ACTIVITY 30.3

Table 30.1 identifies the type of policy measures that governments may use to alleviate poverty. Copy and complete all columns of the table.

Share your table with another student. Add to your table if you need to.

Table 30.1

Type of policy	Policy measure to reduce poverty	Aim	How it may reduce poverty
Fiscal	Increase in unemployment benefit	Raise financial support to the unemployed	Raise income of the unemployed
Supply-side	Increase government spending on training and education	Raise the skills of the unemployed	
Supply-side	Raise the threshold at which people start paying personal income tax	Reduce the personal income tax of those on low wages	
Supply-side	Increase government spending on rail infrastructure	Increase labour mobility	
Supply-side policy	Increase government spending on sea defences		Prevent a fall in the income of low-paid workers in agriculture and tourism
Monetary		Make it more affordable for those on low incomes to buy a house, start a business or pay for training	
Fiscal			Raise the income of the old

Policies to redistribute income

Governments may decide to influence the distribution of income because of concerns that a very uneven distribution may be socially divisive. Those on very low incomes may feel they are not part of society and may join in protests and even riots. A government may also want to ensure that everyone has access to a certain standard of living. When influencing the distribution of income, governments may also be concerned that it does not reduce incentives to entrepreneurs and workers.

Governments can influence the redistribution of income in a number of ways, including:

- **Taxation.** Progressive taxes make the distribution of income more even.

- **The provision of cash benefits.** Unemployment and other cash benefits can help maintain a reasonable standard of living.

- **The provision of free state education and healthcare.** Free state education and healthcare can ensure that everyone has access to these essential services, and it may also offer the people an opportunity to improve their living standards.

- **Other government policy measures.** For example, minimum wage legislation, regional policy and measures to reduce unemployment.

LINKS

There are several policy measures a government may take to reduce poverty – see Chapter 23.2 (Reasons for government spending), Chapter 23.3 (Taxation – Reasons for taxation), Chapter 25.2 (Supply-side policy measures – Education and training) and Chapter 26.3 (Causes and consequences of recession).

ACTIVITY 30.4

In a pair, produce and give a presentation on how a new hospital in your area could help to reduce poverty.

DISCUSSION

Discuss whether you think income should be more evenly distributed in your country.

TIP

Remember the difference between equity and equality. An equal distribution of income might be seen as unfair if people have different needs.

ECONOMICS IN ACTION

Economic growth and poverty

Figure 30.4: The newly built Navi Mumbai Metro Line may encourage economic growth

Economists study the relationship between economic growth and poverty. It is thought that economic growth is necessary but not sufficient to reduce poverty. When economic growth occurs, job opportunities are usually created (see Figure 30.4). Some of those experiencing poverty due to unemployment may be able to gain jobs. The increased demand for workers may raise the wages of a range of workers, including some who were previously low-paid. As well as increasing wages, economic growth can also increase profits and is likely to raise consumer expenditure. The resulting increase in revenue from personal income tax, corporate income tax and sales tax can be spent on projects to reduce poverty, including higher government spending on education and healthcare.

However, economic growth does not always result in lower poverty. Absolute poverty may not be reduced for several reasons. Few new jobs may be created if the increase in total output is largely due to advances in technology. The unemployed may also lack the skills to do any new jobs on offer or may be too ill or too old to do them. In addition, any extra tax revenue may not be spent on reducing poverty.

Economic growth may also not reduce relative poverty. Indeed, it is possible that economic growth may increase relative poverty as those on high incomes may benefit the most.

1   Why may a recession increase both absolute and relative poverty?

2   Why may those on high incomes benefit the most from economic growth?

SUMMARY

You should now know:

- Poverty is measured both in absolute and relative terms.

- The main reasons that account for poverty of people are unemployment and low-paid jobs.

- Among the measures a government may take to reduce poverty and raise living standards include improving education and training, raising aggregate demand, attracting multinational companies and improving healthcare.

- Governments influence the distribution of income through taxation, the provision of benefits, minimum wage legislation, regional policy and measures to reduce unemployment.

Chapter 30 practice questions

1   What might cause a more uneven distribution of income?

   A   an increase in the national minimum wage

   B   an increase in state benefits

   C   a reduction in the top rates of tax

   D   a reduction in unemployment   [1]

2   Why does income inequality tend to be associated with wealth inequality?

   A   it is a disincentive for entrepreneurs and workers

   B   those with high incomes have higher ability to save than those on low incomes

   C   those with high incomes spend a higher proportion of their income than those on low incomes

   D   those with low incomes often inherit wealth   [1]

3   What could cause a decrease in absolute poverty but a rise in relative poverty?

   A   the income of the rich rising by less than those living on low incomes

   B   the income of the rich rising by more than those living on low incomes

   C   the income of the rich falling by less than those living on low incomes

   D   the income of the rich falling by more than those living on low incomes   [1]

4   Which government policy measure may reduce absolute poverty?

   A   a cut in government expenditure on state education

   B   an increase in the rate of interest

   C   granting subsidies to builders of low-cost housing

   D   the imposition of a tax on food   [1]

5 What is the strongest indicator that a family is living in poverty?

    A it spends a higher proportion of income on clothing than the average family

    B it spends a higher proportion of income on food than the average family

    C it spends more in total on clothing than the average family

    D it spends more in total on food than the average family   [1]

                          Total: [5]

6 **a** Define 'absolute poverty'.   [2]

    b Explain **two** reasons why the children of those living in poverty are likely to experience poverty as adults.   [4]

    c Analyse how fiscal policy could reduce income inequality.   [6]

    d Discuss whether or not the introduction of a national minimum wage will reduce poverty.   [8]

                          Total: [20]

CHECK YOUR PROGRESS

How well do you think you have achieved the learning intentions for this chapter? Give yourself a score from 1 (still need a lot of practice) to 5 (feeling very confident) for each learning intention. Provide an example to support your score.

Now I can...	Score	Example
define and explain the difference between absolute poverty and relative poverty		
analyse the causes of poverty: unemployment, low wages, illness, age and environmental factors		
discuss the policies to alleviate poverty and redistribute income: promotion of economic growth, improved education, improved healthcare provision, more generous state benefits, progressive taxation, national minimum wage.		

> # Chapter 31
Population

LEARNING INTENTIONS

By the end of this chapter, you will be able to:

- define birth rate, death rate, net migration, immigration and emigration
- explain how birth rates, death rates and net migration rates can vary between countries
- explain the concept of optimum population
- discuss the effects of increases and decreases in population size and changes in the age and gender distribution of population.

Introduction

Individual countries are facing a number of challenges connected with changes in the size and structure of their populations. For example, Japan is experiencing a decline in population, while Uganda is experiencing a rapid increase in population. The average age of population varies considerably between countries. For example, the average age is 56 years in Monaco, while it is only 15 years in Niger. The birth rate, death rate and net migration vary between countries. Changes in the birth rate, death rate and net migration affect the size of a country's population and its average age and gender distribution. An increase or a decrease in a country's population size can move it towards or away from the number which would result in the highest output per head.

ECONOMICS IN CONTEXT

Too many or too few people?

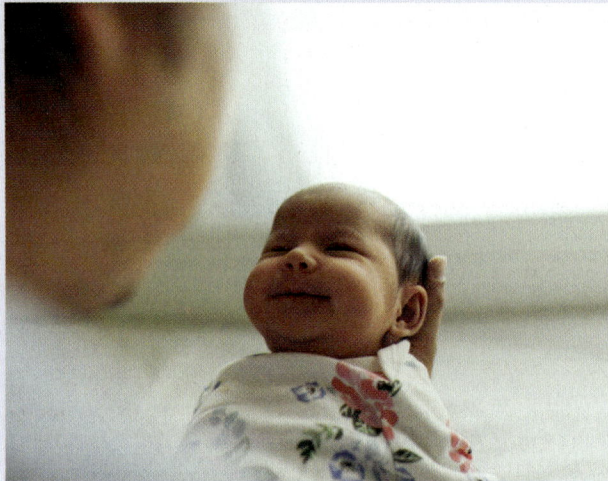

Figure 31.1: Does the world need more or fewer babies?

In November 2022, the world's population reached 8 billion. This was a remarkable increase since 1960 when the world's population was only 2.5 billion. However, the rate of global population growth is slowing down. It is predicted that it will peak in 2086 at 10.5 billion, remain relatively constant until 2100 and then start to decline.

While the populations of some countries, including Egypt, India, Nigeria and Pakistan, are expected to grow at a relatively high rate until 2050, the populations of most countries are growing significantly slower, and some countries are already experiencing a decline in population.

One country with a declining population is Italy. It is predicted that Italy's population will decline by 19% from 59 million in 2023 to 48 million in 2070. Fewer children are being born in the country every year. Women are having children later, and more of them are choosing not to have children. For every 12 deaths that now occur, there are only 7 births. Each year, there are a smaller number of workers to support more pensioners.

Italian governments have tried a variety of measures to increase the number of children each couple has. These include providing a monthly payment to parents for each child they have, provision of childcare and a reduction in tax on baby products. So far, these measures have not proved effective.

Discuss in a pair or group:

1   Do you think the population of the town, city or area you live is likely to increase in the next 20 years?

2   Why might some people decide not to have children?

31.1 Factors that affect population growth

Birth rate, death rate and migration

The size of a country's population can grow as a result of a natural increase or positive net migration, which can also be called net immigration. A natural increase occurs when the birth rate exceeds the **death rate**. For example, the birth rate in Iran in 2023 was 14.8 per 1 000 and the death rate was 5.2 per 1 000, giving a natural rate of increase of 9.6 per 1 000 or 0.96%.

The birth rate is influenced by the average age of the population, the number of women in the population and women's fertility rate (that is, the average number of children per woman).

The death rate is influenced by nutrition, housing conditions, medical care, lifestyles, working conditions and whether the country is involved in military conflict.

Positive **net migration** occurs when **immigration** exceeds **emigration**. This would mean that more people come into the country to live (*immigrants*) than people who leave it to live elsewhere (*emigrants*).

When net migration is negative, it can be referred to as net emigration and occurs when emigration exceeds immigration. This may lower the size of a country's population. Net migration can be measured by the total number of migrants or by the **net migration rate**.

The effects of negative net migration

There are a number of possible economic effects of negative net migration, with more people leaving than entering the country. These are influenced by the size and the nature of the emigration. Some of these include:

- The size of the working population is likely to be reduced. Most emigrants tend to be of working age.

- The remaining labour force will have a greater burden of dependency.

- The average age of the labour force will increase. This may make it less mobile.

- The gender distribution of the population may be affected. In the case of some countries, more males emigrate than females.

- There may be a shortage of skilled workers. For example, doctors may emigrate in search of higher pay and better working conditions. The country they leave will experience a 'brain drain', while the country they go to will experience a 'brain gain'.

- There may be underutilisation of resources. The country may become underpopulated.

- Those who emigrate may send money home to help their relatives. This money is called workers' remittances.

- Workers may gain skills in other countries which could benefit the country, should they return.

KEY TERMS

death rate: the number of deaths per 1 000 of a country's population in a year.

net migration: the difference between immigration and emigration.

immigration: people coming from elsewhere to live in a country.

emigration: people leaving the country to live elsewhere.

net migration rate: the number of net migrants per 1 000 of a country's population in a year.

How birth rates, death rates and net migration can vary between countries

The birth rate is likely to be high when there is a young population in which women start to have children from a young age, the **infant mortality rate** is high, women are not well-educated, most women do not work and it is cheap to bring up children. Other factors leading to a high birth rate are the lack of, or disapproval of, family planning, government cash incentives to have children and a lack of government help to care for the sick and elderly.

In contrast, in a country where it is expensive to have children (because there is a legal requirement to send children to school for a number of years and an expectation that some of them will go on to higher education), and well-paid jobs are open to women, the birth rate is likely to be low. If the government provides state pensions, sickness and disability benefits, people may not feel that they have to have a large family in order to support them.

A country is likely to have a relatively low death rate if its population has healthy diets, enjoys good housing facilities and access to high quality medical care, do not smoke or consume excess alcohol, exercise regularly, enjoy good working conditions and the country is at peace with other countries.

The rate and pattern of net migration is influenced by relative living standards at home and abroad, and extent of control on the movement of people between countries. If living standards abroad are better (or thought to be better) and there is no restriction to immigration by other countries, some people are likely to emigrate. Most migrants tend to be single people of working age.

In deciding what is happening to a country's population size, the relationship between the birth rate, death rate and net migration have to be considered. A fall in the death rate, for example, will not necessarily lead to an increase in population if it is offset by a fall in the birth rate and/or net emigration. Latvia's population, for example, is declining because its birth rate has fallen at a greater rate than its death rate and it is currently experiencing net emigration (see Figure 31.2).

KEY TERM

infant mortality rate: the number of deaths per 1000 live births in a country in a year.

Figure 31.2: Latvia's population is falling

TIP

Be careful not to confuse population growth with economic growth.

ACTIVITY 31.1

You find a report on a country's population with the first page missing. The name of the country does not appear anywhere else in the report, but you know that the economist who wrote it was studying the populations of Cambodia, Hungary, Japan, the Philippines and Tanzania. Using the comments and information provided in the rest of the report, identify the country.

Comments and information

- Children are seen as a cost rather than a source of income.

- A third of the population are aged over 65 and a tenth are aged over 80.

- Despite experiencing net positive migration, the country's population is declining.

- Improvements in healthcare have raised life expectancy in the country to 85.

Your research on the five countries the economist was studying shows:

Country	Average age	Average age at which a mother has first child	Average years of schooling	Birth rate	Death rate	Net migration rate
Cambodia	28	23	7	19	6	−2.7
Hungary	45	28	9	9	9	2.6
Japan	50	32	15	7	12	0.7
Philippines	25	24	13	22	6	−0.1
Tanzania	19	15	9	33	5	−0.3

Write the reasons for your choice in your notebook.

31.2 The effects of changes in the size and structure of populations

The concept of optimum population

The concept of **optimum population** refers to the number of people which, when combined with the other resources of land, capital and existing technical knowledge, gives the maximum output of goods and services per head of the population.

The concept of optimum population is not simply based on the number of people in a country or per square kilometre. The balance between population and resources is of crucial importance. A country with a large geographical area and a small population may still be considered as overpopulated if there is a shortage of land, capital and technical knowledge, relative to the number of workers. In such a case, a government may seek to move towards its optimum population either by introducing measures to reduce its population size or by seeking to increase investment. A country is said to be underpopulated if it does not have enough human resources to make the best use of

KEY TERM

optimum population: the size of the population which maximises the country's output per head.

its resources. In such a case, its government may encourage immigration. Figure 31.3 illustrates the concept of optimum population.

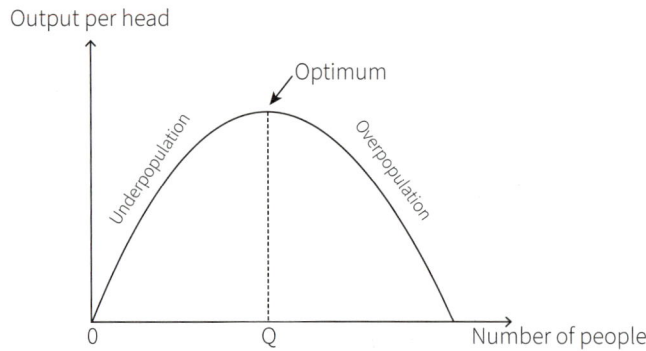

Figure 31.3: The concept of optimum population

In practice, it is difficult to determine a country's optimum population and size of actual population relative to it. This is, in part, because the quantity and quality of resources are changing all the time.

ACTIVITY 31.2

Table 31.1 shows some information about the Democratic Republic of Congo. Using the information, decide if the Democratic Republic of the Congo was moving away from or towards its optimum population. Write an explanation of your decision.

Table 31.1

Year	Population of the Democratic Republic of the Congo (millions)	GDP of the Democratic Republic of the Congo ($ millions)
1995	43	5 640
2000	49	19 090
2005	57	11 960
2010	66	21 570
2015	79	37 920
2020	99	48 720

TIP

It is often thought that countries with low development have large populations. This is not always the case. What they tend to have is a high population growth rate.

LINK

See Chapter 26.2 (Causes and consequences of economic growth – Advantages and disadvantages of economic growth) for the advantages and disadvantages of increasing a country's output.

The effects of increases in population size

The consequences of a growth in a country's population depend on its cause, size of population relative to optimum population and the rate of population growth. Possible benefits of an increasing population include:

- If the population is below the optimum size, the country will be able to make **better use of its resources**.
- The **size of markets will increase**. This should enable firms to take greater advantage of economies of scale.
- There may be an **increase in factor mobility** if the rise has resulted from an increase in the birth rate or immigration. Expanding industries can recruit new workers to the labour force. These people are likely to be familiar with new ideas and methods. If this is the case, firms' training costs will be reduced.
- **Extra demand will be generated.** This is likely to stimulate investment and may lead to the introduction of new technology (see Figure 31.4).
- A **rise in the labour force**, due to positive net migration now and in the future, by a rise in the birth rate. Positive net migration will bring in more workers. More children being born will increase the dependency ratio in the short term but in the long term, will result in more workers.

Despite the possible advantages of an increasing population, there are a number of reasons for a government to be concerned about population growth. These include:

- **Concerns about famine.** If a country is currently overpopulated and agricultural productivity is low, there is a risk that the country may not be able to feed more dependants.
- **Restrictions on improvements in living standards.** Resources which could have been used to improve living standards may have to be allocated to the provision of goods and services for the extra number of dependants in the population. For example, there may be provision of more healthcare facilities but healthcare services per head may fall.
- **Overcrowding.** Increases in population may put pressure on housing and social capital and cause traffic congestion.
- **Environmental sustainability.** More people in a country may result in damage to wildlife habitats, pollution of land and rivers, water shortages and the depletion of non-renewable resources.
- **Pressure on employment opportunities.** If there is an increase in the number of people of working age who lack appropriate skills, the government may have to allocate more resources to education and training. It is important to remember that immigration in itself does not cause unemployment. The number of jobs in existence is not fixed. Although immigration will increase the supply of labour, it will also result in an increase in aggregate demand.
- **Balance of payment pressures.** More dependants in the population may result in a rise in imports and some products may need to be diverted from the export to the home market.

Figure 31.4: A 3D printer. Technological advances can increase the size of a country's optimum population

TIP

Remember that both a high rate of population growth and a low rate of population growth can cause problems for an economy, depending on the causes of the growth and the state of the economy in relation to the country's optimum population size.

DISCUSSION

Discuss whether you think an increase in the size of your country's population would be beneficial.

Ways of reducing the birth rate

A country concerned that its population is growing too rapidly would not want to raise its death rate. It may attempt to reduce immigration and try to reduce the country's birth rate. There are a number of ways it could reduce the birth rate. An effective way is thought to be improvement of the educational and employment opportunities for women. Educated women tend to be more aware of contraceptive methods, delay having children and are likely to restrict their family size in order to be able to combine raising children with work and also because they have higher hopes for their children's future. Better information and increased availability of family planning services will make it more likely that households will be able to limit their family sizes.

Improvement of healthcare and nutrition reduces infant mortality and, in turn, the birth rate. One reason which may explain a higher number of children in families is the concern over their survival. Another reason for having a large family is the need for support in old age. Setting up pension and sickness insurance schemes will reduce the need for family support. A government can raise the cost of having children by raising the school-leaving age. It can also reduce or stop any financial support it gives to families for each child they have and instead provide incentives for families who restrict the number of children. The most extreme measure is to make it illegal to have children above a specified number.

ACTIVITY 31.3

Copy and complete Table 31.2, deciding whether young or older workers are more likely to have each characteristic.

Share your answers with another student.

Table 31.2

Characteristic	Age of worker
1 Experienced	
2 Geographically mobile	
3 Occupationally mobile	
4 Prepared to stay in the job for some time	
5 Received a large amount of on-the-job training	
6 Up to date with advances in technology	

The effects of decreases in population size

The effects of a decrease in population will affect whether a country can make better use of its resources if its population was initially above its optimum population size. The other effects are essentially the reverse of an increase in population. These include a decrease in the size of markets, a possible reduction in labour mobility, a decrease in total demand and a decrease in the size of the labour force. A decrease in population, resulting from fewer dependents, may enable more resources to be allocated to improving the quality rather than the quantity of education and healthcare and may reduce imports. There may also be less overcrowding and less pressure on the environment.

The effects of changes in the age and gender distribution of population

The age distribution is the division of the population into different age groups. In broad terms, the categories are people under 16, those between 16 and 64 and those over 65. In most countries, with people living longer, the average age, is increasing.

The age structure of a population influences its **dependency ratio**. This is:

$$\frac{\text{Number in dependent age groups}}{\text{Number in the labour force}} \times 100$$

The dependant age groups are those below school-leaving age and those above retirement age.

The gender distribution of a population indicates the number of males compared to the number of females. In most countries, more boys are born than girls. However, in a number of countries females outnumber males. This is largely due to women, on an average, living longer than males and higher male infant mortality rates. In some countries, such as the United Arab Emirates (UAE), there are more males in the population than females. This is because more males than females from other countries come to work and live in the country.

> **KEY TERM**
>
> **dependency ratio:** the proportion of the population that has to be supported by the labour force.

The consequences of an ageing population

A number of countries, including Japan, the USA and many EU countries, are experiencing an ageing population. An ageing population is one in which the average age is rising. In Japan, for example, the average age of the population in 2024 was 50 and 31% of the population was aged over 65.

An ageing population can be caused by a fall in the birth rate, a fall in the death rate, negative net migration or a combination of the three. There are a number of consequences of an ageing population, including:

- **A rise in the dependency ratio.** If people are living longer and there are fewer workers because of net emigration, there will be a greater proportion of consumers to workers.

- **A change in the labour force.** Older workers may be geographically and occupationally less mobile. They may, however, be more experienced, reliable and patient.

- **Higher demand for healthcare.** The elderly place the greatest burden on a country's health service.

- **Greater need for welfare services,** such as caring for the elderly at home and in retirement homes.

- **Rise in cost of state and private pensions.**

- **Change in the pattern of demand,** for example, demand for housing for retired people will rise.

Ways of coping with an ageing population

A country that has a higher proportion of elderly workers will put pressure on its government to spend more. If the government does so, it will involve an opportunity cost. The money used, for example, may have been spent on education instead. An ageing population may also raise the tax burden on workers. There are a number of ways a government may seek to reduce these effects. One is to raise the retirement age. This will reduce the cost of pensions and increase tax revenue without increasing tax rates. In a country in which life expectancy is rising, there is some justification for raising the retirement age. Working for a longer period can also increase a worker's lifetime income and, depending on the nature of their work, may keep them physically and mentally healthy for a longer period (see Figure 31.5).

Figure 31.5: People in Japan are living longer

A government may also try to cope with the financial burden of an ageing population by encouraging or making it compulsory for workers to save for their retirement. It may try to raise the productivity of workers by means of education and training. This may involve an increase in government expenditure but, if successful, may generate more tax revenue. In addition, the governments may encourage the immigration of younger skilled workers by issuing more work permits. This will reduce the dependency ratio at least in the short term.

ACTIVITY 31.4

Assume that people are wanting to migrate to your country. In a group, decide what may encourage people to want to live in your country. Write down the reasons in your notebook.

REFLECTION

How confident are you in identifying and explaining a number of the factors that can affect changes in the size of a country's population? If you are still uncertain, can you think of two strategies to increase your understanding?

ECONOMICS IN ACTION

Population differences between Armenia and Qatar

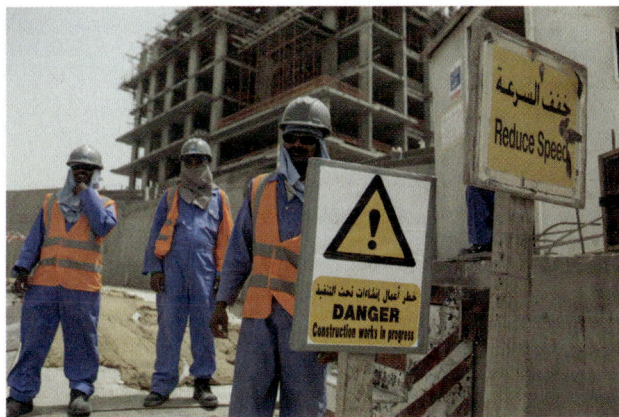

Figure 31.6: Migrant construction workers in Qatar increase the country's population

Studying population structures and changes in those structures can be fascinating. Two countries with interesting population structures are Qatar and Armenia. They have similar population sizes. In 2023, Qatar had a population of 2.75 million and Armenia had a population of 3 million. Their average ages were also relatively similar, at 34 and 39 years, respectively. However, they have some significant differences. Qatar's population is growing while Armenia's population has been declining since 1990.

Qatar has one of the world's highest proportions of migrant workers. In 2023, they accounted for 2 million of the country's population. Most come from Bangladesh, India and Nepal, and the majority of them work in the construction industry. What is particularly unusual is that, because of the high number of migrant building workers, 73% of Qatar's population is male.

In contrast, there are more women than men in Armenia. While the gender balance in most countries is between 49% and 51% female to male, in Armenia it is 54% female. This is because each year, approximately 100 000 people, mostly men, leave the country in search of work. Most go to Russia to work in the construction industry. So, Qatar's population size is increased, and the proportion of women to men is reduced by men entering the country to work in the construction industry. In contrast, Armenia's population size is reduced and its proportion of women to men is increased by men leaving the country to work in the construction industry.

1 Why may immigration into Qatar fall in the future?

2 What benefits may a country gain from some of its population emigrating?

SUMMARY

You should now know:

- A country's population can grow as a result of its birth rate exceeding its death rate and/or as a result of positive net migration.

- The birth rate is influenced by the average age of the population, the number of women in the population and the number of children they have.

- The death rate is influenced by social conditions, lifestyles, medical conditions and the existence or absence of military conflicts.

- People emigrate in search of better living standards and to escape persecution.

- Negative net migration is likely to reduce the size of the labour force, increase the dependency ratio, alter gender distribution, reduce the size of the population and increase money sent home.

- A country is said to be overpopulated if there is an excess of labour relative to land, capital and technical knowledge.

- The effect of an increasing population will depend on its cause, size of the population in relation to the optimum population and the rate of population growth.

- An increase in the size of the population may increase the efficiency of firms, raise factor mobility, increase the demand and make better use of resources.

- A government may be concerned that an increasing population may result in famine, reduced living standards, overcrowding, depletion of resources, environmental problems and an unfavourable balance of payments position.

- Ways of controlling the birth rate include raising the educational and employment opportunities for women, increasing the availability of family planning services, increasing the cost of having children, providing support for the elderly and providing incentives for limiting the family size.

- An ageing population will raise the dependency ratio, change the labour force, burden the health and welfare services, raise the cost of pensions and alter the pattern of demand.

- Among the possible policies that can be used to cope with an ageing population are raising the retirement age, prompting workers to save for their pensions, raising productivity and encouraging immigration of skilled workers.

Chapter 31 practice questions

1   In a country, more males are born than females and yet there are more females than males in the population. How can this be explained?

   A   a higher death rate for females than for males

   B   females living longer than males

   C   more females emigrating than males

   D   the infant mortality rate of females being higher than males   [1]

2   Which is most likely to cause a rise in the average age of a country's population?

   A   a fall in the death rate and birth rate

   B   a fall in the death rate and a rise in the birth rate

   C   a rise in the death rate and a fall in the birth rate

   D   a rise in the death rate and birth rate   [1]

3   What is meant by the 'gender distribution of a population'?

   A   the proportion of females and males in the population

   B   the proportion of people over retirement age in the population

   C   where females and males in the population live

   D   where people over retirement age live   [1]

4   Why may a government want to reduce the growth of its population?

   A   capital is not being fully utilised

   B   the population is below the optimum level

   C   there are worries about the risk of famine

   D   there is low population density   [1]

5   A country has a population of 20m at the start of the year. If its birth rate is 8, how many children will be born during the year?

   A   12 500

   B   16 000

   C   125 000

   D   160 000   [1]

                                                                      Total: [5]

6   a   Identify **two** causes of a natural increase in population.   [2]

   b   Explain why a government may try to reduce the growth of the
       population of its country.   [4]

   c   Analyse how the rate of population growth in a low-income country
       may differ from that of a high-income country.   [6]

   d   Discuss whether or not an economy will benefit from positive net
       migration with immigration exceeding emigration.   [8]

                                                                     Total: [20]

CHECK YOUR PROGRESS

How well do you think you have achieved the learning intentions for this chapter?
Give yourself a score from 1 (still need a lot of practice) to 5 (feeling very confident)
for each learning intention. Provide an example to support your score.

Now I can...	Score	Example
define birth rate, death rate, net migration, immigration and emigration		
explain how birth rates, death rates and net migration rates can vary between countries		
explain the concept of optimum population		
discuss the effects of increases and decreases in population size and changes in the age and gender distribution of population.		

Chapter 32

Differences in economic development between countries

Introduction

Over time most economies develop, allowing poverty to fall, living standards to rise and people to have more choices. For example, between 1980 and 2023 the average life expectancy in Thailand rose from 65 to 79, the infant mortality fell from 47 per 1 000 births to 6 per 1 000, and the percentage of households with a TV rose from 21% to 98%. Economies, however, can develop at different rates. There are a number of possible reasons why countries may experience differences in economic development, A country with a low level of economic development is likely to experience some significant problems.

ECONOMICS IN CONTEXT

Will Burkina Faso make progress?

Figure 32.1: The effect of low rainfall in the Sahel, West Africa

Burkina Faso is a low-income African country in the Sahel, West Africa, which was ranked 184th out of 191 countries in the 2021–2022 HDI Report. All countries would benefit from an improvement in the welfare of their people. This is particularly true of countries which are considered to have a low level of economic development. In 2023, only

19% of Burkina Faso's population had access to electricity, only 10% had adequate sanitation and 40% of the population were living on less than $2.15 a day. Life expectancy was only 61 years, and the country had a high infant mortality rate of 48 and a low literacy rate of 46%.

There are two major threats to the improvement in the lives of people in Burkina Faso. One is terrorist attacks. In 2023, these resulted in some hospitals being closed, restricting access to healthcare, and some schools being closed, interrupting the education of some of the country's children.

The other major threat arises from Burkina Faso being one of the countries most affected by climate change. During the rainy season, the country is suffering more floods which damage housing and, in a country dependent on agriculture, destroys crops and livestock. Agricultural output is also lost due to droughts at other times of the year.

Discuss in a pair or group:

1   How does the quality of life in your country compare with that of Burkina Faso in 2023?

2   What might stop improvements to the lives of people in your country in the future?

32.1 Economic development

Economic development is wider than economic growth. Besides improved living standards, it also involves reducing poverty, expanding the range of economic and social choices and increasing freedom and self-esteem. As an economy develops, the economic welfare of its population increases. At first, the availability of basic necessities increases. Then consumption levels rise beyond those needed for survival, and people have more choice of what to consume, where to live and where to work.

KEY TERM

economic development: an improvement in economic welfare.

The different stages of economic development

Most economies are developing, but their rate and level of development varies. Countries with high income per head also usually have relatively high economic development. They tend to have high living standards, a high proportion of workers employed in the tertiary sector, high levels of productivity and high levels of investment. Countries with lower income per head usually have lower economic development with lower living standards and a number of other characteristics, as explained in Chapter 32.2 (Causes of international differences in economic development).

International organisations classify countries in a variety of ways. The United Nations, for instance, divides countries into four levels of development: very high human development, high human development, medium human development and low human development. The World Bank divides countries into high income, upper-middle income, lower-middle income and low income.

Measures of economic development

It is not easy to measure development, but a number of ways are used. A common one is real GDP per head. This measures an important aspect of development, material living standards, but it does not measure all aspects of development.

A wider measure is the Human Development Index (HDI). As explained in Chapter 29 (Living standards), the index measures the extent to which people in a country achieve a long and healthy life, knowledge and a good standard of living. A figure of 0-1 is calculated for each country. An index of:

- less than 0.550 indicates low development

- 0.550-0.699 medium development

- 0.700-0.799 high development

- above 0.800 very high development.

Some countries are ranked higher in terms of HDI than real GDP per head, for example, New Zealand, Costa Rica, Vietnam and Malawi. Others have a higher real GDP per head ranking than HDI ranking, such as the USA, Guatemala, Pakistan and Zimbabwe.

ACTIVITY 32.1

In a pair, research how an indicator of economic development has changed in your country over a 20-year period. For example, this may be life expectancy, real GDP per head, average years of schooling or the size of the primary sector. Use your findings to produce a poster. You may want to include graphs and photographs on your poster.

32.2 Causes of international differences in economic development

There are a number of reasons why countries have different levels of economic development, including:

- **Differences in income.** Economic development tends to be lower in countries with low real GDP per head. In such countries, some people may struggle to afford a good standard of living. However, this does not mean that all the people in such countries are living in poverty. In fact, some can be very rich.

- **Differences in productivity.** Countries with a low output per worker hour will tend to have low income per head and so may have, for instance, lower education and healthcare.

- **Differences in population growth.** In countries with high population growth there is usually a high dependency ratio, with a high proportion of children being dependent on a small proportion of workers. This means that some of the resources which could have been used to improve the quality of life of the current population have to be used to support the extra members of the population.

- **Differences in the size of the primary, secondary and tertiary sectors.** Economic growth and the quality of people's working conditions tend to be lower the greater the proportion of workers employed in the primary sector. For example, underemployment can be high in agriculture when ten people do the work of six. This, again, lowers productivity.

- **Differences in saving and investment due to differences in income per head.** People living in poverty cannot afford to save and so the savings rate (saving as a percentage of disposable income) of a country where the average income is low is likely to be low. If savings are low, there will be a lack of finance for investment. Countries with a low value of capital goods per worker will be likely to have low income per head.

- **Differences in education and healthcare.** A lack of access to, or low quality of, education and healthcare will reduce the quality of people's lives and will result in low levels of productivity.

- **Differences in the concentration on a narrow range of exports (most of which are primary products).** Countries that export a narrow range of products can be adversely affected by large decreases in demand or decreases in supply. The demand for manufactured goods and services tends to increase more than the demand for primary products as income increases.

- **Differences in natural resources.** Preventing the depletion of non-renewable natural resources will help increase the chance of economic development occurring over generations. Conserving any natural resources which absorb carbon dioxide, such as rainforests, will reduce increases in global warming which would reduce the quality of people's lives. Some countries may have large supplies of natural, renewable sources of energy such as solar power and wind power. This may enable them to generate more energy in an environmentally sustainable way.

As suggested above, the causes of differences in economic development are interrelated. Indeed, countries can be subject to what is known as the underdevelopment trap or the vicious circle of poverty. This problem occurs because low-income countries usually have a low saving rate. This means that most of their resources are used to produce consumer goods. The lack of capital goods keeps productivity and income low, as shown in Figure 32.2.

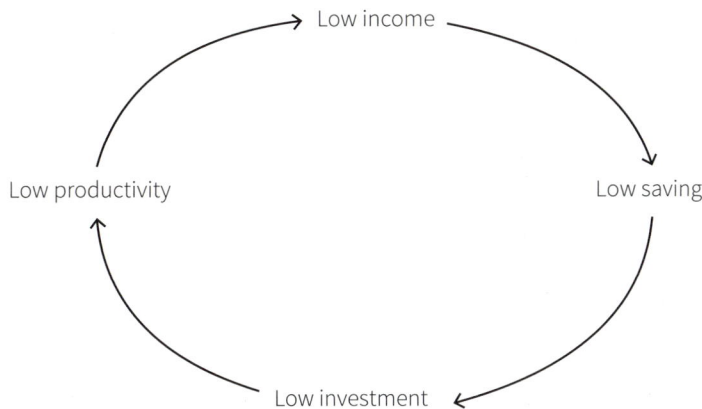

Figure 32.2: The vicious circle of poverty

DISCUSSION

Discuss whether a high real GDP per head always results in high life expectancy.

ACTIVITY 32.2

Table 32.1 shows a comparison of Egypt and Singapore in 2023. In a pair, discuss the extent to which the figures suggest that Singapore achieved a higher level of development than Egypt in 2023.

Write the reasons for your decision in the notebook.

Table 32.1

	Egypt	Singapore
Real GDP per head	$11 700	$91 000
Population under the age of 15	34%	15%
Life expectancy	75	87
Workers employed in agriculture as a percentage of the labour force	20%	0.2%
Doctors per 1 000 of the population	0.75	2.45
Adult literacy rate	74%	98%

Why governments seek to achieve economic development

Governments pursue economic development because they want higher real GDP, higher living standards for their citizens and an expansion of the range of economic and social choices.

Economic growth has the potential to raise material living standards. If higher real GDP consists of both more consumer and capital goods, the country's population should be able to enjoy more goods and services, both now and in the future. Life expectancy may be increased and infant mortality rate may be reduced.

For economic development to be achieved, all people should have access to higher living standards. For this to occur, it is important that the distribution of income does not become too uneven and poverty is reduced.

A reduction in poverty brings benefits both to people living in poverty and to the wider society. Lifting people out of poverty gives them access to (at least) basic necessities, improves their mental and physical health and raises their expectations. People who enjoy better living standards are likely to be more productive, which in turn should lower the country's average costs and make the country more internationally competitive. A reduction in poverty may also reduce pollution. As people become better off, they are more likely to have access to sanitation and environmentally sustainable forms of heating/cooling.

Expanding the range of economic and social choices and increasing freedom and self-esteem includes increasing access to education, healthcare and participation in the political process (see Figure 32.3). This should improve the quality of people's lives and enhance future economic performance. Economic development can create a virtuous circle. As income, education and healthcare increase, saving and investment increase and workers become more productive. This raises international competitiveness, which can lead to even higher output and income.

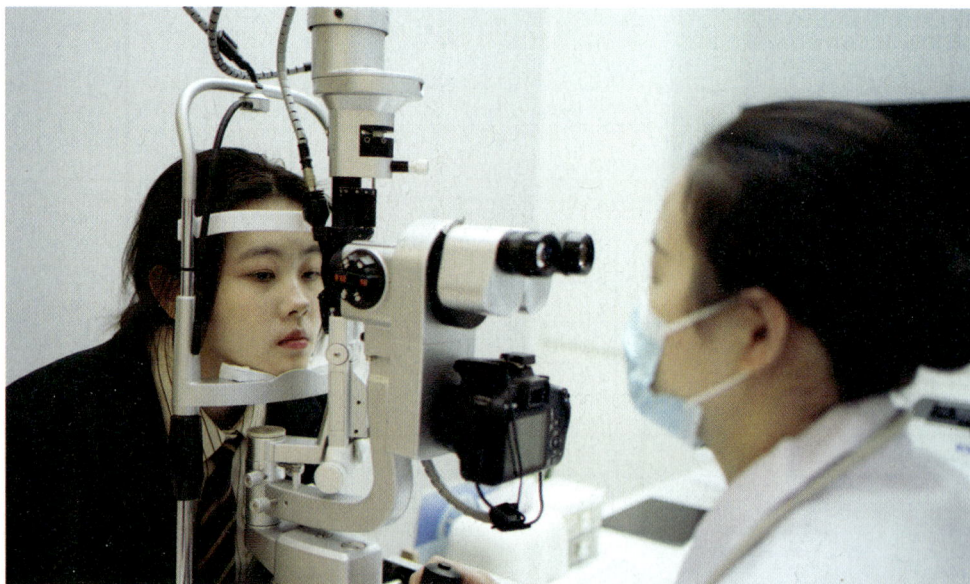

Figure 32.3: Good-quality healthcare promotes economic development

> **TIP**
>
> You could find it useful to consider the development of the economy of your country and the factors influencing its rate of development. This will allow you to apply your understanding of economic development in a real-world context.

The conditions for economic development

Most economists agree that for economic development to occur there needs to be an improvement in the quantity and quality of resources. More investment and improved education, training and healthcare can raise not only real GDP but also the quality of people's lives, their life expectancy and their choices (see Figure 32.4).

Figure 32.4: Better education improves the prospects of a country's children

---

ACTIVITY 32.3

Complete the flowchart which shows how improvements in education in your country could lead to improvements in the education of another country.

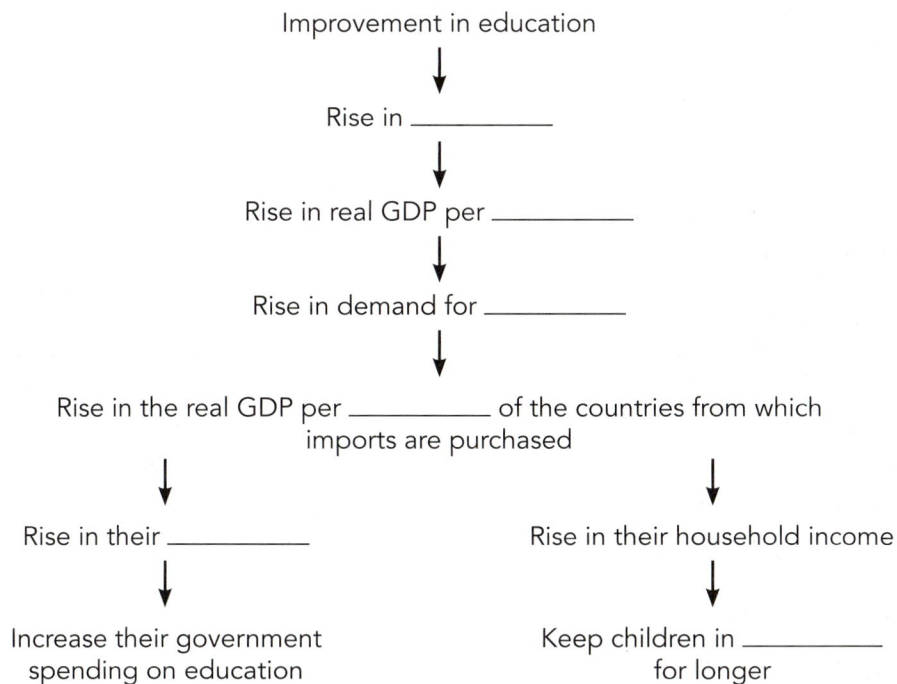

Improvement in education

↓

Rise in _____

↓

Rise in real GDP per _____

↓

Rise in demand for _____

↓

Rise in the real GDP per _____ of the countries from which imports are purchased

↓   ↓

Rise in their _____   Rise in their household income

↓   ↓

Increase their government   Keep children in _____
spending on education   for longer

32.3 Consequences of international differences in economic development

Countries develop at different rates at different times. These differences have implications for each country and for other countries.

Economies with relatively low economic development may face a number of difficulties in seeking to improve their economic performance and living standards. These include:

- **High growth of population.** A high birth rate can result in resources being used, for instance, to feed and educate children. These could instead have been used to increase the country's productive potential and living standards.

- **High levels of international debt.** Many low-income countries have borrowed heavily in the past. In some cases, a large proportion of the country's income is taken up in repaying (and paying interest on) foreign loans. This means the money cannot be used to spend on education, healthcare and investment. So, the opportunity cost of repaying debt may be economic development.

- **Reliance on the export of primary products.** Over a period of time, the price of primary products tends to fall, relative to the price of manufactured goods and services. This means that some low-income countries receive relatively less for their exports, while having to pay more for their imports. Over the last 50 years, a range of prices of primary products, including copper, coffee, cocoa and coal, have been falling. A number of primary markets are dominated by the consuming countries, and these high-income countries use their buying power to keep down the prices of primary products. There have also been significant fluctuations in the price of some primary products due to climate changes and other factors affecting natural resources.

- **Lack of investment in human capital and capital goods.** Lack of expenditure on education, training and capital goods holds back increases in productivity, introduction of new technology and international competitiveness.

- **Emigration of key workers.** Doctors, nurses, teachers, managers and other key workers may seek better-paid employment abroad. Since 1999, for instance, more medical staff have emigrated from Ghana than the country has been able to train. Most of these have emigrated to Canada, the UK and the USA.

- **Trade restrictions on their products.** Tariffs, other restrictions and foreign government subsidies on their own products, make it difficult for low-income countries to sell their products at home and abroad on equal terms. The highest tariffs tend to be imposed by high-income economies on those products, which lower-income economies concentrate on, including agricultural produce and labour-intensive manufactured goods. These tariffs also build up as the goods are processed into higher-value-added goods, so that lower-income economies are discouraged from building up their industries.

- **Unbalanced economies.** Certain markets may be underdeveloped, such as the financial sector. A lack of a developed financial sector is likely to discourage saving and investment.

LINKS

See Chapter 34.4 (Types of trade restrictions) and Chapter 34.6 (Consequences of trade restrictions) for a discussion of their consequences.

ACTIVITY 32.4

A country has a GDP of $7.2 billion and a population of 12 million. The country has low-level infrastructure, emigration of key workers and a relatively high level of corruption. Power and water are not provided for most firms, and there is a lack of good transport links. Firms have to invest in generators. Many professionals, especially doctors, emigrate, taking their skills with them. It also suffers from a lack of access to clean water and from droughts. Only 30% of the population are literate and the average household size is nine.

In a pair, give a presentation in which you explain which problem facing the country is likely to be the main cause of slow economic development in the country. At the end of the presentation, provide your audience with a summary of your points and ask for questions.

REFLECTION

Did producing a summary of the main points in your presentation help to reinforce your learning?

ECONOMICS IN ACTION

Economic development in Luxembourg

Figure 32.5: People living in Luxembourg have a high quality of life

Luxembourg, a small European country, is considered to have a high level of economic development based on a range of economic data. The country has a very high real GDP per head, a high HDI value, long life expectancy and 100% of its people have access to electricity, good-quality sanitation and clean drinking water. Luxembourg has a high positive net migration rate. People come from Belgium, France, Italy, Portugal and Spain to live and work in Luxembourg, attracted by its high level of economic development.

Economists study such economic data over time. For example, while Luxembourg's real GDP per head was ten times greater than the global average in 2023, 50 years before in 1973, it was only five times as great.

Economists also use surveys asking how satisfied people in different countries are with their lives. According to such surveys, Luxembourg comes out as one of the world's best places to live.

There is much agreement among economists about what the information they gather indicates about what causes economic development. These include increasing the quantity and quality of education and healthcare and encouraging firms to rely more on sustainable energy. There is, however, some disagreement about whether it is better to rely on government intervention or market forces operating in the private sector to achieve these changes.

1   What do you think are the four most important indicators of economic development?

2   How may improvements in education and healthcare be linked?

SUMMARY

You should now know:

- Economic development is concerned with improvements in economic welfare. It involves higher real GDP per head, higher living standards, a wider range of choices, more freedom and more self-esteem.

- Economic development can be measured in terms of real GDP per head, although HDI gives a wider measure of development.

- Among the causes of differences in economic development between countries are differences in income, productivity, size of the primary, secondary and tertiary sectors, saving and investment, education and healthcare, concentration on a narrow range of products and natural resources.

- Countries with relatively low economic development may experience a vicious circle of poverty that is difficult to break out of.

- Economic development can introduce a range of benefits to people and enhance a country's ability to develop in the future.

- Countries with low economic development may face a number of problems, including population pressures, international debt, reliance on primary products, lack of investment in human capital and capital goods, emigration of key workers, trade restrictions on their products and unbalanced economies.

Chapter 32 practice questions

1   The table provides information on four countries. Which country is likely to be the most developed?

	Population (m)	Real GDP ($bn)	Life expectancy (years)
A	100	600	58
B	200	2000	70
C	300	2100	58
D	400	3600	70

[1]

2   What is often found in a country with low real GDP per head?

A   a high proportion of the population in higher education

B   a high savings rate

C   a low infant mortality rate

D   a low investment rate   [1]

3   Why is a country's savings rate likely to increase as it experiences economic development?

    A   average income per head will rise

    B   interest rates will rise

    C   investment will decline

    D   the range of saving institutions to choose from will decline   [1]

4   Which would boost an economy's development?

    A   a fall in the average number of years of schooling received by children

    B   a rise in expenditure on the police to tackle a higher rate of crime

    C   a rise in provision of healthcare per head of population

    D   a rise of 2% in nominal GDP and a rise of 8% in inflation   [1]

5   What is most likely to happen as an economy develops?

    A   birth rate rises by more than death rate

    B   output rises by more than the size of the labour force

    C   real GDP rises by less than population

    D   tertiary sector employment rises by less than primary sector employment   [1]

Total: [5]

6   a   Identify **two** indicators of economic development.   [2]

    b   Explain a virtuous circle of economic development.   [4]

    c   Analyse **three** policy measures a government could use to increase economic development.   [6]

    d   Discuss whether or not economic growth will increase economic development.   [8]

Total: [20]

CHECK YOUR PROGRESS

How well do you think you have achieved the learning intentions for this chapter? Give yourself a score from 1 (still need a lot of practice) to 5 (feeling very confident) for each learning intention. Provide an example to support your score.

Now I can ...	Score	Example
discuss the causes and consequences of differences in economic development between countries		
explain the differences in economic development between countries.		

Section 5 practice questions

1   Read the source material carefully before answering all parts of the question.

CASE STUDY: RISE IN LIVING STANDARDS IN CHINA

China fact file		
	1990	2022
Real GDP per head	$343	$12 720
HDI value	0.486	0.768
Cars per 1 000 of the population	9	222

Real GDP per head in China was 36 times greater in 2022 than in 1990. In comparison, the US's real GDP was three times greater over the same period.

The country's Human Development Index (HDI) value rose to 0.768 in 2022. The mean and expected years of education and life expectancy increased. The higher incomes gave people the opportunity to consume more goods and services. Car ownership, for instance, rose to 222 cars per 1 000 of the population and is expected to rise much further in the future.

The rapid growth in the economy has been driven by the expansion of a number of industries, including the aircraft industry, the machine production industry, the healthcare industry and the education industry. At the same time, there has been a decline in the relative importance of agriculture as a source of employment despite the rise in agricultural output. Table 1 shows the percentage of the labour force employed in agriculture and net migration in a number of countries in 2022.

The Chinese government has used a number of policy measures to accelerate economic development. These include giving a subsidy to people in urban areas to bring their income levels up to a minimum standard, the introduction of a rural pension, better health and education services and improved access to safe drinking water in rural areas. These schemes have been funded by the country's progressive taxation system. The nature of tax systems can change over time, including what proportion of tax revenue comes from direct taxes and what proportion comes from indirect taxes.

Table 1: The percentage of the labour force employed in agriculture and net migration in selected countries, 2022

Country	Percentage of labour force employed in agriculture	Net migration per 1 000 population
Bangladesh	35	−2.8
China	22	−0.1
Japan	3	0.7
Laos	56	−1.2
Malaysia	10	1.5
Singapore	0.2	4.1
Sri Lanka	25	−1.4

Refer to the information in the source material in your answers.

a   Calculate how many times greater car ownership was in China in 2022 than in 1990.   [2]

b   Identify **two** industries operating in the secondary sector in China.   [2]

c   Explain what level of development China's HDI figure suggests it had reached in 2022.   [2]

d   Explain **two** reasons why the percentage of workers employed in agriculture may fall while agricultural output increases.   [4]

e   Analyse the relationship between the percentage of people employed in agriculture and net migration.   [4]

f   Discuss whether or not taxation is likely to reduce income inequality in China.   [6]

Total: [20]

2   Read the source material carefully before answering all parts of the question.

CASE STUDY: WE ARE LIVING LONGER

Fact file		
	Republic of Korea 2022	**World 2022**
Birth rate	7.0	17.6
Death rate	7.2	8.0
Net migration rate	2.5	–
Obesity (% of population who are obese)	4.7%	39%

The average age in most countries is increasing, with people living longer. Many countries now have more state pensioners and a smaller proportion of young workers. A study published in 2022 predicted that life expectancy in the Republic of Korea in 2050 would be among the highest in the world at 88 years.

There are thought to be a number of linked reasons why people in the Republic of Korea have, and will continue to have, a long life expectancy. These include good education, good nutrition and widespread access to a good healthcare system. The country has a low level of obesity, a diet rich in vegetables and a relatively small proportion of the population who smoke. The country's economic growth rate averaged 3.0% between 2010 and 2020. The government is seeking to raise the rate in a range of ways, including deregulation, privatisation, increases in the money supply and making it easier for households to take out a mortgage to buy a house.

The Republic of Korea has a relatively even distribution of income. Income inequality can be measured with 100 being the highest degree of income inequality and 0 being a perfectly even distribution of income. Table 2 shows income inequality and life expectancy in six countries.

CONTINUED

Table 2: Income inequality and life expectancy in six selected countries, 2022

Country	Income inequality	Life expectancy (years)
Brazil	53	73
Chile	45	79
Iceland	25	83
Netherlands	26	81
South Africa	62	62
Republic of Korea	33	84

One of the countries with a predicted relatively small increase in life expectancy is the USA. The country has a high obesity rate, a relatively high degree of income inequality and differences in access to good healthcare. In contrast, Switzerland has a lower obesity rate and a more even distribution of income. A larger proportion of people of working age in Switzerland are in the labour force than in the USA. Switzerland, like the USA, is a high-income country. The Swiss, however, seem to have a better work–life balance. Real GDP per head is higher in Switzerland than the USA, but the average Swiss worker works 155 hours less each year. The Swiss are among the happiest people in the world according to the Organisation for Economic Co-operation and Development (OECD).

Refer to the information in the source material in your answers.

a   Calculate the natural change in the Republic of Korea's population in 2022. [2]

b   Identify **two** supply-side policy measures. [2]

c   Explain **one** reason why healthcare costs may rise in the USA. [2]

d   Explain what evidence there is that labour productivity is high in Switzerland. [4]

e   Analyse the relationship between inequality and life expectancy. [4]

f   Discuss whether or not an ageing population is a problem for an economy. [6]

Total: [20]

3   France's HDI has been increasing and its value is above the world's average. Its unemployment rate fell slightly from 8.4% in 2019 to 7.2% in 2023. There is a debate in the country about whether the government should cut or raise its unemployment benefit and other state benefits, including pensions. There is also a discussion about why, despite legislation, there is gender and racial discrimination in the country's labour market.

   a   Identify **two** components of the HDI.   [2]

   b   Explain how discrimination can result in income inequality.   [4]

   c   Analyse how a fall in unemployment in one country can reduce poverty in another country.   [6]

   d   Discuss whether or not an increase in state benefits will reduce poverty.   [8]

   Total: [20]

4   Between 1960 and 2023, Sri Lanka's death rate fell from 11.6 to 7.1. Its birth rate also declined from 37.0 in 1960 to 14.8 in 2023. There were some years, however, when the birth rate rose. For example, it increased from 17.0 to 19.1 from 1998 to 2006. There were also changes in the relative importance of the stages of production in the country over this period. The country has a lack of university places but a high secondary school enrolment.

   a   Identify **two** causes of a decrease in a country's death rate.   [2]

   b   Explain how the relative importance of different stages of production may change as an economy develops.   [4]

   c   Analyse how an increase in the provision of university education could promote development.   [6]

   d   Discuss whether or not an economy will benefit from a rise in the country's birth rate.   [8]

   Total: [20]

> Section 6

International trade and globalisation

> Chapter 33

Specialisation and free trade

LEARNING INTENTIONS

By the end of this chapter, you will be able to:

- define specialisation by country
- analyse the basis for specialisation by country in terms of best resource allocation and/or lowest-cost production
- discuss the advantages and disadvantages of specialisation
- define free trade
- discuss the advantages and disadvantages of free trade.

Introduction

Households in the UK together drink more than 60 billion cups of tea a year. The country, however, produces very little tea. It imports most of the tea from Kenya and Uganda. Kenya imports the oil and most of the machinery it uses. Countries do not produce all the products they consume and they do not consume all the products they produce. They buy goods and services from other countries and they sell some of what they produce to other countries. Engaging in international trade allows countries to specialise.

ECONOMICS IN CONTEXT

India: old and new specialisms

Figure 33.1: IT is a booming industry in India

For centuries, India has been a major producer of spices, including chilli, cinnamon, ginger, pepper, saffron and turmeric. It is now the world's largest producer and exporter of spices. India has a number of advantages in the production of spices. It has a good climate suited to growing spices, workers skilled in their cultivation and processing and a global reputation for high-quality spices.

India is not only a world leader in spices, it is also now the world's largest exporter of IT services. It is one of the leading developers of IT, including in the areas of artificial intelligence (AI) and the internet of things (IoT). The IoT involves the internet links between everyday objects which enable them to exchange data.

The contribution the IT industry makes to India's real GDP continues to grow. In 1998, it only contributed just over 1%, but by 2023 this had increased to 8% and it is forecast that it will rise to 18% by 2050. India has several strengths in IT. These include a large supply of workers with IT and English language skills and government policy measures that promote the IT industry by the setting up of software technology parks for example.

Discuss in a pair or group:

1   What are the possible advantages of concentrating on IT services?

2   Are there any world-leading industries in your country, other than spices and IT if you live in India?

33.1 Specialisation by country

Specialisation by country involves countries concentrating on a limited number of goods and services. Such specialisation is likely to be based on the best resource allocation and low cost of production.

What countries are best at producing is influenced by the quantity and quality of their resources (see Figure 33.2). For example, a country with lots of fertile land, good irrigation, moist climate and a large number of workers may decide to concentrate on producing rice. Its average cost of producing the rice is likely to be low. The best resource allocation will also be influenced by what products are in global demand.

KEY TERM

specialisation by country: countries concentrating on producing a limited number of goods and services that they are best at producing.

A country with a good climate, good beaches and a good supply of labour may decide to concentrate on tourism. In contrast, Singapore, which has a very limited supply of land and a highly skilled labour force, concentrates on financial services.

Figure 33.2: Brazil, the world's leading exporter of coffee, has the right conditions to grow coffee beans

---

ACTIVITY 33.1

Find out what product each of the following three countries specialises in:

1 Chile

2 New Zealand

3 Thailand.

Advantages and disadvantages of specialisation

Advantages and disadvantages for consumers

If countries specialise in what they are best at producing, the output should be higher. The higher output should enable consumers to enjoy more goods and services and so have higher living standards. Specialisation can enable the firms in the country that focus on producing the product to develop skills and techniques in its production. This would raise the quality of the product. Specialisation may also result in lower costs of production and the benefit of this may be passed on to consumers in the form of lower prices.

There is a risk, however, that one country or a small number of countries may gain control of most of the global market for a product and may use its or their power to restrict supply and push up price. The Organization of the Petroleum Exporting Countries (OPEC), a group of the major oil-producing countries, has pushed up the price of oil in the past.

If consumers are buying products from foreign specialists, those firms may not follow the same health and safety standards as in the home country. Any problems that may occur in the countries that are producing the product, including natural disasters, may mean that the products are unavailable, at least for some time.

Advantages and disadvantages for workers

The effect of specialisation on workers will be influenced by what industries a country specializes in. For, example, if a country specialises in rice, pay may be relatively low and workers may experience seasonal unemployment. Specialisation in copper mining may result in poor and dangerous working conditions.

Developing a specialisation is likely to involve a reallocation of resources. This will have different effects on different groups of workers. Workers in the industry that a country is deciding to specialise in will benefit if specialisation results in the industry growing. The greater demand for labour in the industry is likely to increase wages. It may also provide greater job security and more opportunity for job promotion.

However, developing a specialisation may involve a reallocation of resources away from other industries. This may mean that some workers lose their jobs. They may remain unemployed if they are geographically and occupationally immobile.

Advantages and disadvantages for firms

If firms specialise, they can produce the product on a large scale, and this may enable them to take advantage of economies of scale, such as buying and technical economies. Firms can also buy their raw materials from specialist firms which are producing high-quality raw materials at low costs.

Specialisation means that countries have to trade (see advantages and disadvantages for the economy below). Engaging in international trade can help firms in the exchange of new management ideas, information about new products and new technology.

There are, however, a number of disadvantages for firms. If firms become more dependent on other countries as the markets for the products they produce and for the source of their raw materials, they can be adversely affected by events in those countries. For example, foreign governments could put a tax on imports and may restrict the export of raw materials.

Firms could experience a fall in demand. Tastes may change, firms in other countries may become more efficient at producing the product or a substitute product may be developed.

ACTIVITY 33.2

In a pair, research a range of products that you buy regularly. See if you can find out in which country they were made. Take one product and research whether the country is a major producer of the product, what advantages it may have in its production and the benefits firms may gain from producing it.

Produce a leaflet of your findings for other students.

Advantages and disadvantages for the economy

Generally, it is thought that international specialisation and trade increases efficiency and economic welfare. By allowing an economy to concentrate on what it is most efficient at producing, its real GDP should be relatively high. Its output would also be higher than if it used its resources to produce products that the resources are not best suited to making. For example, the USA is a world leader in the development of aircraft technology. The country has some of the most advanced capital equipment and skilled labour. This makes it one of the main manufacturers of aircraft. The USA is a major consumer of coffee, but it only produces a small amount of coffee, in Hawaii and California. This is because it does not have the right climate and its labour is more skilled in producing other products.

Combined with international trade, specialisation can allow an economy to consume outside its production possibility curve (PPC). For example, an economy may be able to produce either 500 cars or 200 tractors. It may initially not specialise and may produce 100 tractors and 250 cars, as shown in Figure 33.3.

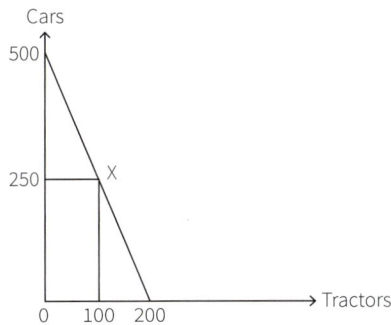

Figure 33.3: PPC for tractors and cars before international trade

The opportunity cost of one tractor is two and a half cars. The economy's resources may be more suited to producing tractors. It may be possible for the economy to export tractors and import cars at a ratio of one tractor for four cars. In this case, the economy could specialise in tractors. It could produce 200 tractors and export 70 tractors. This would enable it to import 280 cars. Figure 33.4 adds a trading possibility curve, which joins 200 tractors and 800 cars. It shows that the economy's consumption of tractors rises by 30 to 130 and its consumption of cars also by 30 to 280.

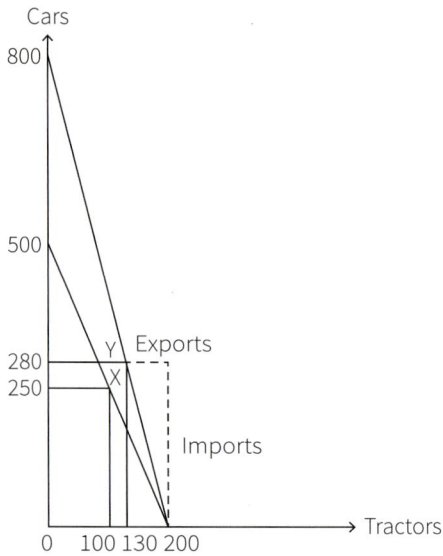

Figure 33.4: Trading possibility curve for tractors and cars

Being able to consume more goods and services can raise living standards and may reduce absolute poverty.

If an economy specialises on the basis of the quality and quantity of its resources, this should mean its resources will not be lying idle. For example, an economy with a large supply of unskilled labour may specialise in industries that are labour intensive and do not require high skills. This can mean that there is little labour unemployment.

As specialisation is based on efficiency, it may also keep the inflation rate relatively low. The economy will be producing products at a relatively low cost and may have the opportunity to import from countries that are efficient at what they are producing.

Specialisation may also enable an economy to build up a reputation in producing a particular product. This could attract both more sales and ancillary (supporting) industries to set up in the country.

It would also boost its sales of exports. In practice, however, it can be difficult to determine what an economy is best at producing and what will be in demand in the future. Indeed, concentrating on a few products is fine if demand for these products remains high and costs of production do not rise. If, however, demand suddenly falls or costs rise, the country can run into difficulties. Structural unemployment may increase if labour is occupationally or geographically immobile. Producing a wider range of products would spread risks.

High transport costs may also offset any cost advantage a country has in producing a product. If the goods are heavy and have to be transported long distances, it may be more efficient for the importing economies to produce them themselves.

DISCUSSION

Discuss why a country may decide not to specialise.

A country has a well-educated labour force and high-speed internet connection. It has large deposits of easily accessible coal, fertile land and a good global reputation for producing chocolate.

In a group of four, you are going to consider what industry the country should specialise in. Write 1–4 on folded pieces of paper and put them in a bag. Each person picks a number from the bag. The number corresponds to the specialisation you are going to argue for:

1   financial services

2   agriculture

3   coal mining

4   chocolate.

After each person has put forward their case and answered questions, take a vote as to which product the country should concentrate on. You may not vote for the product you are representing. When you have finished, write down the arguments for and against specialising in each of the four industries.

33.2 Free trade

Free trade is international trade without any restrictions. When countries specialise, they have to trade. The large-scale production of the goods and services they specialise in will mean that they want to export some of them. They will also have to import those products that their citizens are willing and able to buy but their countries are not producing. If there is free trade, governments will not be using any measures to stop the free movement of exports and imports.

The difference between international and internal trade

Trade involves the exchange of goods and services. International trade, which can also be referred to as external trade, is the exchange of goods and services between countries. In contrast, internal trade is trade within a country. Any trade involves risk and effort. A firm based in one part of the country, selling goods to individuals or firms in another part of the country, has to arrange and pay for transport and may have to wait for the payment for the goods (see Figure 33.5). International trade enables firms to reach a wider market, take greater advantage of economies of scale, source their products from a wider area and earn higher profits. It may, however, provide additional challenges to those posed by internal trade, including different languages and different currencies.

KEY TERM

free trade: international trade without restrictions.

Figure 33.5: Internal trade is often transported by lorry

ACTIVITY 33.4

Decide, in each case, whether the following will increase or decrease the benefits of a country specialising in the production of electric cars.
Copy and complete Table 33.1.

Table 33.1

		Increase/decrease
1	High cost of transporting electric cars to buyers	
2	High number of electric charging points throughout the world	
3	High price of petrol	
4	Large supply of skilled car workers	
5	Low-cost tyre manufacturing firms	
6	Restrictions imposed by other countries on the import of electric cars	

Advantages and disadvantages of free trade

Free trade should allow countries to concentrate on what they are best at producing and hence allow for an efficient allocation of resources. If countries are able to exploit their comparative advantage fully, then world output, employment and living standards should be higher than if resources were less efficiently allocated.

LINK

The disadvantages of free trade are essentially the arguments for protection – see Chapter 34.5 (Reasons for trade restrictions) and Chapter 34.6 (Consequences of trade restrictions).

Selling freely to a global market should enable firms to take greater advantage of economies of scale, raise competitive forces and give them access to more sources of raw materials and components. These effects should lower prices for consumers, raise the quality of products they buy and also enable them to benefit from a greater choice of products.

There are, however, a number of possible disadvantages of free trade. Most people would not want the free movement of demerit goods into their countries. They would want restrictions imposed on such products.

Free trade may make it difficult for new firms and industries to grow to a size where they can take advantage of economies of scale and become internationally competitive. Free trade also does not necessarily mean fair trade. A country's firms may find it difficult to compete with the products of a country which has lower environment standards and whose firms may sell at less than cost because of a government subsidy.

ECONOMICS IN ACTION

Changes in Nauru's specialisms

Figure 33.6: A disused phosphate mine in Nauru where the land is now unsuitable for agriculture

Over time, the products that countries specialise in change. Economists study these changes, in part, to make predictions about how the pattern of countries' production and employment may change in the future.

One country which is experiencing a loss in the advantage it had in one industry and which is facing a threat to another industry is Nauru.

This small island in the South Pacific Ocean used to earn a large amount from selling phosphate. Having mined over 80% of the island's surface and caused considerable air and water pollution, the country's deposits of phosphate have almost run out. Removing the earth's surface to get the phosphate has left most of the island's land unsuitable for agriculture.

A current major source of revenue for the country is selling fishing rights to foreign fishing firms. The seas around Nauru have large stocks of fish, particularly tuna. However, illegal fishing and pollution, including plastic pollution, is reducing its stocks, and there is a risk that the stocks will run out. If this occurs, Nauru's income will fall further.

Nauru's government is trying to develop tourism, but this will not be easy because of the damage done to the land by phosphate mining and the island's remote location. The government is also considering developing its banking industry.

1   Is the decline in Nauru's phosphate industry a disadvantage?

2   What information would an economist examine to decide if a country is likely to be able to develop a successful banking industry?

SUMMARY

You should now know:

- Specialisation by country involves countries concentrating on a limited range of goods and services.

- Specialisation by country is based on the best allocation and low-cost production.

- Specialisation of countries can increase output, reduce costs, increase quality and spread new ideas and technology.

- The risks of specialisation of countries include rival countries' firms may start producing the product, substitute products might be developed, supply problems may be encountered, consumers may become reliant on firms in other countries and trade restrictions may be imposed on their products.

- International trade is the exchange of products across national boundaries.

- Free trade is trade without restrictions.

- Free international trade can raise output, reduce prices and increase choice.

Chapter 33 practice questions

1   Which conditions promote international trade?

   A   difficulties in communication between countries

   B   differences in the quantity and quality of resources in countries

   C   high trade restrictions

   D   high transport costs   [1]

2   A firm which previously had traded internally decides to trade externally. What additional risk will it face?

   A   its costs of production may rise

   B   the government may impose a sales tax on its products

   C   there may be a change in demand for its products

   D   trade restrictions may be placed on its products   [1]

3   The table shows the main source of export earnings with respective products for four countries. What can be concluded from this information?

Country	Product	Percentage of export earnings
W	cars	58
X	copper	63
Y	financial services	70
Z	oil	80

    A   countries X and Z specialise in the production of primary products

    B   countries W and Y specialise in the production of tertiary products

    C   country Z earns most of its export revenue from the sale of secondary product

    D   country Z earns maximum export revenue   [1]

4 What is necessary for a country to benefit from specialisation?

    A   barter

    B   differences in GDP per head

    C   differences in population size

    D   international trade   [1]

5 What is a disadvantage of a country specialising?

    A   it makes it a less attractive location for multinational companies (MNCs)

    B   it makes it more vulnerable to external shocks

    C   it reduces international division of labour

    D   it reduces the range of products available to consumers   [1]

Total: [5]

6 **a** Define 'international trade'.   [2]

    b Explain **two** differences between international trade and internal trade.   [4]

    c Analyse what determines which products countries specialise in.   [6]

    d Discuss whether or not a country should specialise in tourism.   [8]

Total: [20]

CHECK YOUR PROGRESS

How well do you think you have achieved the learning intentions for this chapter? Give yourself a score from 1 (still need a lot of practice) to 5 (feeling very confident) for each learning intention. Provide an example to support your score.

Now I can...	Score	Example
define specialisation by country		
analyse the basis for specialisation by country in terms of best resource allocation and/or lowest cost production		
discuss the advantages and disadvantages of specialisation		
define free trade		
discuss the advantages and disadvantages of free trade.		

> **Chapter 34**
Globalisation and trade restrictions

LEARNING INTENTIONS

By the end of this chapter, you will be able to:

- define globalisation
- explain the causes and consequences of changes in globalisation
- explain the role of multinational companies (MNCs)
- explain the types of trade restrictions/methods of protection: tariffs, import quotas, subsidies and embargoes
- discuss the reasons for trade restrictions
- discuss the consequences of trade restrictions.

Introduction

We buy products from all over the world. We have more choice of goods and services than ever before. More products are being bought and sold between countries, and more firms are producing in other countries. Despite the advantages of international trade, governments put restrictions on what products firms and households can buy from other countries. There are several reasons why governments impose trade restrictions. These restrictions can affect particular industries and also the output, employment, price level and balance of payments of both the countries that impose them and their trading partners. Arguments are put forward both in favour and against using measures to restrict free trade.

ECONOMICS IN CONTEXT

Does the Philippines benefit from international trade?

The Philippines is a country heavily engaged in international trade. It exports nearly a third of the goods and services it produces. It sells a range of products, including office equipment, to other countries. Among its main trading partners are China, Japan, the Republic of Korea and the USA.

More than 40% of the goods and services, including cars, that people in the Philippines consume are imported. The main sources of imports to the Philippines are the same as the destinations of its exports, that is, China, Japan, the Republic of Korea and the USA.

International trade has allowed the Philippines to engage in specialisation to a greater extent and has raised productivity in the country, partly due to increased competition and the spread of technological advances from other countries. However, despite the advantages of free international trade, the government of the Philippines, like all countries, imposes some restrictions on the goods and services that can be imported and exported. For example, the government bans the import of toy guns and hazardous waste. It also imposes taxes on the imports of a range of agricultural products, including rice, cotton and sugar.

Discuss in a pair or group:

1   Why do you think many countries export to and from the same countries?

2   Why may a government want to restrict imports?

Figure 34.1: The Philippines exports high-quality office machinery

---

34.1 What is globalisation?

Globalisation is the process by which the world becomes one market. Barriers may be broken down in terms of where people buy products from and where firms produce. There may also be an increasing number of global brands and **multinational companies (MNCs)**.

34.2 Causes and effects of changes in globalisation

Causes of changes in globalisation

There are times when globalisation occurs at a rapid rate, a slower rate and when there is deglobalisation.

Among the reasons for the greater interconnection between countries are:

- **Reduced transport costs.** Containerisation and larger and more efficient ships, airplanes and trains have lowered the cost of moving goods.

- **Advances in communications.** Consumers can now purchase products online from anywhere in the world and are more in touch with trends in other countries. Executives of MNCs can also keep in close contact with managers of foreign branches.

- **Removal of some trade restrictions.** The general trend has been for tariffs and quotas to be reduced.

- **Movement of multinational companies.** MNCs may open more branches and increase the size of their branches in other countries.

Deglobalisation may occur if there are increases in trade restrictions, higher costs of transport or MNCs close branches in other countries.

Effects of changes in globalisation

Globalisation, and the speed with which it occurs, can have a number of effects:

- **Increases international trade.** This is one of the key features of globalisation. Both exports and imports will increase.

- **Increases competition.** Firms compete with both domestic firms and firms from other countries. Consumers are able to buy a greater range of products at relatively low prices. It also encourages firms to locate some of their production in the most efficient locations, which can lower costs of production.

- **Makes economies more vulnerable to external shocks.** The more economies are integrated through globalisation, the more likely a recession in one economy can have a significant impact on other economies.

- **Restricts government policy, to some extent.** For example, a government may be reluctant to increase the rate of corporate tax for fear that some multinational companies will relocate to other countries.

KEY TERMS

globalisation: the process by which the world becomes increasingly interconnected through trade and other links.

multinational company (MNC): a business organisation that operates in more than one country.

deglobalisation: the process by which the world becomes less interconnected through trade and other links.

- **Causes structural unemployment.** The ability of multinational companies to shift production from branches in one country to other countries can cause industries in some countries to decline. Some workers may also lose their jobs because of the increased competition that is arising from the breaking down of barriers between national markets. This is increasing the importance of occupational mobility.

- **Affects the environment.** Globalisation can improve the environment by encouraging the spread of new, more environmentally sustainable technology including, for example, wind turbine technology. It is possible that multinational companies may use cleaner technology than small firms (see Figure 34.2). Globalisation can also increase public awareness of environmental issues, which can encourage firms to reduce any environmental harm their production methods may cause.

   However, there are concerns that globalisation may threaten environmental sustainability. Greater international trade involves an increase in the transport of goods. Greater use of planes, ships, trains, lorries and other vehicles increases the amount fuel used, which can lead to more greenhouse gas emissions. To transport more goods, more transport infrastructure, including airports, ports, railway lines and roads, is needed, which can destroy natural habitats and reduce animal and plant species. With more goods being transported into and out of countries, there is also the risk that species of animals and plants that may be harmful to a country's native species may be introduced accidentally.

- **Increases migration.** Although most countries impose restrictions on immigration, the movement of people between countries has increased in recent decades. Multinational companies often take some skilled workers to their host countries. Governments tend to be willing to allow highly skilled workers to move to their countries. Some governments may also be willing to allow immigration of unskilled workers if those workers are willing to do jobs that the country's workers are not prepared to do or if an ageing population is resulting in a shortage of workers.

- **Influences income distribution.** Within countries, globalisation moves income from those who cannot adapt to changes in global demand and supply conditions to those who can. In most countries the gap between the income of low-skilled, immobile workers and skilled, mobile workers has increased. The distribution of income between countries favours those which have mobile resources. The gap in the GDP per head in some countries has narrowed while it has increased between other countries. For example, in 1970, the USA had a GDP per head 68 times greater than India. By 2023, this had fallen to 30 times greater. In contrast, the gap in GDP per head between the USA and Niger increased over the same period from 57 times greater to 130 times greater.

- **Influences economic development.** Globalisation can have mixed effects on economic development. The transfer of advances in technology can raise productivity and incomes. It can also improve the quality of education and healthcare throughout the world. However, a more skilled labour force in a low-income country may result in a 'brain drain' with, for example, doctors and nurses migrating to high-income countries. Multinational companies may pay lower wages and impose lower labour standards in their host countries than their home countries. However, these may still be higher than those of some domestic firms in the host country.

Figure 34.2: Electric vehicles and charging points in a firm's warehouse

ACTIVITY 34.1

Decide which changes would increase globalisation and which would reduce globalisation. Copy and complete the table.

		Increase or decrease globalisation	Reasons for increase or decrease
1	A decision by a government to impose trade restrictions on another country's products.		
2	More governments recognising qualifications awarded in other countries.		
3	The development of social media.		
4	An increase in foreign travel.		
5	A reduction in the number of different currencies.		

DISCUSSION

Discuss whether globalisation has benefited your country.

34.3 Multinational companies

A multinational company (MNC) is a business organisation that produces in more than one country. For example, the US-based McDonald's has outlets in many countries, the UK-based Lloyds Bank has branches in a range of countries, the Japan-based Toyota has factories in a number of countries and the Indian-based Tata Group produces in many countries.

Most MNCs are private sector firms, but an increasing number of state-owned enterprises (SOEs) are now producing internationally. For example, the Chinese state-owned oil giant, the China National Offshore Oil Company (CNOOC), operates in a number of countries.

Recent years have seen the growing importance of MNCs. MNCs are increasingly viewing countries throughout the world as their markets and possible locations for production. Besides setting up the operating plants abroad which produce the complete finished good, they are also spreading different parts of the production process to different countries. For example, an MNC producing cars may base its design in a country with a strong tradition in design, its assembly in a country with a skilled but low-cost labour force and its administration and marketing in other countries. In fact, the production process of some products is spread over more than 14 countries.

Advantages and disadvantages of MNCs to host countries

MNCs can have a number of effects on the countries in which they are located, that is their host countries, some beneficial and others harmful. They can increase employment, output and tax revenue, bring in new technology and management ideas and help in development of infrastructure. They may, however, be more prone to pollute and willing to close down plants in foreign countries. Their size and their ability to shift production may mean that they can put pressure on the governments of the host countries in which they have plants to give them tax concessions and not to penalise them for poor safety standards. In addition, although MNCs may increase employment, there is a risk that they may drive domestic firms out of business. The profits they earn may be paid to shareholders in their home countries rather than being reinvested in the host country.

Advantages and disadvantages of MNCs to home countries

MNCs hope to benefit from spreading their operations to more than one country. Producing in countries where products are sold rather than exporting to those countries will reduce the MNCs' transport costs and enable them to keep in close contact with the market. It may also enable them to get around any restrictions on imports, to gain access to cheaper labour and raw materials. They may also receive grants from the governments of the countries in which they set up their franchises. In addition, by selling to a larger market, MNCs may be able to take greater advantage of economies of scale.

The MNCs may send some of the profits they earn in other countries to their home country. This may enable the MNCs to reinvest in their branches at home. The MNCs will also be able to provide some of their workers with the chance to gain experience in working in other countries.

MNCs setting up branches abroad, however, may mean that the host country loses potential jobs and output. It would be difficult, however, to know whether if MNCs could not open branches abroad, they would have opened them in their home country. It is possible that workers in the host country may lose out in terms of their bargaining power. This is because an MNC could resist wage claims by threatening to transfer work to their branches in other countries.

ACTIVITY 34.2

In a group, decide which of the following would attract MNCs to set up in a country.

1 low corporate taxes

2 government grants

3 strict employment laws

4 a good educational system

5 cheap land.

Write your decisions and the reasons for them in your notebook.

34.4 Types of trade restrictions

Trade restrictions are also sometimes known as methods of protection, as they are often used to protect domestic industries from foreign competition. Despite the potential advantages of free trade, every country in the world engages in protection, also called protectionism.

There are several types of trade restrictions that a government of a country or the governments of a group of countries may employ to protect their industries. Some countries are more protectionist than others. Trade restrictions include:

- **Tariff.** A tax can be imposed on imported products. A tariff is also referred to as a customs duty or import duty. Sometimes tariffs are used to raise government revenue, but most commonly they are used to discourage the purchase of imports. Placing a tariff on an imported product raises its price. The tariff is likely to be set at a level which will mean that the imported products will sell at a higher price than domestically produced goods.

- **Import quota.** A limit may be placed on the quantity of a good that can be imported. For instance, a country may limit the number of cars that can be imported into the country at 40 000.

KEY TERMS

tariff: a tax on imports.

quota: a limit placed on imports or exports.

- **Subsidy.** A government may protect its domestic industries from cheaper imports by giving them subsidies. Such help may enable domestic firms to sell at lower prices, which may undercut the price of imports.

- **Embargo.** The import of a product or trade with another country may be banned. A government may want to ban the import of demerit goods. A ban on a trade with a particular country is usually introduced for political reasons.

KEY TERM

embargo: a ban on imports or exports.

TIP

One way to remember the difference between a tariff and a quota: increasing a tariff has the opposite effect to increasing a quota. Increasing a tariff increases protection, while increasing a quota reduces protection.

Besides placing restrictions on imports, governments sometimes impose restrictions on exports. A government may place a tariff or a quota on the export of a good if it is concerned that selling the good abroad will lead to shortages at home and increase prices for domestic consumers. Some governments also restrict exports of raw materials to make it more difficult for foreign firms to obtain them. This may be because both the country's firms and foreign firms use the raw material to produce the same product. In addition, a government may ban the export of a natural resource that it thinks may soon be depleted.

ACTIVITY 34.3

You are acting as an economic adviser to your government. Decide in each case which type of trade restriction you would advise the government to use. Only use a type of trade restriction once. Copy and complete the table.

		Type of trade restriction
1	Domestic producers face competition from larger foreign firms.	
2	Domestic product faces competition from a rival foreign product which has inelastic demand and is superior in quality.	
3	Domestic product sells for $20, while rival foreign product sells for $17.	
4	Foreign product creates significant external costs.	

34.5 Reasons for trade restrictions

A number of reasons are given for protecting domestic industries. Some favour protection of particular domestic industries, while some support protection of all domestic industries.

- **Protect infant (sunrise) industries.** The argument is that such new industries, which have the potential to grow, may be eliminated by foreign competition before they have really started. Giving them some protection may enable them to grow, take advantage of economies of scale and become internationally competitive. It can, however, be difficult to identify the new industries which indeed have such a potential. There is also the risk that the industries will not respond to the opportunity by becoming more efficient but may become dependent on the protection.

KEY TERM

infant (sunrise) industries: new industries with relatively low output and high cost.

- **Protect declining (sunset) industries.** In a dynamic economy, some industries are likely to be declining. If other industries are expanding and labour is mobile, this may not be a problem. However, if labour is immobile and there is a shortage of job vacancies, the decline of a major industry may lead to a significant rise in unemployment. In order to avoid this, a government may decide to protect the industry to allow it to decline gradually. As workers retire and leave of their own accord, the protection can be removed. Owners of the industry, however, may resist the removal of the protection.

- **Protect strategic industries.** These are industries essential for the survival or development of the country. Most governments provide some protection to their agricultural and defence-related industries, to ensure consistency of supplies. A country that is dependent on imports of food and weapons runs the risk of its supplies being cut off due to wars or natural disasters. A government might also consider that protecting the growth of clean energy industries and next generation IT industries may promote the economic development of the country.

- **Avoid dumping.** It is generally agreed that trade restrictions can be imposed to prevent dumping as this is seen as unfair competition. This occurs when foreign firms sell products at a price below the cost of production. Foreign firms may engage in sporadic dumping. Sporadic dumping involves selling excess supplies in other countries, in order to keep the price high in the domestic market. A more damaging motive behind dumping is to drive domestic firms out of the market, gain a large market share and then raise prices. This form of dumping, sometimes called predatory dumping, may benefit consumers in the short run. In the long run, however, it may result in a less efficient allocation of resources and the foreign firms gaining more market power, reducing choice and raising price. This is because it makes it very difficult for domestic firms to compete, even if their costs are lower. Another reason why foreign firms may be gaining an unfair competitive advantage is that they may be enjoying subsidies from their governments. This would again mean that there is not a level playing field.

- **Reduce a deficit on the current account of the balance of payments.** Governments may impose trade restrictions to reduce the gap between import expenditure and export revenue. In the short run, this may be successful. However, in the long run, if the country's firms lack international competitiveness, the deficit will reappear. There is also the risk that other governments will retaliate.

- **Raise tax revenue.** For some countries, revenue from import tariffs and sometimes export tariffs form a significant proportion of total tax revenue. For example, Benin gets more than 40% of its tax revenue from tariffs on imports.

- **Restrict the import of demerit goods.** Most governments ban the import of products that they think are harmful to consumers.

- **Promote environmental sustainability.** A government may impose trade restrictions if it thinks other countries are using protection methods that are environmentally harmful. It is possible that other countries may have lower environmental standards. This may be seen as both a threat to the environment and as unfair competition.

A government may also seek to promote the use of renewable energy by subsidising its own renewable energy industries and by imposing trade restrictions on the import of fossil fuels or the products of countries that make significant use of fossil fuels.

KEY TERMS

declining (sunset) industries: old industries which are going out of business.

strategic industries: industries that are important for the economic development and safety of the country.

dumping: selling products in a foreign market at a price below the cost of production.

LINK

As well as using trade restrictions, there are other government policy measures to reduce a current account deficit – see Chapter 36.4 (Policies to achieve balance of payments stability).

ACTIVITY 34.4

A car firm in Country X is dumping cars in Country Y, which also produces cars. In a group of up to six, you are going to consider whether the government of Country Y should impose a tariff on the import of cars from Country X. Write 1–6 on folded pieces of paper and put them in a bag. Each person picks a number from the bag. The numbers correspond to the roles below:

1   Someone in Country Y planning to buy a car.

2   A worker in the car firm in Country X.

3   A worker in the car firm in Country Y.

4   The owner of the car firm in Country Y.

5   The owner of a car insurance firm in Country Y.

6   A government minister in Country Y.

Before you begin the discussion, individually write down some points you will put forward to support your view. After the discussion, see if you can come to an agreement and write the points that were discussed in your notebook.

REFLECTION

Did carrying out the role-playing exercise help you understand the arguments for and against imposing trade restrictions? Is there an activity, such as producing a mind map, that you think could improve your understanding further?

34.6 Consequences of trade restrictions

Trade restrictions may increase prices in the country that imposes them. Tariffs and quotas are likely to raise the price of imported finished goods and services. By increasing the price of imported raw materials and capital goods, they can increase costs of production. Trade restrictions, by reducing the competitive pressure on domestic firms, may also encourage them to raise their prices. Of course, government subsidies would be likely to reduce the price of both exports and products sold in the home country.

There is the possibility that trade restrictions may lower prices in the country's trading partners. This is because the trading partner's firms may try to lower their costs of production to still be competitive after any tariffs are imposed.

Trade restrictions may increase output and employment in the home country and reduce output and employment in their trading partners in the short run. This is because it may encourage a replacement of imports with domestically produced goods and services. In the long run, however, they may reduce output and employment in both the home country and its trading partners. This is because it can result in a misallocation of resources.

Trade restrictions may reduce a deficit on the home country's balance of payments and increase a deficit on its trading partners' balance of payments. However, if the trade restrictions do not improve the performance of the home country's industries, the relative current account positions may be restored in the long run.

Advantages and disadvantages of restricting free trade

Restricting free trade can protect certain industries. This can bring advantages in allowing infant industries to grow, enabling declining industries to go out of business over time without causing unemployment and ensuring the survival strategic industries. Restricting free trade can also help to prevent dumping and promote environmental sustainability. In some countries, governments receive a significant proportion of their tax revenue from tariffs, and most governments impose trade restrictions on demerit goods.

However, restricting free trade can result in lower choice, higher prices and inefficiency. It also runs the risk of retaliation. If other governments impose trade restrictions in response to another government imposing such restrictions, a **trade war** may develop. For example, one country may impose a tariff of 5% on imported steel. In response, a trading partner that exports steel to the country may impose a tariff of 5% on imported cars from the country. Then the country increases its tariff on imported steel to 9% and its trading partner may raise its tariff on imported cars by 9% or more, and so it goes on. In this circumstance both countries are likely to lose out.

> **KEY TERM**
>
> **trade war:** countries raising trade restrictions in retaliation.

ECONOMICS IN ACTION

Restricting the export of rice

Figure 34.3: Rice production can fluctuate

Economists study trade restrictions on both imports and exports and on both the countries that impose them and on their trading partners. One case examined by economists in recent years was the trade restrictions the Indian government imposed on the export of rice.

India is the world's largest exporter of rice (see Figure 34.3). In 2021, the country accounted for 42% of the world's exports of rice. In September 2022, the Indian government imposed an export tariff on most types of rice grown in the country. Eleven months later, in July 2023, it went further and banned the export of all white rice, except basmati rice.

The Indian government was concerned about the sharp rise in the price of rice in the domestic market. The government wanted to ensure a high supply of rice in the domestic market to keep the domestic price affordable to most people in India. Its trade restrictions did, however, push up the price of rice in importing countries. They also increased the price of wheat on the global market.

1   Why might banning the export of rice increase the price of rice in India in the long run?

2   Why may a rise in the global price of rice increase the global price of wheat?

SUMMARY

You should now know:

- Globalisation is the process by which the world becomes more interconnected through trade and other links.

- Globalisation may occur due to lower trade restrictions, reduced transport costs, advances in communications and the movement of MNCs.

- Globalisation increases international trade, competition, the movement of MNCs and migration. Its impact on the environment, income distribution and economic development is more uncertain.

- MNCs may raise output, employment and tax revenue and bring new technology and management ideas into their host countries but may generate pollution, drive out domestic producers, may shift production to other countries and may unduly influence the government.

- MNCs may increase the profits received in MNCs' home countries, enable them to gain access to cheap raw materials and enlarge the size of their markets, but by setting up branches in other countries, they may reduce potential output and employment in their home countries.

- Four types of trade restrictions are tariffs, quotas, subsidies and embargoes.

- The reasons for imposing trade restrictions include protecting infant, declining and strategic industries, avoiding dumping, reducing a current account of the balance of payments deficit and promoting environmental sustainability.

- Trade restrictions may provide benefits for the home country in the short run while harming its trade partners. The long-run effect will depend on how home industries and the governments and industries of its trading partners respond.

- Trade restrictions can reduce global output by causing a misallocation of resources, but they could also stop some countries engaging in unfair competition.

Chapter 34 practice questions

1   Which is an advantage to a country of having a multinational company producing in that country?

   A   the company depletes non-renewable resources rapidly

   B   the company employs local people

   C   the company reduces its costs by lowering its health and safety standards

   D   the company sends its profits back to the country in which its headquarters is based   [1]

2   Which would reduce trade restrictions in a country?

    A   an increase in quota limits

    B   an increase in tariffs

    C   tighter health and safety standard

    D   the imposition of exchange control   [1]

3   A government has been allowing manufactured goods to enter its country without any trade restrictions. It then decides to impose a 10% tariff on all imported manufactured goods. What effect will this change have on the cost of living and government revenue?

	Cost of living	Government revenue
A	increases	increases
B	increases	reduces
C	reduces	reduces
D	reduces	increases

    [1]

4   Under what circumstances would the protection of infant industries be justified?

    A   if their long-term costs are higher than the revenue earned by them

    B   if they generate substantial external costs

    C   if they have the potential to grow and gain a competitive advantage

    D   if the number of workers they employ will decline over time   [1]

5   What is the main reason for protecting a declining industry?

    A   to avoid unemployment

    B   to increase economic growth

    C   to increase tax revenue

    D   to reduce a deficit on the current account of the balance of payments   [1]

                    Total: [5]

6   **a**   Define an 'infant industry'.   [2]

    b   Explain **two** benefits of free trade for producers.   [4]

    c   Analyse how the imposition of a tariff could prevent dumping.   [6]

    d   Discuss whether or not the presence of a foreign multinational company will benefit a country.   [8]

                    Total: [20]

CHECK YOUR PROGRESS

How well do you think you have achieved the learning intentions for this chapter?
Give yourself a score from 1 (still need a lot of practice) to 5 (feeling very confident)
for each learning intention. Provide an example to support your score.

Now I can...	Score	Example
define globalisation		
explain the causes of changes in globalisation		
analyse the effects of changes in globalisation		
explain the role of MNCs and their advantages to their host and home countries		
explain the types of trade restrictions and methods of production		
analyse the reasons for trade restrictions		
analyse the impact of trade restrictions in the home country and its trading partners		
discuss the advantages and disadvantages of trade restrictions.		

> Chapter 35

Foreign exchange rates

LEARNING INTENTIONS

By the end of this chapter, you will be able to:

- define a foreign exchange rate
- explain the reasons for buying and selling foreign currencies
- analyse how a foreign exchange rate is determined in foreign exchange markets
- discuss the consequences of changes in foreign exchange rates.

Introduction

Currencies are bought and sold like other goods and services. Someone buying imports from Pakistan may buy Pakistani rupees to pay Pakistani firms for the goods or services. This is one of a number of reasons why a person may purchase Pakistani rupees. A rise in demand for a currency is likely to increase its price. Such a change will affect the price of Pakistan's exports and imports.

ECONOMICS IN CONTEXT

The most traded currency

Figure 35.1: The US dollar: an important currency

The US dollar is the most traded currency in the world. A great value and quantity of dollars are bought and sold throughout the year. Why are so many US dollars bought and sold? There are several reasons. One is that the USA sells a high value of exports and purchases a high value of imports. Dollars are earned in exchange for exports and dollars are paid to purchase the imports. Another connected reason is that because the

dollar is such an important currency, it is accepted as a payment between countries other than the USA. Traders throughout the world speculate on whether US dollars will exchange for more or less of other currencies in the future. If they think it will, they will buy more US dollars now.

The importance of the US dollar means that it is easy to find out how much a dollar will buy of another currency. It also means that many economic variables are compared in US dollars. For example, the World Bank and the United Nations, two international organisations, provide information on countries' GDP expressed in terms of US dollars. So significant is the US dollar that when dollars are used in economic data, it is usually assumed that it is US dollars.

Discuss in a pair or group:

1 Do you know anyone who has bought a foreign currency and, if so, for what purpose?

2 Why might another currency account for a higher proportion of all currencies bought and sold in the future?

35.1 What is a foreign exchange rate?

A **foreign exchange rate** is the price of one currency in terms of another currency (or currencies). It is also the value of the currency – that is, how much the currency is worth in terms of another currency (or currencies). For example, a foreign exchange rate of $1 = 65 Indian rupees means that the price of $1 is 65 Indian rupees and that one dollar is worth (would buy) 65 Indian rupees. A foreign exchange rate index is the price of one currency in terms of a basket of other currencies, weighted according to their importance in the country's international transactions. For example, the Japanese effective exchange rate measures the value of the Japanese yen against 15 major currencies, including the US dollar, the Chinese renminbi, the Korean won and the Thai baht.

> **KEY TERM**
>
> **foreign exchange rate:** the price of one currency in terms of another currency or currencies.

ACTIVITY 35.1

Research five of the currencies from the list below. Find out which country uses each currency and the value of the currency in terms of the US dollar.

| cedi | dirham | euro | kip | kwacha | ouguiya | peso |
| rand | real | riyal | rouble | rupiah | shilling | won |

35.2 Reasons for buying and selling foreign currencies

There are a number of reasons for individuals, banks, firms and governments to buy and sell a currency.

- **Trade in goods and services.** For example, a Sri Lankan supermarket may buy washing powder (laundry detergent) from a Japanese firm. The Japanese firm may want to be paid in Japanese yen.

- **Speculation.** This reason accounts for a large proportion of all currency bought and sold. Currency traders buy those currencies they expect to rise in value and sell those currencies they expect to fall in value. The action of speculators can actually bring about the change they are expecting. For example, if currency traders expect the price of the dollar to fall, they will sell it. The increase in the supply of the dollar will be likely to cause its price to fall.

- **Government intervention in currency markets.** A government may leave its country's currency to be determined entirely by market forces. However, there are occasions why governments intervene in currency markets to influence the price of their currencies. For example, if a government wants to increase its country's exports, it may ask its central bank to sell some of its currency to lower its price. Its central bank might also be asked to reduce its interest rate to reduce demand for the currency by people and firms wanting to put money into the country's banks.

- **Payment of profit, interest and dividends between countries.** A branch of a German MNC based in Canada may want to send some of the profits it earns in that country back to Germany. As a result, it may sell some of the Canadian dollars it receives in profit and buy euros to send back to Germany. A German citizen may have a bank account in the UK and may buy shares in some UK firms. The interest and dividends they earn which will be paid in UK pounds may be converted into euros.

- **Workers' remittances.** Some countries have a large proportion of their labour force working abroad. For example, a high number of workers from the Philippines work in other countries, including the USA. These workers send part of the incomes they earn home to their relatives in the Philippines. To do this, they sell dollars and buy Philippine pesos.

- **Investment in capital goods between countries.** MNCs may buy foreign currencies to purchase or build factories, offices or shops in other countries.

Table 35.1 gives examples of the reasons for buying and selling foreign currencies in terms of the demand for and supply for Indian rupees.

> **KEY TERM**
>
> **workers' remittances:** money sent by migrant workers to relatives abroad and money received by relatives from migrant workers in other countries.

Table 35.1: Demand and supply of Indian rupees

Demand for rupees will come from:	The supply of rupees will come from:
• Foreigners wishing to buy Indian goods and services.	• Indians wishing to buy foreign goods and services.
• Foreign-based branches of Indian multinational companies sending back profits to India.	• India-based foreign multinational companies sending profits home.
• Foreign banks buying currencies on behalf of their customers and paying interest on money held by Indian residents.	• Indian banks selling currencies on behalf of their customers and paying interest on money held by foreign people living abroad.
• Foreign firms paying dividends on shares held by Indian residents.	• Indian firms paying dividends on shares held by foreigners.
• Indians working abroad, wishing to send money back home to relatives (workers' remittances).	• Foreigners working in India, sending money home to their relatives (workers' remittances).
• Foreign firms wishing to buy Indian firms and setting up branches in India – **foreign direct investment (FDI)**.	• Indian firms wishing to buy foreign firms and setting up branches in other countries.
• Foreign firms and individuals wanting to buy shares in Indian companies, to save in Indian banks and lend to Indian firms or individuals.	• Indian firms and individuals wanting to buy shares in foreign companies, save in foreign banks and lend to foreign firms and individuals.
• Speculators buying rupees in the expectation that the rupee will rise in value in the future. Significant sums of currency can be traded by speculators.	• Speculators selling rupees because they expect the price of the rupee to fall.

KEY TERM

foreign direct investment (FDI): setting up production units or buying existing production units in another country.

TIP

Think carefully about which curve or curves will shift when there is a transaction involving foreign exchange. Remember, when we buy imports, we sell our own currency and this purchase causes the supply curve to shift to the right.

Figure 35.2 shows the effect of a rise in the Indian rate of interest on the market for Indian rupees. This will encourage foreigners to place money in Indian banks and hence, increase the demand for Indian rupees and raise its price.

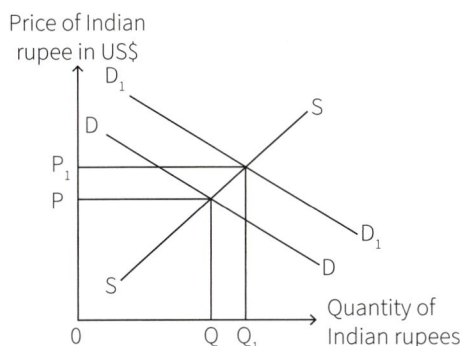

Figure 35.2: The effect of an increase in India's interest rate

---

ACTIVITY 35.2

In each case draw a diagram to show the effect on the market for baht (the currency of Thailand) of:

1   a Japanese multinational company opening up a branch in Thailand

2   more tourists from Thailand going to India on holiday

3   Thai banks lending to Ghanaian firms

4   a reduction in demand for Thai exports.

Check your diagrams with those of another student.

REFLECTION

How confident are you in drawing exchange rate diagrams? What could you do to increase your confidence?

35.3 Determination of a foreign exchange rate in foreign exchange markets

Currencies are bought and sold on foreign exchange markets. Individuals, firms and central banks may buy and sell foreign currencies. The main traders are, however, commercial banks. They buy currencies for their customers and speculate on movements in the price of currencies.

Reasons why foreign exchange rates can change include changes in demand for exports and imports, the rate of interest and speculation.

A floating exchange rate

A **floating exchange rate** is one which is determined by the market forces of demand and supply. If demand for the currency rises or the supply decreases, the price of the currency will rise. Such a rise is referred to as an **appreciation**. In contrast, a **depreciation** is a fall in the value of a floating exchange rate. It can be caused by a fall in demand for the currency or a rise in its supply. Figure 35.3 shows a decrease in demand for Bangladeshi taka, causing the price of the taka to fall.

KEY TERMS

floating exchange rate: an exchange rate which can change frequently as it is determined by market forces.

appreciation: a rise in the value of a floating exchange rate.

depreciation: a fall in the value of a floating exchange rate.

Price of taka in US$

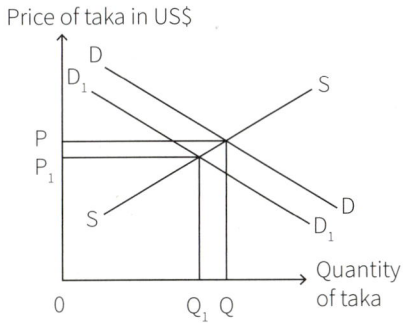

Figure 35.3: A depreciation in the value of the taka

The market for the taka has moved from one equilibrium, where demand and supply were equal, to a new equilibrium, where again demand and supply are equal but at a lower price.

Causes of exchange rate fluctuations

An exchange rate may change as a result of:

- **Changes in demand for exports and imports.** An increase in demand for exports and a decrease in demand for imports would cause the demand for the currency to rise and the supply of the currency to fall.

- **Changes in the rate of interest.** A higher interest rate may attract **hot money flows**. Hot money flows are funds which are moved around the financial markets of the world to take advantage of differences in interest rates and exchange rates. If more people want to place money into a country's banks, it will increase the demand for the country's currency.

- **Speculation.** This can cause significant foreign exchange rate fluctuations. Indeed, if there is a widespread belief that a currency will fall in price, there can be what is called a run on its currency. This is when there is large scale selling of the currency. Such a fall in the foreign exchange rate can be difficult to stop.

ACTIVITY 35.3

In a pair, produce a poster with a line graph showing how your country's foreign exchange rate has varied over the last five years. Write brief bullet points on the poster explaining the main reasons for the changes.

LINK

See Chapter 8.2 (Market equilibrium) for how market equilibrium is determined.

TIP

In explaining how a floating exchange rate is determined, it is useful to draw a diagram. Remember on the vertical axis of an exchange rate diagram, you should express the price of the currency in terms of another currency.

KEY TERM

hot money flows: the movement of money around the world to take advantage of differences in interest rates and exchange rates.

35.4 Effects of changes in foreign exchange rates

Effects of changes in foreign exchange rates on prices and demand for exports and imports

A rise in a country's exchange rate would raise the price of its exports and lower the price of its imports. More precisely, the price of exports rises in terms of foreign currency and the price of imports falls in terms of the domestic currency.

For example, initially 80 Indian rupees may equal $1. In this case, an Indian export valued at 800 rupees will sell in the USA at $10. A USA import valued at $20 will sell in India for 1 600 rupees. If India experiences a rise in its exchange rate against the dollar, it means that rupees will buy more dollars now. The value of the rupee may rise so that 80 rupees equal $2. This significant rise would mean that the Indian export would now sell for $20 in the USA and the $20 import from the USA would sell for 800 rupees in India. If export prices rise, fewer exports will be sold. The effect on export revenue will depend on price elasticity of demand (PED). If demand is elastic, the rise in price will cause a fall in revenue, whereas if demand is inelastic, revenue will rise. In practice, in many export markets there is considerable competition from firms throughout the world and so the demand is elastic.

Effect of a change in the exchange rate on the macroeconomy

A change in the exchange rate, besides affecting exports and imports, may influence economic growth, employment and inflation. A fall in the exchange rate, by lowering export prices and raising import prices, is likely to increase demand for domestic products. This rise in aggregate demand can increase output and employment of the economy if it is not operating at full capacity initially. Figure 35.4 shows real GDP rising from Y to Y_1 as a result of a rise in net exports.

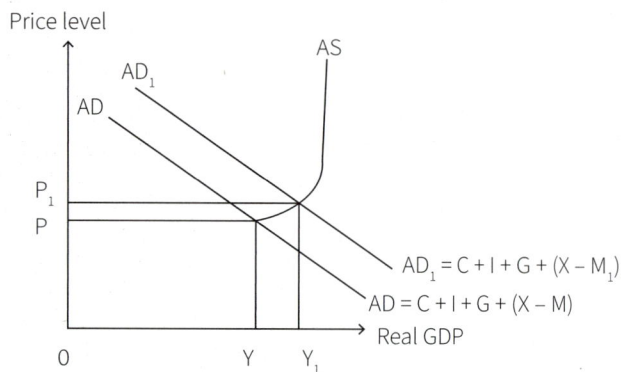

Figure 35.4: The effect of a rise in net exports

> **LINK**
>
> The effect of changes in an exchange rate on export revenue and import expenditure are influenced by the PED for exports and imports – see Chapter 10.4 Determinants of price elasticity of demand (PED and total spending on a product and revenue gained).

> **LINK**
>
> A government may try to influence the foreign exchange rate to achieve its macroeconomic aims. Chapter 24.2 (Monetary policy measures) notes that the foreign exchange rate can be used as a monetary policy measure.

A fall in the exchange rate can, however, increase inflationary pressure for a number of reasons. Imported raw materials will be more expensive, which will raise the costs of production. Finished imported products will also be more expensive. These appear in the country's consumer price index (CPI) and so a rise in their price will directly boost inflation. It will also increase inflation indirectly, by reducing the pressure on domestic firms to keep price rises to a minimum, in order to remain competitive.

DISCUSSION

Discuss whether your country's economy would benefit from a fall in its foreign exchange rate.

ACTIVITY 35.4

The diagram shows the effects of depreciation. Copy and complete the diagram.

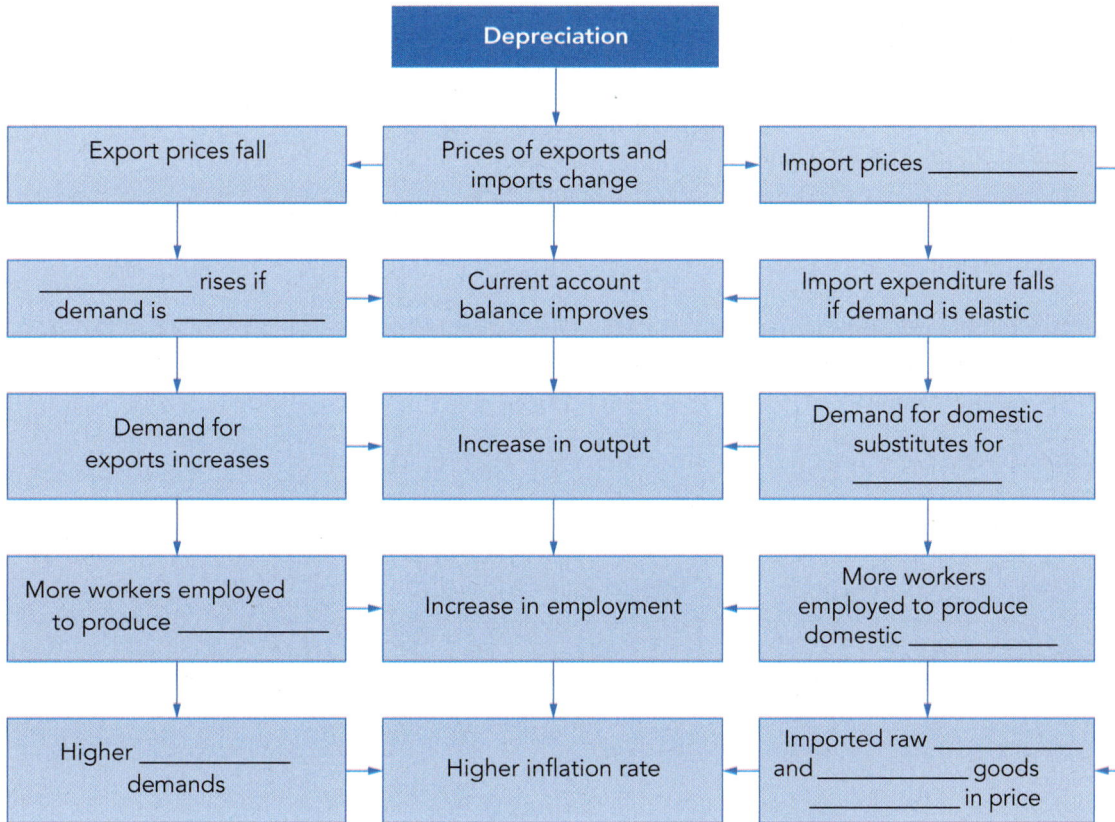

```
                          ┌──────────────────┐
                          │   Depreciation   │
                          └──────────────────┘
                                   │
                                   ▼
┌──────────────────┐    ┌──────────────────┐    ┌──────────────────┐
│ Export prices    │◄───│ Prices of exports│───►│ Import prices     │
│ fall             │    │ and imports      │    │ _____     │
└──────────────────┘    │ change           │    └──────────────────┘
         │              └──────────────────┘             │
         ▼                       │                        ▼
┌──────────────────┐             ▼              ┌──────────────────┐
│ _____ rises  │    ┌──────────────────┐    │ Import expenditure│
│ if demand is     │───►│ Current account  │◄───│ falls if demand   │
│ _____    │    │ balance improves │    │ is elastic        │
└──────────────────┘    └──────────────────┘    └──────────────────┘
         │                       │                        │
         ▼                       ▼                        ▼
┌──────────────────┐    ┌──────────────────┐    ┌──────────────────┐
│ Demand for       │    │ Increase in      │    │ Demand for        │
│ exports increases│───►│ output           │◄───│ domestic          │
│                  │    │                  │    │ substitutes for   │
└──────────────────┘    └──────────────────┘    │ _____     │
         │                       │              └──────────────────┘
         ▼                       ▼                        │
┌──────────────────┐    ┌──────────────────┐             ▼
│ More workers     │    │ Increase in      │    ┌──────────────────┐
│ employed to      │───►│ employment       │◄───│ More workers      │
│ produce _____ │    │                  │    │ employed to produce│
└──────────────────┘    └──────────────────┘    │ domestic _____ │
         │                       │              └──────────────────┘
         ▼                       ▼                        │
┌──────────────────┐    ┌──────────────────┐             ▼
│ Higher _____ │    │ Higher inflation │    ┌──────────────────┐
│ demands          │───►│ rate             │◄───│ Imported raw _____│
└──────────────────┘    └──────────────────┘    │ and _____ goods │
                                                 │ _____ in price  │
                                                 └──────────────────┘
```

ECONOMICS IN ACTION

The cause and consequences of a fall In Brazil's foreign exchange rate

Figure 35.5: Brazil's high inflation rate caused the price of US cars to rise in Brazil

The price of a currency in terms of another currency is determined by changes in the demand and supply of both currencies. Between 2014 and 2023, the price of the Brazilian currency, the real, in terms of the dollar fell. This was largely due to the owners of dollars demanding fewer Brazilian reals, while owners of Brazilian reals were demanding US dollars. One reason for this was Brazil's relatively high inflation rate. Figure 35.6 shows how Brazil's inflation rate was higher than the global inflation rate in every year until 2022. In 2022 and 2023, the price of the Brazilian real in dollars stabilised at 1 real = $0.2.

In 2014, one real could have been exchanged for $0.5. So, a Brazilian wanting to buy a US car priced at $20000 would have had to pay 40000 reais. By 2022, the real would only buy $0.2, so a $20000 car would be priced at 100000 reais.

The fall in the price of the real had several other effects, some harmful and some beneficial, to Brazil. For example, Brazilian airlines had to pay more for fuel, which is priced in dollars, while Brazilian exporting firms experienced an increase in demand for their products. In 2022 and 2023, the increase in demand for Brazilian exports helped to reverse the fall in the price of the real.

1   Why might a country experience a rise in its inflation rate but also a rise in its foreign exchange rate?

2   How might the change in the price of the real in 2022 have affected the behaviour of speculators?

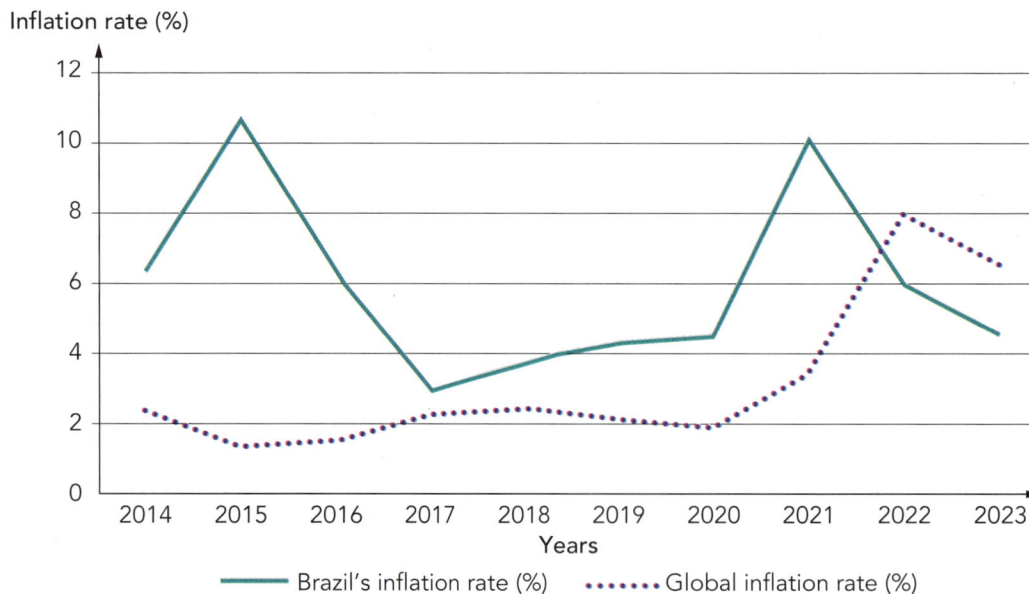

Figure 35.6: Brazil's inflation rate and global inflation rate, 2014–2023

SUMMARY

You should now know:

*   An exchange rate is the price of one currency in terms of another currency (or currencies).

*   The reasons for buying and selling foreign currencies include trade in goods and services, government intervention in currency markets, payment of profit, interest and dividends between countries, workers' remittances, and investment in capital goods between countries.

*   A floating exchange rate is determined by the demand for and supply of the currency.

*   An appreciation is a rise in the value of a floating exchange rate, whereas a depreciation is a fall in its value.

*   An exchange rate may fluctuate due to changes in demand for exports and imports and changes in the rate of interest and speculation.

*   A rise in the exchange rate will increase the price of exports in terms of foreign currency and lower the price of imports in the domestic currency.

*   A fall in the exchange rate would be likely to increase export revenue, reduce import expenditure, boost economic growth and employment but may also tend to increase inflationary pressure.

Chapter 35 practice questions

1   What could cause a fall in the value of the taka, the currency of Bangladesh?

   A   a movement of foreign investment into Bangladesh

   B   a movement of hot money into Bangladesh

   C   decrease in spending by Bangladeshi firms on imported raw materials

   D   increase in the value of bank services purchased by Bangladeshi firms from abroad   [1]

2   What might have caused the change in the value of the Nigerian currency shown in the diagram below?

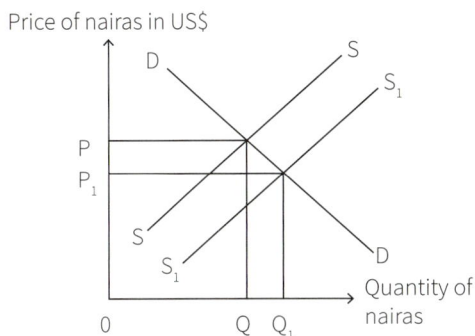

A   foreign firms investing in Nigeria

B   foreigners placing more money in Nigerian banks

C   nigerians buying more imports

D   nigerians speculating that the value of the naira will rise   [1]

3   What combination of factors is most likely to cause a fall in the value of a floating currency?

	Demand for the currency	Supply of the currency
A	increase	increase
B	increase	decrease
C	decrease	decrease
D	decrease	increase

[1]

4   If the value of the pound sterling against the US dollar changes from £1 = $2 to £1 = $1.5, what effect will this have?

A   the USA will import more UK products

B   the value of the pound sterling has risen in price

C   UK exports to the USA will rise in price

D   UK tourists will be able to buy more, for less money, in the USA   [1]

5   Which group of people are most likely to benefit from a fall in the value of the Malaysian ringgit against the Vietnamese dong?

A   Malaysian consumers of Malaysian bicycles made with parts from Vietnam

B   Malaysian consumers of Vietnamese clothes

C   Vietnamese firms that buy imported capital equipment from Malaysia

D   Vietnamese firms that sell most of their output in Malaysia   [1]

Total: [5]

6   a   Define 'depreciation'.   [2]

     b   Explain **two** causes of an increase in a country's foreign exchange rate.   [4]

     c   Analyse how a recession in Country X could affect Country Y's floating exchange rate.   [6]

     d   Discuss whether or not a higher foreign exchange rate will benefit an economy.   [8]

Total: [20]

CHECK YOUR PROGRESS

How well do you think you have achieved the learning intentions for this chapter?
Give yourself a score from 1 (still need a lot of practice) to 5 (feeling very confident)
for each learning intention. Provide an example to support your score.

Now I can...	Score	Example
define a foreign exchange rate		
explain the reasons for buying and selling foreign currencies		
analyse how a foreign exchange rate is determined in foreign exchange rate markets		
discuss the consequences of changes in foreign exchange rates.		

> Chapter 36

Current account of the balance of payments

LEARNING INTENTIONS

By the end of this chapter, you will be able to:

- describe the components of the current account of the balance of payments
- calculate deficits and surpluses on the current account of the balance of payments
- analyse the causes of current account deficits and surpluses
- analyse the consequences of current account deficits and surpluses
- discuss the range of policies available to achieve balance of payments stability and their effectiveness.

Introduction

In 2024, the USA had the largest deficit on the current account of the balance of payments of any country, while China had the largest surplus. A country records income that comes into and goes out of the country. There are four main sources of the income that a country receives from abroad and the income it pays or gives to other countries. Countries record this information in a section of their balance of payments called the current account. This has four parts based on the source of the income. There are a number of reasons why some countries have more income coming in than going out while others have more coming in. Having a deficit or a surplus on its current account of its balance may have several effects on a country's economy.

ECONOMICS IN CONTEXT

What Zambia's current account shows

Figure 36.1: A copper mine in Zambia

All governments keep a record of money coming into and going out of their countries, known as the balance of payments. One part of this is the current account. The current account covers earnings from exports, payments for imports, income and transfers of money between a country and the rest of the world.

The information in the current account can tell us a lot about a country's economy. Examining Zambia's

current account of its balance of payments, for example, shows that more money went out of the country between 2014 and 2018 than came in. It also shows that between 2019 and 2023, the opposite occurred with more money coming into Zambia from abroad than went out.

Looking at the information in more detail, the main reason for this change was Zambia's exports of copper. Zambia is a major producer of copper and earns 70% of its export revenue from selling copper (see Figure 36.1). When there is a high demand for copper, Zambia earns a large amount from exports.

Zambia's current account also shows that the country usually imports a greater value of services than it exports and that a greater value of profit, interest and dividends leave the country than are received from other countries.

Discuss in a pair or group:

1   What are the likely problems involved in recording all the money coming into and going out of a country?

2   Do you think Zambia should try to export a greater range of products?

36.1 Structure of the current account of the balance of payments

The **balance of payments** is a record of all economic transactions between the residents of a country and the rest of the world in a particular period (over a quarter of a year or more commonly over a year). The transactions are made by individuals,

KEY TERM

balance of payments: the record of a country's economic transactions with other countries.

firms and the government. Money coming into the country is recorded as credit items and money leaving the country as debit items. The first section of the balance of payments, and the best known, is the current account.

Components of the current account

The current account shows the income received by the country and the expenditure made by it in its dealings with other countries. It is usually divided into four component sections.

- **Trade in goods** covers exports and imports of goods including cars, food and machinery. If revenue from the exports of goods is less than the expenditure on the imports of goods, the country is said to have a **trade in goods deficit**. This is sometimes called a visible trade deficit. In contrast, a **trade in goods surplus** occurs when export revenue exceeds import expenditure.

- **Trade in services** records payments for services sold abroad and expenditure on services bought from foreign countries. Among the items included are banking, financial services, travel and transportation of goods and passengers between countries. A **trade in service surplus** would mean that service receipts exceed payments for services.

Together the first two component sections give the balance on trade in goods and services.

- **Primary income** (previously called just income) covers income earned by individuals and firms. Primary income records two categories of income flow: compensation of employees and investment income. Compensation of employees includes wages and other benefits earned by residents working abroad minus that earned by foreigners working in the home economy. Investment income covers profit, dividends and interest receipts from abroad minus profit, dividends and interest paid abroad. Investment income is earned on foreign direct investment and financial investment including shares, government bonds and loans. If, for example, a multinational company sends profits out of the country back to its home country, it will appear as a debit item in this section. The receipt of dividends on shares in foreign companies and interest on loans made to foreign firms will be credit items.

- **Secondary income** (previously called current transfers) is transfers of money, goods or services which are sent out of the country or come into the country, but not in return for anything else. It essentially covers gifts. Items include charitable donations, workers' remittances (money sent by migrant workers to relatives abroad and money received by relatives from migrant workers in other countries) and aid from one government to other governments. Workers' remittances are a large item in some countries' secondary income.

Calculation of deficits and surpluses on the current account of the balance of payments

The balances of the four component sections are summed up to give the **current account balance** (also sometimes simply called the current balance). A current account surplus arises when the value of credit items exceeds the value of debit items. If the value of debit items is greater than the value of credit items, there is a current account deficit.

KEY TERMS

trade in goods: the value of exported goods and the value of imported goods.

trade in goods deficit: expenditure on imported goods exceeding revenue from exported goods.

trade in goods surplus: revenue from exported goods exceeding expenditure on imports.

trade in services: the value of exported services and the value of imported services.

trade in service surplus: revenue from exported services exceeding expenditure on imported services.

primary income: income earned by people working in different countries and investment income which comes into and goes out of the country.

secondary income: transfers between residents and non-residents of money, goods or services, not in return for anything else.

current account balance: a record of the income received and expenditure made by a country in its dealings with other countries.

ACTIVITY 36.1

1   A country has imported $27 500m of goods and $14 300m of services. It has exported $30 200m of goods and $16 700m of services. What is the trade in goods and services balance?

2   From the information in Table 36.1, calculate the country's current account balance.

Share your answers with another student.

Table 36.1

	$ millions
Exports of goods	680
Imports of goods	850
Exports of services	240
Imports of services	170
Primary income (net)	−35
Secondary income (net)	22

Changes in exports and imports

There are a number of factors that influence the value of a country's exports and imports.

These include:

- **The country's inflation rate.** If the country has a relatively high rate of inflation, domestic households and firms are likely to buy a significant number of imports. The country's firms are also likely to experience some difficulty in exporting. A fall in inflation, however, would increase the country's international competitiveness and would be likely to increase exports and reduce imports.

- **The country's foreign exchange rate.** A fall in a country's foreign exchange rate will lower export prices and raise import prices. This will be likely to increase the value of its exports and lower the amount spent on imports.

- **Productivity.** The more productive a country's workers are, the lower the labour costs per unit and the cheaper its products. A rise in productivity is likely to lead to a greater number of households and firms buying more of the country's products – so exports should rise and imports fall.

- **Quality.** A fall in the quality of a country's products, relative to other countries' products, would have an adverse effect on the country's balance of trade in goods and services.

- **Marketing.** The amount of exports sold is influenced not only by their quality and price but also by the effectiveness of domestic firms in marketing their products. Similarly, the quantity of imports purchased is affected by the effectiveness of the marketing undertaken by foreign firms.

- **Domestic GDP.** If incomes rise at home, more imports may be bought. Firms are likely to buy more raw materials and capital goods, and some of these will come from abroad. Households will buy more products, and some of these will be imported. The rise in domestic demand may also encourage some domestic firms to switch from the foreign to the domestic market. If this does occur, exports will fall.

- **Foreign GDP.** If incomes abroad rise, foreigners will buy more products. This may enable the country to export more.

- **Trade restrictions.** A relaxation in trade restrictions abroad will make it easier for domestic firms to sell their products to other countries.

LINKS

Countries may impose a variety of trade restrictions for a variety of reasons – see Chapter 34.4 (Types of trade restrictions) and Chapter 34.5 (Reasons for trade restrictions).

ACTIVITY 36.2

Calculate the missing figures in Pakistan's current account for July–December 2023.

Share your answers with another student.

	$ millions
Exports of goods	14 223
Imports of goods	a
Trade in goods balance	−15 366
Exports of services	3 870
Imports of services	4 140
Trade in services balance	b
Trade in goods and services balance	c
Primary income credit	346
Primary income debit	2 977
Primary income (net)	d
Secondary income credit	14 784
Secondary income debit	146
Secondary income (net)	14 638
Current account balance	e

36.2 Causes and consequences of current account deficit

Causes of current account deficit

The factors influencing changes in exports and imports give an indication as to what can cause a current account deficit. One is incomes at home and abroad. A deficit arising from low incomes abroad and/or high incomes at home can be referred to as a cyclical deficit.

A high exchange rate can also cause a current account deficit. This is because it will mean high export prices and low import prices. There may also be structural problems. These can include a problem with the products manufactured by firms in the country, costs incurred to produce them, prices at which they are sold and strategies adopted for marketing them. These can give rise to what is called a structural deficit. A current account deficit may also be the result of a deficit on primary income and/or secondary income.

Consequences of current account deficit

A current account deficit may mean that a country is consuming more goods and services than it is producing. Sometimes we call this a 'country living beyond its means'. A current account deficit can also mean a reduction in inflationary pressure, as there will be a fall in aggregate demand.

A current account deficit does, however, mean that real GDP and employment is lower than possible. If more goods and services were to be produced at home, more workers would be employed and output would be higher.

The significance of a current account deficit depends on its size, duration and cause. A small deficit that lasts for only a short time is unlikely to cause any problem. A deficit that has been caused by the import of raw materials and capital goods, changes in income (domestic and foreign) or a high exchange rate is likely to be self-correcting over time (whatever its size). Imported raw materials and capital goods will be used to produce goods and services, some of which will be exported. Recessions abroad will not last and with a rise in incomes, the country can export more to foreign countries. A deficit on the current account will put downward pressure on the foreign exchange rate. If the rate does fall, exports will become cheaper and imports will become more expensive – as a result, a deficit may be eliminated.

A deficit may also be the result of more primary and secondary income leaving the country than entering it. This may reflect a booming economy, with foreign MNCs making high profits in the country and sending the profits back to their economies and migrant workers earning high wages and sending some of them home to their relatives.

A deficit arising due to a lack of international competitiveness is more serious. This is because it will not be self-correcting. If firms' costs of production are higher due to lower productivity or the quality of the products produced are poor or the products made are not in high world demand, the deficit may persist. In this case, the government may have to introduce policies, particularly supply-side policies, to improve the country's trade performance.

ACTIVITY 36.3

In a pair, research and then produce a podcast on the major trading partners of your country and the reasons for their importance.

36.3 Causes and consequences of current account surplus

Causes of current account surplus

A current account surplus may arise for a number of reasons including:

- **A low foreign exchange rate** will make export prices cheap and import prices expensive.

- **A high quality of domestically produced products** will encourage foreign and domestic citizens to purchase the country's output.

- **High incomes abroad** will enable foreigners to buy a high volume of the country's exports.

- **Low costs of production** may make an economy's products internationally competitive.

- **High investment income earned abroad.** The economy's banks, firms and individuals may be earning more profits, interest and dividends in other economies than is earned by foreigners' assets in the home economy.

- **The receipt of a high level of workers' remittances.** The economy's workers working abroad may be sending more money home to relatives than foreign migrant workers are sending to their relatives.

Consequences of current account surplus

An increase in a current account surplus will increase an economy's aggregate demand and so may lead to a rise in real GDP and higher employment. More money will enter the economy than will leave it and the higher aggregate demand may cause demand-pull inflation if the economy is operating close to full capacity. It also means that the country is consuming fewer products than it is producing.

If an economy is operating a floating exchange rate, an increase in a current account surplus may result in an appreciation in the exchange rate. This is because demand for the economy's currency will exceed its supply.

36.4 Policies to achieve balance of payments stability

Over time, a government is likely to want to achieve balance of payments stability. It will not want to see large and persistent current account deficits or large and persistent current account surpluses. As mentioned above, a current account deficit reduces total demand. A current account surplus means that the people of the country are not consuming as many products as they could afford (see Figure 36.2). To avoid large and persistent current account deficits or surpluses, there are a range of policies a government can use.

Figure 36.2: Empty shopping basket: a current account surplus means that shoppers are not buying all the goods they could afford

Policies to correct a current account deficit

A government will seek to reduce a current account deficit by using policies designed to reduce imports and/or increase exports. It may try to do this directly by imposing import restrictions, subsidising exports and reducing the country's foreign exchange rate. It may also try to reduce imports and increase exports by introducing policies that will lower spending by the country's consumers. Such policies may include increasing income tax, raising the rate of interest and pushing up rates of indirect taxes. The policies may reduce imports and may give domestic firms a greater incentive to export, as they may find it harder to sell at home.

To reduce the chances of a long-run current account deficit, however, a government may decide to use supply-side policies. For instance, education and training may result in lower average costs of production and a rise in the quality of products produced. The government may find that supply-side policy is the most effective approach. This is because the policy has the potential to raise international competitiveness over a longer period of time. It may also avoid some of the disadvantages of other policies, including retaliation (import restrictions), inflation (a lower foreign exchange rate) and higher unemployment (an increase in income tax).

Policies to correct a current account surplus

If a government wants to reduce a current account surplus, it could use the reverse of policies that it would use to correct a current account deficit. It could enable households and firms to purchase more imports by making use of expansionary fiscal policy and monetary policy. For example, a cut in income tax would raise the disposable income of households. This would enable households to buy more goods and services, including imported goods and services.

ECONOMICS IN ACTION

The size of Kyrgyzstan's current account deficit

Figure 36.3: Dried fruits, an important export for Kyrgyzstan

When economists compare the current account position of different countries, they usually compare deficits and surpluses in terms of each country's deficit or surplus as a percentage of its GDP.

In 2022, Kyrgyzstan had what at first appeared to be a small current account deficit in terms of US dollars. Kyrgyzstan has a relatively small economy. It trades mainly with the nearby countries of Kazakhstan, Russia, Uzbekistan and China. Kyrgyzstan exports a range of products including dried fruit, copper and gold (see Figure 36.3).

Table 36.2 shows that Kyrgyzstan's current account deficit was small when compared to the current account deficit of the USA in US dollars. However, when compared as a percentage of GDP and over time, the current account deficit was very large. The table also shows that the USA's current account deficit was more stable than that of Kyrgyzstan.

Economists would want to find out if the deficit would be likely to remain so high. This is because a large current account deficit relative to GDP can have significant consequences. It can mean lower output and lower employment and may cause the exchange rate to fall.

1   Why might an increase in the current account deficit of Russia have a more beneficial effect on Kyrgyzstan than an increase in the current account deficit of the USA?

2   What cause of an increase in Kyrgyzstan's current account deficit would not be a cause of concern?

Table 36.2: The current account deficit of Kyrgyzstan compared with that of the USA, 2015–2022

Year	Current account balance of Kyrgyzstan		Current account balance of the USA	
	$ millions	% of GDP	$ millions	% of GDP
2015	−1 000	−15.8	−408 450	−2.2
2016	−792	−11.6	−396 220	−2.1
2017	−536	−7	−367 610	−1.9
2018	−962	−11.6	−439 850	−2.1
2019	−1 070	−11.4	−441 750	−2.1
2020	374	4.5	−597 140	−2.8
2021	−738	−8	−831 450	−3.6
2022	−5 180	−44.9	−971 590	−3.8

SUMMARY

You should now know:

- The balance of payments is a record of a country's trade and investment with other countries.

- The current account covers trade in goods, trade in services, primary income and secondary income.

- A current account deficit means that expenditure on imports of goods and services, income and transfers received from abroad are greater than earnings from exports of goods and services, income and transfers received from abroad.

- Exports and imports are influenced by changes in the inflation rate, exchange rate, productivity, quality, marketing, income and trade restrictions.

- An increase in a current account deficit may be caused by a change in income at home or abroad, a change in the exchange rate or a change in international competitiveness.

- The significance of a current account deficit depends on its size, duration and cause. A deficit arising from a lack of international competitiveness is the most serious.

- A current account surplus may be caused by a low exchange rate, high quality of domestically produced products, high income abroad and low costs of production.

- An increase in a current account surplus will increase aggregate demand and may raise the exchange rate.

- A government can seek to improve the current account position by encouraging people to buy more domestic and fewer foreign products or by discouraging people from buying products in general. In the long run, supply-side policies are likely to be most effective.

Chapter 36 practice questions

1   Which is an import of a service into Indonesia?

   A   french firms selling insurance to Indonesian firms

   B   indonesian citizens buying cars from the USA

   C   indonesian firms buying land in Germany

   D   tourists visiting Indonesia   [1]

2   Mexican firms sell more oil to the USA and buy more banking services from the UK. How do these changes affect the Mexican balance of payments?

	Trade in goods	Trade in services
A	improves	improves
B	improves	worsens
C	worsens	worsens
D	worsens	improves

[1]

3   Which item is included in the current account of the balance of payments?

   A   the payment of interest on foreign loans

   B   the purchase of shares in foreign companies

   C   the sale of government bonds to foreign residents

   D   the setting up of a branch of a bank in a foreign country   [1]

4   Which is most likely to reduce a deficit on the current account of the balance of payments?

   A   a fall in government expenditure on benefits

   B   a fall in income tax

   C   a rise in consumer confidence

   D   a rise in the value of the currency   [1]

5   What would it mean if a country which engages in international trade has a current account balance of 0?

   A   the debit items on the current account equal the credit items

   B   the government revenue from exports on the current account equals subsidies to exporting firms

   C   the primary income on the current account equals the secondary income

   D   the value of exports of goods on the current account equals the value of imports of goods and services   [1]

   Total: [5]

6   a   Define 'primary income'.   [2]

   b   Explain how a country could have a deficit on its primary income but a current account surplus.   [4]

   c   Analyse how a rise in a country's inflation rate could move a current account surplus into a current account deficit.   [6]

   d   Discuss whether or not an increase in a current account surplus will benefit an economy.   [8]

   Total: [20]

CHECK YOUR PROGRESS

How well do you think you have achieved the learning intentions for this chapter? Give yourself a score from 1 (still need a lot of practice) to 5 (feeling very confident) for each learning intention. Provide an example to support your score.

Now I can ...	Score	Example
describe the components of the current account of the balance of payments		
calculate deficits and surpluses on the current account of the balance of payments		
analyse the causes of current account deficits and surpluses		
analyse the consequences of current account deficits and surpluses		
discuss the range of policies available to achieve balance of payments stability and their effectiveness.		

Section 6 practice questions

1   Read the source material carefully before answering all parts of the question.

CASE STUDY: AFRICAN COUNTRIES BECOME MORE OPEN

Africa fact file	
	2023
South Africa GDP	$406bn
Botswana	$43bn
Agricultural exports as a % of Tanzania's total exports	32%
Workers employed in agriculture as a % Tanzania's total labour force	65%

African countries are becoming more open to international trade. Integration is increasing not only between the 54 countries of Africa, but with the wider world. Transport costs are decreasing, although they are still twice the global average. Tariffs and non-tariff barriers are also declining, but are higher than the global average.

The extent to which African countries are open to international trade and the extent to which their governments engage in trade restrictions varies. Figure 1 shows five African countries' exports and imports as a percentage of GDP compared to the global average.

The export of diamonds has been the main driver of Botswana's economic growth, which has changed the country from one of the poorest countries in Africa to an upper-middle income country. Its heavy reliance on the export of natural diamonds makes it vulnerable to changes in the international market. Natural diamonds are also a non-renewable resource and are now facing competition from synthetic diamonds.

Mauritius and South Africa are also upper-middle income countries. Mauritius has a more diversified economy than Botswana. It produces a range of agricultural products, on a commercial basis, including sugar cane and potatoes, and has growing financial and tourist industries. The government has reduced tariffs significantly, particularly those protecting inefficient industries, and now the country has one of the lowest average tariff rates in the world. South Africa is a relatively large economy which had a GDP of $406 billion in 2023. It uses a range of measures to restrict imports into the economy. For example, it makes widespread use of anti-dumping tariffs as well as quotas, product standards and delays at customs. It is debatable how these measures have influenced the country's international trade.

In 2023, as shown in Figure 1, the country's exports were equivalent to 30% of its GDP, while its imports were equivalent to 28% of GDP.

Rwanda and Tanzania are low-income countries which produce mainly agricultural products. In Tanzania, agriculture accounts for a high proportion of its exports and employment. Tanzania's economic growth has increased in recent years. Lower costs of production have increased the exports of a number of the country's products, including coffee. In Rwanda, a densely populated country with poor infrastructure, many of the population are engaged in subsistence farming. They produce a number of agricultural products, including potatoes and bananas. The governments of both Rwanda and Tanzania are encouraging farmers to spend more on capital goods, and both are being urged by those farmers to increase trade restrictions on agricultural products.

CONTINUED

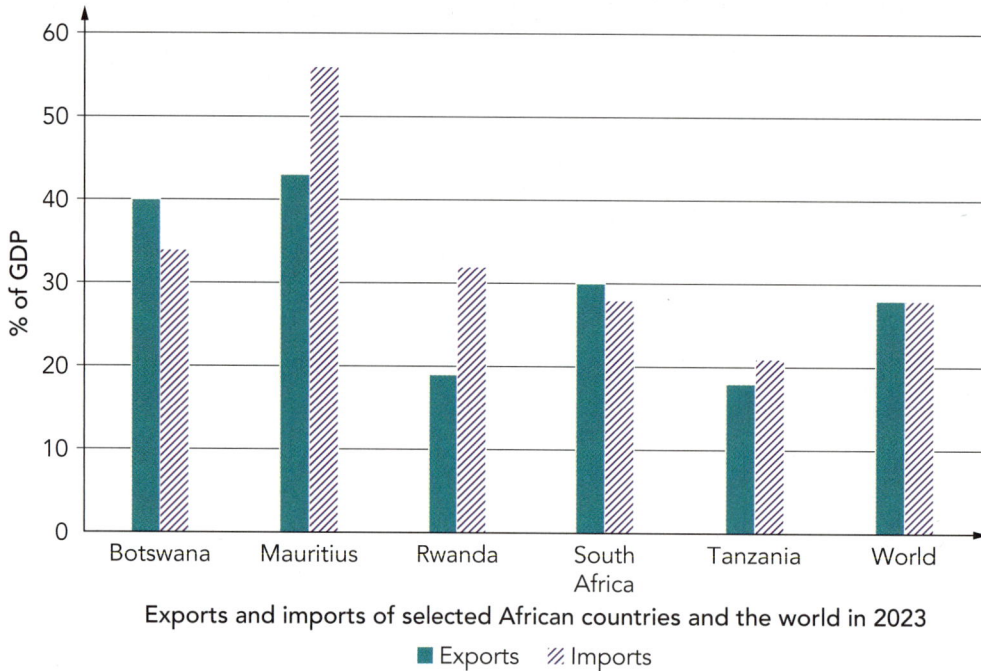

Exports and imports of selected African countries and the world in 2023

■ Exports ▨ Imports

Figure 1: Exports and imports as a percentage of GDP of selected African countries and the world in 2023

Refer to the information in the source material in your answers.

a	Calculate the value of South Africa's imports in 2023.	[2]
b	Identify **two** non-tariff methods of protection.	[2]
c	Explain **one** piece of evidence of globalisation.	[2]
d	Explain **two** possible disadvantages of specialisation.	[4]
e	Analyse which African countries are the most open.	[4]
f	Discuss whether or not the imposition of trade restrictions on agricultural products would benefit Rwanda and Tanzania.	[6]

Total: [20]

2   Read the source material carefully before answering all parts of the question.

CASE STUDY: TRADE LINKS

Nigeria fact file	
	2023
Oil production as % of GDP	6%
Tax revenue from oil as % of total tax revenue	50%
Export revenue from oil as % of total export revenue	80%
Total revenue from the export of goods	$69bn
Total expenditure on the imports of goods	$62.5bn
Current account surplus on the balance of payments	$7.7bn

Nigeria imports a vast range of products, including banking services, food, freight transport, insurance and machinery. Its exports are dominated by oil. The product accounts for 6% of the country's output but 50% of government revenue and 80% of its export revenue. In 2023, the price of oil rose. This increased government revenue and export revenue and caused the country's current account surplus to increase.

The change in the current account position did not stop the country's foreign exchange rate falling significantly, as shown in Table 1. More significant influences on the exchange rate were thought to be the rise in the country's inflation rate and a reduction in the government buying the naira, Nigeria's currency, to support its value.

The rise in the price of Nigeria's oil was a disadvantage for the Indian economy. India is the main destination of Nigeria's exports. Both Nigeria's and India's current account balance fluctuate between deficit and surplus.

In 2023, the Nigerian central bank increased the interest rate to reduce the country's inflation rate. A rise in the interest rate can increase a country's foreign exchange rate and reduce spending by consumers. These two changes can influence the current account balance in opposite directions.

Table 1: Nigeria's inflation rate and foreign exchange rate, 2018–2023

Year	Inflation rate (%)	Foreign exchange rate: price of US dollar in naira
2018	16.5	306
2019	12.1	306
2020	13.2	358
2021	17.1	401
2022	18.9	426
2023	29.1	1492

Refer to the information in the source material in your answers.

    a   Calculate Nigeria's trade in goods balance in 2023.   **[2]**

    b   Identify **two** items that would have appeared in Nigeria's trade in services.   **[2]**

    c   Explain whether demand for Nigerian oil was elastic or inelastic in 2023.   **[2]**

    d   Explain how a rise in consumer spending can cause a current account deficit.   **[4]**

    e   Analyse the relationship between a country's inflation rate and its foreign exchange rate.   **[4]**

    f   Discuss whether or not a rise in a country's interest rate will reduce a current account deficit.   **[6]**

                                                Total: [20]

3   Vietnam is becoming a more open economy. Its government is reducing the protection it gives to domestic industries and is signing more free trade deals. The economy is increasing the resources it devotes to making electrical and electronic products and these have become the country's top export earner.

    a   Define 'free trade'.   **[2]**

    b   Explain **two** reasons for imposing trade restrictions, apart from protecting domestic industries.   **[4]**

    c   Analyse how specialisation at national level can benefit the country's firms.   **[6]**

    d   Discuss whether or not a government should protect its industries from foreign competition.   **[8]**

                                                Total: [20]

4   Between 2018 and 2020, the Mexican peso depreciated against the US dollar. This trend was reversed between 2021 and 2023 when Mexico's foreign exchange rate appreciated. Changes in the country's foreign exchange rate can influence a country's balance on the current account of the balance of payments. The Mexican government was planning to increase its spending on education and training. Some economists suggested that this would reduce the country's current account deficit.

    a   Define 'foreign exchange rate'.   **[2]**

    b   Explain **two** causes of a depreciation in a foreign exchange rate.   **[4]**

    c   Analyse how a decrease in spending on training and education could increase a deficit on the current account of the balance of payments.   **[6]**

    d   Discuss whether or not a depreciation in its foreign exchange rate will reduce a country's deficit on the current account of the balance of payments.   **[8]**

                                                Total: [20]

> Glossary

absolute poverty	a condition where people's income is too low to enable them to meet their basic needs.
actual economic growth	an increase in the output of an economy.
ageing population	an increase in the average age of the population.
aggregate demand (AD)	the total demand for a country's product at a given price level. It consists of consumer expenditure, investment, government spending and net exports (exports – imports).
aggregate supply (AS)	the total amount of goods and services that domestic (local) firms are willing to supply at a given price level.
aggregation	the addition of individual units to arrive at a total amount.
appreciation	a rise in the value of a floating exchange rate.
average fixed cost	total fixed cost divided by output.
average revenue	the total revenue divided by the quantity sold.
average total cost	total cost divided by output.
average variable cost	total variable cost divided by output.
balance of payments	the record of a country's economic transactions with other countries.
barrier to entry	anything that makes it difficult for a firm to start producing the product.
barrier to exit	anything that makes it difficult for a firm to stop making the product.
the basic economic problem	where unlimited wants are greater than finite resources.
birth rate	the number of live births per 1 000 of a country's population in a year.
capital / capital goods	artificial goods used in production.
capital-intensive	the use of a high proportion of capital relative to labour.
casual unemployment	unemployment arising from workers regularly being between periods of employment.
central bank	a government-owned bank which provides banking services to the government and commercial banks and operates monetary policy.
change in supply	changes in supply conditions causing shifts in the supply curve.
change in demand	more or less of a product being demanded at any given price; causes a shift of the demand curve, either to the right or left.
circular flow of income	the movement of expenditure, income and output around the economy.
collective bargaining	representatives of workers negotiating with employers' associations.

commercial bank — a bank which aims to make a profit by providing a range of banking services to households and firms.

competitive market — a market with a number of firms that compete with each other.

complement — a product that is used together with another product.

conglomerate merger — a merger between firms producing different products.

consumer durables — goods purchased by households that last a relatively long time and are purchased infrequently.

consumer goods — goods and services purchased by households for their own satisfaction.

consumer price index (CPI) — a measure of the weighted average of the prices of a representative basket of goods and services.

consumers — people who buy goods and services for their own or their family's use.

consumption — expenditure by households on consumer goods and services.

contraction in demand — a fall in the quantity demanded caused by a rise in the price of the product.

contraction in supply — a fall in the quantity supplied caused by a fall in the price of the product.

contractionary fiscal policy — cuts in government expenditure and/or rises in taxation designed to reduce aggregate demand.

contractionary monetary policy — cuts in the money supply or growth of the money supply and/or rises in the rate of interest designed to reduce aggregate demand.

corporate income (corporation) tax — a tax on profits of a company.

cost-push inflation — rises in the price level caused by higher costs of production.

current account balance — a record of the income received and expenditure made by a country in its dealings with other countries.

cyclical unemployment — unemployment caused by a lack of aggregate demand.

death rate — the number of deaths per 1 000 of a country's population in a year.

declining (sunset) industries — old industries which are going out of business.

decrease in demand — a fall in demand at any given price, causing the demand curve to shift to the left.

decrease in supply — a fall in supply at any given price, causing the supply curve to shift to the left.

deflation — a fall in the average price of goods and services over time.

deglobalisation — the process by which the world becomes less interconnected through trade and other links.

demand — the willingness and ability to buy a product.

demand-pull inflation — rises in the price level caused by excess demand.

demerit goods — products which the government considers consumers do not fully appreciate how harmful they are and so will be overconsumed if left to market forces.

dependency ratio	the proportion of the population that has to be supported by the labour force.	**economically active**	being a member of the labour force.
depreciation	a fall in the value of a floating exchange rate.	**economically inactive**	people of working age who are not in the labour force.
depreciation (capital consumption)	the value of capital goods that have worn out or become obsolete.	**elastic demand**	when the quantity demanded changes by a greater percentage than the percentage change in price.
deregulation	the removal of rules and regulations.	**elastic supply**	when the quantity supplied changes by a greater percentage than the percentage change in price.
direct taxes	taxes on income and wealth of individuals and firms.		
directives	instructions given by the state (government) to state-owned enterprises.	**elasticity of demand for labour**	a measure of the responsiveness of demand for labour to a change in the wage rate.
disinflation	a fall in the rate of inflation.		
disposable income	income after income tax has been deducted and state benefits received.	**elasticity of supply of labour**	a measure of the responsiveness of the supply of labour to a change in the wage rate.
division of labour	workers specialising in particular tasks.	**embargo**	a ban on imports or exports.
dumping	selling products in a foreign market at a price below the cost of production.	**emigration**	people leaving the country to live elsewhere.
earnings	the total pay received by a worker.	**employment**	being involved in a productive activity for which payment is received.
economic development	an improvement in economic welfare.		
economic good	a product that requires resources to produce it and therefore has an opportunity cost.	**enterprise**	risk-taking and key decision-making in business.
economic growth	an increase in the output of an economy and, in the long run, an increase in the economy's productive potential.	**entrepreneur**	a person who takes the risks and makes the key decisions in a business.
		equilibrium price	the price at which demand and supply are equal and there is no surplus and no shortage.
economic system	the institutions, organisations and mechanisms that influence how an economy works and determine how resources are allocated.	**equilibrium quantity**	when the quantity demanded by buyers equals the quantity supplied by sellers, and so there is no surplus and no shortage.

expansionary fiscal policy	rises in government expenditure and/or cuts in taxation designed to increase aggregate demand.	**flat taxes**	taxes with a single rate.
expansionary monetary policy	increases in the money supply and/or the rate of interest designed to increase aggregate demand.	**flexible labour force**	a labour force which adjusts quickly and smoothly to changes in market conditions.
extension in demand	a rise in the quantity demanded caused by a fall in the price of the product itself.	**floating exchange rate**	an exchange rate which can change frequently as it is determined by market forces.
extension in supply	a rise in the quantity supplied caused by a rise in the price of the product itself.	**foreign direct investment (FDI)**	setting up production units or buying existing production units in another country.
external benefits	benefits enjoyed by those who are not directly involved in the consumption and production activities of others.	**foreign exchange rate**	the price of one currency in terms of another currency or currencies.
external costs	costs imposed on those who are not involved in the consumption and production activities of others directly.	**free good**	a product that does not require resources to make it and so does not have an opportunity cost.
external diseconomies of scale	higher average total cost arising from an industry growing too large.	**free rider**	someone who consumes a good or service without paying for it.
external economies of scale	lower average total cost resulting from an industry growing in size.	**free trade**	international trade without restrictions.
eactors of production	the economic resources of land, labour, capital and enterprise.	**frictional unemployment**	temporary unemployment arising from workers being in between jobs.
firm	a business organisation that produces goods and services.	**full employment**	the lowest level of unemployment possible.
fiscal policy	decisions on government spending and taxation designed to influence aggregate demand.	**geographical mobility**	the ability to move from one location to another.
fixed costs	costs which do not change with output in the short run.	**globalisation**	the process by which the world becomes increasingly interconnected through trade and other links.
		government budget	the relationship between government revenue and government spending.
		government budget deficit	government spending is higher than government revenue.
		government budget surplus	government revenue is higher than government spending.

gross domestic product (GDP)	the total output of a country.	**inelastic demand**	when the quantity demanded changes by a smaller percentage than the percentage change in price.
gross investment	total spending on capital goods.		
horizontal merger	the merger of firms producing the same product and at the same stage of production.	**inelastic supply**	when the quantity supplied changes by a smaller percentage than the percentage change in price.
hot money flows	the movement of money around the world to take advantage of differences in interest rates and exchange rates.	**infant (sunrise) industries**	new industries with relatively low output and high cost.
		infant mortality rate	the number of deaths per 1 000 live births in a country in a year.
Human Development Index (HDI)	a measure of living standards which takes into account income, education and life expectancy.	**inferior goods**	a product whose demand decreases when income increases and increases when income falls.
hyperinflation	a very rapid and large rise in the price level.		
immigration	people coming from elsewhere to live in a country.	**inflation rate**	the percentage rise in the price level of goods and services over time.
improvements in technology	advances in the quality of capital goods and methods of production.	**inflation**	a rise in the average price of goods and services over time.
increase in demand	a rise in demand at any given price; causes the demand curve to shift to the right.	**informal economy**	that part of the economy that is not regulated, protected or taxed by the government.
increase in supply	a rise in supply at any given price, causing the supply curve to shift to the right.	**information failure**	a lack of information, inaccurate information or asymmetric information which may result in inefficient choices.
index-linking	changing payments in line with changes in the inflation rate.		
indirect taxes	taxes on goods and services.	**interest**	a payment for borrowing and a reward for saving.
industrial action	when workers disrupt production to put pressure on employers to agree to their demands.	**internal diseconomies of scale**	higher average total cost arising from a firm growing too large.
industry	a group of firms producing the same product.	**internal economies of scale**	lower average total cost resulting from a firm growing in size.

International Monetary Fund (IMF)	an international organisation which promotes international cooperation and helps countries with balance of payments problems.	**market economic system**	an economic system where consumers determine what is produced, resources are allocated by the price mechanism and land and capital are privately owned.
investment	spending on capital goods.		
labour productivity	output per worker hour.	**market equilibrium**	a situation where demand and supply are equal.
labour	human effort used in production.		
labour force	people in work and those actively seeking work.	**market failure**	market forces resulting in an inefficient allocation of resources.
Labour Force Survey	a measure of employment and unemployment in the country's population by means of a survey.	**market price**	the price at which a product is bought and sold.
		market structure	the conditions which exist in a market, including the number of firms.
labour-intensive	the use of a high proportion of labour relative to capital.		
land	natural resources used in production.	**market supply**	total supply of a product.
liquidity	being able to turn an asset into cash quickly without a loss.	**menu costs**	costs involved in having to change prices as a result of inflation.
long run	the time period when all factors of production can be changed and all costs are variable.	**merit goods**	products which the government considers consumers do not fully appreciate the benefits of and so will be underconsumed if left to market forces.
lottery	the drawing of tickets to decide who will get the products.		
market	an arrangement which brings buyers into contact with sellers and which includes all the buyers and sellers.	**mixed economic system**	an economy in which both the private and public sectors play an important role.
market demand	total demand for a product.	**mobility of labour**	the ability of labour to change where or in which occupation it works.
market disequilibrium	a situation where demand and supply are not equal.	**monetarists**	a group of economists who think that inflation is caused by the money supply growing more rapidly than output.

monetary inflation	rises in the price level caused by an excessive growth of the money supply.	**net investment**	gross investment minus depreciation.
monetary policy	decisions on the money supply, the rate of interest and the foreign exchange rate taken to influence aggregate demand.	**net migration rate**	the number of net migrants per 1 000 of a country's population in a year.
		net migration	the difference between immigration and emigration.
money	an item which is generally acceptable as a means of payment.	**nominal GDP**	GDP at current market prices and so not adjusted for inflation.
monopoly	a market with a single supplier.	**normal goods**	a product whose demand increases when income increases and decreases when income falls.
mortgage	a loan to help buy a house.		
multinational company (MNC)	a business organisation that operates in more than one country.	**occupational mobility**	the ability to switch between occupations.
multiplier effect	the final impact on total (aggregate demand) being greater than the initial change.	**opportunity cost**	the best alternative forgone.
		optimum population	the size of the population which maximises the country's output per head.
national champions	industries that are, or have the potential to be, world leaders.	**output**	goods and services produced by the factors of production.
national debt	the total amount the government has borrowed over time.	**perfectly elastic demand**	when a change in price causes a complete change in the quantity demanded.
national minimum wage (NMW)	a minimum rate of wage for an hour's work, fixed by the government for the whole economy.	**perfectly elastic supply**	when a change in price causes a complete change in quantity supplied.
nationalisation	moving the ownership and control of an industry from the private sector to the government.	**perfectly inelastic demand**	when a change in price has no effect on the quantity demanded.
natural monopoly	an industry where a single firm can produce at a lower average cost than two or more firms.	**perfectly inelastic supply**	when a change in price has no effect on the quantity supplied.
negative net investment	a reduction in the number of capital goods caused by some obsolete and worn-out capital goods not being replaced.	**planned economic system**	an economic system where the government makes the main decisions, land and capital are state-owned, and resources are allocated by directives.

potential economic growth	an increase in an economy's productive capacity.
price elasticity of demand (PED)	a measure of the responsiveness of the quantity demanded to a change in price.
price elasticity of supply (PES)	a measure of the responsiveness of the quantity supplied to a change in price.
price fixing	when two or more firms agree to sell a product at the same price.
price mechanism	the way the decisions made by households (buyers or consumers) and firms (sellers) interact to decide the allocation of resources.
price	the amount of money that has to be given to obtain a product.
primary income	income earned by people working in different countries and investment income which comes into and goes out of the country.
primary sector	covers agriculture, fishing, forestry, mining and other industries which extract natural resources.
private benefits	benefits received by those directly consuming or producing a product.
private costs	costs incurred by those directly consuming or producing a product.
private good	a product which is both rival and excludable.
privatisation	the sale of public sector assets to the private sector.

production possibility curve (PPC)	a curve that shows the maximum output of two types of products and combination of those products that can be produced with existing resources and technology.
productivity	the output per factor of production in an hour.
profit maximisation	making as much profit as possible.
progressive tax	tax that takes a larger percentage of the income or wealth of the rich.
proportional tax	tax that takes the same percentage of the income or wealth of all taxpayers.
public corporation	a business organisation owned by the government which is designed to act in the public interest.
public good	a product which is non-rival and non-excludable and so needs to be financed by taxation.
public sector	the part of the economy controlled by the government.
quota	a limit placed on imports or exports.
rate of interest	a charge for borrowing money and a payment for lending money.
rationalisation	eliminating unnecessary equipment and plant to make a firm more efficient.
rationing	a limit on the amount that can be consumed.
raw materials	basic materials used to produce goods.
real GDP	GDP at constant prices and so adjusted for inflation.

real income income adjusted for inflation.

recession a reduction in real GDP over a period of six months or more.

regional unemployment unemployment caused by a decline in job opportunities in a particular area of the country.

regressive tax tax that takes a larger percentage of the income or wealth of those living in poverty.

relative poverty a condition where people are poor in comparison to others in the country. Their income is too low to enable them to enjoy the average standard of living in their country.

resources inputs used to produce goods and services.

savings rate/ratio the proportion of household disposable income that is saved.

scale of production the size of production units and the methods of production used.

scarcity a situation where there are not enough resources to satisfy everyone's wants.

search unemployment unemployment arising from workers who have lost their jobs looking for a job they are willing to accept.

seasonal unemployment unemployment caused by a fall in demand at particular times of the year.

secondary income transfers between residents and non-residents of money, goods or services, not in return for anything else.

secondary sector covers manufacturing and construction industries.

shoe-leather costs costs involved in moving money around to gain high interest rates.

short run the time period when the quantity of at least one factor of production is fixed/cannot be changed.

shortage the amount by which demand is greater than supply (excess demand).

social benefits the total benefits to a society of an economic activity.

social costs the total costs to a society of an economic activity.

socially optimum output the level of output where social cost equals social benefit and society's welfare is maximised.

specialisation the concentration on particular products or tasks.

specialisation by country countries concentrating on producing a limited number of goods and services that they are best at producing.

stable prices the price level in the economy not changing significantly over time.

state-owned enterprises (SOEs) organisations owned by the government which sell products or provide services.

strategic industries industries that are important for the economic development and safety of the country.

strike a group of workers stopping work to put pressure on an employer to agree to their demands.

structural unemployment	unemployment caused by long-term changes in the pattern of demand and methods of production.
subsidy	a payment by government to encourage the production or consumption of a product.
subsistence agriculture	the output of agricultural goods for farmers' personal use.
substitute	a product that can be used in place of another.
sunk costs	cost that cannot be recovered if the firm leaves the industry.
supply	the willingness and ability to sell a product.
supply-side policy	measures designed to increase aggregate supply.
surplus	the amount by which supply is greater than demand (excess supply).
sustainable economic growth	economic growth that does not endanger the country's ability to grow in the future.
tariff	a tax on imports.
tax	a payment to the government.
technological unemployment	unemployment caused by workers being replaced by capital equipment.
tertiary sector	covers industries which provide services.
third parties	those not directly involved in producing or consuming a product.
total cost	the total amount spent on the factors of production used to produce a product.

total revenue	the total amount of money received from selling a product.
trade in goods	the value of exported goods and the value of imported goods.
trade in goods deficit	expenditure on imported goods exceeding revenue from exported goods.
trade in goods surplus	revenue from exported goods exceeding expenditure on imports.
trade in services	the value of exported services and the value of imported services.
trade in service surplus	revenue from exported services exceeding expenditure on imported services.
trade union	an association which represents the interests of a group of workers.
trade war	countries raising trade restrictions in retaliation.
transfer payments	transfers of income from one group to another not in return for providing a good or service.
unemployment	being without a job while willing and able to work.
unemployment rate	the percentage of the labour force who are willing and able to work but are without jobs.
unit cost	the average cost of production. It is found by dividing total cost by output.
unitary elastic	when a change in price causes an equal percentage change in the quantity supplied.
unitary elastic demand	when a change in percentage price causes an equal percentage change in the quantity demanded, leaving total revenue unchanged.

value added	the difference between the sales revenue received and the cost of raw materials used.	**wage-price spiral**	wage rises leading to higher prices which, in turn, lead to further wage claims and price rises.
variable costs	costs that change with output.	**wage rate**	a payment which an employer contracts to pay a worker. It is the basic wage a worker receives per unit of time or unit of output.
vertical merger	the merger of one firm with another firm that either provides an outlet for its products or supplies it with raw materials, components or the products it sells.	**wants**	desires for goods and services.
vertical merger backwards	a merger with a firm at an earlier stage of the supply chain.	**wealth**	a stock of assets including money held in bank accounts, shares in companies, government bonds, cars and property.
vertical merger forwards	a merger with a firm at a later stage of the supply chain.		
vicious circle of poverty	a situation where people become trapped in poverty.	**workers' remittances**	money sent by migrant workers to relatives abroad and money received by relatives from migrant workers in other countries.
wage differential	the difference in wages.		

> Acknowledgements

The authors and publishers acknowledge the following sources of copyright material and are grateful for the permissions granted. While every effort has been made, it has not always been possible to identify the sources of all the material used, or to trace all copyright holders. If any omissions are brought to our notice, we will be happy to include the appropriate acknowledgements on reprinting.

Thanks to Peter Rock-Lacroix for creating the video scripts within this publication.

Thanks to the following for permission to reproduce images:

Cover Eugene Mymrin/GI; *Inside* **Chapter 1** Abstract Aerial Art/GI; Bloomberg Creative Photos/GI; Andresr/GI; Levente Bodo/GI; Alberto Coto/GI; Kaicheng Xu/GI; **Chapter 2** Fhm/GI; DoctorEgg/GI; PacoRomero/GI; Boris Nieuwenhuijzen/GI; Monty Rakusen/GI; Onurdongel/GI; Visionkick/GI; **Chapter 3** Lingqi Xie/GI; Gallo Images/GI; Edwin Tan/GI; Image Source/GI; Aparna Balasubramanian/GI; RyanJLane/GI; **Chapter 4** Senez/GI; Mayur Kakade/GI; Halfpoint Images/GI; Georgeclerk/GI; **Chapter 5** Suttipong Sutiratanachai/GI; Tibor Bognar/GI; Maskot/GI; **Chapter 6** Stefan Cristian Cioata/GI; Thomas Barwick/GI; Rifka Hayati/GI; Susumu Yoshioka/GI; Sylvain Sonnet/GI; **Chapter 7** Ashok Sinha/GI; Mario Marco/GI; Beachmite Photography/GI; Julpo/GI; Bloomberg Creative/GI; Bloomberg Creative/GI; Scyther5/GI; Getty Images/GI; **Chapter 8** Nikada/GI; John Coletti/GI; MediaProduction/GI; Cybrain/GI; Peter Dazeley/GI; Aamir Qureshi/GI; Peter Adams/GI; **Chapter 9** Jackyenjoyphotography/GI; Bugto/GI; IronHeart/GI; Johner Images/GI; Stefania Pelfini, La Waziya Photography/GI; **Chapter 10** Corbis/VCG/GI; Kosamtu/GI; Andresr/GI; Carol Yepes/GI; Noel Hendrickson/GI; Oscar Wong/GI; **Chapter 11** Maurizio Siani/GI; Matspersson0/GI; Edwin Tan/GI; Athima Tongloom/GI; Westend61/GI; **Chapter 12** Eloi_Omella/GI; Tuomas A. Lehtinen/GI; Maskot/GI; Matthew Horwood/GI; Renata Angerami/GI; Picha Stock/GI; **Chapter 13** Horasiu Vasilescu/GI; Stockbyte/GI; Jose A. Bernat Bacete/GI; Singkham/GI; Frans Lemmens/GI; **Chapter 14** Tim Grist Photography/GI; Fcafotodigital/GI; Figure 14.2 National Preventive Health Strategy 2021–2030 © Commonwealth of Australia as represented by the Department of Health 2021 (CC-BY); Craig Hastings/GI; RBB/GI; imageBroker/Lilly/GI; Philippe Colombi/GI; **Chapter 15** Prasit photo/GI; Oscar Wong/GI; Ali Trisno Pranoto/GI; LukaTDB/GI; TiagoBaiao/GI; SDI Productions/GI; SimpleImages/GI; **Chapter 16** Theerasak/GI; Abdirashid Abdulle Abikar/GI; EmirMemedovski/GI; P. Lubas; **Chapter 17** Image Source/GI; Mayur Kakade/GI; ShaunWilkinson/GI; Fatcamera/GI; Image Source/GI; Zeljkosantrac/GI; Tetra Images/GI; **Chapter 18** ArtistGNDphotography/GI; Raja Islam/GI; Monty Rakusen/GI; Ed Lallo/GI; Simon Maina/GI; **Chapter 19** wragg/GI; Iantfoto/GI; FG Trade Latin/GI; Scharfsinn86/GI; **Chapter 20** Richard Drury/GI; Maskot/GI; Monty Rakusen/GI; Images By Tang MIng Tung/GI; Maskot/GI; Science Photo Library/GI; **Chapter 21** ImageBroker/Raimund Kutter/GI; Ankit Sah/GI; Kosamtu/GI; Kali9/GI; Oscar Wong/GI; **Chapter 22** Piranka/GI; Antonio Hugo Photo/GI; Andresr/GI; Calvin Chan Wai Meng/GI; **Chapter 23** Klaus Vedfelt/GI; Norbert Zingel/GI; Sutthichai Supapornpasupad/GI; Reza Estakhrian/GI; Peeterv/GI; **Chapter 24** Matthias Kulka/GI; Peeterv/GI; Peng Song/GI; Bloomberg/GI; **Chapter 25** Koiguo/GI; Ultra.F/GI; Lorado/GI; Jean-Francois Monier/GI; **Chapter 26** Franz Aberham/GI; Yaorusheng/GI; Grant Faint/GI; Mauroof Khaleel/GI; **Chapter 27** Westend61/GI; Peter Cade/GI; Hispanolistic/GI; Mediterranean/GI; Halfpoint Images/GI; Jennifer Heslop/GI; Thomas Barwick/GI; **Chapter 28** Gary Yeowell/GI; FatCamera/GI; Artmarie/GI; Javier Ghersi/GI; Table 28.1 Office for National Statistics (ONS), released 11 March 2024, ONS website, article, Consumer price inflation basket of goods and services; **Chapter 29** Alexander Spatari/GI; Maskot/GI; Jamie Grill/Tetra Images/GI; Figure 29.3 Based on Human Development Report 2021/2022, Table 2 Human Development Index trends, 1990–2021, pages 277–280, © UNDP 2022; Paola Giannoni/GI; Johnnygreig/GI; Table 29.2 *Human Development Report 2021/2022*, Table 1 Human Development Index and its components, pages 272–275, © UNDP 2022; **Chapter 30** Karl Hendon/GI; David Weyand/GI; Eymen Uzunkok/GI; Travelpix Ltd/GI; Puneet Vikram Singh/GI; **Chapter 31** Alexander Spatari/GI; Tuan Tran/GI; Dallas and John Heaton/GI; Wladimir Bulgar/GI; Yoshiyoshi Hirokawa/GI; Sam Tarling/GI; **Chapter 32** Yuichiro Chino/GI; Martin Harvey/GI; Wengen Ling/GI; Nickylloyd/GI; Tibor Bognar/GI; **Chapter 33** Wuttipong Charoensub/GI; Mayur Kakade/GI; Helen Camacaro/GI; John Lamb/GI; Hadi Zaher/GI; **Chapter 34** Grotmarsel/GI; Plan Shooting 2/Imazins/GI; Adventtr/GI; Carlos Duarte/GI; **Chapter 35** MR.Cole_Photographer/GI; Simpleimages/GI; Andreswd/GI;

Chapter 36 Yuichiro Chino/GI; Mabus13/GI; Jackyenjoyphotography/GI; Emad Aljumah/GI; Activity 36.2 State Bank of Pakistan, Summary Balance of Payments, March 2024

Key GI = Getty Images

Videos are created using images from Getty Images

Video 1 Japatino/GI; Yana Tatevosian/GI; Danita Delimont/GI; Duncan1890/GI; Lordhenrivoton/GI; Lewis Mulatero/GI; Comezora/GI; Suriyapong Thongsawang/GI; Carol Yepes/GI; Tommy/GI; David Malan/GI; Pavel Gospodinov/GI; Tommy/GI; Jadwiga Figula/GI; Matthias Kulka/GI; Winslow Productions/GI; DNY59/GI; Vladgrin/GI; **Video 2** Grant Faint/GI; SrdjanPav/GI; Andresr/GI; Onurdongel/GI; Richard Drury/GI; Robas/GI; Ricardo Lima/GI; Tuul & Bruno Morandi/GI; Peter Zelei Images/GI; Peterpencil/GI; Ilkermetinkursova/GI; Valentinrussanov/GI; Westend61/GI; Hinterhaus Productions/GI; Longhua Liao/GI; Issarawat Tattong/GI; Westend61/GI; Alvarez/GI; Edwin Tan/GI; Deepak Sethi/GI; Daniel de la Hoz/GI; Ilbusca/GI; Westend61/GI; Evandrorigon/GI; Sarote Pruksachat/GI; Andresr/GI; Recep-bg/GI; ljubaphoto/GI; Westend61/GI; Jdillontoole/GI; Mjhollinshead/GI; Martin Barraud/GI; Kali9/GI; **Video 3** Solstock/GI; Zak00/GI; Designer29/GI; Bubaone/GI; Phototechno/GI; **Video 4** Fcafotodigital/GI; Virojt Changyencham/GI; Photo_Concepts/GI; Linearcurves/GI; Peter Dazeley/GI; Fatcamera/GI; **Video 5** Filo/GI; Mindful Media/GI; Peanutpie/GI; **Video 6** D3sign/GI; Milorad Kravic/GI; Thomas Barwick/GI; Fingermedium/GI; Digipub/GI; Daniela Garling/GI; RLT_Images/GI; Deepak Sethi/GI; Solstock/GI; Fatcamera/GI; 4x6/GI; Jessicaphoto/GI; Juanmonino/GI; Robert Brook/GI; **Video 7** Jordi Salas/GI; Nnehring/GI; Posteriori/GI; Sarayut Thaneerat/GI; Eakphoto/GI; Martin Harvey/GI; Sepia Times/GI; Jayk7/GI; Pgiam/GI; Shomiz/GI; Zap Pix/GI; Anilyanik/GI; Deepak Sethi/GI; Kinga Krzeminska/GI; D3sign/GI; Urbazon/GI; Jayk7/GI; Professionalstudioimages/GI; **Video 8** Owngarden/GI; Andresr/GI; Wang Yukun/GI; Daniel Bosma/GI; Westend61/GI; Vithun Khamsong/GI; Steve Proehl/GI; Nnehring/GI; MTStock Studio/GI; FG Trade/GI; Sorbetto/GI; Monty Rakusen/GI; Westend61/GI; **Video 9** Maskot/GI; KTSdesign/GI; Johannes Mann/GI; Andrew Brookes/GI; PixeloneStocker/GI; Tolgart/GI; Chun han/GI; Rengim Mutevellioglu/GI; Imaginima/GI; Mario Marco/GI; Markswallow/GI; Bgblue/GI; Javier Zayas Photography/GI; Tommy/GI; Jimmyjamesbond/GI; **Video 10** Erhui1979/GI; Filo/GI; Bgblue/GI; Courtneyk/GI; Nora Carol Photography/GI; Leopatrizi/GI; Jordan Lye/GI; Hiraman/GI; Nickylloyd/GI; **Video 11** -Victor-/GI (x2); Appleuzr/GI (x2); Fingermedium/GI; Fonikum/GI (x2); Sorbetto/GI; Lvcandy/GI; Fonikum/GI; Enis Aksoy/GI; **Video 12** Peterpencil/GI; Victor/GI; Rambo182/GI; Appleuzr/GI; Hadynyah/GI; Teatrambicia/GI; Sungjin Kim/GI; Maskot/GI; Robert Brook/GI; Maskot/GI; Mattjeacock/GI; **Video 13** Victor/GI; Hans-Peter Merten/GI; Santiago Urquijo/GI; Per-Anders Pettersson/GI; Mariusz Kluzniak/GI; Tim Grist Photography/GI; Peeterv/GI; A-Clip/GI; Maskot/GI (x2); Buena Vista Images/GI; Arnitorfason/GI; Deejpilot/GI; Ingunn B. Haslekaas/GI; **Video 14** Alistair Berg/GI; Cheunghyo/GI; Nikada/GI; Comezora/GI; Prapass Pulsub/GI; Bloomberg Creative/GI; Grant Faint/GI; Alex Potemkin/GI; Sierrarat/GI; Pierre Longnus/GI; Kathy Collins/GI; Frankramspott/GI; Appleuzr/GI; Malte Mueller/GI; Philippe Lissac/Godong/GI; **Video 15** Doctoregg/GI; Bgblue/GI; Alistair Berg/GI; Image Source/GI; Mustafahacalaki/GI; Propic/GI; MR.Cole_Photographer/GI

> Index

Note: Page numbers in **bold** refer specifically to tables, and those in *italics* to figures.

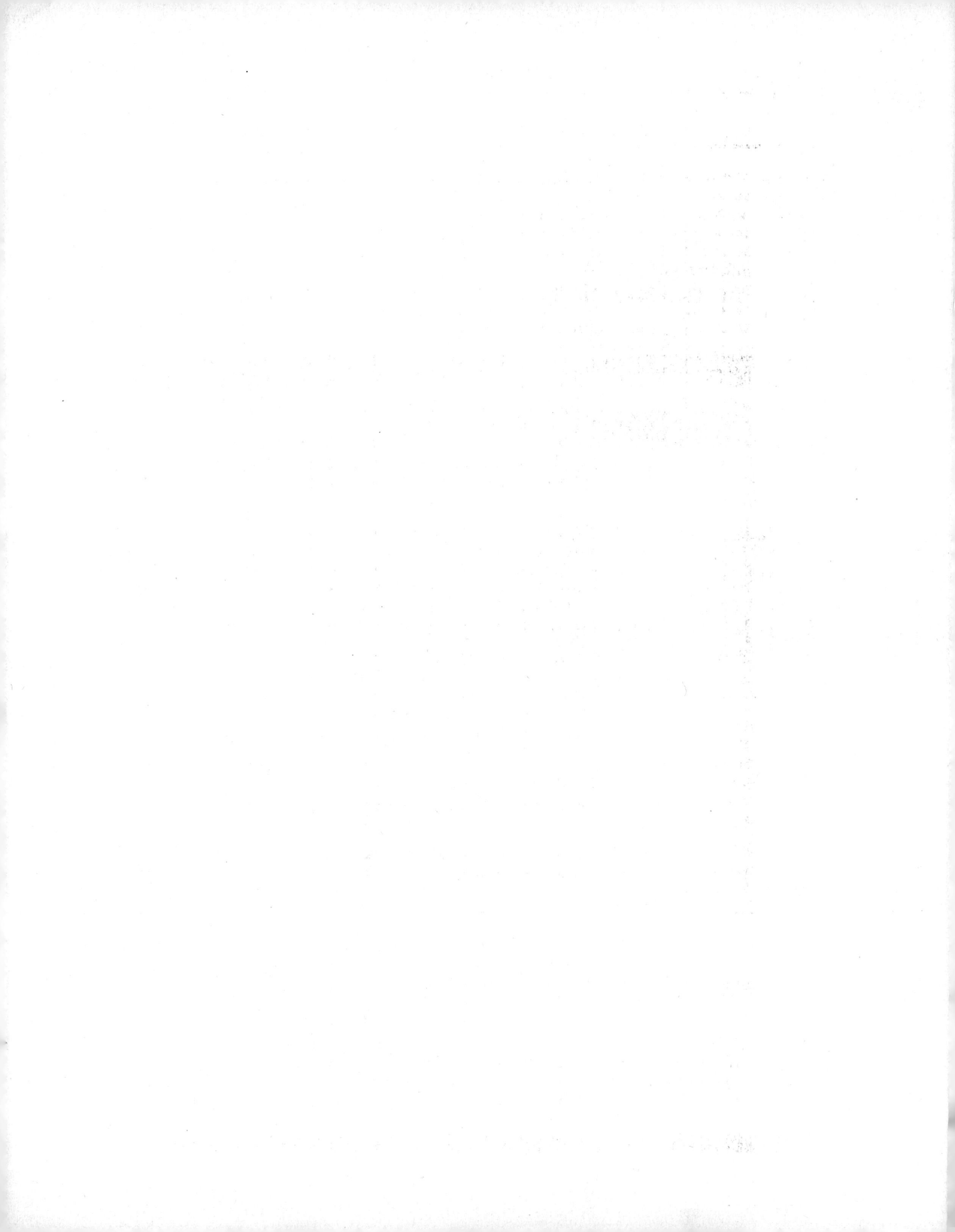